The Economy of Florida

J. F. (Dick) Scoggins
Ann C. Pierce
Editors

Bureau of Economic and Business Research
College of Business Administration
University of Florida
Gainesville

1995

UNIVERSITY OF
FLORIDA

The Economy of Florida

ISBN 0-930885-06-6

Preface

David Denslow is an "idea man." A spell-binding lecturer, a noted scholar and a genuinely nice person he is as well, but above all, he is an idea man. It came therefore as no surprise in 1989, while serving as chairman of Governor Bob Martinez's Council of Economic Advisors, that David Denslow had another one of his great ideas. Why not use the expertise of the council and the facilities of the Bureau of Economic and Business Research (BEBR) at the University of Florida (UF) to write a book about the economy of Florida? The book would cover the most important economic sectors of our large and growing state. Not only would it provide relevant statistics, it would also give insightful analyses and informed prognoses by experts in the varying sectors.

Dave enlisted the assistance of several members of the BEBR staff, most notably Anne Shermyen (then associate director) and Ann Pierce, director of Information/Publications Services. The end result was *The Economy of Florida, 1990 Edition*. That edition was an immediate success. It was not only useful to government policymakers, but it also proved useful to journalists, educators and the business community as well.

In 1994 the task of assembling a new edition was handed to Ann Pierce and me. We have attempted to produce an entirely new book that analyzes an even broader spectrum of economic sectors. Not having been members of the Governor's Council of Economic Advisors, we decided to solicit contributions from a list of experts whose professional affiliations span the state.

The first and most comprehensive chapter is by Carol T. West, director of the Forecasting Program of the BEBR. Carol oversees the quarterly and long-term economic forecasts for the state and the twenty-three regions and MSAs as well as the long-term forecasts for each of the sixty-seven counties in Florida. She is uniquely qualified to give an informed overview of such a large and diverse state economy as ours.

We next present a chapter on population by Stan Smith. It is safe to say that to understand how our economy works, there is no more crucial aspect than its rapidly growing population and that there is no greater living authority on this subject than Stan Smith. As director of the Population Program of the BEBR, he is the official nose-counter for the state.

No book on the economy of Florida would be complete without a chapter on the labor force, since it represents the single most important factor of production as well as the largest source of personal income. Larry Kenny, chairman of the economics department at the University of Florida, explains the reasons why wage rates in Florida are relatively low.

Carolyn Herrington at the Learning Systems Institute at Florida State University (FSU) and Yasser Nakib at the University of Delaware map out the daunting task our state faces in the area of public education. Shrinking resources and expanding demand make for an interesting chapter, if not for a comforting one.

Much to the chagrin of our state residents, crime has had a significant impact on our economy. Bruce Benson and David Rasmussen, both at FSU, show that the current policies dealing with this problem may not be as desirable as some alternatives.

Marc Smith of the Shimberg Center for Affordable Housing at UF provides a chapter on the importance of housing in the state's economy and future needs in this sector.

The subject of meeting our electricity demands is handled by Thomas Moore and William Ashburn, both of the Tampa Electric Company. Thomas Moore also provides us with an interesting chapter on the future of the mining industry in Florida.

As any peruser of the literature knows, there is an environmental cost of economic growth. Wally Milon of the Institute of Food and Agricultural Sciences at UF explains the policies in place for dealing with the problem and discusses their likely effects.

No other industry has gone through as much institutional change in the last decade as banking. Mark Flannery and Joel Houston, both in the Department of Finance, Insurance and Real Estate at UF, explain the regulatory and market forces at work here and assess the likelihood of future change.

Like the economies of most other states, Florida's has increasingly depended on technology. The implications of the information age and the likely changes in the regulatory environment are discussed in a chapter on telecommunications by Sanford Berg, executive director of the UF Public Utility Research Center.

A growing population requires an ever-expanding infrastructure. While public transportation and road construction require enormous sums of capital. Gary Brosch of the Center for Urban Transportation Research at the University of South Florida (USF) in Tampa details the process by which funds are generated for this purpose and outlines the likely consequences of inadequate funding.

Since the end of the Cold War our nation's economic priorities have changed. The de-emphasis of the military has had profound impacts on federal expenditures and Florida's economy. David Lenze of the BEBR describes the future impact of base closings and other defense cutbacks.

Having the largest proportion of elderly citizens makes the health care crisis especially acute for Florida. Gary Fournier of the economics department at FSU and Ellen Fournier, a legislative analyst for the Florida Senate, describe the importance of health care to the economy and the recent policy developments.

Since World War II tourism has been a major component of the Florida economy. David Williams, president of Florida Economics Consulting Group, presents evidence of the industry's importance and its future growth potential.

Florida is a multicultural state with an important strategic location in the Caribbean. Thomas Fullerton of the BEBR is an expert on Latin American economies. He provides us with a chapter on international trade and investment.

I authored the chapter on state and local government finance. Our state's numerous fiscal crises and long-running political squabbles concerning funding gave rise to the need for such a chapter.

As our population grows, the problems associated with urban areas grow with it. In the final chapter, Bill O'Dell and Marc Smith of the UF Shimberg Center for Affordable Housing and Larry Winner of the statistics department use the history of the explosive growth of Orange County as an illustrative example of what lies ahead for other communities in Florida.

The statistical tables provided at the end of the volume were compiled by Susan Floyd and Gayle Thompson. Since they produce the *Florida Statistical Abstract* on an annual basis they are well qualified for this task. Dot Evans, our publications production specialist, administered the graphics and layout. Carol McLarty assisted with maps. Niki Kordus designed the cover.

Many thanks to all the other people who helped with the production of this volume. I hope it proves as instructive to use as it was to edit.

J.F. (Dick) Scoggins
Associate Director
Bureau of Economic and Business Research
University of Florida
Gainesville, Florida

Contents

Regional Heterogeneity of the Florida Economy

1

Carol T. West
Professor of Economics
Forecasting Program Director
Bureau of Economic and
Business Research
University of Florida
Gainesville, Florida

It is a "land of swamps, of quagmires, of frogs and alligators and mosquitos. . . .No one would want to immigrate there, even from hell."

1840--Senator John Randolph of Virginia, opposing admission of Florida to the Union.[1]

A century and a half later in 1990, Florida's population was more than double that of Virginia. In the post-World War II U.S. economy, "Florida" has been synonymous with "growth." The spectacular and steady expansion of the state's economy lifted it from a relatively small economic/demographic entity in 1940--its 1.9 million population ranked it twenty-seventh among states--to a major U.S. regional economy of 14.0 million persons in 1994, the fourth most populous state in the nation. While the number of residents has risen sevenfold, the number of nonagricultural jobs has escalated at almost twice that rate, from 420 thousand in 1940 to 5.6 million in 1994. Employment growth has been sufficient to absorb the waves of job-seeking inmigrants, rising labor force participation rates and an internal shift from a rural to an urban economy. Florida's unemployment rate has averaged 0.4 percentage point below the national rate since 1948. Indeed, the state has become more than a significant regional economy

---

[1]Quoted in Blizin 1995.

within the national economy. It has become a significant economy judged by global standards. Its $225.1 billion gross state product in 1991 surpassed that of 190 countries in the world and was exceeded in size by only 17.

The sources of growth have been diverse, their impacts on different areas of the state uneven and some geographical regions were completely missed by the extended boom. As a consequence, Florida has emerged not as a homogeneous economic entity but as a collection of disparate regional economies, highly diversified in economic base structure, demographic composition, growth rates, level of economic well-being and vulnerability to swings in the national and international economies.

Today, understanding Florida has become a complex task of understanding the heterogeneous regional economies encompassed within historical borders of the state. Such regional heterogeneity has a long history in the state, predating by a century its postwar growth explosion. Regional dissention originally led many Floridians in the mid-nineteenth century to agitate for its entry as two separate states--East Florida and West Florida. Maintaining the political balance of free and slave states, however, necessitated that it enter as a single state jointly with the admission of the free state of Iowa. Growth since then has only created more regions and more intrastate regional diversity.

This chapter considers Florida as a collection of twenty-three regional economies--the twenty Metropolitan Statistical Areas and the nonmetropolitan counties grouped into three regions (northeast, northwest and south-central). It is a perspective that alters the view of Florida derived from statewide aggregated statistics and national/state comparisons. For example:

■ Is Florida a "state of senior citizens"? In the 1990 Census, 12.5 percent of U.S. residents were 65+ years of age but in Florida the proportion was 18.5 percent, the highest state average in the nation. Yet, in 1990 over 40 percent of Floridians lived in regions of the state in which the proportion of population 65+ years of age was less than 1.5 percentage points above the national average or was below the national average.

■ Is Florida a "Hispanic state" ? In the 1990 Census, the proportion of Floridians of Hispanic heritage was 12.2 percent while the national average was only 9.0 percent. Yet in 1990, 84 percent of Floridians lived in regions in which the proportion of population of Hispanic heritage was less than the national average.

■ Is the typical Floridian "economically as well off or better off than the average U.S. citizen"? In 1990, Florida per capita income exceeded the national average. Yet in 1990, almost three-quarters of Floridians lived in regions with per capita incomes below the national average. In 1993, none of Florida's sixty-seven counties had average earnings per job equal to or above the national average.

■ Is the Florida economy "recession-proof"? By standard measures of employment growth volatility, Florida job expansion has been clearly more stable than that of the nation. Yet in 1989, over 90 percent of Florida workers were employed in regions destined to suffer greater peak-to-trough job declines in the 1990-91 recession than characterized the nation as a whole.

■ Does Florida have a "water problem"? Among the fifty states, Florida ranks in the top six in average annual precipitation, fifth in inland surface water, second in coastal water and first in groundwater supplies. Yet, 60 percent of Floridians live in regions that have imposed water use restrictions in the last year; over 98 percent live in regions that have enacted water consumption controls in the last five years.

These apparent contradictions derive from the heterogeneity of Florida's regions and regional growth. No region "looks like the statewide average" and intrastate regional extremes distort the statewide averages, allowing experiences of the majority to contradict the average. State policy needs to recognize this diversity so that problems are not missed and statewide "cures" do not inflict unfair regional economic burdens. Equally important, it needs to unite diverse demographic cultures and economic markets into a common strength. A century and a half ago, David Levy, Florida's territorial delegate to the U.S. Congress, persuaded divided east and west factions to put aside differences and not miss the opportunity to enter the Union as a single state. Not missing opportunities because of diversity remains a challenge for state leaders today and the number of factions has increased markedly.

Sources of Florida Growth and Regional
Heterogeneity of Economic Bases

Reasons for Florida's extraordinary growth are multiple--some reflective of other rapidly growing regions in the U.S. and some peculiar to this southeastern state. It has been part of the general movement of older manufacturing out of the North Central and Northeast parts of the United States to the South and West in response to traditional economic incentives--relative wages, relative wage pressure from unionization, relative power costs. In addition, the rise in manufacturing of goods with low transport cost-to-value ratios has diminished the comparative attraction of dense population and industrial centers, permitting firms to realize competitive cost advantages of lower wages associated with natural amenities in many southern and western regions.

Natural resource development contributed to the state's postwar growth. The wartime innovation of frozen orange juice concentrate escalated citrus production. The development of the Bone Valley phosphate formation in central Florida--a unique geologic structure mined at exceptionally low cost--by 1980 made Florida the supplier of 35 to 40 percent of the world's phosphate. National defense policy contributed to growth through establishment and expansion of naval and air bases along the Atlantic coast and Gulf of Mexico. National defense interacting with lack of development also generated growth. On May 11, 1949, President Truman signed Public Law 60 creating the Long-Range Proving Ground on Canaveral for missile development, insuring future Florida growth derived from the U.S. defense and space programs. The reasons for selection of Canaveral were its coastal location, its comparatively cheap land cost and its undeveloped and almost uninhabited state. Human life would not be threatened by missile experimentation.[2] Beginning in the late 1970s the state's traditional defense and space activity in military bases and the Cape Canaveral program were augmented by a sharp rise in manufacturing defense contracting. Department of Defense prime contracts for Florida firms grew at an average rate of 18.5 percent per year between 1977 and 1987.

---

[2]For more detailed history of Cape Canaveral, see Jahoda 1976.

Manufacturing expansion, natural resource development and national defense and space spending directly created employment growth that was then accelerated by workforce-attached migration, yielding a cumulating simultaneous interaction of job increases and population increases. During the 1980s, this accelerator was further fueled by regional recession in other parts of the United States. As Florida remained relatively unscathed by depressions in oil and metal mining and agriculture, the comparative economic attraction of the state increased, luring more job-seekers from the troubled economies of Texas and the Midwest.

Finally, and of special significance in Florida postwar history, have been exogenous shifts in population (non-workforce-attached migration) and rising U.S. real per capita incomes that have encouraged rapid development of retiree/seasonal visitor /recreation-based economies in attractive coastal locations. The influx of retirees was stimulated particularly by medical advancements that lengthened life spans and the retirement period of the life cycle; development of the technology of home air conditioning (making the state more attractive for year-round residence); and the increased coverage of Social Security and private pensions, enhancing the financial independence and mobility of the older age cohort.

These various sources of growth have impacted Florida regions unevenly, leaving the state with a heterogeneous collection of regional economies. In simplified terms, each region can be thought of as having a set of key sectors bringing in dollars from outside the area and a second set of sectors serving the needs of the local population. The former, the economic base or export base of the region, are often identified as the growth-driving forces of the area. If activity in the economic base expands, employment and wages increase. The new income is spent at least partially in the local area, raising the level of local-serving employment; ultimately, growth in both sectors may attract new migrants, snowballing the expansionary process. The opposite occurs when the economic base contracts.

Conceptually identifying the economic base of an area is far simpler than empirically measuring it. Early regional economics simply defined it as the commodity-producing industries of agriculture, mining and manufacturing, on the implicit assumption that these are the sectors that sell outside the local market, thereby bringing external dollars into the regional economy. However, such external dollars can also be provided by tourist expenditures, pension disbursements, income from investments elsewhere that accrues to residents, and Social Security payments and military incomes paid by the federal government. Furthermore, specialized financial sectors, wholesaling services, medical services and retailing outlets may attract clientele from outside their local market, thereby becoming part of the economic base. Such sectors often have both export-base and local-serving components that are difficult to disentangle. Finally, the economic base varies according to how broadly a region is defined. For example, state government is "local-serving" when the state as a whole is considered as the region of analysis. However, for a smaller substate market in which a state prison is a major employer, the state government sector is part of the economic base, the prison being funded primarily by revenues contributed by other regions of the state.

Although it is impossible to delineate exactly a region's economic base, the distribution of sources of income indicates variation in the bases across areas. Table 1 identifies eight sectors that potentially contribute to a local economic base. The list is not exhaustive since, as noted above, many other industries can have export-base components. Conversely, the listed sectors are not necessarily exclusively, or even predominantly, export base in each given local economy. What are significant are clear deviations of income share from the national or state norm.

The substantial role of retirees in Florida's economic base is indicated by the state's unusually high share of income in dividends/interest/rent, which accrue in unusual proportions to older persons. Most of the income in the combined category is interest (83 percent nationally in 1988 and 79 percent in Florida) and dividends (15 percent nationally in 1988 and 19 percent in Florida). The dominance of older persons as recipients of this income is indicated by personal income tax statistics--e.g., in 1986, filers 65 years of age or older accounted for 12.6 percent of tax returns and 11.8 percent of adjusted gross income, but 48.7 percent of dividends received and 53.7 percent of interest received.

Column 1 in Table 1 and data on the proportion of population over 65 in Table 2 imply especially large retirement-related components in the economic bases of ten of the twenty-three substate areas--Daytona Beach, Ft. Lauderdale, Ft. Myers-Cape Coral, Ft. Pierce-Port St. Lucie, Naples, Ocala, Punta Gorda, Sarasota-Bradenton, West Palm Beach-Boca Raton and the south/central nonmetropolitan economies. In eight of these areas, dividends/interest/rent account for more than 30 percent of gross income compared with only 17 percent nationally and the share exceeds 40 percent in three regions--Naples, Sarasota-Bradenton and West Palm Beach-Boca Raton. Although the share is below 30 percent in Daytona Beach and Ocala, both these regions have unusually large proportions of income in retirement-related transfer payments, indicating the significant role of retirees in these two economies. It should be noted that the data do not permit identifying "snowbirds"--visitors coming regularly to Florida for extended stays--but snowbird and retirement populations are generally related, so the seasonal visitors probably significantly augment the retiree bases in these ten regions.

Offsetting the unusual role of retirees in Florida's economic base is an unusually low share of income from earnings in mining and manufacturing. Only Brevard County's 15.33 percent of gross income from manufacturing and mining exceeds the national average. In comparison with the state aggregate, local economic bases unusually weighted toward manufacturing/mining also include Lakeland-Winter Haven, Ocala, Orlando and the northeast and northwest nonmetropolitan counties.

In eighteen of the twenty-three Florida regions, labor earnings from tourist-related industries account for a larger share of gross income than in the U.S., with the data verifying the particular dominance of tourism in Orlando. Even though far above state and national averages, Orlando's 11.4 percent of gross income from tourist-impacted sectors appears low when confronted with the conventional wisdom that Orlando was developed on "a pair of mouse ears."

Several factors explain the conflict between quantitative data and popular qualitative perception. First, wages are low in tourist-related sectors--more than two jobs in tourism in Orlando are needed to

Table 1. 1990 Sources of Gross Income*
(percent)

Area	Dividends, interest, and rent	Transfer payments	Agriculture	Mining and manufacturing	Labor earnings Tourist-related**	Labor earnings Finance, insurance, real estate, health services, wholesale trade	Labor earnings Federal civilian and military	Labor earnings State government	Other earnings
United States	16.98	14.09	1.41	14.01	3.89	14.69	3.20	3.42	28.31
Florida	25.60	15.43	1.57	6.30	5.03	14.41	2.82	1.62	27.22
Metropolitan Statistical Areas									
Daytona Beach	28.63	22.57	1.12	5.73	5.88	9.54	0.87	1.11	24.55
Ft. Lauderdale	31.78	14.59	0.46	5.09	4.83	14.82	0.93	0.63	26.86
Ft.Myers-CapeCoral	34.00	16.62	1.38	2.29	5.10	11.86	0.89	0.91	26.95
Ft. Pierce-Port St. Lucie	38.35	15.47	5.36	3.25	3.76	9.57	0.63	0.81	22.79
Ft. Walton Beach	14.78	20.20	0.28	4.63	4.66	8.03	23.29	0.76	23.37
Gainesville	14.86	14.41	0.84	4.11	4.23	15.60	3.49	16.87	25.59
Jacksonville	14.36	13.93	0.66	6.85	4.17	19.99	8.65	1.10	30.29
Lakeland-Winter Haven	19.48	16.91	4.46	11.67	4.08	13.08	0.86	1.49	27.97
Melbourne-Titusville-Palm Bay	18.46	17.18	0.52	15.33	3.84	9.13	4.65	0.62	30.27
Miami	19.29	13.09	0.76	5.68	4.94	19.55	2.40	0.89	33.37
Naples	46.89	9.76	3.94	1.65	5.48	9.78	0.49	0.34	21.68

Area	Dividends, interest, and rent	Transfer payments	Agriculture	Mining and manufacturing	Tourist-related**	Finance, insurance, real estate, health services, wholesale trade	Federal civilian and military	State government	Other earnings
						Labor earnings			
Ocala	23.42	22.98	2.20	8.45	4.18	11.86	0.82	1.55	24.54
Orlando	15.43	12.84	1.51	8.61	11.39	15.62	3.04	1.03	30.54
Panama City	14.27	20.45	0.4I	5.55	6.69	10.50	12.59	1.18	28.36
Pensacola	13.66	20.65	0.51	7.76	3.55	12.38	14.28	1.75	25.47
Punta Gorda	39.21	24.44	0.98	1.09	3.17	10.26	0.49	0.70	19.64
Sarasota-Bradenton	41.25	16.55	1.56	4.70	4.00	10.25	0.68	0.51	20.51
Tallahassee	12.44	12.34	0.93	3.18	3.92	12.93	1.77	23.58	28.91
Tampa-St. Petersburg Clearwater	23.05	17.67	0.94	6.75	4.36	16.30	2.28	1.15	27.51
West Palm Beach-Boca Raton	43.51	11.03	2.39	5.67	3.94	11.47	0.67	0.71	20.62
Nonmetropolitan Areas***									
Northeast	14.49	25.11	4.82	12.30	3.41	6.28	2.00	8.17	23.42
Northwest	14.81	30.58	3.18	9.49	4.16	6.07	1.78	6.10	23.83
South/Central	32.35	19.65	7.31	3.51	4.72	7.75	1.91	1.47	21.33

*Gross income is personal income minus the earnings adjustment for residential plus personal contributions to social insurance. **Tourist-related earnings are defined as combined earnings in SIC 55 (automobiles/gasoline stations), 58 (restaurants/bars), 70 (hotels/motels) and 79 (amusements/recreation). ***Northeast: Baker, Bradford, Columbia, Dixie, Gilchrist, Hamilton, Lafayette, Levy, Madison, Suwannee, Taylor and Union counties. Northwest: Calhoun, Franklin, Gulf, Holmes, Jackson, Jefferson, Liberty, Wakulla, Walton and Washington counties. South/Central: Citrus, De Soto, Glades, Hardee, Hendry, Highlands, Indian River, Monroe, Okeechobee, Putnam and Sumter counties.

generate the equivalent wages of one typical job in manufacturing. Consequently, share of income is less than share of employment. Second, data in Table 1 do not measure the full impact of an economic-base sector on the total economy. Each primary industry stimulates growth in other sectors by its demands on construction, transportation, wholesaling, business services, etc., and thus the tentacles of tourism extend far deeper into the Orlando economy than the data of Table 1 alone suggest. Third, conventional wisdom is not entirely correct. Growth in Orlando has also been propelled by high-tech and defense manufacturing and by the growth demands of smaller urban and rural regions of central Florida. Orlando provides specialized services, air transportation access and wholesaling to rapidly growing smaller local economies around it.

A similar situation characterizes Gainesville, Jacksonville, Miami and Tampa-St. Petersburg-Clearwater. Each has proportions of income in combined finance/insurance/real estate, health services and wholesale trade that exceed state and national norms. As in Orlando, part of the economic base of these metropolitan areas is provision outside the MSA of sophisticated services and trade that require large markets for economic viability. These industries cater not only to local residents and businesses but to smaller economies in the region that are below the size threshold for self-provision of specialized industries. Additionally in Jacksonville, national-serving insurance industries lift that region's share of income in the financial, health and wholesale sectors to almost 20 percent.

The diversity of local areas is highlighted particularly by the disparate significance of agriculture, federal government and state government across regions. Earnings in each sector account for a relatively small proportion of total income both nationwide and in the state, but for much larger proportions in specific local economies of Florida. Only 1.4 percent of national income is from earnings in agriculture, but more than 5 percent of income in Ft. Pierce-Port St. Lucie and the south/central nonmetropolitan area is derived directly from this industry.

Military bases bolster economic activity in the north. Federal civilian and military income is 3.2 percent of national income and 2.8 percent of state income, but in Jacksonville, Panama City,

Pensacola and Ft. Walton Beach the proportions are respectively 8.7 percent, 12.6 percent, 14.3 percent and 23.3 percent. Additionally, these regions attract military retirees. Ft. Walton Beach, Panama City and Pensacola each has a large share of income in retirement transfer payments but a low proportion of population over 65 years of age. A large fraction of the transfer-payment income goes to retired military personnel, who typically leave active duty at a younger age than civilian workers retire from their jobs.

State government is the key economic-base sector of Gainesville and Tallahassee, accounting for 16.9 percent of income in the former and 23.6 percent in the latter compared with under 1.8 percent in all other metropolitan areas. State government prisons, institutions for the mentally ill, etc., dominate in individual rural counties and provide 6.1 percent of income in the northwest nonmetropolitan area and 8.2 percent in the rural northeast.

Because of the variation across regions in key sectors, few substate regions, if any, have historically paralleled state growth. Few resemble the statewide average in demographic composition, regional economic inequality abounds, national business cycles unevenly buffet regional markets and geographic concentration of growth has enhanced environmental pressures on the state's fragile ecosystem.

Regional Heterogeneity of Florida Population

All Florida regions have experienced population growth more rapid than that of the nation overall since 1970. However, as documented in Table 2, average annual rates of increase have varied considerably around the state from over 7 percent in Naples and Punta Gorda to under 2 percent in Jacksonville, Pensacola and the northwest nonmetropolitan area. The substantial role that net inmigration from other states and from abroad has played in growth is evidenced by the fact that in 1990 only 30.5 percent of Florida residents were Florida natives while in the nation overall, 61.8 percent of the population resided in their state of birth. Only rural northern regions reflect the national average and the proportion of population that is native is particularly low, approximately 20 percent or less, in the

Table 2. 1990 Population Characteristics
of Florida Regions

Area	Population (1,000s)	Average annual growth rate 1970-1990 (percent)	Percent over 65	Percent native*	Percent black	Percent Hispanic
United States	248,709.9	0.99	12.6	61.8	12.1	9.0
Florida	12,937.9	3.25	18.3	30.5	13.6	12.2
Metropolitan Statistical Areas						
Daytona Beach	399.4	4.23	23.0	26.0	9.0	4.0
Ft. Lauderdale	1,255.5	3.53	20.8	23.3	15.4	8.6
Ft. Myers-Cape Coral	335.1	5.89	24.8	20.9	6.6	4.5
Ft. Pierce-Port St. Lucie	251.1	5.93	23.6	25.2	12.2	4.3
Ft. Walton Beach	143.8	2.47	9.3	26.7	9.1	3.1
Gainesville	181.6	2.77	9.3	47.7	19.0	3.7
Jacksonville	906.7	1.98	10.9	44.8	20.0	2.5
Lakeland-Winter Haven	405.4	2.88	18.6	41.8	13.4	4.1
Melbourne-Titusville-Palm Bay	399.0	2.82	16.6	24.8	7.9	3.1
Miami	1,937.1	2.11	14.0	26.5	20.6	49.2
Naples	152.1	7.13	22.7	19.0	4.6	13.6
Ocala	194.8	5.25	22.2	35.2	12.8	3.0
Orlando	1,224.9	4.33	12.9	29.1	12.0	8.2
Panama City	127.0	2.63	12.0	39.1	10.8	1.8
Pensacola	344.4	1.74	11.3	42.3	16.2	1.8
Punta Gorda	111.0	7.18	33.8	13.5	3.8	2.5
Sarasota-Bradenton	489.5	4.09	30.4	20.7	5.8	3.1
Tallahassee	233.6	2.50	9.0	54.6	30.1	2.4
Tampa-St. Petersburg-Clearwater	2,068.0	3.12	21.6	28.3	9.0	6.7
West Palm Beach-Boca Raton	863.5	4.60	24.4	22.9	12.5	7.7
Nonmetropolitan Areas**						
Northeast	217.0	2.50	13.6	63.5	19.0	1.7
Northwest	164.4	1.76	15.3	60.5	17.4	1.3
South/Central	533.2	3.97	23.4	34.7	9.4	6.9

*Percent native for the United States is the proportion of population residing in their state of birth. Percent native for Florida and Florida areas is the proportion of population that is native Floridians.

**Nonmetropolitan county groupings are defined in the footnote to Table 1.

four southwestern metropolitan areas of Sarasota-Bradenton, Ft. Myers-Cape Coral, Punta Gorda and Naples.

Similar high regional variation characterizes area proportions of population who are 65+ years of age, who are black and who are Hispanic. Nine of the twenty-three regions have proportions of elderly population near or below the national average of 12.6 percent. The state's high overall average results from proportions topping 20 percent in eleven areas and exceeding 30 percent in two of the latter. High proportions of black population are concentrated in northern regions of the state (both rural and metropolitan) and Miami. Most extreme is the regional concentration of Hispanic population. Twenty-one of the twenty-three areas have proportions of Hispanic population below the national average of 9.0 percent. The relatively high statewide average of 12.2 percent derives from a proportion nearing 50 percent in Dade County. The latter is home to 15 percent of the state's total population but over 60 percent of the state's population of Hispanic heritage.

Demographic diversity adds richness to the fabric of the state's population, but some of the potential benefits of this richness are negated by the extremely uneven concentration of population subgroups in different regions. Instead of "diversified Florida" we have "elderly Florida" concentrated in southern coastal regions, "Hispanic Florida" concentrated in Dade County, "native Florida" in rural northern areas, etc. Lack of more homogeneous blending results in regional cultural and economic rifts and poses particular problems for formulating and passing statewide policies.

Regional Economic Inequality

Florida's overall postwar development has improved its relative economic well-being as measured by per capita income. In 1950 the state's per capita income was 14.4 percent below the national average, a gap that closed to 12.2 percent in 1960, 6.4 percent in 1970, 1.2 percent in 1980 and near zero in recent years. As shown in Table 3, by 1990 state and national per capita incomes were almost identical. Over time, the factors contributing to these statewide gains have varied and are summarized in Table 4.

Table 3. Economic Characteristics of Florida Regions

Area	1990 Per capita income (dollars)	1989 Percent of families living in poverty	1993 Per capita taxable real property (dollars)	Average annual growth rate of nonagricultural employment 1969-1993 (percent)	Variability of employment growth 1970-1993*
United States	18,675	10.0	NA	1.90	0.980
Florida	18,802	9.0	31,449	4.21	0.772
Metropolitan Statistical Areas					
Daytona Beach	15,718	7.8	29,815	4.80	0.712
Ft. Lauderdale	22,287	7.1	33,463	5.10	0.775
Ft. Myers-Cape Coral	19,438	6.1	49,785	6.94	0.614
Ft. Pierce-Port St. Lucie	20,442	7.1	45,219	6.01	0.730
Ft. Walton Beach	16,153	7.8	21,269	4.73	0.642
Gainesville	16,080	14.4	16,106	4.37	0.564
Jacksonville	18,055	8.9	24,451	3.16	0.718
Lakeland-Winter Haven	15,278	9.4	19,175	3.41	0.953
Melbourne-Titusville-Palm Bay	17,678	6.3	27,762	2.89	1.582
Miami	17,632	14.2	29,562	2.59	1.135
Naples	27,235	6.4	82,372	7.82	0.810
Ocala	14,543	10.8	20,186	5.69	0.603
Orlando	17,491	7.1	33,984	6.33	0.774
Panama City	14,981	11.2	24,563	4.32	0.591
Pensacola	14,969	12.9	16,417	3.02	0.569
Punta Gorda	17,325	5.2	44,754	7.93	0.659
Sarasota-Bradenton	23,267	5.5	41,536	5.70	0.710
Tallahassee	15,788	11.7	20,000	4.30	0.593
Tampa-St. Petersburg-Clearwater	17,984	7.8	26,108	4.66	0.705
West Palm Beach-Boca Raton	29,132	6.2	51,095	5.42	0.723
Nonmetropolitan Areas**					
Northwest	12,039	16.2	18,310	3.15	0.684
Northeast	11,943	16.1	12,718	3.00	0.747
South/Central	16,789	10.4	35,019	4.58	0.666

NA Not available.

*Measured as the square root of

$$\sum_{i-1970}^{1993} \left(\frac{ai - ti}{ti}\right)^2 / 24$$

where ai is actual employment growth rate in year i and ti is long-run trend employment growth rate in year i.

**Nonmetropolitan county groupings are defined in the footnote to Table 1.

Table 4. Income Gains in Florida:
Average Annual Growth Rate
(percent)

	1950-1960	1960-1970	1970-1980	1980-1990
Real Per Capita Income	2.17	4.12	2.09	1.86
Real Nonagricultural Wages and Salary Per Employee	2.30	2.56	-0.37	0.36
Real Per Capita Dividends/ Interest/Rent	4.71	5.59	3.31	3.24
Real Per Capita Transfer Payments	2.65	7.63	5.59	1.70
Labor Force Participation	0.13	-0.28	0.44	0.80

Fundamentally, there are three ways to affect real per capita income: (1) put higher proportions of persons to work (increase labor force participation); (2) generate higher earnings per job; (3) raise nonlabor income per capita (investment earnings, transfer payments, etc.). From 1950 to 1970, labor force participation was not a factor affecting income growth in Florida. Declining male participation offset rising female participation, leaving the aggregate state rate unchanged.

In the 1950s and 1960s, rising real earnings per job topping 2 percent annual rates of increase significantly boosted per capita incomes. The decade of the fifties was a period in which relatively high-paying manufacturing and construction jobs grew more rapidly than total jobs. Improved job quality was less of a factor in the sixties but earnings per job nonetheless advanced more rapidly than inflation. The gain was propelled by growth of over 2 percent per year in the real minimum wage. Despite the rising proportion of higher-paying jobs experienced in the previous decade, the Florida employment distribution was still unusually concentrated in lower-paying retail trade and service jobs. In 1960, these sectors accounted for 38 percent of the state's nonagricultural employment but only 14 percent of national employment. Consequently, raising earnings in minimum wage employment lifted Florida relative to the nation. Since the end of the sixties, earnings per job have not contributed to real per capita income gains in the state. Adjusted for inflation, the minimum wage has eroded over 25 percent since 1970, providing less support at the lower end of the earnings scale. Efforts to attract higher-paying manufacturing employment did not alter the industrial distribution of jobs sufficiently to raise average paychecks and national manufacturing downsizing in the eighties left fewer such jobs to be attracted. Florida real earnings per job fell in the 1970s and rose less than half a percentage point per year in the 1980s.

The main factor lifting Florida per capita income to a par with that of the nation was the state's phenomenal gains in per capita nonlabor income. In real terms, the latter rose 85 percent in the decade of the sixties and 56 percent in the decade of the seventies. The two-decade gain outpaced that of the nation by almost 30 percent. The Florida increases reflect the fact that nonlabor income accrues disproportionately to older citizens and retirees simply brought their entitlements and investment portfolios with them when they flocked to the state in the sixties and seventies. Between 1960 and 1980, Florida imported its per capita income parity with the nation.

During the decade of the eighties, retirees played less of a role in enhancing statewide averages. While their proportion in the state's population had increased over two percentage points per decade in the previous two ten-year periods, it was almost unchanged between 1980 and 1990. The financial and real estate market excesses of the eighties helped sustain increases over 3 percent per year in real per capita dividend/interest/rent earnings but real per capita transfer payment growth dropped from over 5.5 percent in the seventies to under 2 percent in the eighties. Florida per capita growth in the two components combined was 2.4 percent per year, slightly below the national average of 2.6 percent.

Despite the marked decline in real per capita transfer payment gains and minimal advances in earnings per job, inflation-adjusted per capita income in Florida rose almost 2 percent per year during the 1980s. In that decade, aggregate labor force participation was especially significant. During the 1970s, the participation rate increased as proportions of females in the labor market continued to rise and the previous decline in male participation abated. However, during that decade greater numbers of workers were partially offset by the decline in real earnings per job. Although real earnings growth was slow in the 1980s, it did not negate the rise in labor force participation. During the last decade, male participation grew slightly-- less than two percentage points--and that of women without children at home rose almost six percentage points. The major change, however, was the rise in working mothers. Labor force participation of women with preschool children jumped from 50.7 percent in 1980 to 63.2 percent in 1990 and that of women with school-age children increased from 64.8 percent to 77.0 percent.

The nature of historical per capita income growth in the state has resulted in a very uneven distribution of income across regions of Florida. Wealthy retirees (and their property income and transfer payment entitlements) tended to cluster in particular southern metropolitan regions. The higher-paying manufacturing jobs that were attracted to Florida were not evenly disbursed across the state and higher-salaried transportation and wholesaling jobs naturally concentrate in larger metropolitan regions. By 1990, per capita income in Florida was $18,802, slightly above the national average of $18,675. But underlying the statewide figure were huge regional disparities ranging from 36 percent below the national norm in the rural northeast to 56 percent above the national norm in Palm Beach County.

Some special measurement factors contribute to low per capita income figures in northern regions in Table 3. For example, Ft. Walton Beach, Panama City and Pensacola each has relatively large numbers of military personnel whose earnings alone do not fully reflect shopping and housing benefits available on military bases. Students at the University of Florida are a significant proportion of the Gainesville population but the income they receive from their parents is not allocated by official statistics to Alachua County. Similarly, concentrations of institutionalized populations in some of the northern rural counties may distort the measure. However, such special factors account only partially for the low per capita incomes in these regions and do not at all explain why the Ocala metropolitan area's per capita income is 23 percent below the statewide average. Removing the institutionalized populations from the calculations of per capita income in the rural northeastern and northwestern areas still leaves their figures only two-thirds that of the state.

Consideration of regional cost-of-living differences does partially mitigate the regional income inequality. Using formal measures, inequality of the regional distribution of real per capita income is currently 22 percent less than that of nominal per capita income. However, the significance of cost-of-living differences has been diminishing over time. In the early 1970s, adjusting for regional price variations reduced inequality by 50 percent.[3]

The major factor determining Florida's regional income inequality is the extraordinary inequality in the regional distribution of income from wealth--an inequality more than seven times that of aggregate income. Such sources of income are associated with high-income families and individuals and their uneven dispersion within the state. The role of the unequal distribution of very high incomes in determining the distribution of per capita incomes tends to limit the usefulness of the latter as an indication of personal and family economic conditions. One area may have a much lower per capita income than another simply because the wealthiest segment of its population is not as well off as the wealthiest segment of the other, even though households and persons in the middle and lower ends of the income distributions are similar in both areas. If the only difference reflected in per capita incomes is how rich the rich are, there is little cause for concern. Indeed, variation across Florida regions in median household income is 30 percent less than that of per capita income.

However, more disturbingly, low per capita incomes are associated with high incidences of poverty in the state. Eight of the nine regions with the lowest per capita incomes are all characterized by proportions of families in poverty that exceed the state average, reaching as high as 16 percent in rural northern areas. With the exception of Lakeland-Winter Haven, all these areas with low per capita incomes and substantial pockets of poverty are in the northern part of the state. Perhaps more than any other data, these statistics highlight the extent to which postwar economic development of Florida has not fully embraced its northern portion.

Altering economic inequality is currently focused on improving wages. From a practical economic perspective, other historical

---

[3]The income inequality measure used here is the information-theoretic-based statistics in Theil 1967.

sources of per capita income growth in Florida are waning in momentum. Given the large increases that have occurred in labor force participation, scope for further gains is lessened. Labor force participation in the state is projected to grow under 3 percent between 1990 and 2005 compared with over 14 percent between 1975 and 1990. The 1980s bubble in financial and real estate markets has burst. Projected per capita growth in wealth income for the period 1990-2005 is less than one-sixth that of the 1980s. The supply of potential retirees to lure to the state (with their wealth income and transfer-payment entitlements) is dwindling as the young retiree population begins to draw upon the smaller cohort of individuals born in the depression. Florida's proportion of population over 65 is forecast to increase by less than one percentage point between 1990 and 2005. From a practical political perspective, the current trend is to stem the rise of transfer payments as a solution to the poverty problem and to focus on improving the ability of the labor market to provide above-poverty incomes for individuals and families.

Like average per capita incomes, average wage levels vary considerably around the state. But unlike per capita income, all average wage levels are below the national norm. Average 1993 earnings per job across the sixty-seven counties of Florida varied from a low of $15,500 in Hardee County (41 percent below the U.S. mean) to a high of $26,300 in Palm Beach County (less than one percent below the U.S. mean). Major factors influencing regional wages in general are cost of living, taxes, industrial structure of employment, unionization of employees, quality of the labor force, demographic characteristics of the labor force, regional amenities and disamenities, job security and labor availability. Interregional migration of labor forces wages to compensate for some regional differences. Workers residing in areas with a high cost of living, oppressive taxes, an unattractive climate, a boring geography, a high crime rate and a high probability of job loss won't stay there long unless pay rates on the job make up for those disadvantages.

Some of these factors are less significant within Florida than between Florida and other states. For example, the major tax differential between Florida and most other states is the lack of a state income tax here. This lowers Florida wages relative to those of

Table 5. Causes of Variation in 1993 Average Earnings Per Job Across Florida Counties

Cause	Percent of total variation contributed by variation in cause
Cost of Living	22.1
Industry Structure	16.2
Education of the Labor Force	13.5
Pool of Available Labor	6.8
Proportion of Labor Force That Is Female	6.2
Job Security	5.4
Area Crime Rate Disamenities	5.2
Area Water Amenities	3.2
Experience of the Labor Force	3.1
Other Factors	18.3

other states but has no impact on wage disparities within the state. Similarly, climate differences are relatively minor within Florida but all residents clearly derive positive climate benefits compared with citizens of many other states. Some factors do not vary substantially among regions. For example, work experience is a major factor explaining wage variation among workers of different age cohorts but the average experience level of an entire labor force varies less across regions, so experience explains less of the interregional differentials. Some factors are difficult to measure--What is the value of a mountain in Colorado compared with a seashore in Florida? Some factors are measurable but data for them have not been collected. For example, there are measures of the proportion of the workforce that is unionized in different states but not in different regions of Florida.

While it is impossible to account for all wage variations, measurable differences across regions of Florida explain over 80 percent of intercounty differences. As summarized in Table 5, a large number of factors contribute significantly.[4] Variation in the cost of living is the single most important factor determining variation in average

---

[4]Analysis of Florida wages was first reported in West 1995.

pay per job. It accounted for over a fifth of the differences in average county wages in 1993.

Average pay differs substantially across industries. At the extremes in Florida, average earnings per job in agriculture and retail trade lag the mean by almost 40 percent and those in mining exceed the mean by over 50 percent. County differences in the concentration of high-paying and low-paying industries account for 16.2 percent of intercounty average wage variations.

Quality of the labor force has two dimensions, experience and education. As noted above, average experience varies relatively little across regions so it plays a relatively minor role in determining intercounty wage disparities. In contrast, differences in the education of the labor force account for 13.5 percent of intercounty wage variation. Adding an additional year of education to the labor force increases average county cost-of-living-adjusted wages approximately 10.5 percent. But not all additional years count equally. National studies based on individuals have consistently found that when the additional year results in high school graduation it has a much larger positive effect on wages than other single-year additions to schooling (Hashimoto and Raisian 1985 and Weiss 1988). This same phenomenon is observed in studying average wages across Florida counties. Regional wages are particularly depressed by a high proportion of high school dropouts in the labor force.

The most common demographic findings in wage differential research are that women and blacks earn less on average. Some recent studies have found lesser significance of race but the gender gap persists. In Florida, a higher proportion of females in the county labor force significantly lowers average earnings per job (and accounts for 6.2 percent of the intercounty variation) but the proportions of blacks or other minorities do not have a statistically significant impact.

Basic laws of supply and demand manifest themselves in rising wages in tight labor markets and slowed earnings growth in markets with a large available pool of labor. Over time, labor migrates from the depressed job markets to the robust ones, tending to restore the regional balance. At any point in time, however, the process is incomplete and downward pressure on wages is observed in the former markets and upward pressure in the latter ones. Across the counties of Florida, differences in labor availability contribute 6.8 percent of the observed variation in earnings per job.

Large amenity factors such as climate that distinguish Florida from other states do not vary substantially among areas of Florida. Significant, however, are variations in water amenities (both coastal and inland) and crime-rate disamenities. Jointly, these quality-of-life considerations account for 8.4 percent of the intercounty wage variation. Not only are workers willing to trade higher quality of life for average wage, they are similarly willing to trade higher job security for average wage. Intercounty differences in average job security explain 5.4 percent of the intercounty average wage differences.

When the causes of regional variation are compensating factors, there is little need for public concern. Individuals are willing to accept lower average wages for lower cost of living, higher job security, more area amenities and lack of area disamenities. When all aspects of compensation are considered together, those individuals are not worse off than workers with higher pay that is offset by higher cost of living, lesser job security and fewer amenities.

Of more policy concern are the factors that reflect labor market discrimination and interregional differences in human capital. With regard to the latter, it is important to note that from a dynamic perspective, the role of education in determining area wages is larger than suggested by the figures in Table 5. The 13.5 percent of variation in wages across counties accounted for by education of the labor force in Table 5 is the direct effect--more particularly, the effect given the impact of industrial structure. But over time, education in turn impacts industrial structure--a poorly educated labor force discourages location of high-wage industries in the region. Across Florida counties, the indirect effect of education enhances the direct effect by 64 percent. It is a vicious cycle--if only low-paying jobs with low educational requirements are available, educational attainment is discouraged but if educational attainment is low, high-paying industry is discouraged. Breaking the low-wage cycle in parts of the state and turning it into a cumulative growth cycle with educational attainment and job quality reinforcing each other is a current policy challenge.

Regional Heterogeneity and the Business Cycle

By standard measures of employment-growth instability, the Florida economy has been less buffeted than that of the nation by business cycles. Indeed, the state has enjoyed the enviable situation of a higher mean and lower variability in the rate of job creation. Between 1969 and 1993, annual job growth in the state averaged 4.21 percent, more than double the national average of 1.90 percent. The variability of Florida's growth, however, was only four-fifths that of the aggregate U.S.

As shown in Table 3 on page 14, all regions of the state posted above-national-average job growth rates and twenty of the twenty-three regions have experienced growth-rate variability at least 15 percent below the national average. Both growth rates and growth-rate variability, however, have ranged widely across substate regions. Only five areas are characterized by average rates of increase within half a percentage point of the state mean—the three northern metropolitan areas of Gainesville, Panama City and Tallahassee, the Tampa-St. Petersburg-Clearwater MSA and the south/central nonmetropolitan region. Employment growth rates in other areas have clearly exceeded or clearly fallen short of the Florida average.

Dominated by less cyclically sensitive state government employment, job-growth variability in the Gainesville and Tallahassee metropolitan areas has been far below the national norm, approximately 40 percent less. Similar stability has characterized the panhandle metropolitan areas of Panama City and Pensacola. At the other extreme, the historically cyclically sensitive mining and manufacturing industries in Lakeland-Winter Haven have endowed it with a variability similar to that of the nation overall. Two regions exceed the national average in employment-growth variability--Melbourne-Titusville-Palm Bay and Miami. Dade County's volatility is historically attributable to highly uneven population change, a consequence of reversals in retiree migration and sporadic influxes of Latin immigrants. More recently, banking and airline industry restructuring has unusually concentrated large-firm closures in that metro area. Even more extreme, however, has been the Brevard County cyclicality induced by shifts in federal funding of space-related activities.

Although measures of employment-growth variability that are calculated over decades of data are lower for most areas of the state compared with the nation, few would now contend that Florida is "recession-proof." In the recent 1990-91 recession, peak-to-trough employment decline in the state was 2.65 percent, well above the national average of 1.48 percent. Of the twenty-three regions in the state, only three experienced no job loss--the Ft. Walton Beach and Tallahassee MSAs and the northwest nonmetropolitan area. The south/central nonmetropolitan area experienced an under-one-percent job loss and the Panama City MSA paralleled the nation with a 1.48 percent employment reduction. The remaining eighteen regions all posted percent employment declines more severe than in the U.S. overall. While two of the four largest cutbacks (declines of 4 percent or more) were in the traditionally more volatile Polk and Dade county economies, two were also in the apparently nonvolatile metropolitan areas of Ft. Pierce-Port St. Lucie and Tampa St. Petersburg-Clearwater. Concomitantly, the unemployment rate rose 3.76 percentage points in Florida compared with a lesser 2.73 points in the nation. The unemployment rate climbed more than the national rate in over two-thirds of the state's regions.

Despite the historical volatility measures, the recent experience is not an anomaly. Data limitations do not permit analysis of substate cyclical sensitivity prior to approximately 1970, but earlier postwar periods of employment volatility can be examined for the state overall. It is clear that Florida's relative cyclicality is increasing. For the two decades 1948-1969, the U.S. measure of employment volatility was 1.065; it fell slightly to 0.980 in the subsequent 1969-1993 period. In contrast, Florida's climbed dramatically, from 0.466 in the former period to 0.772 in the latter period. Closer examination of the data reveals that the increase in state volatility is primarily attributable to increased severity of slowdowns/downturns. Indeed, Florida was once apparently "recession-proof" but that is no longer the case.

Some changes in the Florida economy have enhanced its vulnerability to economic downturns--e.g., diversification into defense manufacturing during the latter part of the seventies and the 1980s left it particularly sensitive to cutbacks in that production with the ending of the Cold War. More basically, however, the character of U.S. recessions has been changing.

While abstract business-cycle theory attempts to model broad commonalities of cyclical downturns, empirically each has been found to have unique precipitating and exacerbating factors. Florida has long been sensitive to some sets of these and not sensitive to others. It was relatively insensitive to specific factors of the early postwar recessions but sensitive to those of 1975, 1982 and 1991. At a minimum, Florida's economy has always at least noticeably slackened during a national recession. At a minimum, national demand for exported Florida goods and services declines to some degree. From the state's perspective, the difference among recessions has been whether the only impact was indirect--slower overall national demand--or whether the specific exacerbating factors especially impinged upon the Florida economy.

Domestic supply shocks played a critical role in the 1960 and 1970 recessions--the steel strike in the former and the automobile and General Electric strikes in the latter. With virtually none of its economic base concentrated in production of these goods, the Florida economy was untouched directly. The severe 1958 national recession was of similar ilk but it derived from domestic demand cutbacks following an exceptional automobile buying boom. Consumption and housing continued to grow peak-to-trough in the 1954 recession and nonresidential fixed investment declined only a small 1.6 percent. The major factor then was a 17.3 percent decline in federal government spending following the end of the Korean War. With private spending and housing investment still relatively healthy and without a manufacturing base in defense materials, again Florida was relatively unscathed by direct precipitating factors.

The mid-1970s saw a new type of postwar national recession--an international supply shock resulting in double-digit inflation and consequent severe credit crunches. Florida's tourist industry was pummeled directly by the gasoline shortages and rising prices of fuel. The credit crunch resulted in an unprecedented postwar collapse in housing. Nationally, the peak-to-trough decline in residential fixed investment was almost 30 percent. In the five previous postwar recessions, housing investment had grown in three, fallen 2.7 percent in one and declined 10.9 percent in another. Like rising gasoline prices, national housing-market collapse also directly impacted Florida. Not only had the state been riding a construction boom in the early years of the 1970s--and hence was particularly vulnerable to a construction-led recession--but without a robust national housing market potential inmigrants to the state could not sell their homes and hence, postponed a move. Net migration to the state declined 64.5 percent, exacerbating the downturn in Florida. Recessions in Florida were no longer confined to specific areas of manufacturing and federal space research; recessions were phenomena that also affected regions of the state dependent upon construction, tourism, retiree spending and simply net inmigration--almost all regions of the state. In 1981-82, housing-market decline again played a central role but in this case it was engendered by an explicit policy decision to wring inflation out of the economy, a decision that maintained severe credit constraints well into the recession. The cycle of construction collapse, housing-market collapse, population-mobility collapse was repeated and again Florida did not emerge unscathed.

In the most recent recession, Florida once more found itself vulnerable to specific precipitating factors--construction curtailments following reversal of the 1981 tax code, reduced availability of development funding as a consequence of the savings and loan crisis and the inevitable adjustment to excess supply of office buildings and apartments. In addition, consumer spending cutbacks were unusually precipitous. Nationally, consumer spending fell almost one percent peak to trough compared with a previous postwar recession average of an 0.8 percent gain. With an economy particularly dependent upon retail and service spending and a state tax base unusually concentrated in sales taxes, both Florida private and public sectors were exceptionally impacted. National housing market bubbles burst. Housing value declines in the Northeast had severe effects on Florida, since the Northeast is a critical feeder region of migrants to the state. Net inmigration to Florida fell over 50 percent, repeating the experiences of 1975 and 1982. And finally, the build-up of defense manufacturing, which buffered the Florida economy in the 1980 and 1982 recessions, proved to be a liability in the post-Cold War 1991 recession.

The "steel and automobile" recessions of the early postwar period are fading into history and are unlikely to be repeated. Since the early seventies employment in these industries has declined 30 percent and growth in production of their goods elsewhere on the globe has reduced domestic-economy dependence on domestic production. Industry unionization has declined and the unions that continue are sensitive in their demands to the new international competition. The more recent construction/financial market/real estate cycles of the postwar period appear far more likely to be the repeated phenomena. In addition, there will be new precipitating factors reflecting the evolving world economy. To the extent that Florida strives to participate in and succeeds in benefiting from the growth potential that evolution brings, Florida will continue to expose itself to the inevitable cyclical downturns that correct the excesses of unbridled expansion.

Regional Heterogeneity and the Florida Environment

In most rapidly growing areas, deterioration of the environment becomes an issue and there are indeed many environmental problems common to growth regions--e.g., congestion, aesthetically unattractive strip development, loss of biodiversity from habitat destruction, automobile pollution, solid waste and hazardous waste accumulation, inland water pollution from cumulative sewage and industrial waste dumping and urban stormwater runoff. Florida has been acutely experiencing these costs of development. Additionally, it is burdened by coastal erosion, a problem not pertinent to rapidly growing landlocked states. Such erosion results from armoring beaches with bulkheads, jetties, seawalls and groins to protect oceanfront properties, destroying natural dunes by poor construction practices and human trampling, and artificially trapping sand by altering the configuration and depth of inlets. Even among other rapidly growing coastal states, Florida's environmental costs of development have intensified. For example, waters of the Keys contain the only living coral reef off the continental United States; hence Florida uniquely faces the problem of protecting the reef from ocean waters fouled by agricultural runoff, garbage and sewage and from the destruction wrought by fishermen and divers.

Florida's environmental vulnerability extends beyond isolated biological/geological phenomena such as the reef; only relatively recently has it been recognized that the state's growth and regional pattern of growth has threatened the stability and continued viability of its entire hydrologic cycle. Of primary significance is loss of wetlands--grounds shallowly submerged for much of the year. Currently, only about half of the state's historic wetlands remain. They are a significant homeostatic mechanism in the state's hydrologic cycle. They act as recharge areas for underground waters and improve water quality as their microbe/soil/plant ecosystems filter the water; they attenuate floods; and through surface evaporation, the wetlands provide a source of rainfall for the heavily populated and developed parts of south Florida. Drainage of the wetlands to provide for economic growth has a long history, dating back to the mid-1880s. Indeed, the 1850 federal Swamp and Overflowed Lands Act gave the Everglades to Florida with the proviso that it be drained. While wetlands were initially drained to provide land for railway development, to attenuate flooding and to control mosquitos, subsequent drainage was undertaken to expose the rich peat earth for agricultural development and, ultimately, to provide buildable land for expanding population and commercial interests, especially in the southern part of the state.

Loss of the regulatory function of the state's wetlands has impaired the fragile ecosystem's ability to provide potable water. More than 90 percent of the state's drinking water comes from underground and geology dictates that this dependence on underground water will continue. Even though Florida receives approximately sixty inches of rainfall per year, reservoir systems are infeasible--the virtually flat terrain prohibits efficient collection of the surface water. The regional heterogeneity of population growth and development--particularly its postwar concentration in the southern areas of the state --has exacerbated the problem, leaving much of the population now subject to ongoing water-availability crises. Not only were wetlands drained in the south to provide buildable land but the southeastern portions of the state--now heavily populated Palm Beach, Broward, Dade and Monroe counties--are completely dependent upon the Biscayne Aquifer for fresh water supplies. And the Biscayne Aquifer is considerably smaller than the combined aquifers that supply regions to the north of these areas. Intense development was not located where the largest available water supplies to support that growth existed.

Development itself retards aquifer recharge, since water that would formerly have seeped into the ground now runs off roofs and pavement into stormwater systems. The combination of development where less abundant water supplies naturally existed and the reduction in recharge of these systems both from paving over land and from loss of interior wetlands has resulted in the rate of underground water pumping exceeding the rate of recharge in numerous regions of the state. As underground water levels drop, the state's highly permeable sandy soils and limestone substrata act like a sponge, absorbing adjacent ocean waters and thus salinating the freshwater supply.

More recent development in the central portion of the state has additionally pressured the water supply. Historically, these regions were abundant in central Florida scrub—sandy, hilly lands of sand pine and small oak. The scrub areas are regions of particularly high water-recharge, their well-drained soils being especially efficient in replenishing the underground water supplies. Those same characteristics, however, also made scrub areas the most desirable for development. As a consequence, much of Florida's once plentiful scrub land has been destroyed and fragmented, further deteriorating the ability of the state's ecosystem to sustain groundwater supplies.[5]

Basic statistics on the availability of water in Florida render almost unbelievable the notion that the state has a water-supply problem. The current problems derive from two sources: (1) historical lack of understanding of Florida's fragile hydrological ecosystems--a lack of understanding that permitted draining wetlands, developing scrub lands, killing the habitat of seagrasses, trampling dunes and dredging waterways; and (2) the choice to concentrate development in regions of the state least capable environmentally of supporting massive growth. Current ecological knowledge has led to a myriad of

---

[5]For more extensive presentation of environmental issues in Florida, see Partington, Jr., et al. 1987 and Lord 1993. See Duplaiz and Ward for reviews of the state's water resources.

University of Florida   *Bureau of Economic and Business Research*

preservation efforts in Florida that go beyond the familiar protection of species biodiversity and the control of pollution. Preservation of the environment has been incorporated into mandated regional growth management plans. It is debated whether given the historical damage, current initiatives are sufficient in scope and enforcement. It is debated whether controlling land use unfairly deprives landowners of development rights. While many of these complex issues remain unresolved, awareness of them has heightened dramatically in the last quarter century and preserving Florida's environmental capacity to grow will remain a central policy issue for the state and its regions for decades to come.

A Look Ahead

There is no evidence that regional diversity in Florida is diminishing. Its now 150-year history as a state has shown only that as growth occurs, more regions--and different regions--emerge. Long-run forecasts for regions of the state suggest little trend toward greater homogeneity--forecast regional demographic characteristics remain diverse, few reductions in regional economic inequality are anticipated, business cycles will continue to buffet substate markets with different degrees of severity and regional variations in environmental sensitivity to growth are permanent.

This regional heterogeneity is a strength, allowing one "Florida" to in fact be many "Floridas" attractive to a variety of ages, cultures and economic pursuits. The cost of this diversity is the difficulty posed for state policy formulation. How do we redistribute economic burdens and gains as policies impinge differentially on varied regions and populations in the state? More fundamentally, it raises a basic issue of whether we want "people prosperity" or "place prosperity." Do we attempt to consciously divert growth to lagging regions or do we attempt to provide residents of languishing regions the skills to prosper in more vibrant areas and encourage their migration to these more robust economies?

References

Blizin, J. 1995. "David Levy Yulee: The Man Who Gave Statehood to Florida." *Florida Living* (March), pp. 26-27.

Duplaiz, N. 1990. "South Florida Water: Paying the Price" and Ward, F. "Florida's Coral Reefs Are Imperiled." *National Geographic* 178:1, pp. 89-132.

Hashimoto, Masanori, and John Raisian. 1985. "Employment Tenure and Earnings Profiles in Japan and the United States." *American Economic Review* 75 (September), pp. 721-35.

Jahoda, G. 1976. *Florida.* New York: W.W. Norton and Company.

Lord, Linda A. 1993. *Guide to Florida Environmental Issues and Information.* Winter Park: The Florida Conservation Foundation.

Partington, W.J. Jr., et al. 1987. *An Official Guide to Florida Environmental Issues: 1987.* Winter Park: The Florida Conservation Foundation, Inc.

Theil, H. 1967. *Economics and Information Theory.* Amsterdam: North-Holland.

Weiss, Andrew. 1988. "High School Graduation, Performance and Wages." *Journal of Political Economy* 96, pp. 785-820.

West, Carol T. 1995. "How to Fatten Paychecks." *Florida Trend* 17 (January), pp. 8-9.

Population Growth and Demographic Change

2

Stanley K. Smith
Professor of Economics
Director
Population Program Director
Bureau of Economic and
Business Research
University of Florida
Gainesville, Florida

There are many "Floridas." There are the farms and small towns of north Florida, with families that have lived there for generations. There are the burgeoning commercial and industrial centers of central Florida, creating new jobs and attracting young workers and their families. There are the retirement villages of southwest Florida, attracting thousands of migrants from northern states each year. There are the rapidly growing ethnic communities of southeast Florida, with their cultural diversity and melting-pot ambience. Congested cities spill into sparsely populated rural areas, tremendous affluence abuts grinding poverty, newcomers mingle with old-timers. Florida is not a single entity, but rather a composite of many diverse parts, each with its own unique identity.

These parts are tied together by one common characteristic: rapid population growth. Florida has been one of the most rapidly growing states in the nation for many years and is expected to continue growing rapidly in the future. Although some parts of the state have grown more rapidly than others, no part has completely escaped the impact of rapid population growth. Isolated beaches have sprouted high-rise condominiums, swamps have become shopping malls, quiet country roads have been transformed into super highways, sleepy villages have become bustling cities. Rapid population growth has had a tremendous impact on virtually all aspects of life in Florida

Table 1. Florida Population Growth 1990-1994

Year	Population	Decade Change	Percent Change
1900	528,542	----------	-----
1910	752,619	224,077	42.4
1920	968,470	215,851	28.7
1930	1,468,211	499,741	51.6
1940	1,897,414	429,203	29.2
1950	2,771,305	873,891	46.1
1960	4,951,560	2,180,255	78.7
1970	6,791,418	1,839,858	37.2
1980	9,746,324	2,954,906	43.5
1990	12,937,926	3,191,602	32.7
1994	13,878,905	940,979	7.3

Sources: U.S. Bureau of the Census, *1980 Census of Population*, PC80-1-All, February 1982. Bureau of Economic and Business Research, *Florida Estimates of Population, April 1, 1994*, University of Florida 1995.

and no public issue can be fully understood without a firm grasp of the state's population dynamics.

Historical Trends

In 1900 Florida was one of the smallest states east of the Mississippi River, with a population of barely half a million (Table 1). By 1994 its population had grown to almost 13.9 million, making it the fourth-largest state in the United States. Growth rates during the twentieth century have ranged between 29 and 79 percent per decade, far above the 10-20-percent growth rates for the United States as a whole. Compared to other states, Florida's growth rates have ranked among the four highest in every decade since 1920. In fact, Florida's population increase during the 1980s (3.2 million) was larger than the total 1990 population of twenty-four states.

One direct result of rapid population growth has been the steady increase in Florida's representation in the U.S. House of Representatives, which is determined by the number of residents counted in each decennial census. Florida had only 3 of 391 seats in 1900, but had 15 of 435 by 1970. Rapid growth during the 1970s and 1980s

Figure 1. Map of Florida and Its Regions

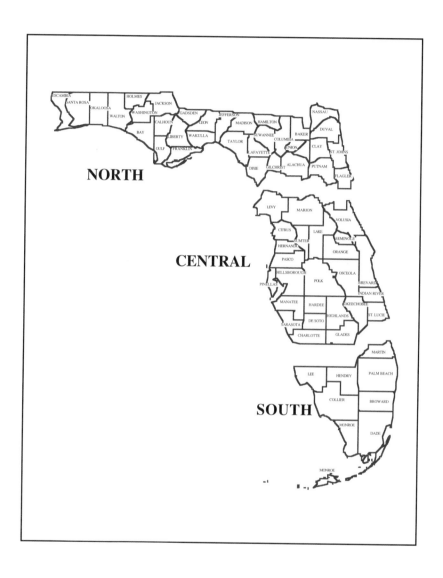

Table 2. Distribution of Florida's Population
by Region 1990-1994

Year	North Number	North Percent	Central Number	Central Percent	South Number	South Percent
1900	349,593	66.1	152,917	28.9	26,032	4.9
1910	458,396	60.9	248,896	33.1	45,367	6.0
1920	520,484	53.7	352,354	36.4	95,632	9.9
1930	606,322	41.3	606,959	41.3	254,930	17.4
1940	723,485	38.1	738,207	38.9	435,772	23.0
1950	951,332	34.3	1,052,561	38.0	762,412	27.7
1960	1,302,820	26.3	2,008,377	40.6	1,640,363	33.1
1970	1,542,567	22.7	2,776,230	40.9	2,472,621	36.4
1980	1,926,777	19.8	4,161,665	42.7	3,657,882	37.5
1990	2,386,335	18.4	5,803,582	44.9	4,748,009	36.7
1994	2,585,598	18.6	6,256,337	45.1	5,036,970	36.3

Sources: T. Stanton Dietrich, *The Urbanization of Florida's Population: An Historical Perspective of County Growth, 1830-1970*, Bureau of Economic and Business Research, University of Florida, 1978. Bureau of Economic and Business Research, *Florida Estimates of Population, April 1, 1994*, University of Florida 1995.

gave Florida 4 extra seats each decade, for a current total of 23. The Florida delegation is now larger than that of all other states except California, New York and Texas. Greater political clout at the national level is one clear result of Florida's rapid population growth.

The geographic distribution of Florida's population has changed dramatically during the twentieth century. Figure 1 shows a division of Florida into three regions: the north is everything above the Alachua-Marion county line and the south is everything below Lake Okeechobee; the central region is everything in between. In 1900, two-thirds of Florida's residents lived in the northern region of the state and fewer than one in twenty lived in the southern region (Table 2). Duval was the largest county, with a population of 39,733. Dade (which in 1900 included present-day Dade, Broward, Palm Beach and Martin counties) had fewer than 5,000 residents.

Since 1900 a tremendous southward shift has occurred. Fueled by agricultural and industrial growth, tourism, retiree migration and an expanding transportation system, the populations of central and

Table 3. Population Growth Rates
by Region 1990-1994

Decade	North	Central	South	Florida
1900-1910	31.1	62.8	74.3	42.4
1910-1920	13.6	41.6	110.8	28.7
1920-1930	16.5	72.3	166.6	51.6
1930-1940	19.3	21.6	70.9	29.2
1940-1950	31.5	42.6	76.1	46.1
1950-1960	36.9	90.8	113.8	78.7
1960-1970	18.4	38.2	50.7	37.2
1970-1980	24.9	49.9	47.9	43.5
1980-1990	23.8	39.4	29.8	32.7
1990-1994	8.4	7.8	6.1	7.3

Sources: T. Stanton Dietrich, *The Urbanization of Florida's Population: An Historical Perspective of County Growth, 1830-1970*, Bureau of Economic and Business Research, University of Florida, 1978. Bureau of Economic and Business Research, *Florida Estimates of Population, April 1, 1994*, University of Florida 1995.

south Florida mushroomed while the population of north Florida lagged (Table 3). Between 1900 and 1980, growth rates averaged 89 percent per decade in the southern region, 53 percent in the central region and only 24 percent in the northern region. By 1980, 43 percent of the state's population lived in the central region, 37 percent in the southern region and 20 percent in the northern region.

Recent trends, however, indicate that the southward shift in Florida's population has come to an end. During the 1970s the central region grew more rapidly than the southern region for the first time in this century. During the 1980s the central region grew much more rapidly than the southern region and the northern region grew almost as fast. Since 1990, the northern region has been the fastest growing in the state, the southern region the slowest growing. By 1994, 45 percent of the state's population lived in the central region, 36 percent in the southern region and 19 percent in the northern region. The southern region's share of state population has declined since 1980 and although its numbers will continue to increase, its share will most likely decline slowly in future years. In terms of the geographic distribution of its population, Florida has passed an important turning point in its history.

Figure 2. Annual Births and Deaths in Florida
Since 1950

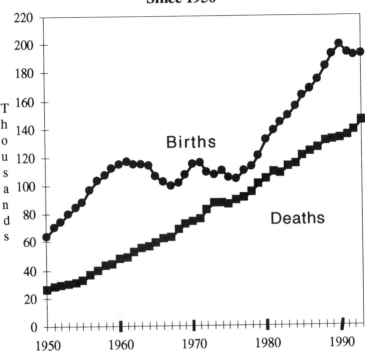

Components of Growth

What accounts for Florida's rapid population growth? There are only three components of growth: births, deaths and migration. A population grows through births and in-migration and declines through deaths and out-migration. The overall expansion or contraction of a state's population thus depends on its combination of births, deaths, in-migrants and out-migrants.

Births. Figure 2 shows the annual number of births and deaths in Florida since 1950. The Baby Boom had a major impact on Florida's population, as the annual number of births almost doubled between 1950 and 1960. This increase was caused both by rapid population growth and by a substantial increase in the average number of births per woman. During the 1960s and early 1970s the number of births per woman declined dramatically but overall population growth kept the total number of births at a fairly constant 100,000 to 120,000 per year.

Since the mid-1970s, the annual number of births has again risen steadily, reaching 199,000 in 1990. This increase was caused by continued population growth, small increases in the average number of births per woman and the aging of the Baby Boom generation, which raised the proportion of women in their prime childbearing years. The number of births has declined a bit since 1990 and will most likely fluctuate between 190,000 and 200,000 per year during the 1990s as the Baby Bust generation born in the 1960s and 1970s replaces the Baby Boomers as women in their prime childbearing years. Births will increase again after the turn of the century, reflecting continued population growth and the aging of persons born since the mid-1970s.

Deaths. Deaths in Florida have followed a totally different pattern than births. Instead of fluctuating up and down, annual deaths have increased steadily from 27,000 in 1950 to 145,000 in 1993. There are two major reasons for this steady increase. First is the much larger population, which has grown five-fold since 1950. Second is population aging. Florida's older population has grown tremendously in recent decades, both in absolute numbers and as a proportion of total population. Since mortality rates are much higher for older people than younger people, an aging population adds substantially to the number of deaths. Deaths in Florida are projected to continue rising steadily in future years.

Natural Increase. The excess of births over deaths is called natural increase. This is the growth that comes from within a population itself, independent of in- and out-migration. The natural increase of Florida's population rose steadily during the Baby Boom, peaking at almost 69,000 in 1959. It then began to fall, reaching 15,000 by 1976. The increase in births since the mid-1970s caused natural increase to rise again, reaching 66,000 in 1990. It has fallen since 1990 and current projections of births and deaths imply that it will continue falling, approaching zero in about fifteen years. After that time, deaths will outnumber births in Florida. There are already twelve counties in Florida in which there are more deaths than births.

Migration. If natural increase is very small (or negative), it follows that population growth must depend primarily (or totally) on

Figure 3. Net Migration and Natural Increase in Florida 1950-1994

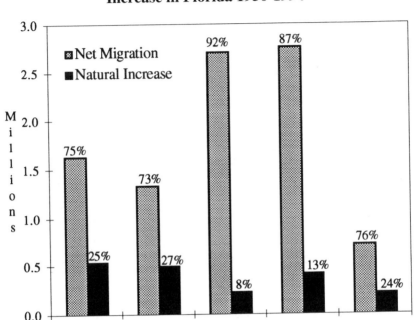

migration. Net migration is the difference between the number of people moving into an area and the number moving out. The net migration stream into Florida in recent decades has been huge, averaging more than 160,000 per year during the 1950s, 130,000 per year during the 1960s and 270,000 per year during both the 1970s and 1980s. In each of the last four decades, Florida has grown more by net migration than any other state except California.

Net migration has declined considerably since 1990, averaging only 180,000 per year from 1990 to 1994. This was primarily the result of the recession in the early 1990s, which slowed the rate of job growth in Florida and made it more difficult for potential migrants to sell their homes in other states. Net migration should pick up again over the next few years, although it is not likely to return to the levels seen in the boom years of the 1970s and 1980s.

Figure 3 shows natural increase and net migration in Florida between 1950 and 1994. During the 1950s and 1960s net migra-

Table 4. Florida's Migration Flows 1955-1960, 1965-1970, 1975-1980, 1985-1990

	1955-1960	1965-1970	1975-1980	1985-1990
Number of Interstate Migrants				
In	1,157,937	1,214,673	1,801,362	2,130,613
Out	381,141	641,168	978,135	1,058,931
Net	776,796	573,505	823,227	1,071,682
Number of Immigrants from Abroad	85,302	184,526	238,831	389,868

Note: Data are not available for persons leaving the United States.

Sources: U.S. Bureau of the Census, *1960 Census of Population*, "Mobility for States and State Economic Areas," Subject Reports PC(2)-2B, September 1963. U.S. Bureau of the Census, *1970 Census of Population*, "Mobility for States and the Nation," Subject Reports PC(2)-2B, June 1973. U.S. Bureau of the Census, *1980 Census of Population*, "Geographic Mobility for States and the Nation," Subject Reports PC80-2-2A, September 1985. U.S. Bureau of the Census, Journey to Work and Migration Statistics Branch, 1990 Census Special Tabulation.

tion accounted for about three-quarters of Florida's population growth. During the 1970s and 1980s it accounted for around 90 percent. This proportion is higher in Florida than any other state, not only because of the large migration flows into the state but also because of the low rate of natural increase. If current projections of births and deaths prove to be accurate, net migration will account for all of Florida's population growth within about fifteen years.

It is clear that migration has been--and will continue to be--the most important cause of Florida's population growth. Table 4 shows that 1.1 million people moved to Florida from other states between 1955 and 1960, 1.2 million between 1965 and 1970, 1.8 million between 1975 and 1980 and 2.1 million between 1985 and 1990. The number of foreign immigrants also has increased steadily, from 85,000 between 1955 and 1960 to 390,000 between 1985 and 1990. Clearly, a large and increasing number of persons have found Florida an attractive place in which to live.

Table 5. State of Origin of Florida In-migrants
1965-1970, 1975-1980, 1985-1990

	1965-1970		1975-1980		1985-1990	
Rank	State	Number	State	Number	State	Number
1	New York	189,446	New York	364,450	New York	361,295
2	Ohio	83,347	Ohio	135,219	New Jersey	150,954
3	Georgia	71,210	New Jersey	134,150	Ohio	120,121
4	New Jersey	70,868	Pennsylvania	104,710	Texas	114,454
5	Illinois	69,653	Illinois	102,192	Illinois	102,286
6	Michigan	67,813	Michigan	95,246	Michigan	99,552
7	Pennsylvania	60,715	Georgia	75,596	Pennsylvania	99,491
8	California	53,247	Massachusetts	63,383	California	94,940
9	Alabama	43,067	California	60,531	Georgia	91,891
10	Virginia	42,235	Virginia	57,794	Massachusetts	81,684

Sources: U.S. Bureau of the Census, *1970 Census of Population*, "Mobility for States and the Nation," Subject Reports PC(2)-2B, June 1973. U.S. Bureau of the Census, *1980 Census of Population*, "Geographic Mobility for States and the Nation," Subject Reports PC80-2-2A, September 1985. U.S. Bureau of the Census, Journey to Work and Migration Statistics Branch, 1990 Census Special Tabulation.

Table 4 also shows that large numbers of people have moved out of Florida: 381,000 between 1955 and 1960, 641,000 between 1965 and 1970, 978,000 between 1975 and 1980 and 1,059,000 between 1985 and 1990. (These numbers refer only to interstate migrants; data on persons leaving the United States are not available). This is not unusual. All states have substantial numbers of people moving in and out, responding to shifting employment and educational opportunities, job transfers, changes in personal preferences, changes in family status (e.g., marriage or divorce) and so forth. Migration out of rapidly growing states is often particularly high because those states have large numbers of especially migration-prone persons. It is not surprising, then, that more people left Florida between 1985 and 1990 than left all but three other states.

What are the major origins and destinations of Florida's migrants? Table 5 shows the leading states of origin for the last three decades. New York was the leading state by a wide margin in each decade. Ohio, New Jersey, Pennsylvania, Illinois and Michigan were other large northern states to rank consistently among the top ten. Georgia was the only southern state to rank in the top ten in all three decades.

Table 6. State of Destination of Florida Out-migrants
1965-1970, 1975-1980, 1985-1990

	1965-1970		1975-1980		1985-1990	
Rank	State	Number	State	Number	State	Number
1	Georgia	77,849	Georgia	103,782	Georgia	119,073
2	California	57,655	Texas	81,402	California	71,766
3	New York	37,798	California	69,922	North Carolina	67,399
4	Texas	36,556	North Carolina	51,749	New York	64,214
5	Alabama	32,956	New York	49,452	Texas	55,878
6	Virginia	31,852	Alabama	46,682	Virginia	55,125
7	North Carolina	31,836	Virginia	42,971	Ohio	51,789
8	Ohio	27,877	Tennessee	40,908	Alabama	44,215
9	South Carolina	22,303	Ohio	40,431	Pennsylvania	38,888
10	Tennessee	21,307	Illinois	30,741	Tennessee	38,082

Sources: U.S. Bureau of the Census, *1970 Census of Population*, "Mobility for States and the Nation," Subject Reports PC(2)-2B, June 1973. U.S. Bureau of the Census, *1980 Census of Population*, "Geographic Mobility for States and the Nation," Subject Reports PC80-2-2A, September 1985. U.S. Bureau of the Census, Journey to Work and Migration Statistics Branch, 1990 Census Special Tabulation.

States from the Northeast and Midwest regions accounted for 61 percent of all domestic migrants into Florida in 1965-1970, 68 percent in 1975-1980 and 61 percent in 1985-1990. States from the South accounted for 32 percent, 25 percent and 31 percent in those three time periods, respectively. The West accounted for less than 10 percent of Florida's in-migrants in all three time periods.

The destinations of Florida's out-migrants differ considerably from the origins of its in-migrants (Table 6). Georgia was the leading destination in all three time periods; California, Texas, Virginia, North Carolina, Alabama and Tennessee also ranked consistently in the top ten. New York and Ohio were the only northern states to rank in the top ten in all three time periods. About half of Florida's out-migrants moved to other southern states; the other half moved in approximately equal numbers to the Northeast, Midwest and West regions. As is true for most states, a large proportion of the people leaving Florida are heading for other Sunbelt states.

Table 7 shows the age distribution of Florida's migrants for the 1950s, 1960s, 1970s and 1980s. Contrary to popular belief, most persons moving to Florida are young rather than elderly. At least

Table 7. Age Distribution of Florida's Interstate Migrants 1955-1960, 1965-1970, 1975-1980, 1985-1990

	1955-1960		1965-1970		1975-1980		1985-1990	
Age	Number	Percent	Number	Percent	Number	Percent	Number	Percent
				In-Migrants				
5 - 14	229,671	19.8	218,795	18.0	239,280	13.3	262,841	12.3
15 - 24	191,176	16.5	232,531	19.1	337,385	18.7	331,356	15.6
25 - 34	196,996	17.0	187,576	15.4	336.456	18.7	465,005	21.8
35 - 44	162,799	14.1	130,365	10.7	190,474	10.6	318,539	15.0
45 - 54	113,971	9.8	110,127	9.1	157,447	8.7	198,523	9.3
55 - 64	117,463	10.1	139,182	11.5	253,586	14.1	238,556	11.2
65+	145,861	12.6	196,097	16.1	286,734	15.9	315,793	14.8
Total	1,157,937	100.0	1,214,673	100.0	1,801,362	100.0	2,130,613	100.0
				Out-Migrants				
5 - 14	83,964	22.0	148,338	23.1	239,280	17.1	152,895	14.4
15 - 24	82,695	21.7	162,680	25.4	241,873	24.7	199,876	18.9
25 - 34	94,636	24.8	146,557	22.9	273,021	27.9	305,472	28.8
35 - 44	56,358	14.8	78,812	12.3	116,616	11.9	167,649	15.8
45 - 54	26,776	7.0	43,352	6.8	62,654	6.4	78,200	7.4
55 - 64	16,894	4.4	24,670	3.8	46,161	4.7	50,712	4.8
65+	19,818	5.2	36,759	5.7	70,439	7.2	104,127	9.8
Total	381,141	100.0	641,168	100	978135.0	100	1,058,931	100.0
				Net Migration				
5 - 14	145,707	18.8	70,457	12.3	71909.0	8.7	109,946	10.3
15 - 24	108,481	14.0	69,851	12.2	95512.0	11.6	131,480	12.3
25 - 34	102,360	13.2	41,019	7.2	63435.0	7.7	159,533	14.9
35 - 44	106,441	13.7	51,553	9.0	73858.0	9.0	150,890	14.1
45 - 54	87,195	11.2	66,775	11.6	94793.0	11.5	120,323	11.2
55 - 64	100,569	12.9	114,512	20.0	207425.0	25.2	187,844	17.5
65+	126,043	16.2	159,338	27.8	216295.0	26.3	211,666	19.8
Total	776,796	100.0	573,505	100.0	823227.0	100.0	1,071,682	100.0

Sources: U.S. Bureau of the Census, *1960 Census of Population*, "Mobility for States and State Economic Areas," Subject Reports PC(2)-2B, September 1963. U.S. Bureau of the Census, *1970 Census of Population*, "Mobility for States and the Nation," Subject Reports PC(2)-2B, June 1973. U.S. Bureau of the Census, *1980 Census of Population*, "Geographic Mobility for States and the Nation," Subject Reports PC80-2-2A, September 1985. U.S. Bureau of the Census, *1990 Census of Population*, Public Use Sample Tapes.

half the in-migrants were younger than age 35 in all time periods; only 12-16 percent were age 65 and older. However, young persons also account for most of Florida's out-migrants. In each time period, more than 60 percent of all persons leaving the state were younger than age 35. The high proportion of migrants made up by young

Table 8. Primary Reason for Moving to Florida by Age: In-migrants in 1992 and 1993
(percent distribution)

Age	N	Employ-ment	Climate	Family	College/Military	Other	Total
18-24	54	37.0	11.1	22.2	16.7	13.0	100.0
25-34	96	54.2	11.5	11.4	11.5	11.4	100.0
35-44	62	40.3	19.4	12.9	11.3	16.1	100.0
45-54	31	41.9	35.5	12.9	0.0	9.7	100.0
55-64	38	7.9	65.8	13.2	0.0	13.1	100.0
65+	18	5.6	61.1	16.7	0.0	16.6	100.0
Total	299	38.1	25.4	14.4	9.0	13.1	100.0

Source: Bureau of Economic and Business Research, University of Florida, unpublished data from 1992 and 1993 Florida household surveys.

persons is a common finding in migration studies. Migration rates are high for young adults because they are not as closely bound to an area by job or family ties as older adults and they face longer lifespans over which to reap the economic benefits of moving.

Relatively few older persons move out of Florida. Only 10-15 percent of out-migrants during the last four decades were age 55 and older. Consequently, the net migration stream into Florida has been heavily skewed toward the older ages. For example, between 1985 and 1990 there were 57 out-migrants for every 100 in-migrants younger than age 55; for persons age 55 and older, there were only 28 out-migrants for every 100 in-migrants. Migration is the major cause of Florida's population aging since 1950.

Why do people move to Florida? The obvious answer is sun, surf and sand. In many instances, however, that is not the correct answer (Table 8). Climate has a relatively minor impact on migration for younger people. For people younger than age 45, employment (e.g., job transfer, take a new job, look for work) is by far the major reason for moving to Florida. The impact of climate on migration increases steadily with age, however, and for persons above age 55 climate is by far the major reason for moving to Florida.

To summarize, Florida's population growth is due primarily to high rates of net in-migration. Huge numbers of people have moved to Florida during the twentieth century (especially in recent decades) and there are no signs that these numbers are yet beginning to decline. Job opportunities, climate and other amenities have attracted people to Florida, and the development of home air conditioning undoubtedly played a role as well (84 percent of Florida's homes were air conditioned in 1980, a higher proportion than in any other state). These migrants have had a major impact on Florida, radically altering many of its demographic and socioeconomic characteristics.

Changes in Demographic Characteristics

The make-up of Florida's population has changed considerably during the twentieth century (Table 9). One change has been the switch from a predominantly male to a predominantly female population. In 1900 there were 109 males for every 100 females in Florida. By 1990 this ratio had been reversed: 107 females for every 100 males. A similar change occurred for United States as a whole, but the change was more pronounced in Florida because of its older age structure. This change was caused primarily by the greater increase in the lifespan of females than males. In 1900, females outlived males by an average of three years (51 vs. 48); by 1990, the difference was seven years (79 vs. 72). The numerical dominance of females is especially strong in the older age groups. In 1990 there were 135 women for every 100 men age 65 and above in Florida; above age 85, there were 200 women for every 100 men.

There has also been a major change in the racial composition of Florida's population. At the turn of the century, 56 percent of Florida's population was white and 44 percent was black (persons of other races accounted for only 0.1 percent). Although the number of blacks increased in every decade since 1900, the number of whites increased much more rapidly, causing a steady decline in blacks as a proportion of total population. By 1990, whites accounted for 84 percent of Florida's population; blacks, 14 percent; and persons of other races, 2 percent. This change was the direct result of migration: the vast

Table 9. Distribution of Florida Population by Age, Sex and Race 1900-1994

	1900	1910	1920	1930	1940	1950	1960	1970	1980	1990	1994
					Percent						
Male	52.1	52.4	51.1	50.2	49.7	49.3	49.2	48.2	48.0	48.4	48.4
Female	47.9	47.6	48.9	49.8	50.3	50.7	50.8	51.8	52.0	51.6	51.6
White	56.3	58.9	65.9	70.5	72.8	78.2	82.1	84.3	85.4	84.8	84.5
Black	43.7	41.0	34.0	29.4	27.1	21.7	17.8	15.3	13.8	13.7	14.0
Other	0.1	0.1	0.1	0.1	0.1	0.1	0.1	0.4	0.8	1.5	1.5
<Age 15	38.6	35.7	33.4	29.8	25.1	26.2	29.6	25.8	19.3	18.8	19.2
Age 65+	2.6	2.8	4.2	4.8	6.9	8.6	11.2	14.6	17.3	18.2	18.5
					Years						
Median Age	20.4	21.9	23.9	25.8	28.9	30.9	31.2	32.2	34.7	36.4	37.5

Sources: T. Stanton Dietrich, *The Urbanization of Florida's Population: An Historical Perspective of County Growth 1830-1970*, Bureau of Economic and Business Research, University of Florida, 1978. U.S. Bureau of the Census, *1980 Census of Population*, PC80-1-B11, August 1982. U.S. Bureau of the Census, *1990 Census of Population and Housing*, STF1-A (adjusted). Bureau of Economic and Business Research, University of Florida, unpublished data.

majority of persons moving to Florida during the twentieth century has been white.

Perhaps the most important demographic change in Florida during the twentieth century has been the change in age structure. In 1900 the median age of Florida's population was 20.4, younger than for the United States as a whole (22.9). During the next fifty years falling birth rates made both populations considerably older. By 1950 the median age had reached 30.9 for Florida and 30.2 for the United States. In both populations, 8 to 9 percent were age 65 and older.

After 1950 a tremendous shift occurred. The national population became younger while Florida's population became older. The median age of the United States population declined to 28.0 by 1970, while Florida's rose to 32.2. The United States population became younger because the Baby Boom produced millions of children during the 1950s and 1960s. Since Florida had its own Baby Boom, why did its median age rise instead of fall? Again, the answer lies with migration: the net migration stream into Florida during the 1950s and 1960s was so heavily weighted toward the older ages that it more than offset the rejuvenating effects of the Baby Boom.

Since 1970, declining birth rates and increasing longevity have led to older populations in both Florida and the United States. (In Florida, the in-migration of older persons has continued to play a role.) By 1990 the median age for the United States was 32.9; for Florida it was 36.4, the highest of any state's. In addition, 18.2 percent of Florida's population was age 65 and older compared to 12.6 percent for the United States. This proportion was higher in Florida than in any other state. In twelve of the state's sixty-seven counties, more than 25 percent of the population is above age 65; eight additional counties have between 20 and 25 percent above age 65.

Florida's age structure is one of its unique demographic features. It has a major impact on child care, health care, education, employment, housing demand, voter behavior and many other important issues. Florida today foreshadows the United States age structure in thirty or forty years, and Florida's attempts to deal with an aging population will be instructive for the nation as a whole.

Comparing Florida with Other States

How does Florida's population compare to that of other states? As shown in Table 10, Florida's population grew by almost 3.2 million between 1980 and 1990, more than that of any other state except California. This represented a 33 percent increase, the fourth-highest growth rate of any state. Population growth has made Florida a highly urbanized state, as 85 percent of its population lived in urban areas in 1990 compared to 76 percent nationally.

Florida has by far the oldest population of any state in the United States. The median age (36.4) and proportion age 65+ (18.2 percent) are higher in Florida than in any other state, while the proportion younger than age 15 (18.6 percent) is lower than in any state except the District of Columbia. Average household size (2.46) is also lower in Florida than in any state except the District of Columbia, reflecting the large number of older persons living alone or with one other person.

Only 35 percent of Florida's residents were born in the state, compared to 67 percent nationally. This is a lower proportion than in any

Table 10. Demographic and Socioeconomic Characteristics, Florida and the United States 1990

Characteristics	Florida	Rank	United States
Population Size	12,937,926	4	248,709,873
Population Growth 1980-1990 (Number)	3,191,602	2	22,164,068
Population Growth 1980-1990 (Percent)	32.8	4	9.8
Percent Urban	84.8	9	75.9
Median Age	36.4	1	32.9
Percent Younger Than Age 15	18.6	50	21.5
Percent Age 65+	18.2	1	12.6
Average Household Size	2.46	50	2.63
Percent Black	13.6	16	12.1
Percent Hispanic	12.2	7	9.0
Percent Born in Same State	34.9	50	67.1
Percent Foreign-born	12.9	4	7.9
Percent in Labor Force (Age 16+)	60.4	47	65.3
Percent High School Graduates (Age 25+)	74.4	37	75.2
Percent College Graduates (Age 25+)	18.3	30	20.3
Per Capita Income (1989)	14,698	18	14,420
Median Household Income (1989)	27,483	29	30,056
Percent of Families in Poverty (1989)	9.0	26	10.0

Source: U.S. Bureau of the Census, *1990 Census of Population and Housing*, CPH-1-1, CPH-5-1 and Summary Tape Files 1C and 3C.

state except Nevada, reflecting the high rate of migration into Florida. Thirteen percent of Florida's residents were foreign-born, more than in all but three other states. Florida has the sixteenth-largest proportion of blacks (13.6 percent) and the seventh-largest proportion of Hispanics (12.2 percent) of any state.

Only 60 percent of Floridians age 16 and older are in the labor force, a lower proportion than in all but four other states. This reflects the impact of the many retirees who have moved to Florida. Florida has lower proportions of high school and college graduates than the United States as a whole. This is also due partially to Florida's age structure, as older people generally have lower levels of educational attainment than younger people.

Florida's income levels are similar to those for the United States. Florida has a slightly higher per capita income ($14,698) than the nation as a whole but has a lower median household income ($27,483).

The proportion of families in poverty is also lower in Florida than nationally (9 versus 10 percent). These differences are not large and Florida's income and poverty levels rank about in the middle of the pack when compared to those of other states.

Florida can thus be characterized as a large, rapidly growing, highly urbanized state with high proportions of blacks, Hispanics, older people and migrants from other states and abroad. It has low proportions of children and labor force participants and has a very low average household size. Levels of educational attainment are somewhat lower in Florida than in most states but income and poverty levels are similar to those in the rest of the United States.

A Look Ahead

The future of Florida's economy, culture, political structure and natural environment is intimately tied to its population growth. Successful planning thus requires a realistic assessment of future population growth. Table 11 summarizes the most recent projections of Florida's population. The population is expected to continue growing rapidly, although not as rapidly as during the 1970s and 1980s. The Florida population is projected to grow by about 2.5 million in each of the next three decades, reaching 20.3 million by 2020. It is also expected to continue aging. The proportion age 65+ remains fairly flat over the next two decades but the proportion age 45-64 increases very rapidly, from 20 percent of total population in 1990 to 28 percent in 2010. The first of the Baby Boomers reach age 65 in 2010 and the proportion age 65 and above then begins to increase rapidly, reaching 21 percent by 2020.

The number of children (younger than age 15) is expected to continue rising, faster than the rest of the population until 2000 but more slowly thereafter. Consequently, that age group will comprise a declining proportion of total population after the year 2000. The proportion in the prime working ages (15-64) will remain stable until 2010, at 62 to 63 percent of the total population. From 2010 to 2020 this proportion drops to 61 percent, reflecting the more rapid growth in the older population.

Table 11. Florida's Population by Age in 1970, 1980 and 1990, and Projections for 2000, 2010 and 2020

Age	1970 Number	Percent	1980 Number	Percent	1990* Number	Percent
<15	1,749,907	25.8	1,876,774	19.3	2,428,671	18.8
15-24	1,073,293	15.8	1,622,767	16.7	1,682,627	13.0
25-44	1,508,628	22.2	2,450,189	25.1	3,920,704	30.3
45-64	1,468,249	21.6	2,109,021	21.6	2,549,998	19.7
65+	989,366	14.6	1,687,573	17.3	2,355,926	18.2
Total	6,789,443	100.0	9,746,324	100.0	12,937,926	100.0

Age	2000 Number	Percent	2010 Number	Percent	2020 Number	Percent
<15	3,015,404	19.4	3,266,096	18.2	3,713,600	18.2
15-24	1,853,437	11.9	2,278,100	12.7	2,364,290	11.6
25-44	4,209,947	27.1	4,097,835	22.8	4,688,009	23.0
45-64	3,557,017	22.9	5,008,308	27.9	5,302,856	26.1
65+	2,891,579	18.6	3,308,223	18.4	4,280,946	21.0
Total	15,527,384	100.0	17,958,562	100.0	20,349,701	100.0

*The age numbers for 1990 are based on the Census Bureau's modified census counts, which differ slightly from the numbers shown in other publications.

Sources: U.S. Bureau of the Census, *1980 Census of Population*, PC80-1-B11, Table 20, August 1982; U.S. Bureau of the Census, *1990 Census of Population and Housing*; SFT1A (adjusted). Bureau of Economic and Business Research, University of Florida, unpublished data.

The movement of the Baby Boom generation through the population's age structure over time has been likened to a pig being swallowed by a python: no matter where it is, its impact is visible and substantial. The huge number of babies born during the 1950s became the elementary school children of the 1960s, the high school and college students of the 1970s and the young adults of the 1980s. They will become the middle-aged work force of the 1990s and early twenty-first century, and the retirees of the second and third decades of that century. Their influence will be felt throughout their lifetimes, affecting politics, education, healthcare, recreation, housing, the labor market, the Social Security system and virtually every other facet of American life. The impact of that generation can scarcely be overemphasized, in Florida or any other state.

The century-long decline in blacks as a proportion of Florida's total population has ended. This proportion has stabilized at around 14 percent and will most likely edge up slightly in coming decades. This turnaround has been caused by higher rates of natural increase for blacks than whites and by increases in net in-migration for blacks. The impact of this change will be strongest among school-age children because the black population is much younger than the white population.

It is also likely that Florida's Hispanic population will continue to soar. In 1970 Florida had 451,000 Hispanic residents, representing 6.6 percent of the total population. By 1990 this number had grown to 1.6 million, more than 12 percent of the total population. Cubans form the largest proportion of Florida's Hispanic population (43 percent in 1990, down from 55 percent in 1980); in fact, Florida has more residents of Cuban origin than all other states combined. Given Florida's proximity to Latin America and the strong economic and cultural ties that have developed in recent decades (especially in south Florida), it is likely that Florida's Hispanic population will continue growing rapidly during the 1990s and beyond.

It is impossible to guarantee the accuracy of these population projections, of course. Unexpected changes could occur in mortality rates, fertility rates and especially migration rates. It is a near certainty that Florida's population will continue to grow rapidly, however, and will continue to age and to become more ethnically diverse. The primary challenge facing the state in the coming years will be to maintain its attractive quality of life in face of the constant demands for expansion and change created by rapid population growth.

The Labor Market

3

Lawrence W. Kenny
Professor and Chair
Department of Economics
and
J. F. (Dick) Scoggins
Associate Director
Bureau of Economic and
Business Research
University of Florida
Gainesville, Florida

There are many misconceptions about southern labor markets and about the Florida labor market in particular. It is true that wages in Florida are lower than the national average, in part because the desirable climate and lower pollution levels of most of Florida are nonwage attractions for job seekers. However, negative factors such as crime and the high cost of land can push wages up. Government can do little to change the cost of land, which rises with population growth. However, the possibility does exist for government to affect the wage structure by reducing crime and pollution. There will be policy options for local and state governments to consider as Florida enters the twenty-first century.

Why Do Floridians Have Lower Wages?

In 1993, the average annual pay in the United States was $26,362 (U.S. Department of Labor 1994b).[1] In contrast, the typical Florida worker took home a paycheck that totaled 10.6 percent less, or $23,571.

---

[1]The figure is calculated by dividing the total annual pay of employees covered by unemployment insurance programs by the average monthly number of these employees.

Table 1. 1990 Educational Profile
of Individuals 25 or Older
(percent)

Profile	Florida	United States
0 to 4 years of elementary school	2.5	2.7
5 to 8 years of elementary school	7.0	7.7
1 to 3 years of high school	16.1	14.4
4 years of high school	30.1	30.0
1 to 3 years of college	26.0	24.9
4 years of college or more	18.3	20.3

Source: Bureau of the Census, *1990 Census of Population.*

Why are wages lower in Florida? Some would argue that lower wages in the South are the result of distinct regional labor markets. Under this explanation, southern workers are getting a worse deal than workers in other regions. But if that is the case, workers should be leaving the South in droves. Instead, a multitude of workers are migrating to the South, especially to Florida.

Do the lower wages, then, reflect poorer skills, a lower cost of living, more desirable living conditions or a smaller membership in unions? Do these factors fully account for the lower wages in Florida?

Skills. More-skilled workers receive higher wages. The skills that workers bring to the job have been gauged by several yardsticks, including education, age, sex, race and ethnic background. Florida's labor force differs from the U.S. labor force in several interesting ways.

In 1990, the educational attainment of Florida's population was strikingly similar to that of the nation, as can be seen in Table 1. There was, however, a little less diversity in the number of years spent in school by Floridians. Relatively fewer Floridians had gone only to elementary school or had graduated from college. The difference between educational attainment in Florida and in the nation is estimated to lower average income in Florida by 0.7 percent.[2] The

___

[2] 1993 median income for each of these educational groups has been multiplied by the fraction in that category. The data source for median income is *Current Population Reports*, Series P-60-188, February 1995.

Table 2. 1990 Age Profile of Civilian Labor Force
(percent)

Age	Florida	United States
16-19	5.3	5.6
20-24	10.2	11.0
25-54	68.6	69.6
55-64	10.3	9.4
65-69	2.3	1.8
70+	1.7	1.2

Source: Bureau of the Census, *1990 Census of Population.*

reduction in income from having fewer college graduates more than offsets the increase in income from having fewer with only an elementary education.

Older workers generally have more labor market experience, which is associated with greater knowledge and thus higher earnings. On the other hand, elderly workers often put in fewer hours and accordingly have smaller annual earnings. Table 2 shows that the age profile of Florida's civilian workers in 1990 was   similar to the age distribution of civilian workers in the nation. However, Florida's unusually large elderly population is reflected in its labor force and workers over age 54 represent a 1.9 percent larger share in Florida than in the nation. Young workers under age 25 correspondingly comprise a slightly smaller share of Florida's workforce. On net, the small differences in the age distribution of workers are estimated to have no effect on Florida salaries.[3]

The sexual composition of Florida's labor force is also similar to that of the nation. Female workers account for 46.2 percent of workers in Florida and 45.8 percent of the nation's workforce (U.S. Department of Labor 1994a). Women receive lower annual incomes, at least partly because they work fewer hours and have less experience in the labor market. The slightly higher representation of women in

---

[3]1993 median income for each of these age groups has been multiplied by the fraction in the category.

Florida's workforce is estimated to result in 0.2 percent lower earnings.[4]

Florida, like every southern state, has a large black population: 13.1 percent of the workforce compared to only 10.2 percent of workers nationally (U.S. Department of Labor 1994a). Under segregated school systems, the spending per black child was far below the spending per white child (Nechyba 1990). Thus, black children in this era acquired fewer skills than their white counterparts. Although school segregation was struck down in 1954, many of today's black workers attended segregated school systems and have suffered their ill effects. Smith and Welch (1989) report that in 1980 the ratio of the weekly wage for black males with a twelfth-grade education to that of white males was 0.789. When this earnings ratio is applied to the racial mixes in Florida and in the nation, the larger black population in Florida is estimated to pull Florida earnings down by 0.6 percent.

Hispanics in 1993 made up a much larger part of Florida's workforce (14.0 percent) than of the U.S. workforce (7.8 percent) (U.S. Department of Labor 1994a). This reflects the large influx of Cubans when that country became communist and the sizeable migration from nearby Central and South America. Many recent immigrants are not fluent in English. The labor market penalizes people who do not speak the modal language well, and McManus, Gould and Welch (1983) have found that Hispanics with poor English have lower earnings than Hispanics with good English. In fact, they have some evidence that poor English accounts for all of the earnings differential between Hispanics and Anglos, after controlling for schooling, labor market experience and residence in a metropolitan area. Long (1977) estimates that Hispanics with a Cuban background and the same education, age, location, hours worked and marital status as whites earn 89 percent as much as Anglos. Mexican-Americans earn 72 percent as much as comparable Anglos. In 1990, 45.0 percent of Hispanics in Florida were from Cuba but only 5.7 percent of U.S. Hispanics were Cuban (Bureau of the Census 1990). If the earnings ratio for Mexican-Americans is applied to non-Cubans, these figures imply that the larger Hispanic population in Florida reduces average earnings by 0.7 percent.

---

[4] 1993 median incomes for men and women have been multiplied by the fraction in each category.

None of the skill comparisons favors Florida. The smaller variance in educational attainment and the greater importance of women, blacks and Hispanics in the labor force together lower Florida salaries by 2.2 percent.

Location. There are sizable geographical differences in income. Recent studies have used the theory of compensating wage differentials to explain these differences. In a simple version of this theory, competition among firms for workers leads to wage differentials that give workers the same level of happiness in each job. This implies that wages must be higher in cities that are more expensive and otherwise equally desirable. Kenny and Denslow (1980) found some evidence supporting the strong prediction that wages fully adjust for geographic differences in the cost of living; i.e., cities that are 10 percent more expensive, other things equal, have 10 percent higher wages. Wages are also expected to rise to compensate workers for living in a less desirable climate and a more polluted or crime-ridden city. What impact do the cost of living, climate, pollution and crime have on salaries in Florida?

Most of the geographical variation in the cost of living is due to land prices. Urban areas bid land away from agricultural use, so to understand how urban land prices are determined we must first understand how agricultural land prices are determined. Agricultural land prices reflect fertility, rainfall, length of growing season and proximity to markets. In 1992, the average value per acre of land and buildings in agriculture in Florida was $2,037. The population-weighted average value of agricultural land in the U.S. was $1,684.[5] An increase in the value of agricultural land leads to higher rural and urban land prices, which raise the cost of living and produce a compensating increase in salaries. Kenny and Denslow found that salaries are higher in locations where agricultural land is more expensive. The higher value of agricultural land in Florida is estimated to raise salaries by 0.4 percent.[6]

---

[5]The state values of agricultural land have been weighted by the state populations. This more closely approximates the value of land than does the unweighted value of agricultural land. Source: *1992 Census of Agriculture.*

[6]Kenny and Denslow's regression coefficient was multiplied by the difference in agricultural land prices in 1969 dollars.

Land in urbanized areas is more valuable than land in rural areas because urban land has been bid away from agricultural uses. Wages are expected to be higher in urbanized areas to compensate for the higher cost of living there, and Kenny and Denslow found evidence that this is indeed the case. A higher fraction of Florida's population lives in urban areas (0.848) than is so for the nation (0.752). Kenny and Denslow's estimates imply that this would lift salaries in Florida by 0.6 percent.

Some urbanized areas are more expensive than others. A three-bedroom, two-bath house in Los Angeles commonly costs $500,000 but rarely costs more than $100,000 in Lakeland, Florida. There is a greater demand for land with a centralized location in metropolitan areas with larger populations, which drives up the cost of land and thus leads to higher wages. Many scholars have found that wages are higher in larger cities. Floridians live in smaller metropolitan areas than typically are found in the nation. Although 8.0 percent of the U.S. population lives in cities with at least one million people, there are no Florida cities this large. The typical U.S. metropolitan area has 737,687 people and the average Florida metropolitan area has 618,636. By Aggarwal's (1988) estimates, this difference in the size of metropolitan areas reduces Florida wages by 0.2 percent.

Together, the higher price of agricultural land, the more extensive urbanization and the smaller size of metropolitan areas in Florida are estimated to raise wages in the state by 0.8 percent.

We have seen that the higher cost of land makes the cost of living higher in Florida. But land prices are not the only factor. Local labor is an important input for many locally produced services such as haircuts, restaurant meals and physician visits. If barbers, waitresses, nurses and physicians are willing to accept lower wages to obtain the more attractive climate and cleaner air found in Florida, then the cost of their services, and thus the cost of living, will be lower in Florida.

The analysis that follows estimates the total effects of climate, pollution and crime on wages. Included in each total effect is the direct effect reflecting preferences (for example, how much someone is willing to give up for a warmer winter) and the indirect effect associated with the resulting change in the cost of living (for example, the lower cost of restaurant meals because restaurant workers are willing to work for lower wages in cities with warmer winters).

The climate is an important determinant of earnings. Aggarwal, in an extensive study of the relationship between climate and earnings in U.S. metropolitan areas in 1980, found that wages are lower in cities with warmer winter climates. This evidence from the labor market implies that the average worker prefers warmer winters. She also finds that cities such as San Francisco, with an average July temperature of 62 degrees Fahrenheit, are too cold in the summer and that Florida is too hot in the summer. Given equal winter climates, wages are lowest at an average July temperature of 77 degrees (Baltimore, Los Angeles, New York), which means that this is the summer climate that is ideal for the typical worker.

The center of the U.S. population in 1990 was approximately halfway between St. Louis and Springfield, Missouri. The center of Florida's population in 1990 was near Lakeland, in central Florida. The climates for these two areas will be used to estimate the effects of climate on Florida earnings. The average January temperature in St. Louis - Springfield is 30.1 degrees and in Lakeland is 61.0 degrees. According to Aggarwal's estimates, this difference in winter climates lowers wages in Florida by 11.6 percent. On the other hand, workers require some compensation to put up with Florida summers. July temperatures are 78.5 degrees in St. Louis - Springfield and 82.4 in central Florida. Aggarwal's estimates imply that the hot summers increase wages in Florida by 2.9 percent. Florida calls itself the Sunshine State and indeed is a relatively sunny location. The sun shines on central Florida 65.5 percent of the time, compared with 61.1 percent for the nation. Blomquist, Berger and Hoehn (1988) find that workers are willing to accept a lower salary to work in a sunnier location. Their estimates imply that the sunnier climate in Florida results in 0.5 percent lower wages. On net, climate causes Florida salaries to be 9.2 percent lower.

One benefit from having very little manufacturing is lower pollution. Florida, being mostly a peninsula, also receives very little pollution from nearby states. These factors help explain why Florida's average total suspended particulate level is 3.9 percent lower than the nation's.[7] Roback (1982) has found that wages rise to compensate for more particulates in the air. According to her estimates, the lower air pollution in Florida leads to 0.1 percent lower wages.

Florida provides an attractive environment for crime. Its tourists are easy targets. Prowling outside in January is more pleasant in Florida, and its hot summers may cause tempers to erupt. Florida, with its long coastline, also is the gateway for much of the illegal drug traffic into this country. The violent crime rate in Florida is 62 percent higher than in the nation. Blomquist, Berger and Hoehn (1988) have found that wages rise to compensate workers for living in cities with higher violent crime rates. Their estimates imply that the higher crime rate in Florida causes wages to be 3.4 percent greater.

Land costs, climate, pollution and crime all have a sizeable effect on salaries in Florida. The higher cost of land and crime rate lead to higher salaries, which are more than offset by the reduction in salaries due to Florida's attractive climate and cleaner air. On net, locational factors cause wages to be 5.1 percent lower in Florida.

Unions. Unions are much less important in Florida than they are nationally. In 1989, only 9.0 percent of Florida's manufacturing workforce was unionized, compared with 23.8 percent for the nation (U.S. Department of Commerce 1993). The cost of organizing a union is higher in Florida because of the right-to-work law and the small size of the typical establishment in a state with very little manufacturing. Unions, through the threat of strike, are able to raise wages above their competitive levels. Lewis (1963) estimates that unionization raises wages by 10 percent on average. The relative small membership in unions in Florida thus would cause earnings to be 1.5 percent smaller.

Total explained differences. The estimated wage differentials due to differences in skills, location and unionization are summarized in Table 3. The factors that have been discussed so far are estimated to cause wages in Florida to be 8.8 percent lower than in the nation. As

---

[7]Florida's mean is a weighted average of the 1992 annual total suspended particulate levels reported in different cities, where the weights are county populations. These data come from the *Florida Statistical Abstract* 1993. The U.S. mean is the mean particulate level reported in *Statistical Abstract of the United States* 1994.

Table 3. Explanation of Earnings Differential
Between Florida and U.S. Workers
(percent)

Educational Attainment	-0.7
Ag	0
Sex	-0.2
Black	-0.6
Hispanic	-0.7
Land Values	0.8
Climate	-9.2
Pollution	-0.1
Violent Crime	3.4
Unions	-1.5
Total Explained Difference	-8.8
Unexplained Residual	-1.8
Actual Difference	-10.6

noted above, wages actually are 10.6 percent lower in Florida. Thus, the remaining 1.8 percent difference is unaccounted for. Given the potential error in this kind of analysis, the 1.8 percent residual is quite small and provides some reassurance that our analysis is on target.

We have not taken into account every factor that could affect wages. For some, such as proximity to the ocean and effectiveness of the school system, it is difficult to quantify the effect on wages. The fact that wages in Florida are lower than we have been able to account for may be partly due to the low level of academic achievement of Florida's primary and secondary school students.

Another perspective. The skills acquired through schooling and on-the-job training lead to better jobs in occupations and industries with higher salaries. Unionization is more common in some industries and occupations. Examining the occupational and industrial mixes allows us to view the sources of lower wages in Florida from a slightly different perspective.

The industrial mix in Florida and the United States is given in Table 4. Florida's workers are more concentrated in retail and whole-

Table 4. 1992 Industry Profile of Employed Workers
(percent)

Industry	Florida	United States
Agriculture	2.7	2.7
Mining	0.1	0.6
Construction	5.1	6.0
Manufacturing	9.0	17.0
Transportation, Communication and Public Utilities	5.9	7.0
Wholesale Trade	5.4	4.1
Retail Trade	21.1	16.7
Finance, Insurance and Real Estate	6.6	6.6
Services	36.9	34.7
Government	7.0	4.8

sale trade and in government, which provide services for Florida's large elderly population and for the influx of tourists into the state. Florida has only a little more than half the nation's share of workers in manufacturing. Florida's workers are more concentrated in low-paying sectors (retail trade has particularly low salaries), which pulls their income down by 3.6 percent.[8]

The distributions of occupations for Florida and the nation are shown in Table 5. Because of the importance of tourists and the elderly, Florida's labor force is disproportionately represented by sales and service workers and their managers. Craft workers, operative and professional workers (including scientists and engineers) are less common in this state, which has little manufacturing. Differences in the occupational distributions would produce very little difference in earnings. These differences would give Floridians 1.6 percent higher salaries.[9]

[8]1991 average annual wages and salaries for each industry has been multiplied by the fraction in that category. The data source for salaries is *Statistical Abstract of the United States* 1993.

[9]1992 median income for each of these occupation groups has been multiplied by the fraction in that category. The data source for median income is *Statistical Abstract of the United States* 1994.

Table 5. 1993 Occupational Profile of Employed Workers
(percent)

Occupation	Florida	United States
Executive, Administrative and Managerial	13.2	12.9
Professional Specialty	13.1	14.2
Technicians and Related Support	3.5	3.4
Sales	13.8	12.0
Administrative Support, including Clerical	15.5	15.6
Service Occupations	15.9	13.8
Precision Production, Craft and Repair	10.8	11.1
Machine Operators, Assemblers and Inspectors	3.8	6.2
Transportation and Material Moving	3.9	4.2
Handlers, Equipment Cleaners, Helpers and Laborers	3.5	3.9
Farming, Forestry and Fishing	3.1	2.8

Source: U.S. Department of Labor, Bureau of Labor Statistics, *Geographic Profile of Employment and Unemployment, 1993.*

Conclusion. There is no evidence that the Florida labor market is a distinct labor market operating in isolation from other regions in the country. Instead, we have been successful in explaining why wages are lower in Florida. About a quarter of the differential is attributable to lower skills. Florida's workers are a little less educated and are comprised of more women, blacks and Hispanics. The workforce is correspondingly concentrated in low-paying industries. Almost two-thirds of the wage differential is due to locational factors. Florida's desirable climate pulls wages down by more than 9 percent. This is offset somewhat by the high crime rate and expensive land. Finally, wages are a little lower in Florida because unions have a weaker presence in the state.

A Look Ahead

What does the future hold for the wage gap between Florida and the nation? The answer to this question hinges on what will happen to skills, the cost of living, pollution, crime and unionization and to the wage premiums associated with these factors and climate.

Many of Florida's new workers are young people who have just entered the labor market. There is some evidence that Florida high school seniors have not learned as much as the typical U.S. high school senior. The average SAT scores in several states in 1992-93 are shown in Table 6. The combined average verbal and mathematical score varies by nearly 100 points across states. Some of the highest scores are found in New England and the lowest scores are found in the South. Florida's performance beats Georgia and the Carolinas. Nevertheless, combined SAT scores were 20 points lower in Florida than in the nation. If SAT scores are adjusted for differences across states in the fraction who take the test, Florida's SAT scores are only 14 points, or 1.6 percent, below the national average. The results of the 1992 National Assessment of Educational Progress paint a similar picture. Florida fourth- and eighth-grade reading and mathematics scores are 2.3 to 3.2 percent below U.S. average test scores. These findings indicate that Florida's workforce is less skilled than the national workforce with the same number of years spent in school and thus commands lower wages. There are several possible explanations for the poor performance of Florida students.

First, it appears that Florida is devoting fewer real educational resources to its students. The fact that teacher salaries in Florida are only 89.1 percent as high as teacher salaries nationally suggests that Florida is hiring less qualified teachers.[10] Additionally, the pupil-teacher ratio is higher in Florida (14.4) than in the nation (12.6). Current expenditure per pupil in average daily attendance is 95.1 percent as high in Florida as in the U.S (U.S. Department of Commerce 1993) and would be lower if Florida did not utilize more administrators and support staff than other states.

---

[10]Recall that Florida's locational advantages would lead workers to accept a 5.1 percent lower salary to work in Florida.

Table 6. Scholastic Achievement

Area	Average Proficiency Score 1992 Mathematics 4th Grade	Average Proficiency Score 1992 Mathematics 8th Grade	Average Proficiency Score 1992 Reading 4th Grade	SAT Score 1992-93 Verbal	SAT Score 1992-93 Math	SAT Score 1992-93 Percent Taking
United States	217	266	216	424 (424)	478 (478)	43
California	207	260	203	415 (416)	484 (485)	47
Connecticut	226	273	223	430 (439)	474 (485)	88
Delaware	217	262	214	430 (436)	465 (472)	68
Florida	212	259	209	416 (419)	466 (469)	52
Georgia	214	259	213	399 (404)	445 (451)	65
Hawaii	213	257	204	401 (404)	478 (482)	56
Indiana	220	269	222	409 (414)	460 (465)	61
Maine	231	278	228	422 (428)	463 (470)	69
Maryland	216	264	212	431 (437)	478 (485)	66
Massachusetts	226	272	227	427 (436)	476 (486)	81
New Hampshire	229	278	229	442 (450)	487 (496)	78
New Jersey	226	271	224	419 (427)	473 (482)	76
New York	217	266	216	416 (423)	471 (479)	74
North Carolina	211	258	213	406 (410)	453 (458)	60
Pennsylvania	223	271	222	418 (425)	460 (467)	70
Rhode Island	214	265	218	419 (426)	464 (471)	71

Continued . . .

Table 6. Scholastic Achievement
(Continued)

| Area | Average Proficiency Score 1992 | | | SAT Score 1992-93 | | |
| | Mathematics | | Reading | | | |
	4th Grade	8th Grade	4th Grade	Verbal	Math	Percent Taking
South Carolina	211	260	211	396 (400)	442 (447)	61
Texas	217	264	214	413 (414)	472 (473)	45
Virginia	220	267	222	425 (430)	469 (475)	63

Note: States include those that participated in the National Assessment of Educational Progress in 1992 and in which at least 30 percent of high school graduates took the SAT test. SAT scores in parentheses have been adjusted for differences in the percent taking the test.

Source: Center of Educational Statistics, *Digest of Education Statistics, 1994.*

Second, analysis of the earnings gap attributes lower earnings in Florida to a larger black and Hispanic population when educational attainment and age are held constant. The explanations provided for the black and Hispanic wage differentials initially seem inadequate to account fully for the lower SAT scores in Florida. School systems today are integrated and many Hispanic schoolchildren have been raised in the United States and speak English well. There may, however, be an intergenerational explanation. Parents who attended poor school systems or who do not speak English well are less capable of helping their children with their schoolwork and their children learn less.

Third, the opportunity cost of studying in terms of recreational activities foregone may be higher in temperate Florida than blustery New England. If this is the case, Florida children may devote fewer hours to study than other children, which lowers learning.[11]

---

[11]Kenny (1980) finds time devoted to study to be an important determinant of performance on standardized tests.

Table 7. Percentage of Youths Enrolled in School in 1990

Age	Florida	United States
15-17	90.4	92.4
18-19	60.5	65.5
20-24	30.8	33.6

Source: Bureau of the Census, *1990 Census of Population.*

Table 8. Percentage of Youths Employed in 1990

Age	Florida	United States
16-19	43.6	40.3
20-24	67.8	70.3

Source: Bureau of the Census, *1990 Census of Population.*

Whatever the explanation, Florida schoolchildren are leaving high school with fewer skills than U.S. children. This ultimately is reflected in lower wages but it is difficult to quantify the effect.

Young people in Florida are also remaining in school for fewer years and participating in the labor market in greater numbers than is the case in the U.S. School enrollment in 1990 is shown in Table 7. The biggest gap between Florida and the nation is found in the high school years. This reflects the fact that in recent years Florida has had one of the lowest high school completion rates in the nation. Employment rates in 1990 are depicted in Table 8. A higher fraction of Florida youths is employed despite the greater difficulty of finding work in a low-wage state such as Florida in the presence of a minimum wage.

The SAT test score and educational enrollment statistics are quite disturbing, for they suggest that the gap in skills between Florida and the rest of the nation is growing, not narrowing. If true, the wage gap will widen in the future.

Florida's population is expected to increase greatly in future years. This will have several effects. First, the greater demand for land will raise land prices. As Florida becomes a relatively more expensive location, the wage gap will become smaller. Second, crime rates are higher in large urban areas. As Florida becomes more urbanized and its metropolitan areas grow, crime rates also will increase. Wage rates will rise to compensate for the higher crime, narrowing the wage gap. Third, pollution is expected to increase as more factories and cars foul the air. This also will decrease the wage gap between Florida and the nation.

Directions. There are several ways in which policy can affect wages. Government can have some impact on workers' skills and on the environment in which they work.

Better skills are the product of a better educational system. This can be achieved by devoting more resources to education and utilizing those resources more efficiently. Higher salaries would attract more effective teachers into Florida's primary and secondary schools. Replacing salary scales with an incentive system that rewards better teachers would foster good teaching. Unlike most other states, Florida has countywide school districts. Kenny and Schmidt (1994) estimate that if this restriction on school district formation were eliminated, Florida would have had 567 school districts in 1980 instead of its 67 districts. Doing away with countywide districts thus would result in much smaller districts, where parents are more likely to oversee school operations, and would result in more competition among districts. Husted and Kenny (1995) have shown that test scores are higher in states with more competition among school districts. Kenny and Schmidt (1994) found that in states unconstrained by competition spending was higher, perhaps going to unnecessary administrators and support staff. These results suggest there may be significant benefits from eliminating countywide districts and perhaps also from adding magnet schools and instituting vouchers. At the college level, Florida spends much less on each college student than do the better state university systems. A larger budget would enable Florida university students to get the additional attention that comes with smaller classes. According to McManus, Gould and Welch (1983), Hispanics earn less than comparable Anglos because they are not fluent in English. This suggests that there may be a sizeable payoff to programs that enhance proficiency in English.

Wages are lower in Florida because of the more desirable climate and the lower pollution and are higher because of the greater crime and more expensive land. There is nothing government can do to affect the climate, and land costs are determined by population density. But government can reduce crime and pollution. The wage differentials reported here provide some measure of the value that consumers place on this.

References

Aggarwal, Archana. 1988. "Interaction between Land and Labor Markets." Unpublished Ph.D. dissertation. Gainesville: University of Florida.

Blomquist, Glenn C., Mark C. Berger and John P. Hoehn. 1988. "New Estimates of Quality of Life in Urban Areas." *American Economic Review* 78 (March), pp. 89-107.

Husted, Thomas A., and Lawrence W. Kenny. "Evidence from the States on the Political and Market Determinants of Efficiency in Education." University of Florida Department of Economics Working Paper 94-95-10.

Kenny, Lawrence W. 1980. "The Effects of Family and School Upon Cognitive Achievement." *Research in Population Economics* Volume II, pp. 99-113.

Kenny, Lawrence W., and David A. Denslow, Jr. 1980. "Compensating Differentials in Teachers' Salaries." *Journal of Urban Economics* 7 (April), pp. 98-207.

Kenny, Lawrence W., and Amy B. Schmidt. 1994. "The Decline in the Number of School Districts in the U.S.: 1950-1980." *Public Choice* 79 (April), pp.1-18.

Lewis, H. Gregg. 1963. *Unionism and Relative Wages in the United States*. Chicago: University of Chicago Press.

Long, James E. 1977. "Productivity, Employment Discrimination, and the Relative Economic Status of Spanish Origin Males." *Social Science Quarterly* 58 (December), pp. 357-373.

McManus, Walter, William Gould and Finis Welch. 1983. "Earnings of Hispanic Men: the Role of English Language Proficiency." *Journal of Labor Economics* 1 (April), pp. 101-130.

Nechyba, Thomas. 1990. "The Southern Wage Gap, Human Capital, and the Quality of Education." *Southern Economic Journal* 57 (October).

Roback, Jennifer. 1982. "Wages, Rents, and the Quality of Life." *Journal of Political Economy* 90 (December), pp. 1,257-78.

Smith, James P., and Finis R. Welch. 1989. "Black Economic Progress after Myrdal." *Journal of Economic Literature* 27 (June), pp. 519-564.

United States Department of Commerce, Bureau of the Census. *1990 Census of Population.* Washington, D.C.

_____. 1993, 1994. *Statistical Abstract of the United States.* Washington, D.C.

United States Department of Labor, Bureau of Labor Statistics. 1994a. *Geographic Profile of Employment and Unemployment, 1993.* Bulletin 2327.

United States Department of Labor. 1994b. News release 94-454.

University of Florida, Bureau of Economic and Business Research. 1993. *Florida Statistical Abstract.* Anne H. Shermyen, ed. Gainesville: University Press of Florida.

_____. 1994. *Florida Statistical Abstract.* Ann C. Pierce, ed. Gainesville: University Press of Florida.

Education

4

Carolyn D. Herrington
Associate Professor
Learning Systems Institute
Florida State University
Tallahassee, Florida
and
Yasser A. Nakib
Assistant Professor
University of Delaware
Research Fellow
Finance Center of the
Consortium for Policy
Research in Education (CPRE)
Newark, Delaware

The educational system in Florida is the fourth largest system in the country and the largest single activity of state government. People outside the field of education often fail to appreciate the sheer size of the educational enterprise in Florida. It enrolls over two million students and total operating costs will pass the $11 billion mark in 1995-96. In many communities, the public school system may be the largest industry, employing more people than any other single company. Most children spend six hours a day, nine months a year for thirteen years in public schools. Many more attend additional years in the state's twenty-eight community colleges and nine state universities. These same schools also offer services to the very young and the very old. The facilities are used for a broad range of civic activities ranging from serving as voting booths to hurricane relief shelters. The educational system--from prekindergarten to graduate training--impacts daily upon the lives of most children and large numbers of adults. The state's educational system determines in no small way the cultural, economic and social well-being of a state and the quality of life of its citizens.

The educational system in Florida is a study in contrasts and contradictions. Similar to other southern states, in the period since World War II, Florida's educational system has been marked by persistent improvements in its teaching force, its facilities and the achievements of its students. However, its political, governmental and taxation structures remain rooted in the traditions of the old South--agrarian and conservative (Koppich, Cobbe, Herrington and Zimpfer 1991). While many states have increasingly professionalized their educational governance systems, Florida has retained a highly politicized system, opting for the greater responsiveness of the political process over the greater professionalism of educators (Schuh and Herrington 1990).

The next decade promises explosive increases in the numbers of children in school, increasingly strident demands for higher performance and the need for huge infusions of public funds. Yet Florida carries into the next century a legacy of deferred expenditures, high levels of child poverty and an education performance record that repeatedly places it in the bottom half compared to other states. The state also faces dramatic changes in the types of children it will be greeting at the schoolhouse door. The children who will be entering Florida schools over the next twenty years will be more physically, culturally, linguistically and racially diverse than current students (Herrington et al. 1991). Not only do these new demographics pose formidable challenges to professional educators to meet the curricular and instructional needs of a new generation of children, they also bring to the surface a host of thorny and potentially divisive issues regarding the role and scope of schools in our society. Who are the schools to serve? Whose standards should they enforce? Whose values should they transmit?

Questions of quality have been persistent (Office of the President, Florida Senate 1983). Indicators of system performance show mediocre student achievement as measured by the Scholastic Aptitude Test (SAT) and by the high levels of remediation required of beginning college students. The business community has become a prominent voice in demanding change, claiming that the skills of the entry-level workforce are insufficient to the demands of the workplace. Criticism of the quality of the educational system, particularly in the public schools, has acquired an even more urgent tone in the face of growing competition in manufacturing and services from other countries. Large trade deficits, the loss of significant portions of the manufacturing sector to international competitors and the inability of the wages of lower-skilled workers to keep apace with the cost of living have placed new urgency on the issues of quality schooling and adequate preparation for work (National Commission on Excellence in Education 1983, Hudson Institute 1987).

State policymakers have responded repeatedly, though inadequately, to these events. Florida, like many Sunbelt states, has tried to strengthen its economic base. With an economy largely dependent on tourism and agriculture, it had been hit hard by the recession of 1974-75 and emerged determined to diversify its economic base by building a more substantial industrial sector. All four governors over the last two decades have had ambitious economic development programs designed to bolster and diversify the state's economy through different strategies including attracting high-technology and light manufacturing firms seeking to relocate in the South and developing a major international presence. Because a quality educational system was seen as an important amenity with which to compete among other states and other countries, these economic development programs were accompanied by equally ambitious educational reform programs including greater funding, basic skills testing, longer school days, more parental participation and stiffer standards for teacher certification, high school graduation and advancement within the college system (Koppich, Cobbe, Herrington and Zimfer 1991).

Despite ambitious reform activities and significantly increased expenditures, indicators of educational performance have not registered needed improvements. Furthermore, the state is facing huge increases in its school-age population which will place unprecedented demands upon its fiscal and capital infrastructure. Over the next few years, critical decisions will need to be made by the state's citizens and their elected officials as to how Florida will accommodate the anticipated growth in numbers and diversity of its school-age population as well as how to continue the struggle for educational excellence.

Table 1. Florida Education System Size and Growth

Sector	Enrollment	Projected 10-Year Growth (percent)
PreK-12	2.3 Million 1995-96	27.3 1990-91/1999-00
Community Colleges	325,043 Fall 1993	41.9 1993-94/2002-03
State Universities	191,148 Fall 94	33.7 1991-92/1999-00

Sources: Martha Miller, *Updated PreK-12 Projections, Florida Public Schools*, Florida Department of Education, 1993; Edward Cisek, *Projected FTE Enrollments, Florida Community Colleges*, Florida Division of Community Colleges, 1993.

Increased Enrollments and Increased Diversity

Florida has one of the largest and one of the fastest growing student populations in the country. It currently ranks fourth in the country in the size of its K-12 student population and enrollment growth is over four times the national average. It ranks eighth in higher education enrollment (Postsecondary Education Planning Commission 1992).

Between 1990 and the year 2010, the number of children in Florida ages 0 to 19 will increase from 3.2 million to 4.1 million, a 29.3 percent increase in two decades (Weller 1991). (However, the adult population will outstrip the child population in growth, increasing by 42.2 percent in the same period.) These staggering growth rates translate into equally high enrollment increases in the public school system. In the 1995-96 school year, the state's public school enrollments (FTEs) are projected at 2.3 million. Another half million students are enrolled in Florida's universities and community colleges. It is estimated that by the year 1999-2000, public school enrollments will have increased 27.3 percent over the 1990 enrollment (see Table 1).

The pressures of growth will be even greater in the higher education sector. Starting in 1995-96 and continuing throughout the next decade, the graduation of the Baby Boom Echo from high school is projected to increase dramatically the size of the traditional college-age population. Between 1990 and the year 2010, Florida public high school graduates are projected to increase from 88,000 to 136,000, a 54.5 percent increase over a twenty-year period as the leading edge of the Baby Boom Echo leaves the public schools. Between 1993 and 2002, community college enrollments (FTEs) are estimated to increase 41.9 percent. The state university system is estimating an equally staggering growth rate of 33.7 percent between 1991-92 and 1999-2000. The challenges associated simply with meeting the needs for personnel, facilities and instructional materials created by this phenomenal rate of growth are straining the state's capacity. It is predicted that in the year 2000 alone, 11,500 new public school teachers will be needed to meet the increased enrollments. This growth is also occurring at a time when the number of households with children is declining as the population ages and as other demands on public resources are growing.

The growth in the number of students is running parallel to a concurrent growth in the type of students the educational system is being asked to serve. Increasingly, Florida's schools are receiving students who are members of racial and ethnic minority groups. Some of these students enter school with nonexistent, or only rudimentary, command of the English language. Historically, these students have been more difficult and more expensive to educate and the system has been less successful in educating them. Table 2 shows the fiscal impact of growth in these areas in the public school system. Between 1983-84 and 1995-96, the number of K-12 basic FTEs (students who are not considered to have special education needs) is expected to grow from 1.3 million to 1.7 million or at a rate of 29.8 percent. The at-risk FTEs will increase at a radically greater rate-- 743 percent. Exceptional educational FTEs (handicapped and gifted students) will increase 143 percent.

Currently, 38.6 percent of the total prekindergarten through twelfth grade school population belong to racial and ethnic minority groups. Between 1974-75 and 1993-94 the percentage of Hispanic students

Table 2. Unweighted Public School FTEs
by Program Groups

Fiscal Years	K-12 Basic	Percent-age of Total Enroll-ment	At Risk*	Percent-age of Total Enroll-ment	Excep-tional	Percent-age of Total Enroll-ment	Total
1983-84	1,331,138	93	23,224	2	74,200	5	1,428,562
1988-89	1,506,277	91	51,311	3	106,226	6	1,663,814
1992-93	1,650,890	85	137,468	7	144,618	8	1,932,976
1993-94	1,671,264	84	163,210	8	153,021	7	1,987,495
1994-95	1,699,612	83	177,350	9	167,862	8	2,044,824
1995-96**	1,727,702	82	194,695	9	180,862	9	2,103,259

*Includes Educational Alternatives, Dropout Prevention and English as Second Language (ESOL).

**Projected.

Source: December 1994 Enrollment Estimating Conference.

as a proportion of the total prekindergarten through grade twelve population more than doubled from 6.4 percent to 13.8 percent. During this same period, the white student population declined ten points, from 70 percent of the total to 59.6 percent of the Florida public school population and the proportion of African-Americans increased only about two percentage points from 22.5 percent to 24.8 percent. Minority enrollments in higher education fall behind those of the K-12 sector. In Fall 1994, state university enrollments were 75.6 percent white, 12.0 percent African-American and 12.4 percent Hispanic. The community college enrollments for Fall 1993 were 70.4 percent white, 11.7 percent African-American and 12.9 percent Hispanic (see Table 3). The percentage of minority students will continue to increase, by the year 2010 making up a majority of Florida's students and achieving the highest minority growth rate in the country. Furthermore, by the year 2015 minority students will comprise the majority of entry-level workers.

Given the influx of immigrant students to Florida's schools, it is not surprising that increasing numbers of students begin their education with limited facility in English. These students enter Florida as refugees from war, civil strife and economic hardship in Central and South America, Southeast Asia and other locales. In the 1994-95

Table 3. Enrollment by Race/Ethnicity
in Florida's Public Education System
(percent)

	White	African-American	Hispanic
Public Schools (PreK-12) 1993-94	59.6	24.8	13.8
Community Colleges Fall 1993	70.4	11.7	12.9
State Universities Fall 1994	75.6	12.0	12.4

Source: MIS Office, Division of Public Schools, State Board of Community Colleges and State University System.

school year, over 85,000 students were enrolled in bilingual or English as a Second Language programs--a six-fold increase since 1987. Of the students participating in these classes, most were Hispanic.

Dade County presents a striking example of the state school system's linguistic diversity. In this south Florida county, more than one-quarter of public school students were born in foreign countries. One hundred and twenty countries of origin and more than sixty-five different languages are represented by Dade County students. Spanish outranks English as the primary language of parents of Dade County public school students with English and Creole ranking second and third, respectively. In 1994-95, Dade's 43,684 children enrolled in English as a Second Language represented 14 percent of all its pupils.

Another challenge of diversity for Florida is the growth in the number of children with disabilities in the school system. In Fall 1993, public school special education classes had an enrollment of 329,201. Between 1986 and 1993, students in need of special education increased by more than half (55 percent) in Florida. The passage of the 1976 Education for All Handicapped Children, Public Law 99-142, mandated that all school systems provide appropriate educational opportunities for all children, no matter how severely disabled. This law has resulted in an increase in the number of public school students with disabilities, the range and severity of disability of students being served and the settings in which schools serve these children. Many special education students are individuals who, in an earlier era, would have received little or no formal education. The state offers classes for both the educable and trainable mentally handicapped; programs for physically, visually, emotionally and profoundly handicapped students; and students requiring physical and occupational therapy, and speech, language and hearing impaired. Florida schools now have the continuing challenge to craft appropriate developmental and academic programs for these children. In Florida, the special education category also includes programs for the gifted.

Mobility is a more recent trend that may have disturbing consequences for education. Florida has one of the most mobile populations in the country. It ranked second only to Nevada in the net migration rate between 1980 and 1989 (26.2 percent), second only to California in the number of people moving into the state between 1985 and 1990 (2.5 million) and second in the number of people who moved into a different house in the five-year time period between 1985 and 1990. In fact, in the majority of Florida's sixty-seven counties including all the heavily populated counties, 50 percent or more of the people moved to a different house within the same five-year period. The Sarasota County School District recently found that only 20 percent of its high school graduates had been enrolled in the district's elementary schools. When children change schools frequently they not only change teachers but also subjects, textbooks and skill expectations. Even within a school district, students who move within a year might be starting over academically. Principals comment that mobile children tend to be insecure, that instructional staff have difficulty assessing and monitoring the students' school progress and that clerical staff are burdened by the paperwork of requesting records and originating new ones. Sadly, mobility is higher in schools that serve poor children, according to a recent study of mobility in Dade County schools (Harkey

1992). Thus, to the academic problems associated with poverty are added those associated with mobility.

New Demands: More Schooling and Higher Skills

Another area of pressure is preparing students for employment. Most of the information we have on the workplace of the future indicates that future jobs in Florida will favor the better educated. Employment in occupations in which workers need less education will decline as a proportion of total employment. Jobs are expected to continue to be available for those with only a high school education; however, persons who do not finish high school will find it more difficult than those with more education to find a job, particularly a job with good pay and chances for advancement. They will continue to have more labor market problems and less opportunity for the training needed to adapt to the continuing changes in employment. Much of today's economy is an information economy. To function effectively, people must process information and make decisions. Not only have traditional services jobs like bank clerks been automated, but even in manufacturing the operator, a "laborer" in name only, uses automation to monitor information, control production flows and plan maintenance work. All these shifts have stimulated increasing demand for educated workers.

According to *Workforce 2000*, a report recently commissioned by the Florida Department of Labor and Employment Security, among the fastest-growing occupational groups in the country, 68 percent of technical positions require postsecondary training while 24 percent of service workers and 47 percent of sales workers require additional schooling beyond high school. When the need for a high school diploma is added to the educational equation, the numbers become 98 percent, 73 percent and 87 percent, respectively. This difference reflects the new basic literacy needed for the jobs of the future. This is a literacy composed of the skills of acting and thinking strategically in dynamic settings. Occupational categories requiring less than high school education are declining.

If we rank jobs according to skills, rather than education, the rising requirements are even more dramatic. When jobs are given

Table 4. Percent of Existing and New Jobs
by Skill Ratings*

Jobs	Skill Ratings					
	0.7-1.4	1.5-2.4	2.5-3.4	3.5-4.4	4.5-5.4	5.5-6.4
Existing	9	31	35	18	5	1
New	4	23	34	28	11	2

*Examples of representative job skill ratings are: Lawyers, 5.2; Teachers, 4.2; Construction, 3.2; Farmers, 2.3; Helpers and Laborers, 1.3.
Source: Hudson Institute 1987.

numerical ratings according to the math, language and reasoning skills they require, only 27 percent of all new jobs fall into the two lowest skill categories yet 40 percent of current jobs require these limited skills. By contrast, 41 percent of new jobs require the highest skills, compared to only 24 percent of the current jobs (see Table 4).

Student and System Performance

How successful is the Florida school system in preparing its students for adulthood? One means to gauge how well the graduates of Florida's public schools perform academically is to review the results of a testing requirement of entering college students. All students entering Florida state universities or community colleges must take one of four tests to assess their skill levels in reading, writing and mathematics. If they perform below the established cut-off scores, they are required to enroll in college preparatory courses and must pass the courses before they may enroll in college-level courses. In 1993-94, 78 percent of Florida's entering college students scored at or above the cut-off in reading and writing and 70 percent scored at or above the cut-off in mathematics. Altogether, only 58 percent of the students were deemed ready for college-level coursework in all three areas. Performance differs significantly by ethnicity. African-Americans' passing rates for all three areas were 36 percent. Hispanic rates were 42 percent. The cut-off scores are not high. The cut-off scores for two of the four tests that students may choose to

Table 5. Passing Rates for College Entry-Level
Placement Tests, 1993-94
(percent)

Students	Math	Writing	Reading	All Three Tests
All	69.7	77.6	77.7	57.8
White	75.9	85.8	87.3	67.9
African-American	52.8	59.3	58.2	36.3
Hispanic	61.1	67.1	63.6	42.4

Source: Taylor Cullar, *Readiness for College: A Postsecondary Feedback Report to Florida's Public High School and School Districts, 1993-94*, Florida Department of Education, 1995.

take, the SAT and ACT, are 740 and 14, respectively. These tests indicate that large numbers of Florida students are graduating from high school and entering college without the foundation for successful college-level work (see Table 5).

The most widely used college admissions test in the United States is the SAT. It is not a test of achievement but is designed to assess a student's ability to successfully undertake college-level work. The exam is meant, in other words, to be predictive of performance in college, not evaluative of achievement in high school. The Scholastic Aptitude Test consists of two sections, verbal (reading comprehension, composition, etc.) and mathematics. It is possible to score 800 points on each section, for a total possible composite score of 1600. Florida students in 1994 had an average composite (reading and mathematics combined) score of 879. The national composite average was 902. This represents a decline since 1986 of sixteen points. The U.S. average declined over that same time period by four points (see Table 6).

There has been a steady increase in the number of minority students in Florida taking the SAT, as well as the number of minority test-takers as a percentage of total SAT takers in the state. Between 1978 and 1994, the number of African-American Florida high school students taking the SAT increased from 8.7 percent to

Table 6. Performance of Florida and United States Students on the SAT 1977-1994

| Year | Florida | | United States | |
	Percent-age of Graduates Taking Test	Combined Score	Percent-age of Graduates Taking Test	Combined Score
1977	35.7	879	31.0	899
1978	34.4	888	31.6	897
1979	35.7	890	31.7	894
1980	36.5	887	32.3	890
1981	38.3	887	32.9	890
1982	38.0	889	32.6	893
1983	39.0	887	33.5	893
1984	39.9	890	35.0	897
1985	45.7	884	36.5	906
1986	44.6	895	37.7	906
1987	48.4	893	40.0	906
1988	50.2	890	41.0	904
1989	47.0	887	39.8	903
1990	46.0	884	39.5	900
1991	48.0	882	40.0	896
1992	48.2	884	41.8	899
1993	50.4	882	41.7	902
1994	50.7	879	42.2	902

Source: Martha Miller, *Information on SAT Scores: 1994 College-Bound Seniors, Florida and the U.S.*, Florida Department of Education, 1994.

13.3 percent of total SAT takers. Between 1978 and 1994, the percent of Hispanic high school students among those taking the SAT rose from 3.7 to 15.1. Overall, 31 percent of Florida's SAT takers were members of racial and ethnic minority groups, which have historically scored below the mean. The comparable national statistic is 22 percent. With the exception of Asians, minority-group students tend to score lower on the SAT than do white students. The composite SAT score for white students in Florida in 1994 was 926; for African-American students, it was 729; and for Hispanics, 837 (see Table 7).

Table 7. Performance of Florida Students on the SAT
by Race and Ethnicity 1994

Race/Ethnicity	Composite SAT Score
White	926
African-American	729
Hispanic	837

Source: Martha Miller, *Information on SAT Scores: 1994 College-Bound Seniors, Florida and the U.S.,* Florida Department of Education, 1994.

Funding for Florida Schools

For 1995-96, the State of Florida appropriated approximately $11.1 billion to operate its educational system including prekindergarten programs; elementary, middle and high schools; state universities and community colleges; and adult, community and vocational education programs. Per-student spending in Florida, after rising significantly in the seventies and early eighties, is now failing to keep up with growth. After allowing for inflation and rising numbers of students, state general-revenue spending per pupil is beginning to fall. In 1985-86, per-student general revenue spending for public schools was $1,760; in 1994-95 spending was $3,350. However, if adjusted for inflation, 1994-95 spending is worth only $1,645, a 7 percent decline over the ten-year period. Higher education has experienced an even more dramatic decline. Between 1989 and 1993, state university per-student funding not adjusted for inflation declined from $7,200 to $5,200, or 27.8 percent. In 1992-93, Florida ranked in the middle of other states (twenty-third) in public school revenue per pupil (ADA) and in current expenditures per elementary and secondary pupil (twenty-sixth). However, it ranked somewhat lower in effort. In per-pupil expenditures for public elementary and secondary schools as a percent of per capita income, Florida ranked thirty-first. Some of the discrepancy between expenditures and effort is explained by the demographic structure of Florida. It has the highest median age of any state (37.2), meaning that a larger proportion of its citizens is not of school age. Comparative teacher

Table 8. Financing Education in Florida:
Interstate Rankings 1992-93

Indicators	Florida's Interstate Ranking
Revenue Per Elementary and Secondary Pupil	23
Expenditure Per Elementary and Secondary Pupil	26
Expenditure Per Pupil for Elementary and Secondary as a Percent of Per Capita Income	31
Estimated Average Teacher Salaries	27
Pupil-Teacher Ratio (1991)	15
State Per Pupil Support of Higher Education (1990-91)	15
State Appropriation for Higher Education Per Capita	45

Sources: Brizius and Foster, *States in Profile, 1994*, Alexandria, Virginia: State Policy Research, 1994; MIS Office, Division of Public Schools, State Board of Community Colleges and State University System.

salary rankings also place Florida in the middle of other states, twenty-seventh in estimated average salaries as reported by the National Education Association. Another more positive indication of effort is the pupil-teacher ratio. Florida's 17.6 ratio in 1991 places it fifteenth in the country (See Table 8).

Comparative state rankings in higher education show relatively similar findings. State support of higher education on a per-pupil basis placed Florida fifteenth in the country with $4,497 for 1990-91. However, Florida drops to forty-fifth in state appropriations for higher educaton as a percent of per capita income.

One of the major problems facing many states is the geographic distribution of educational funding. Because the second major source of funding for public schools is local property taxes, the availability of funds may differ considerably from locale to locale as property values vary. The discrepancies in local wealth and the resultant threat of inequitable resources for schools has been one of the most difficult issues that educators and policymakers have faced. The issues became contentious nationwide in the early 1970s when a series of court rulings asserted that states were to fund educational systems independent of local wealth. Florida adopted the Florida Education Finance Program (FEFP) in 1973 to assure equitable educational opportunity throughout the state. The FEFP is a funding formula designed to recognize variations in the value of local property tax bases as well as variations in program cost factors, district cost differentials and differences due to sparsity and dispersion of student population in per-student cost for equivalent educational programs.

There are two outstanding features of the FEFP. The first is that the majority of local tax effort, the required local effort, is equalized. The result is that the effect on students of differing fiscal capacity among districts based on local property wealth is reduced. A district with a high level of assessed property value receives a proportionately smaller share of state revenues; a district with a low level of value receives a larger share. Florida has one of the most equalized systems of public school funding in the country. In 1992-93, approximately 97.17 percent of the $8.3 billion provided for operation of Florida's schools was equalized across the districts.

The second outstanding feature of the FEFP is its use of the individual student participating in a particular educational program as the base for financial support. The level of funding for the FEFP is generated primarily by multiplying the number of fulltime equivalent students (FTE) in each of the educational programs by cost factors to obtain a weighted FTE (WFTE). The WFTE is then multiplied by a base student allocation and by a district cost differential as well as a number of other calculations. The result of the computation determines the total funding for the FEFP, both state and local funds. Program cost factors are calculated on a three-year average, are specified by the Legislature and reflect the relative cost differences among the educational programs in FEFP. The base cost factor is 1.000, which represents the cost for the basic programs for Grades 4-8. The cost factors for all other educational programs, such as Specific Learning Disability, Vocational-Technical Programs and Dropout Prevention, are indexed to 1.000.

The last few years have seen a number of structural constraints that have resulted in per-student funding setbacks. The recession of the 1990s clearly showed the vulnerability of the state's tax base to recessionary cycles. By constitutional prohibition, Florida cannot impose a state personal income tax nor can it impose a state property tax. The state has traditionally relied mostly on sales and, to a lesser degree, corporate income taxes. The volatility of the sales tax under the pressures of a recession has undermined the stability of educational funding at the state level.

Another complicating factor is the recent increase in the caseload of other program areas, increases over which the state has limited control. Demographically fueled increases in dependent populations, federal mandates covering Medicaid and court orders binding service delivery in juvenile justice, mental health, foster care and corrections among others have all increased the percentage of the state budget going to these areas and limited state budgeting flexibility. For example, Medicaid expenditures by the state have been increasing at over 30 percent annually in recent years. In 1985-86, education accounted for 62 percent of state general-revenue spending; by 1994-95, this had slipped to only 50 percent. Conversely, the appropriation for Medicaid represented 6.2 percent of general revenue in 1985-86 and grew to 17 percent by 1994-95. Corrections as a percentage of state general revenue spending increased from 5.0 percent to 7.9 percent over the same ten-year period.

In 1992, Florida voters approved two constitutional amendments that will have significant impact on the state's ability to raise funds for education. The first requires the state to establish a budget stabilization fund amounting to 5 percent of the general revenue fund by fiscal year 1998-99. This will further limit state budgetary discretion by requiring that the state lay aside over $600 million in the next five years. Second, property tax assessment increases will be restricted to 3 percent annually. Furthermore, two years later, voters overwhelmingly approved a tax cap that limits state government budgetary growth to the average increase in personal income over a three-year period. Higher education is particularly vulnerable to declines in state budgeting flexibility because, unlike the K-12 sector, enrollment may be capped.

In 1987 the state started operating lottery games with the net proceeds dedicated to educational funding, including the college and university systems. It is widely alleged that the lottery has hurt educational finance mostly because of the degree of substitution that those proceeds allow with general revenue funding (Stark, Wood and Honeyman 1983). However, education's share of the general revenue fund was in decline even before funds from the lottery were included in 1988-89. The lottery may have hurt educational finance the most by fostering a misconception by the public that lottery revenues are meeting educational funding needs. This may inadvertently relieve pressure to seek additional revenues to support the expanding school system.

A related issue is the so-called tax gap. It has been estimated that the state has a tax gap (defined as the difference between the amount of state taxes that are legally owed and what the state collects) of over a billion dollars. The property tax in particular has come under close scrutiny. In Florida, sixty-six counties have elected appraisers. Dade County has an appointed official. A series of reviews--a statewide grand jury report, two recent state audits and an internal revenue department study--suggests that the property appraisal system may be seriously flawed. Some legislators are reluctant to support new taxes while collection rates on currently owed tax revenue are low. However, legislative proposals to improve tax enforcement through additional funding for collection enforcement and through increasing penalties are politically unpopular and have met with only modest success to date.

Finally, the political will to increase funding for education may have been diluted in the face of a lack of improvements stemming from past funding increases. Florida, like most other states, increased the per-pupil funding for education steadily and significantly between 1960 and 1990 and yet there is little evidence that the increased resources have purchased increased achievement. In this sense, the education sector faces a serious productivity problem (Hanushek 1994). In 1959-60, Florida expended $318 per student. This increased to $732 in 1969-70, $1,889 in 1979-80 and $4,997 in

Table 9. Expenditure Per Pupil in Florida
1959-60 to 1989-90
(dollars)

	1959-60	1969-70	1979-80	1989-90
Expenditure	318	732	1,889	4,997
Percent Change		130.2	158.1	164.5
Percent Change 1959-60 to 1989-90				1,471.3
Expenditure (Constant 1989-90 Dollars)	1,373	2,461	3,198	4,997
Percent change		79.2	29.9	56.3
Percent change 1959-60 to 1989-90				263.9

Source: National Center for Education Statistics, *Digest of Education Statistics*, U.S. Government Printing Office, 1992.

1989-90, or approximately 1,470 percent over the period. When the same figures are calculated holding constant for inflation, the increase is reduced to 264 percent, which nevertheless is significant (see Table 9). The Florida data are similar to national data, which indicate that, holding constant for inflation, U.S. expenditures per pupil increased 206 percent in the same thirty-year period (Odden 1992).

Some of the increased expenditures can be explained by the inclusion of a broader array of students such as those with severe handicaps who were excluded from public education prior to the 1980s; by the inclusion of racial minorities who had received an inferior education under a *de jure* system of segregation; by the increasing administrative requirements of greater federal and state regulations and by a broader programmatic reach (such as programs in driver education, health education, etc.).

Still, it is of concern that the large increases in funding have not been accompanied by some increases in achievement. Recent analyses of education achievement in the United State suggest that even though the decline in achievement widely referenced in the seventies seems to have abated, achievement levels have simply been restored to the levels of the sixties; there has been no net increase (Hanushek 1994, Odden 1992). Increasingly many educators and researchers are arguing that in the absence of radical changes in the way schools are structured and governed, increasing funds will not increase learning (Branson 1987, Finn 1991, Chubb and Moe 1990, Odden 1992, Hanushek 1994). One of the greatest challenges facing the educational system will be to convince elected officials that infusions of new funds will make a difference. This is a burden of proof that educators have never had to bear before.

Maintaining Equity

In addition to concerns regarding the resources for education, another challenge facing Florida will be to retain the fundamental equity of the state's funding formula. Pressure to allow locally strong areas to raise their own local taxes independently during periods of state budget cutbacks may be hard to resist. Such pressures did materialize during the budget cutbacks of the early nineties. Sarasota and Alachua County school boards sought legal authority to increase their own discretionary local millage. The Supreme Court, however, confirmed the Legislature's authority to cap discretionary millage. Bills introduced in the 1995 Legislature indicate the mounting pressures. One would allow local school boards to levy taxes up to the 10 mill maximum in the state constitution. Most districts are between 8.5 and 9.5 mills. (This includes a two-mill local-option levy for capital expenditures.) It is estimated that there will be a $2 billion shortfall in 1995-96 in the Public Education Capital Outlay Trust. To address this, another bill would increase the maximum discretionary millage that school boards can levy for capital purposes from 2.0 to 2.5 mills. A final proposal would allow each school district to levy a document stamp tax of up to 15 cents per $100 on deed and other real estate documents. Yet another bill would allow each school board to put to a referendum a half-penny increase in the county sales tax. In choosing this option, a district would have to freeze the property-tax rate for the operating fund for three years. Only the latter bill passed.

However, it is clear that as stress on statewide revenue sources increases, local districts that do have additional revenue-generation capacity will exert increased pressure to be allowed to tap their local sources. If given permission, the state will be increasingly liable to court challenges to the system's fairness.

Public Support for Public Education

Public support for education in Florida is strong as indicated in recent public opinion surveys. Although there is a widespread belief that the citizens of Florida would prefer a cut in state government spending rather than an increase in taxes, they seem willing to bear a greater tax burden to support certain programs, education in particular (Scoggins and Horn 1994). A majority favors increased expenditures for education even if it increases taxes. The survey data indicate that 64 percent of Floridians prefer that local education spending be increased, 21 percent prefer no change and 8 percent prefer a decrease. A majority of those questioned, 53 percent, would prefer that education spending be increased even if it meant an increase in their local taxes. Only 4 percent would prefer a decrease in education spending even if it did not cause a decrease in their local taxes.

However, different groups of adults have different preferences. In general the greater the age of the respondents, the less they preferred increased spending on education. Compared to the rest of the respondents, adults with children in public schools have a greater preference for increased spending as do adults with relatively high income levels and educational attainment (see Table 10).

Finally, the survey provided evidence that the existing level of education expenditures per capita affects one's preferences. Adults who live in counties with relatively high education expenditures per capita have a lesser preference for increased spending than adults who live in counties with relatively low per capita expenditures. However, the level of education expenditures per student has no effect on preferences. Neither does gender.

Table 10. Floridians' Preference for Increased Spending On Education Even if Taxes Are Increased
(percent)

	By Age					
	18-24	25-34	35-44	45-54	55-64	>65
Against	32.66	35.50	32.34	39.00	53.32	42.09
For	57.91	57.42	60.62	55.42	35.55	35.38

	By Income						
	<$10,000	$10,000 to $14,999	$15,000 to $19,999	$20,000 to $24,999	$25,000 to $34,999	$35,000 to $44,999	>$45,000
Against	46.20	43.95	43.69	44.19	43.84	35.64	34.47
For	41.73	43.20	43.36	50.05	51.34	55.94	61.61

	By Educational Attainment					
	<9th	High School	High School Graduate	College	College Graduate	Graduate School
For	51.25	46.66	42.46	35.14	42.59	31.23
Against	33.73	39.44	46.62	57.84	52.71	62.92

Source: Scoggins and Horn 1994.

School Reform Thrusts

Over the next decade Florida and its citizens will be struggling to manage skyrocketing growth in its systems of schools and colleges; to foster the intellectual, social and personal growth of students of varied backgrounds and varying abilities; to prepare a generation of adults able to meet the demands of a more competitive workplace and to increase the productivity of a system historically resistant to change. The struggles to do this will result in intense and often acrimonious debate over the role of government, on the burdens of taxation, on the rights of parents, families and communities and the requirements of economic security. The next decade will see higher levels of stress on the system, continuing challenges to the prevailing consensus on its roles and mission, and greater demands for accountability. The citizenry's historic ambivalence about the role of public education will surface repeatedly in these debates and will severely test the state's century-old commitment to publicly subsidized mass education. These issues can be discussed under three categories: quality, accountability and equity.

Quality. The quality of the state's educational system has dominated the public debate on education for the last twenty years and shows no sign of abating. While one generation has always claimed that academic standards are being compromised by the upcoming generation, the availability of a relatively reliable metric such as the SAT has given particular credence to those allegations over the last few decades. This evidence of decline, or at least the failure to improve, is coinciding with an unsettling decline in America's economic hegemony in the world economy resulting in a new urgency to issues of academic rigor. Reasons for the lack of improvement vacillate between blaming a more permissive society and blaming an unresponsive educational bureaucracy.

Three strategies are currently being pursued in Florida to reverse the trend. The central strategy is to deregulate the practice and funding of education by giving more discretion to actors at the school level such as principals, teachers and parents. While this approach is relatively inexpensive to pursue, it is unproven and will probably vary in success widely from site to site.

A second approach is assuring that students who are lacking in other materials or social resources receive the services they need, such as health and social services, to compensate for the deficiencies and to support their educational efforts. While this approach has a strong research base to substantiate it and will certainly improve the learning potential of students if adequately implemented, it is expensive and it risks upsetting public perceptions regarding the role of schools and their mission in the community. Finally, over the next twenty years, it is clear that the advances in electronic technologies that have improved productivity in other economic sectors will be applied to education to try to improve the quality of learning. This reform strategy's success will depend on how well the new processes are integrated into the existing facilities, personnel and practices and how quickly academic gains can be shown to justify the massive infusions of equipment and training that are required.

Accountability. This has been a perennial issue in education since the 1960s (Herrington, Johnson and O'Farrell 1992; Kimbrough, Alexander and Wattenbarger 1982). Increases in the amount of dollars required to operate schools and in the percentage of overall state funds dedicated to education have been accompanied by increases in demands for accountability of how the funds are spent and on how well the system is performing. Educators have frequently seen the demands for accountability as poorly disguised attempts to ferret out poor-performing components in the system and justify punitive actions against them. They argue that teaching is a collaborative process and thus accountability-based or incentive-based formulations cannot accurately tie outcomes to individual employees or components and flawed attempts result only in deprofessionalization and low morale. Policymakers and elected officials, however, in their roles as trustees of public education, consider it their responsibility to attempt to "account" for how well the system is performing. This tension has coexisted for over twenty years and though the level of tension and accompanying rhetoric will probably increase over the next decade, a resolution is unlikely because the technology for evaluating outcomes is woefully inadequate and the knowledge linking inputs to outputs is nonexistent (see Herrington 1995).

Florida has attempted for over twenty years to create assessments by which to measure student performance with lamentable results. It has varied the nature and intensity of inputs without any success in linking the inputs to changes in the system. Furthermore, the correlation between student achievement and family income is so high that declaration of intentions to hold educators accountable are often not acted upon by policymakers out of fear that they may end up punishing the most vulnerable students. Furthermore, and perhaps even more fundamental, a consensus on what constitutes the mission of schooling (which is necessary for any evaluation of success or failure) is lacking in any operational terms.

However, debates concerning the quality of education, while not easy to resolve, at least center around means, not ends. There does, at least, exist a high level of consensus that students need to learn more.

Issues involving equity may prove even more intractable because they involve more deeply held convictions. The increasing diversification of the clients that the school system is attempting to serve threatens its cohesion and unity. New pressures on the school system to reflect the diversity of the population are colliding with traditional beliefs that one of the major purposes of public schooling is the socializing of diverse peoples into a cohesive populace with a sense of common purpose and shared commitment. As the school population becomes more diverse, the demands for special instructional content and instructional approaches and assessments surface. Advocates for racial and linguistic minorities, for individuals with disabilities and for low-income students allege that classroom strategies and instructional materials need to be tailored to meet the needs or interests of particular groups. However, the knowledge, the technology and any broad-based consensus is lacking on separatist approaches. For example, New York State attempted to define the unique learning styles of African-Americans but the results were extremely controversial and were believed by some to be a re-creation of race-based stereotypes (Hacker 1989). Students with disabilities and their parents and teachers have been engaged in a fierce debate over the last few years regarding the efficacy of maintaining separate instructional strategies and placements or opting for "mainstreaming." Fragmenting wedges threaten to further divide ethnically and linguistically diverse students, students with exceptional learning requirements and physical limitations, urban versus suburban interests, households with children versus those without and holders of conservative versus liberal positions on the role of schooling in character development. The future direction and cohesiveness of Florida's educational enterprise will be determined, in no small part, by the interplay of these fragmented and fragmenting constituency groups and their relative successes in forcing responses from elected and administrative leaders.

A Look Ahead

The purpose of public school has always been complex. We are unquestionably entering an age in which the demands being placed on the educational system are outstripping the public consensus on its role and the existing funding capabilities. While there is broad consensus on the need for an educated citizenry in a democracy and the need for a trained workforce able to capably assume entry-level employment, there is little consensus on the relative weight given these two objectives. There is even less consensus on new areas of responsibilities not traditionally a part of public schooling such as services to the severely handicapped whose mental functioning is very limited, the provision of basic health and social services to children and their families through the school system and issues surrounding values education, sex education and services to very young children. The latter, in particular, are issues that have come to the education sector because of a weakening of the other social institutions such as the family, communities and religious groups.

Florida's education system must creatively confront a number of challenges if it is to fulfill its obligation to the state's children in the years ahead. Managing growth--in other words, simply making available sufficient classroom space for the burgeoning student population swelling the schools' and colleges' attendance rolls--presents a complex challenge. Financing this growing, increasingly diverse education system presents a companion challenge. The current taxation base in Florida is failing to keep pace with growth and needs to be restructured. Enhancing educational opportunity for all students is a task to be undertaken and a continuing challenge to be met. Keeping the public eye fixed on education in a state in which school-age children--nonvoters all--comprise just 16 percent of the population is yet another challenge. How the state confronts these educational challenges and takes advantage of the possibilities will have a profound and lasting effect on the health and well-being of Florida and its children well into the next century.

References

Branson, R. K. 1987. "Why the Schools Can't Improve: The Upper Limit Hypothesis." *Journal of Instructional Development* 10:4.

Chubb, J., and T. Moe. 1990. *Politics, Markets and America's Schools*. Washington, D.C.: The Brookings Institution.

Finn, C. 1991. *We must take charge: Our schools and our future*. New York: Free Press.

Hacker, A. 1989. "Affirmative Action: The New Look." *The New York Review of Books* (October), pp. 63-76.

Hanusheck, E.A. 1994. *Making Schools Work: Improving Performance and Controlling Cost*. Washington, D.C.: The Brookings Institute.

Harkey, L. 1992. Interim Report of the Senate Education Committee. Tallahassee: Florida Senate.

Herrington, C.D. et al. 1991. *Condition of Children in Florida*. Tallahassee: Center for Policy Studies in Education.

Herrington, C.D. 1995. "School-Level Resource Allocation Analyses: Implications for State Policymakers" in L. Picus, ed., *Where Does the Money Go? Resource Allocation in Elementary and Secondary Schools*. Corwin Press.

Herrington, C.D., R. Johnson and M. O'Farrell. 1991. *Twenty Years of Accountability Legislation in Florida*. Tallahassee: Learning Systems Institute.

Hudson Institute. 1987. *Workforce 2000: Work and Workers for the 21st Century*. Indianapolis.

Kimbrough, R., K. Alexander and J. Wattenbarger. 1982. "Government and Education" in M. Dauer, ed., *Florida Politics and Government*. Gainesville: University Press of Florida.

Koppich, J., L. Cobbe, C.D. Herrington and P. Zimpfer. 1991. "Education," in C.D. Herrington et al., *Condition of children in Florida*. Tallahassee: Center for Policy Studies in Education.

National Commission on Excellence in Education. 1983. *A nation at risk*. Washington, D.C.: Department of Education.

Odden, A. 1992. "School Finance and Education Reform: An Overview" in A. Odden, ed., *Rethinking School Finance*. San Francisco: Jossey-Bass.

Office of the President. *The RAISE Program and Educational Reforms Enacted by the 1983 Florida Legislature*. Tallahassee: The Florida Senate.

Postsecondary Education Planning Commission. 1992. Issue Brief: Demographics. Tallahassee.

Schuh, J., and C.D. Herrington. 1990. *Elected vs. Appointed Superintendents*. Tallahassee: Center for Policy Studies in Education.

Scoggins, J. F., and R. Horn. 1994. "Popular Attitudes Change Toward Local Public Finance in Florida." *Economic Leaflets* Vol. 53 No. 10. University of Florida: Bureau of Economic and Business Research.

Weller, R. 1991. "Demographic and Economic Profile" in C.D. Herrington et al., *Condition of children in Florida*. Tallahassee: Center for Policy Studies in Education.

Crime and Punishment

5

Bruce L. Benson
Distinguished Research Professor
Department of Economics
and
David W. Rasmussen
Director
Policy Sciences Center
Professor of Economics
Florida State University

Mark Twain once said that what you think you know that isn't true can cause more harm than what you don't know. Some people apparently "know" that building more prisons is the answer to Florida's crime problem. Others know that controlling guns will do the job. Proposed solutions abound: hire more police, treat juvenile offenders as adults, give violent offenders tougher sentences, impose life sentences on multiple offenders, and so on.

This chapter emphasizes that criminal justice policy involves a complex system composed of offenders, the public, police, courts, corrections and the Legislature. No single quick-fix is likely to solve the problems of the criminal justice system and no haphazard combination of policies is likely to do so either. Because the system is so complex and because all the parts are interconnected, some "solutions" will actually create pressures on other parts of the system that undermine, rather than enhance, public safety.

Four sections follow this introduction. A discussion of crime trends in Florida in the next part suggests the state's crime problem is not new and that crime rates have actually been falling throughout this decade. The second section describes the criminal justice sys-

Figure 1. Florida Offenses per 100,000
Population 1971-1993

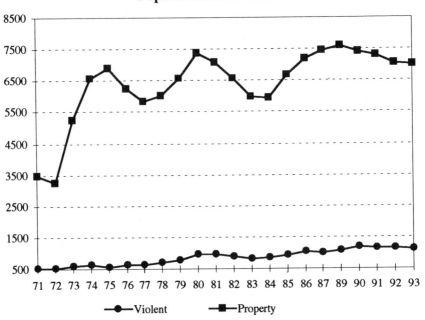

Note: Violent offenses consist of murder, rape, robbery and assault. Property offenses include burglary, larceny and auto theft. Data for 1988 are not comparable to those for other years and are not included in the table.

Source: Florida Department of Law Enforcement, *Crime in Florida*, various years.

tem as seen by offenders, a perspective that illustrates how interdependent the system is and why dramatic but simple solutions are not likely to yield the expected benefits. Florida's proposed prison building program is then analyzed from this perspective in part three, which is followed by concluding comments.

How Severe Is Florida's Crime Problem?

Some observers contend that Florida's crime crisis may be created more by sensational headlines than by a sharp increase in crime. Figure 1 supports this view: it shows violent and property crime rates in Florida over the 1971-1993 period. The property crime rate in 1993 was lower than it was in 1980 and lower than in every year

Figure 2. Change in the Number of Crimes
in Florida 1990-93
(percent change)

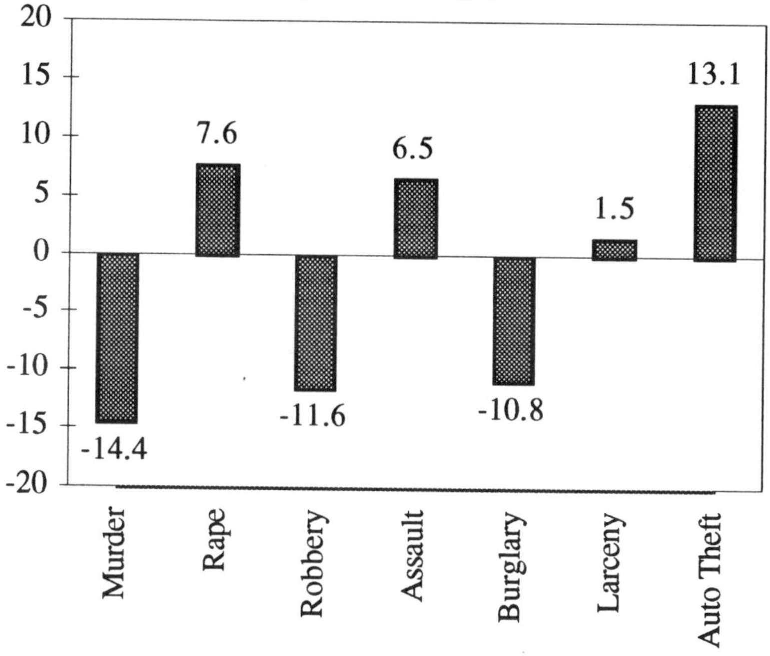

Source: Florida Department of Law Enforcement, *Crime in Florida*, various years.

since 1986. Violent crime rose relative to population until 1990 but there has been a slight decline since then. Figure 2 shows recent trends in crime. Since 1990 the numbers of reported murders, robberies and burglaries have fallen while incidents of rape, assault, larceny and motor vehicle theft have risen.

Despite the current frenzy of interest in the crime issue, crime statistics are not actually much different than they were when other issues such as the Gulf War or the economic recession were available to grab headlines. Crime is a serious issue, of course; it is just not a new issue. The overall crime rate rose steadily through the 1970s, more than doubling during the decade. The rate fell during the early 1980s but the last half of the decade saw crime rates increasing once again, reaching a record high in 1989. Thus, the falling rates in the 1990s reflect reductions below the 1989 peak but they remain well above their mid-1980s levels and more than double their 1970 level.

Since most crimes are not actually reported, these reported crime rates may be misleading. Reliable data on victimization in Florida are not available but national trends suggest that violent and property crimes have actually been falling for some time. Beginning in 1980 property crimes (burglary, larceny and motor vehicle theft) began a downward trend: by 1992 the victimization rate for these crimes was 35.3 percent below its 1979 level.[1] Violent crimes reached a peak in 1981 of 35.3 per thousand persons and fell to 28.1 in 1986. By 1992 the number had risen again, to 32.1 per thousand, a 14.2 percent increase.

These trends do not support a crisis mentality. Of course, the aggregate crime and victimization rates may be hiding other trends. Perhaps offenders are increasingly violent. This does not appear to be true, however. The number of murders in Florida has fallen each year from 1989 to 1993. Robberies are very high by comparison to most of the 1980s but they too have declined somewhat from their peak in 1990. Reported violent crimes of all types in Florida in 1993 were at about the same level as in 1990, largely due to an increasing number of assaults that were reported. Increasing violence apparently is not the source of the new crime crisis.

Perhaps violent crime is increasingly random, then, which would mean that people are increasingly uncertain about how to avoid crime. This uncertainty could cause increased apprehension and a crisis frame of mind. The randomness of crimes is difficult to measure with any available statistics, however. One indicator of randomness is whether the crime is committed by a stranger as opposed to an acquaintance or relative. Victim surveys indicate that the proportion of total attacks by strangers has fallen by about 8 percent since 1980. This does not prove that crime in general is less random, of course, but it does suggest that perceptions of increased randomness are probably

---

[1]Reported crime rates did not fall so dramatically during this time period because of an upward trend in the proportion of crimes reported to the police. Reporting of property crimes rose by almost 14 percent from 1979 to 1992.

exaggerated, just as perceptions of sharp increases in crime over the last three years are exaggerated.

Victimization data come from national surveys and Florida's situation is not necessarily the same as the nation's. For instance, Florida's crime rates are clearly higher than the national average. Indeed, state-by-state comparisons suggest that Florida is "Number 1" in crime. Some experts point out that Florida's reported crime rates (number of reported crimes divided by population) are not really comparable to those of many other states because Florida's population figures understate the number of potential crime victims by about a million people, the average number of people visiting Florida each day.

The question of whether Florida is really "Number One" in crime or only, say, "Number Five" when the crime rate is properly measured, is really irrelevant. Whether all of these victims are Florida citizens or visitors to the state is immaterial. The fact is that crime is a serious problem whether we consider it relative to what is happening elsewhere in the country or relative to Florida's own historical crime levels, but it is not a new problem and it is not getting worse.

The number of crimes reported does not reveal the full extent of the problem, of course. The fact is that crime creates tremendous costs for all Floridians even if they are not directly attacked or victimized. In fact, virtually everyone in the state is implicitly a crime victim. Most of us pay taxes to support the criminal justice system. Many of us pay to make our homes, businesses and other property more secure. We buy insurance against property crimes and the insurance rates we pay are high because we live in Florida where reported crime is high. We send our children to schools whose funding has been reduced relative to what it would be because state and local governments feel compelled to spend more on crime control. Large numbers of us lose business because tourists decide to go someplace else or stay home rather than travel to the nation's crime center. And the list could go on to include any number of other direct and indirect costs of crime.

Given the tremendous costs we are already bearing because of crime, the cost-effectiveness of any new policy initiatives should be of paramount concern. Are new prison beds worth the added costs? Are tougher sentences or gun control laws or any of the other proposals really going to make a significant difference? In order to answer these questions, we must understand how the criminal justice system works and how it affects the behavior of criminals.

The Criminal Justice System

Most criminal offenders are like other people in one important way: they respond to incentives. This is why deterrence works. Considerable evidence suggests that, by and large, criminals implicitly weigh the expected benefits of an offense against the expected costs when they are choosing to commit a crime (see Rasmussen and Benson 1994, Chapter 3). One potentially important cost of committing a crime is the punishment the criminal expects, but this is different from the punishment that convicted criminals actually receive. The expected punishment for a crime is not the actual sentence given to convicted criminals. Instead, the expected punishment is determined by the probabilities of a series of events occurring.

First, the crime must be reported to or be observed by police. According to the Bureau of Justice Statistics' most recent victimization survey, only about 39 percent of all Index I crimes are reported in the United States, although reporting varies by crime type--from 92 percent for motor vehicle theft to 15 percent for crimes of larceny resulting in losses of less than $50.

Second, the police must arrest the criminal. The probability of arrest for a particular crime depends on many circumstances specific to the crime, of course; among them are the skill of the criminal, luck, how observant the victim and/or witnesses are, the response time of police, and so on. Clearance rates provide an estimate of the probability of arrest for reported crimes. Using Florida data, clearance rates range from a high of 68 percent for murder to a low of 15 percent for motor vehicle theft.[2]

---

[2]The data used in this section come from Benson, Rasmussen and Mast 1994, who employ 1992 data. Although new sentencing guidelines now in place will change the incarceration estimates, the important relationships explained here will not be affected by recent changes in criminal justice policy.

Third, the offender must be charged and prosecuted after being arrested. Many people who are arrested are not prosecuted due to insufficient evidence, mistakes in arrests (e.g., arresting the wrong person, violation of due process rules by police, etc.), charges being dropped by the victim (e.g., as in many assault cases involving family members) or delays in the processing of the case. Recent estimates suggest that for Florida there is a 68 percent and 82 percent chance of prosecution given arrest for robbery and burglary, respectively.

Fourth, the prosecution must be successful before a sentence is imposed. The probability of conviction can be approximated by the ratio of convictions to the number of persons accused. The probability of conviction is very high, ranging from 0.84 for murder to 0.92 for burglary in Florida during 1992, suggesting that this is one area of the criminal justice system that works relatively well. Offsetting this impression is the fact that prosecutors probably have a good idea of the chances of conviction before they actually file accusations. Perhaps more significantly, about 98 percent of these Florida convictions were obtained by plea or charge bargaining, a practice dictated by the shortage of court resources relative to the number of accused persons. Since offenders will agree to a plea bargain only if they have something to gain--a reduced expected punishment--many of these convictions are for lesser crimes and/or fewer crimes than were actually committed.

Fifth, given a conviction, the criminal will be sentenced but prison is only one of a number of alternatives. Building more prisons so incarcerated offenders serve 75 or 85 percent of their sentences may have little impact if most offenders do not expect to go to prison but instead expect probation, for instance. The probability of imprisonment after conviction for burglary and robbery is estimated to be 26 percent and 46 percent, respectively, in 1992, for example.

Average prison sentences vary by crime, ranging from 21.8 years for murder in Florida during 1992 to 4.1 years for theft and fraud, but most prisoners can expect to serve only a portion of their full sentences. The portion of sentences served by Florida prisoners varied by crime type in 1992--from a low of 33.6 percent for theft to 45.8 percent for sexual offenses.

Figure 3. Calculating Expected Prison Sentences

(1) Probability of Victim Reporting	X	(2) Probability of Arrest	X	(3) Probability of Prosecution
X	(4) Probability of Conviction	X	(5) Probability of Imprisonment	
X	(6) Average Prison Sentence	X	(7) Portion of Sentence Served	

In sum, Figure 3 shows the expected prison sentence for a criminal is (1) the probability that a victim or witness will report the crime, times (2) the probability of arrest given the reporting of the crime, times (3) the probability of being prosecuted given arrest, times (4) the probability of conviction given prosecution, times (5) the probability of a prison sentence given conviction, times (6) the average prison sentence for the crime, times (7) the portion of sentence served.

A rough approximation of the calculation just described has been made for some crimes using 1992 Florida data. Table 1 provides these estimates for robbery and burglary. At the time they are planning their crime, burglars can expect to spend about 13 days in prison, while robbers can expect the cost of their crimes to be roughly 66 days in prison. Similar calculations suggest that violent crimes against persons have relatively high expected penalties: a murderer can expect to spend roughly 2.99 years in prison and a sexual offender can expect about 338 days. Property offenses may be common in Florida because there is a very low expected penalty to deter potential offenders. In addition to the low expected price of burglary, those engaged in theft face an expected 4.5 days in prison while auto thieves can expect about 10 days.

Table 1. Estimates of Expected Prison Sentences
in Florida 1992

	Robbery	Burglary
Probability of victim reporting	0.70	0.60
Probability of arrest	0.25	0.15
Probability of prosecution	0.68	0.82
Probability of conviction	0.85	0.92
Probability of imprisonment	0.46	0.26
Average prison sentence (in years)	8.60	5.50
Portion of sentence served	0.45	0.37
Expected prison time (in days)	65.70	12.80

Source: Benson, Rasmussen and Mast 1994.

Clearly, the expected prison terms for many crimes committed in Florida are very low. This is one reason for the high level of crime in Florida. But what will an expansion in prison capacity do to the expected punishment? Assume that prisoners end up serving 85 percent of their sentences and nothing else changes. A burglar would then expect to spend 30.1 days in prison. The expectation for a larcenist would go up to 11.4 days and for an auto thief it would reach 24.7 days. The reason that these expectations remain so low is that the probabilities of reporting, arrest and/or imprisonment are very low. Significant increases in deterrence are likely to require changes in these probabilities rather than simply the building of more prison beds.

Let us divide the law enforcement equation in Figure 3 into three separate, but not mutually exclusive, policy options. The first option includes policies geared toward preventing a crime from happening, an example being community policing efforts that increase the presence of law enforcement on the street.[3] To the extent that it is practical to do so, preventing crime is obviously the most effective policy because all the costs of victimization and those of the legal system are avoided. Preventing crime involves a partnership of the public

---

[3]There is some evidence that police presence on the street (community policing) is in fact more effective at lowering crime than having officers patrolling in cars. See Sherman 1983.

and private sectors. Private citizens can do much to stop crime by avoiding high-risk situations, locking cars and not providing would-be thieves with easy targets, and by purchasing private protection such as dead bolts on doors and alarm systems. The public sector can prevent crime via law enforcement activity (policy options two and three) or by increasing the legal earning opportunities of crime-prone persons.

The second policy option to combat crime focuses on efforts to increase the chances that offenders will be convicted of the crimes they commit. These include the first four events in Table 1: the probabilities of reporting, arrest, prosecution and conviction. The chance of a robber being convicted for a single offense is about 10 percent, according to the data in Table 1; for burglars it is about 7 percent. There is considerable evidence that increasing the chances of being caught more effectively deters criminals than a longer prison sentence. In this crucial area Florida, like the rest of the nation, provides little deterrence to property offenders.

Perhaps we are attracted to the third policy option, using increasingly severe prison sentences to deter crime, because offenders are not likely to be apprehended for the typical offense. Long sentences for chronic criminals prevent them from committing new crimes against the public but the fact remains that the low probability of conviction will compromise the effectiveness of this policy option. Yet, Florida has chosen to commit billions of dollars to the construction and operation of new prisons to combat crime. Given the apparent inability of police (in all jurisdictions) to increase the chances of arrest and conviction when the victim does not know the offender, we are left with a fundamental policy issue: is there an alternative strategy in which the anticrime dollars spent can affect more than a small fraction of all offenders?

Can Criminal Justice Policy Be More Cost Effective?

This question is particularly germane for the next few legislative sessions since the 1994 Legislature committed about $1.3 billion to build and operate new prisons over a four-year period. Substantial evidence suggests that this prison construction plan will not be the most cost-effective way to fight crime in our state. A review of this evidence suggests that reallocating some of the resources devoted to new prisons can make Floridians safer than they will be if the current plan is implemented.

Comparing the effectiveness of Florida's $1.3 billion prison expansion plan to an alternative that would add fewer prison beds and expand intermediate sanctions--nonprison punishments that are more severe than probation--requires that we focus on one critical question: will the last prison beds constructed do more to reduce crime than using the money on intermediate sanctions? If not, public safety in Florida is better served by transferring resources out of prison construction to these alternatives. The policy question then becomes: what portion of the $1.3 billion should be shifted to most effectively fight crime?

Three issues that help answer this question are discussed here. First, what benefits can be expected from the plan to build over 14,000 new prison beds? Second, what are the practical alternatives to building these beds? And finally, how many resources planned for prison construction in Florida could be better spent on intermediate sanctions?

The Benefits of Adding Prison Beds. Sentencing offenders to prison offers three potential benefits: rehabilitation, deterring offenders from future crime and, if these fail, incapacitation of criminals to assure public safety. First of all, it is hard to detect the rehabilitative powers of prison. Many observers have argued that the opposite occurs in prison; these institutions actually can be criminogenic, leading offenders to become more dangerous to society than they were before doing time. Grogger (1991), in a careful study of California offenders, provides empirical support for this argument. Closer to home, the National Council on Crime and Delinquency's evaluation of Florida's community control program shows that drug offenders going to prison are much more likely to recidivate than those facing intermediate sanctions (Benson and Rasmussen 1994). This is not really news, of course; advocacy of the rehabilitation effects of prison has not been heard in Florida's public debate on crime. Indeed, the goal of Florida's prison construction program clearly focuses on incapacitation. The stated purpose of having more prison beds is to assure that all offenders serve at least 75 percent of their sentences, up from an average figure of 33 percent in 1989 and 43 percent in 1993.

A fundamental implication of the research on deterrence is that the probability of punishment discourages crime more effectively than the severity of punishment. A study of recidivism among drug offenders in Florida (Kim et al. 1993), for example, found that a prison sentence had a greater deterrence effect than probation but that increasing the length of sentence had no effect on the chances of an offender being caught for a repeat offense. According to this study, which used the actual crime records of over 5,000 drug offenders in Florida, increasing the time served for the drug offenders, who account for about 20 percent of the status population, would yield no individual-specific deterrent effects. For nondrug offenders the evidence is less clear, although the criminogenic effects of prison reported above are consistent with the idea that there are no specific deterrence effects of longer prison sentences.

Whether longer prison terms will deter other potential offenders is also questionable. After all, many factors influence the decision to commit crimes. The psychological make-up and life experiences of the individual may be of critical importance, for instance. Economic opportunities are also significant determinants of crime. A person who does not have a job and does not have the skills necessary for obtaining a secure high-paying job is much more likely to engage in all kinds of crime than a person with a well-paying secure job. But determinants of crime such as these cannot be influenced directly by the criminal justice system (at least until an individual has committed an offense and comes under the control of the criminal justice system, which could then encourage education, job training, etc.). Expected punishment is a determinant of crime but as explained above, the probability of punishment (e.g., victim reporting, arrest and prosecution) is more important than the severity of punishment.

If Florida's commitment to keeping all offenders in prison for 75 or 85 percent of their sentences will not rehabilitate or deter offenders, we are left with the third potential benefit of more prisons: incapacitation. Offenders in prison are not able to commit crimes against the public. For repeat violent offenders this is an unambiguous benefit and these offenders should be given the highest priority use for prison space. Incapacitating many of Florida's inmates for a longer time may provide significant social benefits but it is also true that for many others these potential benefits are probably not worth the costs.[4] For example, locking up drug-involved offenders, perhaps even a portion of those who commit some property crimes, may be of little benefit to Floridians if the drug habit that is a root cause of the individual's problems remains untreated. There is ample evidence that drug treatment under court compulsion (e.g., drug courts) can be cost-effective relative to prison.

Importantly, it is not clear that the projected increases in incapacitation will be in fact achieved over the long run. The drive to increase prison sentences for all prison inmates in Florida is rooted in the understandable frustration of citizens when violent offenders are released early, only to commit heinous crimes again. Unfortunately, the aspects of the criminal justice system that led to prison crowding, as explained by Rasmussen and Benson (1994), are not altered by building more prison beds. The expanded prison system soon will be overcrowded since prosecutors and judges will find good reasons to incarcerate more people. Indeed, the preceding discussion suggests a good reason: raising the probability of imprisonment might deter potential criminals. Therefore, more prison capacity will tempt prosecutors and judges to get tougher on some criminals, in part because they previously may have put some offenders into community control whom they would have preferred to put in prison had it not been for the widely noted prison overcrowding problem.[5] And some in the system might feel they can be more punitive toward offenders who violate the terms of their community control sentences, thereby increasing prison intakes from this source. The result will be familiar if prison overcrowding is not tolerated: inmates will be released early and the percentage of sentence served will fall from

---

[4]See Benson and Rasmussen 1994 and Austin 1994 for a discussion of punishments that are an alternative to prison for some offenders.

[5]In FY1993-94, 54,758 persons were sentenced to probation, 16,230 sentenced to community control and 25,806 sent to prison (Criminal Justice Estimating Conference, Final Report, July 21, 1994).

the 85 percent goal that originally motivated the prison building program. This raises the prospect that overcrowding will again occur and far sooner than anyone expects, given the massive construction effort.

Thus, building more prison beds will not be a panacea for Florida's crime problem. Inmates are not likely to be rehabilitated by their experience in prison and longer incarceration is not a significant deterrent for many people already in our prisons. The prospect of long sentences will not serve as effective general deterrence either, unless significant increases are realized in the probabilities of crime reporting, arrest and prosecution. Incarcerating violent offenders who are likely to repeat will obviously increase public safety but many non-violent felons are in our prisons. Given these facts, it is likely that at least some of the beds in Florida's proposed prison expansion will yield modest benefits over their cost. We now consider the extent to which public safety would be enhanced by substituting some intermediate punishments for a portion of the 14,000 prison beds to be constructed during the next four years.

Trading Prison Beds for Intermediate Sanctions. Here is the trade-off. Invest, say, $100 million in building and operating new prison beds or increase the number of offenders put into intensive supervision and treatment programs. Florida's prison bed construction plan is an explicit commitment to increase punishments for felons who are generally well into a criminal career. Benson and Rasmussen (1994) present substantial evidence that it would be cost effective to divert some of Florida's planned prison construction for 1994 through 1998 to community control programs. What portion should be diverted to get the most benefits per dollar expenditure is the policy issue.

Allocating available prison beds to the most dangerous felons is an obvious first step in developing a cost-effective criminal justice strategy. Many drug offenders have been put in Florida's prisons, reaching a peak of 37 percent of prison admissions in 1989. Although the link between drug abuse and crime was believed to be very close, there is strong evidence that suggests a large portion of drug offenders are not otherwise a threat to the community. The RAND Corporation's (Everingham and Rydell 1994) study of the relative effectiveness of supply and demand strategies to control cocaine use suggests that treatment of heavy users is much more cost effective than domestic law enforcement, which includes such activities as cocaine seizures, seizing assets of drug dealers and incarcerating suppliers of drugs. RAND concludes that treatment is about seven times more cost effective than traditional enforcement efforts. Everingham and Rydell explain this conclusion:

> ...treatment of heavy users is more cost-effective than supply-control programs. One might wonder how this squares with the (dubious) conventional wisdom that, with treatment, "nothing works." There are two explanations. First, evaluations of treatment typically measure the proportion of people who no longer use drugs at some point after completing treatment; they tend to under-appreciate the benefits of keeping people off drugs while they are in treatment—roughly one-fifth of the consumption reduction generated by treatment accrues during treatment. Second, about three-fifths of the users who start treatment stay in their program less than three months. Because incomplete treatments do not substantially reduce consumption, they make treatment look weak by traditional criteria. However, they do not cost much, so they do not dilute the cost effectiveness of completed treatments.

This does not mean that all law enforcement efforts against drug offenders should be stopped in favor of intermediate sanctions geared toward rehabilitation and treatment, of course. First, there is a limit to how much treatment can be done. Second, drug treatment under compulsion of traditional law enforcement efforts is effective and widens the net of people brought into programs that treat drug dependency, but many criminals are not drug dependent and even more have chosen a criminal path for reasons unrelated to drugs.

Diverting nonviolent drug offenders from prison beds to cheaper and more effective treatment programs is a cost-effective way to increase the time chronic offenders spend in prison. This strategy is being used in Florida. Prison admissions for drug offenses have fallen precipitously since 1992: there were 3,381 drug admissions in the first quarter of FY1992-93 but only 1,227 in the same quarter of 1994-95, a 64 percent decline. A recent study by Austin (1994) reported that the process of diverting drug offenders from prisons is not yet complete, noting that at least 4,000 inmates in our state could safely be diverted from the prison system to alternative punishments.

Since 1990, Florida's criminal justice system has put more offenders on community control and fewer people into prison. Annual prison admissions have fallen since 1990, from a peak of 43,330 in FY1989-90 to an estimated 25,700 in FY1993-94. Despite putting fewer people in prison each year, crime rates have fallen (see Figures 1 and 2). This apparent contradiction between lower crime rates and a declining incarceration rate is resolved, at least in part, by the fact that the most dangerous felons are still going to prison and are being held there longer. By being more selective in who is incarcerated, the average percentage of sentence served rose about 30 percent from June 1990 to June 1994 (from 33.1 percent to 43.1 percent) and the average actual time served rose 78 percent (from 13.8 months to 24.6 months).

The political appeal of having prisoners serving 75 or 85 percent of their sentences is obvious but a more important issue revolves around which prisoners are to be incarcerated for these long sentences. If building more prison beds means that we revert to putting more nonviolent drug offenders in prison for a long time, we will have squandered resources that could be used in better ways to increase public safety. The most visible part of our public debate on criminal justice policy has been too narrowly focused on prison construction, while in reality the last four years has seen a more efficient use of our prison space and a modest decline in the crime rate.

Florida has limited public resources, so more prison beds means there will be fewer resources elsewhere in the criminal justice system. Some tradeoffs are stark. If the consequence of adding more prison space is fewer police or prosecutorial resources and a lower probability of conviction, for example, expected sentences of criminals could fall even lower than they are now, thereby undermining the effect of the added prison beds. Using our scarce criminal resource dollars to build and operate more prisons is an implicit commitment to stop persons who have established a criminal career rather than to increase the punishments of budding criminals who might be diverted from a criminal career. Youthful offenders and those first convicted for property crimes are not going to be sent to prison. Instead, they most likely will receive no punishment at all, encouraging some of them to believe that crime pays.

Alternative sanctions are less expensive and, unlike prisons, they can be used to increase the severity of punishment for first or second offenses, thereby offering the possibility of derailing a potential criminal career. A common complaint of law enforcement is that repeat youthful offenders are put back on the street immediately after they are arrested. Building more prisons, which might represent to these youth very severe punishment in the future after many more offenses, is not likely to curtail their immediate illegal behavior. Indeed, by not showing them that their acts have immediate and undesirable consequences, we are probably accomplices in the creation of criminal careers. Further, most drug-using felons indicate that their criminal careers started long before they used drugs, suggesting that firm action against first- and second-time offenders might also deter their introduction to drug use that further reduces the chances that they will become productive citizens (Rasmussen and Benson 1994, p.58). Thus, one cost of putting too many of our criminal justice resources into adult-prison construction is a reduction in early intervention such as more stringent supervision and drug treatment before offenders build a criminal record that puts them in prison. The folk wisdom of "a stitch in time saves nine" may offer an important insight for the most cost effective allocation of funds to be spent on punishing offenders in Florida.

A Look Ahead

Aggregate crime rates in Florida have been declining since 1990. Felons in our prison system are now serving a bigger portion of their sentences and the average time served rose over 78 percent between 1990 and 1994. Fear of crime is nevertheless the major policy issue, leading the Legislature to spend billions of dollars on the construction and operation of new prisons. Prisons concentrate our scarce public dollars on the punishment of established criminals when the most pressing need in Florida might be a surer and swifter punishment of offenders at the beginning of their criminal careers. Although there is no panacea for Florida's crime problem, cost-effective policy must consider the entire criminal justice system rather than emphasizing any single component. From this perspective, our current commitments to build more prison beds should be reconsidered.

References

Austin, James. 1994. *Prisoners Who Don't Need to be Imprisoned: An Assessment of Florida's Inmates Eligible for Intermediate Sanctions* (November 8). Washington, D.C.: National Council on Crime and Delinquency.

Benson, Bruce L., and David W. Rasmussen. 1994. *Intermediate Sanctions* (November). A Report to the Task Force to Reform Criminal Justice in Florida.

Benson, Bruce L., David W. Rasmussen and Brent Mast. 1994. *Crime in Florida* (March). Tallahassee: Florida Chamber of Commerce.

Everingham, Susan S., and Peter Rydell. 1994. *Modeling the Demand for Cocaine.* Santa Monica, California: RAND Corporation.

Grogger, J. 1991. "Certainty vs. Severity of Punishment." *Economic Inquiry* 21 (April), pp. 297-309.

Kim, Iljoong, Bruce L. Benson, David W. Rasmussen and Thomas W. Zuehlke. 1993. "An Economic Analysis of Recidivism among Drug Offenders." *Southern Economic Journal* 60 (July), pp. 169-183.

Rasmussen, David W., and Bruce L. Benson. 1994. *The Economic Anatomy of a Drug War: Criminal Justice in the Commons.* Lanham, Maryland: Rowman and Littlefield.

Sherman, Lawrence W. 1983. "Patrol Strategies for Police" in James Q. Wilson, ed., *Crime and Public Policy.* San Francisco: Institute for Contemporary Studies Press.

Housing 6

Marc T. Smith
Associate Director
Shimberg Center for
Affordable Housing
University of Florida
Gainesville, Florida

As Florida has experienced rapid growth, the state's housing stock has needed to grow and expand to meet the need. The resultant housing construction has several implications that are important to any attempt to characterize the state's housing stock. The growth has also meant that housing production has played an important role in the economy of the state.

This chapter addresses three aspects of housing in the state of Florida. First, data from the U.S. Census are used to compare housing characteristics across counties and for the census years 1970, 1980 and 1990. Second, a relatively untapped data source, county property appraiser data, is used to examine differences in housing characteristics and house prices across counties. Finally, policy issues in the state are discussed.

Housing Characteristics by County: Census Data

Table 1 presents data for each county in the state for the years 1970, 1980 and 1990 as drawn from the various decennial U. S. Censuses. Five characteristics of the housing stock are included: number of housing units, percentage of rental units, percentage of mobile homes, percentage of units older than thirty years and percentage of single-family housing units. An analysis of these characteristics illustrates both the impact of growth on Florida over the

Table 1. Housing Characteristics by County
1970, 1980 and 1990

Counties and Years	Number of Housing Units	Percent of Rental Units	Percent of Mobile/ Trailer Homes	Percent of Units Less Than 30 Years	Percent of Single Family Units
Alachua					
1990	79,022	41.3	13.3	81.7	51.6
1980	58,896	41.7	10.6	84.9	57.6
1970	33,519	36.4	7.6	83.8	68.6
Baker					
1990	5,975	19.2	43.2	82.8	51.8
1980	4,525	20.6	22.9	81.6	70.3
1970	2,324	26.3	14.8	74.6	81.8
Bay					
1990	65,999	25.6	16.8	81.0	57.5
1980	40,447	27.5	13.1	82.1	65.6
1970	26,742	28.1	9.6	83.4	77.3
Bradford					
1990	8,099	20.4	29.7	73.6	62.9
1980	7,213	19.8	18.8	74.7	72.7
1970	4,591	21.8	8.3	80.6	85.8
Brevard					
1990	185,150	26.8	11.5	87.0	62.3
1980	113,077	25.6	10.7	94.3	65.6
1970	77,871	25.5	7.9	94.9	70.9
Broward					
1990	628,660	26.9	4.4	84.2	44.2
1980	477,468	24.7	4.5	95.5	46.1
1970	245,799	24.6	4.0	96.1	60.8
Calhoun					
1990	4,468	17.5	29.5	67.9	66.3
1980	3,474	18.9	16.7	68.0	79.4
1970	2,710	21.7	8.7	73.2	88.6
Charlotte					
1990	64,641	15.3	16.1	93.0	66.3
1980	33,940	12.7	18.6	95.1	69.1
1970	13,046	12.9	10.6	92.7	81.6
Citrus					
1990	49,854	13.7	31.5	93.9	62.2
1980	27,361	11.7	28.2	94.4	67.2
1970	9,707	10.8	14.0	90.9	80.7
Clay					
1990	40,249	24.3	18.1	89.5	66.5
1980	23,576	21.8	13.4	89.6	73.6
1970	10,445	26.6	11.3	86.5	76.7

Continued . . .

Table 1. Housing Characteristics by County
1970, 1980 and 1990 (continued)

Counties and Years	Number of Housing Units	Percent of Rental Units	Percent of Mobile/ Trailer Homes	Percent of Units Less Than 30 Years	Percent of Single Family Units
Collier					
1990	94,165	19.5	10.8	94.7	42.9
1980	49,795	19.7	13.3	96.9	43.7
1970	16,081	24.3	11.1	96.9	60.0
Columbia					
1990	17,818	23.0	34.0	78.1	55.5
1980	13,505	23.8	19.9	76.8	69.4
1970	8,446	25.4	10.1	74.9	81.1
Dade					
1990	771,288	41.0	2.4	68.5	50.0
1980	663,343	41.8	2.1	82.5	48.6
1970	450,119	43.6	2.2	85.5	56.2
De Soto					
1990	10,310	20.7	36.4	79.3	52.8
1980	7,334	21.4	27.2	75.3	63.8
1970	4,041	27.1	8.1	61.9	83.1
Dixie					
1990	6,445	10.6	53.0	84.2	44.0
1980	3,282	16.9	31.3	82.5	64.3
1970	1,875	28.7	13.7	79.2	82.3
Duval					
1990	284,673	34.4	7.7	67.0	62.7
1980	226,637	34.5	5.9	76.8	66.2
1970	174,149	30.1	4.2	79.1	75.1
Escambia					
1990	112,230	31.0	9.4	72.6	68.7
1980	87,994	28.7	7.4	78.7	75.5
1970	65,085	27.4	5.3	80.6	82.7
Flagler					
1990	15,215	18.3	12.4	93.8	75.2
1980	5,714	19.1	13.2	91.2	70.9
1970	1,841	28.3	7.9	86.5	73.2
Franklin					
1990	5,891	12.0	20.7	74.1	67.9
1980	3,579	17.2	18.0	71.2	73.7
1970	3,017	20.8	6.6	69.4	86.0
Gadsden					
1990	14,859	22.0	26.9	67.1	65.0
1980	13,193	23.4	12.7	67.0	75.4
1970	10,000	30.0	4.8	59.0	89.9

Continued . . .

Table 1. Housing Characteristics by County
1970, 1980 and 1990 (continued)

Counties and Years	Number of Housing Units	Percent of Rental Units	Percent of Mobile/ Trailer Homes	Percent of Units Less Than 30 Years	Percent of Single Family Units
Gilchrist					
1990	4,071	11.7	49.0	86.7	48.3
1980	2,360	12.8	29.4	83.3	65.8
1970	1,249	20.3	16.7	75.5	80.5
Glades					
1990	4,624	13.6	58.2	88.8	36.8
1980	2,456	23.6	37.0	85.8	55.4
1970	1,392	28.3	20.0	82.5	68.6
Gulf					
1990	6,339	14.6	25.2	66.1	68.5
1980	4,159	18.9	14.3	75.8	79.2
1970	3,725	19.9	4.1	81.7	90.9
Hamilton					
1990	4,119	20.2	36.9	70.3	56.1
1980	3,224	21.0	20.7	68.1	71.8
1970	2,557	27.6	11.4	65.0	85.3
Hardee					
1990	7,941	19.5	31.6	72.0	61.7
1980	7,006	21.9	15.8	75.6	76.8
1970	4,697	25.3	8.4	65.7	86.4
Hendry					
1990	9,945	24.7	40.9	87.7	50.6
1980	6,737	28.4	30.4	85.9	59.1
1970	3,969	35.4	16.6	81.3	67.5
Hernando					
1990	50,018	13.1	24.3	94.7	70.0
1980	21,502	12.6	25.7	93.2	70.1
1970	7,578	16.0	12.2	88.8	82.0
Highlands					
1990	40,114	16.2	27.6	85.8	59.0
1980	21,597	21.5	18.1	84.5	67.4
1970	12,309	24.0	10.6	79.4	75.7
Hillsborough					
1990	367,740	32.6	11.5	78.0	58.9
1980	260,559	30.3	9.7	82.3	65.5
1970	168,292	25.5	6.8	78.8	76.7
Holmes					
1990	6,785	16.4	27.7	72.8	68.9
1980	5,701	16.5	12.5	71.1	81.9
1970	4,062	19.1	7.9	67.0	88.2

Continued . . .

Table 1. Housing Characteristics by County
1970, 1980 and 1990 (continued)

Counties and Years	Number of Housing Units	Percent of Rental Units	Percent of Mobile/ Trailer Homes	Percent of Units Less Than 30 Years	Percent of Single Family Units
Indian River					
1990	47,128	20.1	14.4	85.5	57.9
1980	28,351	20.3	13.0	90.6	59.8
1970	13,769	23.9	6.1	87.0	78.5
Jackson					
1990	16,320	20.4	25.1	66.0	68.5
1980	14,445	22.3	13.0	67.9	80.3
1970	11,375	24.4	5.2	66.5	90.7
Jefferson					
1990	4,395	21.1	30.7	65.4	62.4
1980	3,832	22.2	15.8	60.8	77.1
1970	2,679	29.5	5.9	63.2	91.2
Lafayette					
1990	2,266	14.7	41.4	78.1	55.6
1980	1,576	19.5	25.9	71.5	72.0
1970	1,036	20.9	13.9	62.4	84.6
Lake					
1990	75,707	18.2	35.6	80.7	52.7
1980	49,818	18.3	26.2	83.4	62.7
1970	28,044	21.5	12.3	79.1	77.1
Lee					
1990	189,051	20.6	17.3	91.7	52.0
1980	108,633	19.6	17.5	93.5	54.8
1970	42,196	21.2	12.4	89.5	70.6
Leon					
1990	81,325	39.7	12.3	83.0	55.5
1980	59,255	40.2	10.3	87.9	56.3
1970	32,572	38.1	9.6	86.3	66.5
Levy					
1990	12,307	14.9	46.0	83.4	50.3
1980	8,607	16.4	28.5	83.7	64.4
1970	4,721	23.2	11.8	75.6	82.4
Liberty					
1990	2,157	15.2	40.6	74.7	58.3
1980	1,777	17.5	22.1	69.2	69.6
1970	1,287	18.2	7.8	73.1	90.1
Madison					
1990	6,275	21.1	30.9	66.2	62.8
1980	5,551	22.8	14.5	67.0	76.9
1970	4,252	31.8	5.9	65.3	90.3

Continued . . .

Table 1. Housing Characteristics by County
1970, 1980 and 1990 (continued)

Counties and Years	Number of Housing Units	Percent of Rental Units	Percent of Mobile/ Trailer Homes	Percent of Units Less Than 30 Years	Percent of Single Family Units
Manatee					
1990	115,245	23.0	22.7	82.5	47.9
1980	82,798	19.3	21.7	88.3	52.9
1970	41,789	17.9	21.7	85.0	63.7
Marion					
1990	94,567	20.2	30.8	88.9	57.4
1980	51,691	20.9	21.5	87.1	67.2
1970	25,830	21.1	11.1	81.7	81.9
Martin					
1990	54,199	18.3	14.4	90.4	53.6
1980	31,576	18.2	16.6	93.5	53.5
1970	11,745	20.0	18.7	88.9	67.4
Monroe					
1990	46,215	27.3	21.5	75.9	47.9
1980	36,295	27.8	17.7	83.9	51.4
1970	19,933	38.5	16.0	79.6	53.1
Nassau					
1990	18,726	18.6	30.5	81.1	53.6
1980	13,009	18.3	23.4	84.2	59.4
1970	6,677	21.1	11.1	76.0	81.1
Okaloosa					
1990	62,569	32.2	9.7	84.9	66.0
1980	42,899	32.7	10.9	91.4	65.7
1970	27,218	36.1	13.0	93.5	70.8
Okeechobee					
1990	13,266	21.2	50.4	89.8	42.9
1980	8,322	24.9	33.3	90.8	58.4
1970	3,687	33.0	15.6	84.3	74.7
Orange					
1990	282,686	36.7	7.1	79.8	61.1
1980	183,373	35.0	6.7	86.5	65.4
1970	116,961	29.5	4.9	87.2	76.1
Osceola					
1990	47,959	28.0	20.1	88.7	56.1
1980	22,946	24.6	22.9	83.0	59.1
1970	10,300	22.3	16.0	74.4	72.4
Palm Beach					
1990	461,665	22.2	4.7	86.7	49.7
1980	286,784	21.8	5.1	90.0	49.4
1970	135,131	29.6	5.0	86.3	60.5

Continued . . .

Table 1. Housing Characteristics by County
1970, 1980 and 1990 (continued)

Counties and Years	Number of Housing Units	Percent of Rental Units	Percent of Mobile/ Trailer Homes	Percent of Units Less Than 30 Years	Percent of Single Family Units
Pasco					
1990	148,965	15.6	27.1	92.2	60.4
1980	96,681	12.4	20.3	94.8	71.1
1970	34,201	12.8	17.0	91.9	77.0
Pinellas					
1990	458,341	25.6	11.4	74.1	52.7
1980	360,980	24.9	9.4	87.3	58.1
1970	225,544	22.8	9.8	86.3	69.5
Polk					
1990	186,225	24.7	27.8	77.6	55.5
1980	126,742	26.7	15.9	79.9	67.8
1970	79,631	26.4	9.5	77.5	78.2
Putnam					
1990	31,840	16.6	42.8	79.5	50.4
1980	21,653	18.1	27.0	79.0	65.1
1970	12,900	20.6	10.8	74.2	81.7
St. Johns					
1990	40,712	24.3	15.9	82.0	58.7
1980	22,503	20.7	14.5	75.1	68.8
1970	11,581	22.8	6.6	64.4	82.0
St. Lucie					
1990	73,843	21.9	15.6	87.9	61.5
1980	38,441	27.4	15.7	89.0	62.5
1970	18,734	31.7	5.9	89.5	72.9
Santa Rosa					
1990	32,831	22.5	19.7	83.8	70.3
1980	20,222	21.6	12.3	87.1	78.7
1970	12,079	24.5	9.7	85.6	82.4
Sarasota					
1990	157,055	19.0	13.3	85.0	60.2
1980	112,196	17.9	12.9	92.3	60.1
1970	54,936	18.6	10.4	92.5	70.3
Seminole					
1990	117,845	30.3	4.3	90.1	69.5
1980	67,544	25.5	4.8	91.8	74.8
1970	28,415	22.0	5.0	86.0	82.2
Sumter					
1990	15,298	15.8	48.2	83.8	46.4
1980	10,464	16.2	32.9	83.9	61.0
1970	5,270	19.1	13.0	79.7	84.4

Continued . . .

Table 1. Housing Characteristics by County
1970, 1980 and 1990 (continued)

Counties and Years	Number of Housing Units	Percent of Rental Units	Percent of Mobile/ Trailer Homes	Percent of Units Less Than 30 Years	Percent of Single Family Units
Suwannee					
1990	11,699	17.8	42.3	79.6	51.3
1980	8,602	20.3	25.7	73.5	67.1
1970	5,227	23.3	11.2	68.1	84.5
Taylor					
1990	7,908	17.4	32.7	72.0	62.4
1980	6,339	22.2	14.0	73.0	77.7
1970	4,976	20.9	8.9	73.0	86.7
Union					
1990	2,975	26.9	39.1	77.6	52.2
1980	2,352	30.6	21.0	71.2	70.2
1970	1,737	35.0	9.7	64.5	84.5
Volusia					
1990	180,972	23.8	11.9	79.5	64.7
1980	121,532	24.4	11.2	83.6	65.7
1970	70,289	23.0	6.8	79.7	74.8
Wakulla					
1990	6,587	13.1	43.7	85.7	54.0
1980	4,878	13.5	33.5	83.1	62.6
1970	2,637	14.1	10.3	83.3	84.8
Walton					
1990	18,728	12.1	22.4	81.7	57.2
1980	10,456	13.9	14.4	77.4	75.0
1970	6,025	18.3	7.7	73.9	89.3
Washington					
1990	7,703	16.3	27.2	71.9	68.9
1980	5,884	15.6	14.1	70.7	80.3
1970	4,216	17.6	7.5	70.4	87.8

Sources: Bureau of the Census, *1990 Census of Housing, Detailed Housing Characteristics, Florida*, Table 66, pp. 156-162; *1990 Census of Housing, General Housing Characteristics, Florida*, Table 49, pp. 160-166; *1980 Census of Housing, Detailed Housing Characteristics, Florida*, Table 49, pp. 265-268; *1970 Census of Housing, Housing Characteristics, for States, Cities, and Counties Florida*, Table 62, pp. 240-256.

twenty-year period and the differences in the housing stock and its usage across counties.

Number of Housing Units. Virtually all counties in the state of Florida experienced a large increase in the number of housing units between 1970 and 1990 and no county had fewer units in 1990 than in 1970. Increases on the order of 500 percent or more were experienced in Charlotte, Citrus, Collier, Flagler and Hernando counties. Others experiencing large percentage increases included Lee, Martin, Osceola, Pasco, St. Lucie and Seminole counties. Some of the larger counties added a significant number of units but the large base from which they started in 1970 reduced the impact of their growth in percentage terms. Among the counties with numerical increases of over 100,000 housing units between 1970 and 1990 are Brevard, Broward (almost 400,000 units), Dade, Hillsborough, Orange, Palm Beach (over 300,000 units), Pinellas, Polk, Sarasota and Volusia.

Rental Housing. Florida is predominantly a homeownership state. Comparing first across counties in 1990, the proportion of rental units ranged from a high of 41.3 percent in Alachua County to a low of 10.6 percent in Dixie County. The large rental stock in Alachua County is not surprising given the presence of the University of Florida. The rental percentage is also high in Dade County, a major urban county, and Leon County, seat of state government and Florida State University. Low percentages of rental occupancy are found, in addition to Dixie County, in other nonmetropolitan counties including Citrus, Franklin, Gilchrist, Glades, Gulf, Lafayette, Levy, Wakulla and Walton. Hernando's rental occupancy is also below 15 percent. Of the sixty-seven counties in Florida, fifty-one have less than 25 percent of their housing stock in rental usage, considerably below the national average of almost 36 percent in 1990.

Following the national trend in which rental housing was occupied by about 37 percent of the population in 1970 and 36 percent in 1990, percentages of rental housing have not changed much in Florida counties over the 1970-to-1990 period. Declines of more than 10 percent in the proportion of total housing occupied as rental housing were experienced in Dixie, Flagler, Glades, Hendry, Madison, Monroe and Okeechobee counties. No increases of as much as 10 percent were reported; the largest increase was 8.3 percent in Seminole County.

Manufactured Housing. Manufactured housing has played a major role in the provision of housing in Florida in recent years. Data provided by the Florida Manufactured Housing Association, Inc., indicates that since 1978, manufactured home sales as a percentage of the total of both single-family housing starts and manufactured home sales have ranged between 15 percent (in 1992) and 31 percent (in 1982). The average has been approximately 20 percent. In 1992, the percentages by county ranged from 0 to 90 percent (in Hendry County), with ten counties having 50 percent or more. About 50 percent of all manufactured home sales occur in three counties, with Polk and Marion counties being the leaders.

Census statistics confirm the importance of manufactured or mobile homes. The percentage that mobile homes comprise of the housing stock is highest in Glades County, with 58.2 percent mobile homes. Other rural counties also have high percentages of mobile homes, with those over 40 percent including Baker, Dixie, Gilchrist, Hendry, Lafayette, Levy, Liberty, Okeechobee, Putnam, Sumter, Suwannee and Wakulla. The lowest percentage is Dade County with only 2.4 percent of the housing stock. Urban counties generally have lower percentages of mobile homes than rural counties.

The percentage of mobile homes in the total housing stock has increased significantly in many counties between 1970 and 1990. For example, in Baker County mobile homes have increased from 14.8 percent of the total housing stock in 1970 to 43.2 percent in 1990; in De Soto the increase was from 8.1 percent to 36.4 percent; in Dixie County from 13.7 to 53.0 percent; in Gilchrist from 16.7 to 49.0 percent; in Levy from 11.8 to 46.0 percent; in Liberty from 7.8 to 40.6 percent; in Okeechobee from 15.6 to 50.4 percent; in Sumter from 13.0 to 48.2 percent; in Suwanee from 11.2 to 42.3 percent; and in Wakulla from 10.3 to 43.7 percent.

Age of Housing Units. The fourth column of Table 1 reports the percentage of housing units in each county that were less than thirty years old in 1970, 1980 and 1990. On a national level, about 60 percent of the housing units were less than thirty years old in 1970 and about 58 percent in 1990. The growth of Florida and resultant level of construction necessary to meet the demands of the population migrating to the state is apparent as the age of the housing stock is considerably less than the national average. Counties with 90 percent or more of their housing stock built in the last thirty years include Charlotte, Citrus, Collier (94.7 percent), Flagler, Hernando,

Lee, Martin, Pasco and Seminole counties. A number of other counties have over 80 percent of their housing stock less than thirty years old, including Clay, Glades, Marion, Okeechobee and Osceola counties with percentages over 88 percent. Counties with lower percentages of housing less than thirty years old include predominantly nonmetropolitan counties. Counties with below 70 percent of their housing units less than thirty years old include Calhoun, Duval, Gadsden, Gulf, Jackson, Jefferson and Madison.

Few counties have undergone major changes in their percentages of housing units less than thirty years old between 1970 and 1990. Counties in which the housing stock has become appreciably older (greater than 10 percentage points) include Broward, Dade, Duval and Pinellas, all large urban counties, and Gulf, a nonmetropolitan county. Counties experiencing a greater increase than 10 percentage points in housing units less than thirty years old, indicating a newer housing stock, include De Soto, Gilchrist, Lafayette, Osceola, St. Johns, Suwannee and Union, a mix of nonmetropolitan and smaller, rapidly growing metropolitan counties.

Percentage of Single-Family Units. The final variable from the census indicates the types of housing units found in the county. Single-family units can be owner- or renter-occupied. The highest proportion of single-family units in 1990--75.2 percent--was in Flagler County. At the other extreme, only 36.8 percent of the units in Glades were single-family structures. Most counties have experienced a significant decline in the percentage of single-family units between 1970 and 1990, although the single-family unit remains the dominant housing form in most counties.

Summary of Census Housing Characteristics. This brief review of Florida counties shows a diverse state. While growth has impacted all areas of Florida, some have experienced very rapid growth while in other areas the change has been less dramatic. The growth counties, and therefore the ones that have had the greatest changes in their housing stock, are generally in the southern, coastal areas of the state or around Orlando. Slower-growth areas are generally in the interior and northern portions of the state. Considerable differences in housing-stock characteristics are also apparent between urban counties and rural, nonmetropolitan counties.

Housing Characteristics: County
Property Appraiser Data

County property appraisers prepare the property tax roll in a county each year. For this purpose they gather a rich data set that includes information for each property on the type of land use from among 100 land use categories, the most recent and second most recent sales prices and dates, current assessed value, year built, size of lot, size of unit and exemptions. The latter includes use of the homestead exemption, which indicates that the unit is occupied by the owner. There are limitations to the data in that all records are not complete in all counties. For example, in Alachua and St. Johns counties only five years of data are available. Data are not available at all for some counties. However, the data this source does provide are not otherwise available.

The appraiser data are used to calculate the mean and median house price for owner-occupied single-family homes shown in Table 2 and to further characterize differences in the housing stock across counties. The table includes data for metropolitan and representative nonmetropolitan counties.

Housing Prices. The most recent and second most recent sales price values and dates were used to develop a series on the mean and median sales price by county for the period 1982-1991, the latter being the most recent year for which a full year of data is available. The 1982 and 1991 means and medians are shown in the table.

The sales price data further illustrate the differences between urban and rural counties and between coastal and noncoastal counties. The highest mean prices in 1991 are in five coastal counties, four of which are not major urban areas. Monroe County has the highest mean price of $154,606; Martin County's was $134,950; Collier's was $133,375; Palm Beach's was $133,072; and the mean price in St. Johns County was $124,398. Comparing mean and median prices indicates that the mean is pulled up by sales of very expensive homes, as the mean prices are considerably above the median prices of $128,000 in Monroe; $110,500 in Martin; $113,500 in Collier; $109,400 in Palm Beach; and $100,000 in St. Johns County.

Table 2. Mean and Median Single-Family Housing
Values by Selected County 1991 and 1982

Counties	Mean		Real Change in Mean	Median	
	1991	1982		1991	1982
Alachua	77,748	71,246	-0.0228	70,000	65,000
Bay	69,480	52,894	-0.0029	64,000	47,500
Bradford	52,837	44,468	-0.0089	46,450	43,400
Brevard	84,424	64,973	-0.0128	75,000	58,600
Broward	107,822	87,146	-0.0111	90,900	74,000
Charlotte	63,646	52,331	-0.0127	58,700	48,950
Citrus	58,871	50,582	-0.0223	55,000	45,000
Clay	85,761	65,852	-0.0165	79,500	62,500
Collier	133,375	89,355	0.0148	113,500	70,500
Columbia	59,098	41,560	-0.0089	55,700	37,000
Dade	114,295	86,384	-0.0111	90,450	70,000
De Soto	64,262	36,804	-0.0094	50,000	31,500
Duval	84,102	57,332	-0.0019	76,300	51,500
Escambia	63,646	52,331	-0.0232	58,700	48,950
Gilchrist	44,757	34,600	-0.0089	46,250	35,000
Hernando	73,803	53,563	-0.0189	67,050	52,000
Hillsborough	87,075	61,403	0.0001	78,000	57,550
Lake	77,624	55,770	-0.0113	74,400	50,000
Lee	93,093	65,265	0.0117	78,450	59,950
Leon	84,798	64,983	-0.0099	74,800	59,600
Manatee	93,407	65,519	-0.0064	85,000	59,500
Marion	64,725	48,866	-0.0118	59,444	45,000
Martin	134,950	81,502	0.0176	110,500	66,500
Monroe	154,606	90,139	0.0106	128,000	75,000
Nassau	85,573	49,713	-0.0011	79,500	41,750
Okeechobee	57,535	37,348	-0.0094	49,950	32,500
Orange	97,059	64,972	0.0011	87,800	58,750
Osceola	82,667	53,483	0.0009	79,900	47,650
Palm Beach	133,072	NA	NA	109,400	NA
Pinellas	92,633	63,662	-0.0127	77,500	55,500
Polk	69,574	57,958	-0.0188	63,900	52,500
St. Johns	124,398	103,236	-0.0108	100,000	84,000
St. Lucie	71,063	56,899	-0.0134	66,000	52,900
Sarasota	110,723	75,047	-0.0048	86,000	66,500
Seminole	106,310	83,093	-0.0128	92,400	75,000

NA Not available.

Source: Author calculations based on county property appraiser data. Data prepared by ARMASI, Inc.

Other counties with high mean prices in 1991 include a mix of urban, suburban and coastal counties such as Broward at $107,822; Dade at $114,295; Sarasota at $110,723; and Seminole at $106,310. All of these counties also have mean prices in 1991 that greatly exceed their median prices in that year, indicating individual sales of high-priced homes. Other counties with mean sales prices over $90,000 include Lee, Manatee, Orange and Pinellas.

At the other extreme, counties with the lowest mean house prices are generally those that are rural, slow growing and located in the interior of the state. The lowest mean sales price--$44,757--was in Gilchrist County. With a $46,250 median, Gilchrist's mean is pulled down by the sale of low-priced units with apparently few if any high-priced ones selling.

Other counties with low mean prices relative to the state as a whole include Bradford County with a mean of $52,837; Citrus at $58,871; Columbia at $59,098; and Okeechobee County at $57,535. Even Marion County, a rapid-growth county through the 1980s, has a low mean house price of $64,725. This indicates another division in the state, as southern counties tend to have higher mean sales prices than do northern counties. Charlotte County is an exception among coastal counties with its mean sales price of $63,646 in 1991. Among major metropolitan areas, mean housing prices are generally lowest in the counties of the Tampa Bay area. Among other metropolitan counties, Escambia and Polk have the lowest mean housing prices.

Housing Price Appreciation. All counties in Florida experienced increases in housing prices between 1982 and 1991. To minimize the distortion that results from changes in house size over time, the average price per square foot was calculated for the counties included above for 1982 and 1991. For Hillsborough, Lee and Martin counties, home square footage was not available so changes in the mean sale price were used to calculate percentage changes.

While using price per square foot allows adjustment for differences in the size of houses that sell each year, it does not control or adjust for other differences in the quality of the units such as age, location and lot size. Statistical methods to adjust for these differences are available but are not possible with the data on hand.

Using the property appraiser data, the average sale price per square foot for each county and year was calculated using data on all homestead property transactions. There are several significant points to be made from this analysis. First is the wide range of average prices per square foot across counties, from a low in 1991 of about $28 in Marion and Polk counties to a high of almost $115 in Monroe County and over $70 in several other counties.

The average change in price per square foot was reduced by the amount of general inflation each year over the study period to calculate the "real" rate of appreciation in property values. These results are shown in Table 2. Surprisingly, the mean real rate of appreciation per year in value over the period was negative for most counties in Florida; i.e., property values did not increase as much as inflation during the period. However it should be noted that 1991 was a recession year, which may make these negative appreciation rates very short-lived phenomena. Exceptions included Collier, Lee, Martin, Monroe and Orange counties. Inflation averaged about 3.6 percent during the period, so that adding that number to the reported mean "real" appreciation will yield a measure of the actual or nominal appreciation in house prices.

The series on average sales price per square foot presents interesting information on the range of housing values across Florida counties and the differences in movement of those prices over time. Not surprisingly, growing counties and those (such as Monroe) in which development is constrained have experienced the greatest appreciation. Large urban counties, in general, have the highest average prices.

Condominiums. The role of condominiums in providing housing is another indicator of the differences in housing stock across counties (see Table 3). As expected, condominiums are an important source of housing in coastal counties where a number of retirees live but not in interior counties. There were 1,096,697 condominium housing units in the state in 1991 as compared to 3,067,031 single-family units, according to the Florida Department of Revenue's *Ad Valorem Tax Report*. Of these condominium units, about 628,000, or 57 percent, were located in three southeast Florida counties: Dade (218,855), Broward (193,574) and Palm Beach (216,376). Over 45

Table 3. Number of Parcels
by Category 1992

Counties	Single-Family Residential	Mobile Homes	Condo-miniums	Vacant Residential
Alachua	39,385	4,142	3,158	12,690
Baker	2,536	1,187	0	1,640
Bay	37,424	4,342	8,938	20,078
Bradford	4,549	1,245	18	2,681
Brevard	116,071	10,699	22,803	94,313
Broward	248,360	4,385	193,574	32,582
Calhoun	2,295	492	0	1,763
Charlotte	43,404	5,410	9,506	133,449
Citrus	31,616	13,071	1,447	79,639
Clay	26,623	5,767	1,098	18,248
Collier	35,726	2,830	49,988	51,798
Columbia	8,521	2,570	44	6,202
Dade	305,937	387	218,855	34,613
De Soto	4,570	2,423	272	4,275
Dixie	2,325	2,793	0	5,705
Duval	178,995	8,177	7,214	26,827
Escambia	72,968	4,403	3,650	19,279
Flagler	11,706	1,058	1,454	47,256
Franklin	4,091	712	0	5,092
Gadsden	8,572	1,610	0	5,800
Gilchrist	1,366	1,315	0	4,592
Glades	1,378	2,264	32	4,036
Gulf	4,292	1,203	36	4,000
Hamilton	1,800	539	0	5,343
Hardee	3,838	1,463	259	1,304
Hendry	4,334	3,029	139	20,834
Hernando	34,611	8,471	630	42,430
Highlands	22,529	4,957	1,426	69,243
Hillsborough	206,721	11,671	19,753	32,890
Holmes	2,947	726	0	2,032
Indian River	26,767	1,042	10,618	22,536
Jackson	8,768	1,353	0	11,909
Jefferson	1,678	505	0	913
Lafayette	725	384	0	1,551
Lake	36,524	16,550	2,407	18,517
Lee	89,736	11,573	46,646	237,809
Leon	48,062	4,855	951	17,274
Levy	5,417	4,700	125	25,544
Liberty	1,203	366	0	906
Madison	2,815	751	0	2,843

Continued . . .

Table 3. Number of Parcels
by Category 1992 (continued)

Counties	Single-Family Residential	Mobile Homes	Condo-miniums	Vacant Residential
Manatee	43,979	8,462	21,845	11,791
Marion	49,092	17,262	5,146	125,606
Martin	25,199	2,839	13,373	11,284
Monroe	20,116	6,021	6,459	28,550
Nassau	9,440	3,652	2,211	8,889
Okaloosa	39,590	1,753	4,031	14,712
Okeechobee	4,965	4,494	158	14,955
Orange	169,085	3,732	22,918	35,032
Osceola	27,887	3,678	4,931	32,760
Palm Beach	169,201	3,890	216,376	44,939
Pasco	85,186	27,936	11,104	21,372
Pinellas	222,542	3,185	86,241	22,698
Polk	96,386	23,412	6,482	58,561
Putnam	14,568	11,885	143	58,067
St. Johns	23,382	3,938	6,777	17,738
St. Lucie	46,833	3,343	11,028	61,104
Santa Rosa	23,576	4,589	863	28,240
Sarasota	82,546	7,372	39,933	81,308
Seminole	83,754	2,043	7,716	15,172
Sumter	6,239	4,496	106	4,242
Suwannee	4,390	2,670	0	11,241
Taylor	4,677	1,811	0	4,217
Union	863	585	0	562
Volusia	106,636	6,703	19,464	71,552
Wakulla	3,317	2,318	64	9,568
Walton	8,754	2,167	4,287	16,917
Washington	3,643	760	0	14,857
Totals	3,067,031	320,416	1,096,697	1,956,370

Source: Florida Department of Revenue, *Florida Ad Valorem Valuations and Tax Data*, 1994.

percent of all the housing units in Palm Beach County in 1991 were condominiums.

While other coastal counties do not have numbers of the magnitude of those in the three southeast counties, condominiums do play a major housing role. In Collier County, its 49,988 condominium units comprise over 50 percent of the total housing stock. Counties in which condominiums total over 20 percent of the housing stock include Bay, Indian River, Lee, Martin, Sarasota and Walton. An additional eight counties have more than 10 percent of their housing stock in condominiums.

Condominiums generally do not represent an affordable alternative to single-family units in Florida, unlike other portions of the country where condominiums are often viewed as a "steppingstone" to single-family homeownership. The mean price of condominium units sold in 1991 was $137,646 in Monroe County, $120,735 in Collier County, $103,535 in Sarasota County, $102,521 in Palm Beach County and more than $75,000 in all counties except Broward and Pinellas among those in which condominiums are more than 10 percent of the housing stock. The relatively high price of the condominium stock in Florida appears to reflect the steep premium paid for the ocean accessibility that comes with many of them.

At the other extreme and indicating the role that condominiums play as an urban and coastal housing alternative, there are no condominium units in sixteen Florida counties including a number of northern and rural counties. Five other counties have fewer than 100 condominium units. The counties without condominiums seem to parallel those in which manufactured housing is important. However, the numbers of mobile homes shown on Table 3 undercount the actual number because only those recorded as real property, located on a lot owned by the homeowner, are included in the property appraiser file.

New Construction by County. The *Florida Ad Valorem Valuations and Tax Data* report includes data on new construction as a percent of total taxable value. These data were compiled for each county for the ten-year period of study. New construction as a percentage of total taxable value ranges from a low of under one percent in Hamilton, Lafayette and Washington counties to a high of 7 percent in Osceola County.

Additional data on new construction of single-family homes is provided as a result of the Florida Energy Efficiency Code for Building Construction (FEECBC), which requires builders to submit forms to local governments detailing the energy-conserving characteristics of residential buildings constructed in the state. Between 1987 and

1993, approximately 500,000 buildings were documented. A one percent sample of these forms was drawn to analyze the features of newly constructed single-family units across the state.

The average single-family unit contained 2,037 square feet of conditioned space. Masonry and frame were the most common materials, with 39.6 percent and 34.9 percent of the total, respectively. Only 12.9 percent of the units had no heating, ventilating and air conditioning ducts installed, and 98.9 percent of the units contained central cooling equipment. The heat pump was the dominant heating form, with 57.4 percent of the total. Electric strip heating was the second most common with 37.1 percent of the total. Almost all (93.4 percent) water heating systems used electricity.

Housing Policy Issues: Unit Needs

The following two sections examine the issues of housing needs in the state from two perspectives. First, the need for additional housing units in Florida will be examined. The final section will then explore housing affordability in the state.

The need for housing units is driven by three factors: growth in the number of households, maintaining an equilibrium vacancy rate that allows mobility for the population, and replacement of housing units removed from the housing inventory. There is an interrelatedness to these variables as the number of households that form is in part determined by the number (and cost) of housing units available for occupancy. In addition, the demand for housing units is a determinant of the conversion of existing buildings to housing use or the loss of housing from the inventory.

The Florida Department of Community Affairs has developed a projection methodology to estimate the basic housing unit construction needs in the state through the year 2000. This methodology is described and the projections by county are included in the *Draft State of Florida Consolidated Plan, March 1995*. The county-by-county numbers are included as Table 4. It is estimated that there will be a total of 6,727,541 households in the state in the year 2000. Including a removal rate for existing units, the total number of new units needed between 1990 and 2000 is estimated to be 2,146,758.

Table 4. Vacant Residential Lots 1993 and Basic Construction Needs 1990-2000

Counties	Vacant Residential Lots	Housing-unit Construction Needs
Alachua	12,690	33,773
Baker	1,640	1,144
Bay	20,078	28,756
Bradford	2,681	2,369
Brevard	94,313	55,592
Broward	32,582	155,878
Calhoun	1,763	2,021
Charlotte	133,449	36,237
Citrus	79,639	35,500
Clay	18,248	19,274
Collier	51,798	39,436
Columbia	6,202	6,615
Dade	34,613	117,277
De Soto	4,275	2,554
Dixie	5,705	2,224
Duval	26,827	47,705
Escambia	19,279	23,072
Flagler	47,256	11,069
Franklin	5,092	1,506
Gadsden	5,800	1,844
Gilchrist	4,592	655
Glades	4,036	573
Gulf	4,000	1,779
Hamilton	5,343	1,611
Hardee	1,304	1,414
Hendry	20,834	4,272
Hernando	42,430	41,467
Highlands	69,243	22,684
Hillsborough	32,890	114,262
Holmes	2,032	1,137
Indian River	22,536	33,725
Jackson	11,909	1,710
Jefferson	913	822
Lafayette	1,551	628
Lake	18,517	25,632
Lee	237,809	88,361
Leon	17,274	822
Levy	25,544	5,501
Liberty	906	595
Madison	2,843	886
Manatee	11,791	47,332

Continued . . .

Table 4. Vacant Residential Lots 1993 and Basic Construction Needs 1990-2000 (continued)

Counties	Vacant Residential Lots	Housing-unit Construction Needs
Marion	125,606	39,346
Martin	11,284	34,662
Monroe	28,550	15,944
Nassau	8,889	5,261
Okaloosa	14,712	18,042
Okeechobee	14,955	4,131
Orange	35,032	152,730
Osceola	32,760	28,551
Palm Beach	44,939	207,874
Pasco	21,372	128,582
Pinellas	22,698	122,783
Polk	58,561	50,695
Putnam	58,067	9,746
St. Johns	17,738	14,520
St. Lucie	61,104	23,043
Santa Rosa	28,240	11,238
Sarasota	81,308	59,406
Seminole	15,172	70,571
Sumter	4,242	5,536
Suwannee	11,241	2,920
Taylor	4,217	1,115
Union	562	1,174
Volusia	71,552	58,087
Wakulla	9,568	1,543
Walton	16,917	13,915
Washington	14,857	2,954
Totals	1,956,370	2,104,083

Source: Florida Department of Community Affairs, *Draft State of Florida Consolidated Plan, March 1995* and Florida Department of Revenue, *Florida Ad Valorem Valuations and Taxation Data*, 1994.

The county-by-county numbers indicate the greatest need for new housing between 1990 and 2000 will be in Broward, Dade, Hillsborough, Lee, Orange, Palm Beach, Pasco and Pinellas counties. In fact, over 50 percent of the housing construction needs are in these eight counties.

The next question is whether there is space suitable and available to provide these units. Growth management regulations including concurrency restrictions, environmental concerns and other regulations potentially restrict the supply of buildable land. One indication of the supply is the number of vacant residential parcels recorded by the county property appraisers and displayed in Table 4. Several counties have large backlogs of platted lots that are presumably available for development. The total number of vacant residential parcels in Florida--1,956,370--is close to the required number of new residential units needed as projected by the Department of Community Affairs. The number of available sites exceeds the number of units needed if it is assumed that more than one unit is built on some of the parcels. However, with the exception of Lee County, which has 237,809 vacant residential parcels, these backlogs of vacant parcels do not match the locations where new units are needed.

Other than in Lee County, the largest numbers of vacant land parcels are found in Brevard, Charlotte, Citrus, Collier, Highlands, Marion, Polk, Putnam, St. Lucie, Sarasota and Volusia counties. These counties all have more than 50,000 vacant parcels, and including Lee County have over 57 percent of all vacant residential parcels in the state. Most are rapid-growth counties, with a mix of coastal and interior locations. Counties with large projected needs for housing units presently have vacant residential parcels considerably below the numbers needed to meet the projected demand.

A final factor affecting future housing construction in the state is the rate of replacement needed for existing units. With the recent rapid growth of Florida, a number of housing units have been built over the past thirty years. As units reach thirty or so years old, they typically begin to require significant maintenance expenditures to maintain their quality. State and local jurisdictions may need to track the quality of the housing stock and consider means to encourage upkeep and maintenance of existing units. Existing units are the major source of housing inventory in any given year.

Housing Policy Issues: Housing Affordability

The Florida Department of Community Affairs has prepared a draft of the "1995 State of Florida Consolidated Plan," which will be submitted to the U. S. Department of Housing and Urban Development. One of the tables in the plan quantifies the housing needs of low- and moderate-income households in the state. The needs are based on tabulations from the *American Housing Survey*, a sample survey conducted every other year by the U.S. Census Bureau.

Housing needs of three types are documented in the consolidated plan table: cost burden, substandard and overcrowding. Cost burden is calculated according to two standards--the household is paying more than 30 percent or more than 50 percent of income for housing costs. Cost burden is the predominant housing need in the state. According to the tabulations of the Florida Department of Community Affairs, there are 1,123,911 low- and moderate-income households in the state, about 22 percent of Florida's households, that are paying more than 30 percent of their income in housing expenses. Of those households, 551,737 (about 11 percent) are spending more than 50 percent of their income on housing costs. Households spending more than 30 percent of income on housing costs include 614,947 renter and 508,964 owner households. In contrast to cost burden, overcrowding is experienced by 166,235 households and 225,976 households are in substandard housing. Substandard housing is defined as housing units built before 1940, so the measure may not be an accurate reflection of substandard housing. Some households experience more than one form of housing need, so that many of the households with overcrowded and/or substandard housing units also are experiencing cost burdens.

It seems clear from these numbers that housing affordability is a major problem confronting Florida. While overcrowding and housing condition are problems, considerably more households are confronted with cost burden problems.

Housing Affordability Indices. As an alternative method of examining housing affordability, and as a means of making comparisons across counties, housing affordability indices were calculated for each of the counties included in Table 2. The construction of the affordability index follows the National Association of Realtors methodology, which examines the ability of a household with median income to afford a median-priced home. The calculations assume a mortgage loan of 80 percent of the house price at the current mortgage rate and a qualification standard that the mortgage payments can be no more than 25 percent of household income. The household median income for a county is divided by the income needed to qualify for a loan on the median-priced home and that number is multiplied by 100 to determine the index. Median income by county is from the numbers prepared by the U.S. Department of Housing and Urban Development for administering housing programs including the federal Low Income Housing Tax Credits program. An index number equal to 100 indicates that the median-income household can just afford the median-priced home. Index numbers less than 100 indicate the degree to which the median-income household is unable to afford the median-priced home. Index numbers greater than 100 indicate a relatively affordable housing market.

Table 5 displays the calculated affordability indices for 1991, the year for which median house prices are available. The mortgage rate is assumed to be 9.3 percent, determined by the Federal Housing Finance Board to be the average effective rate for 1991. The affordability index does not consider whether a household has sources of funds to make the required downpayment and, by examining only the medians, does not look at differences in the distributions between house prices and incomes that may result in households below the median not being able to afford a house. The method also does not consider rental housing. With these limitations in mind, it may be best to examine the affordability indices more as an indication of relative affordability across counties rather than as a definitive indication of housing affordability. Note also that the index is a function of the assumptions concerning the loan-to-value ratio and interest rate and other terms of the mortgage loan.

Using the indices as an indicator of relative housing affordability across Florida counties, the result is similar to previous conclusions about the differences between metropolitan and nonmetropolitan, and between coastal and noncoastal counties. The only county with a 1991 affordability index below 100, indicating that the median-income household could not afford the median-priced house, was Monroe County. Land availability problems and development constraints contribute to giving that county the highest median prices in the state but incomes are not similarly high, perhaps due to the service nature of employment in the Keys.

Table 5. Affordability Index by Selected County 1991

Counties	Median Price ($)	Median Income ($)	Affordability Index
Alachua	70,000	35,100	157.326
Bay	64,000	28,900	141.680
Bradford	46,450	35,100	237.089
Brevard	75,000	39,300	164.408
Broward	90,900	42,200	145.660
Charlotte	58,700	31,200	166.766
Citrus	55,000	25,800	147.180
Clay	79,500	36,300	143.262
Collier	113,500	41,900	115.827
Columbia	55,700	30,800	173.495
Dade	90,450	38,000	131.815
De Soto	50,000	26,400	165.663
Duval	76,300	36,300	149.270
Escambia	58,700	31,000	165.697
Gilchrist	46,250	23,900	162.135
Hernando	67,050	33,800	158.164
Hillsborough	78,000	33,800	135.961
Lake	74,400	29,100	122.719
Lee	78,450	35,600	142.380
Leon	74,800	34,200	143.455
Manatee	85,000	33,100	122.180
Marion	59,444	26,400	139.343
Martin	110,500	35,600	101.083
Monroe	128,000	36,300	88.979
Nassau	79,500	36,300	143.262
Okeechobee	49,950	28,100	176.507
Orange	87,800	38,900	139.010
Osceola	79,900	38,900	152.754
Palm Beach	109,400	43,800	125.617
Pinellas	77,500	33,800	136.838
Polk	63,900	30,200	148.285
St. Johns	100,000	36,300	113.893
St. Lucie	66,000	35,600	169.238
Sarasota	86,000	36,800	134.258
Seminole	92,400	38,900	132.090

Source: Author calculations based on median prices from Table 2 and U.S. Department of Housing and Urban Development estimates of median income.

Martin County's affordability index of 101 is the only other that is below 110. Martin County is a coastal area with a high median house price. Other counties with indexes below 125 include Collier,

Lake, Manatee and St. Johns, all coastal counties except Lake, which is in the metropolitan area surrounding Orlando. Palm Beach County, an urban, coastal county, has an index of 125.7. Even these counties appear relatively affordable in a national context, as the national affordability index reported by the National Association of Realtors for 1991 was 112.9 (as reported in "U.S. Housing Market Conditions," U.S. Department of Housing and Urban Development, Policy Development and Research, November 1994).

The highest index number is 237 in Bradford County. This county north of Gainesville is the only county with an index over 200; it has the lowest median price of the counties included in the analysis. Other counties with index numbers above 170 include Columbia and Okeechobee. Nonmetropolitan counties not included in the analysis would likely be found in this group.

The remaining counties had affordability indices of between 125 and 170 in 1991. Included are a mix of coastal and interior, metropolitan and nonmetropolitan counties. This pattern indicates that counties with high median house prices also have high median incomes and vice versa. It might therefore be argued that a household with an income below the mean may be better off living in a low housing-price county where housing will be more affordable.

Looking Ahead

Florida has grown rapidly during the past two decades, and to accommodate that growth the housing stock has expanded dramatically. As a result, the housing stock in the state is fairly young. The extent of housing construction has also meant that the construction industry has been a major employer in the state. The expansion of the housing stock has been accompanied by changes in its character as it has become less dominated by single-family homes and mobile or manufactured housing has increased in importance.

This chapter has also shown the diversity of the housing stock in Florida. Using data from the census and the county property appraisers, as well as other appropriate sources, it has shown that differences exist between coastal and interior counties and between metropolitan and nonmetropolitan counties. For example, condominiums are most likely to be found in coastal counties, while mobile homes are more frequently found in interior and nonmetropolitan counties. Mean and median housing prices for single-family homes are higher in coastal and metropolitan counties. The affordability index calculated has its lowest values in coastal counties, indicating that these are the least affordable locations in the state.

As Florida looks to the future, with population growth expected to continue, the state will need to continue to provide new housing units to accommodate the needs. Certain counties are likely to continue to be locations that are experiencing the most rapid growth; these are likely to be coastal and metropolitan areas. The availability and cost of sites for development may be an emerging future issue as growth management and other regulations continue to impact on site availability and the cost of development. As the housing stock built to house the surge of population ages, occupants of the housing units will need to maintain them to assure that they do not fall into substandard condition.

Appendix
County Property Appraiser Data

Data Sources

The Florida Department of Revenue publishes *Florida Ad Valorem Valuations and Tax Data* each year. This publication contains information by county on the number of parcels, total assessed value of property, number of homesteaded properties and their total value and number of parcels receiving exemptions other than homestead. Additional data from this source included new construction as a percentage of the total value of property in a county each year and the percentage of property sold each year. The publication also includes data on the millage rates in each county.

Historical data on the Consumer Price Index were obtained from published sources and projections of inflation were obtained from those prepared by the Florida Consensus Estimating Conference. Demographic data on population, population growth rate and age structure of the population, useful in understanding the differences between counties, were taken from the *Florida Statistical Abstract*.

Finally, data on all sales transactions of homesteaded properties from 1982 to 1991 were created from property appraiser tapes. Summary data on each transaction were produced by ARMASI, Inc., and included the sale price, assessed value, square footage of the unit, year of sale and year built.

Price Series by County

The first step in the analysis was to prepare a series of average price change in each county for each year between 1982 and 1991. This series uses both the most recent and second most recent sales price and date as recorded on the tape. The quality of the data appears to be lower in a significant number of counties earlier than 1982 due to missing observations and other problems.

To calculate the mean and median price, it was necessary to eliminate observations that were not usable. The first group of these was those for which no price was recorded for the transaction. Remaining observations were then run through a series of "screens" to eliminate problem observations. The first screen was to eliminate sales in which the price is too low and represents either a recording error or a non-arms-length transaction (all sales of less than $10,000 eliminated). A similar screen was necessary to eliminate observations in which the square footage of the house is unreasonable, so that observations with square footage below 600 square feet were eliminated.

Particularly in growing counties, sales are recorded in which the price is lower than the assessed value of the property. These observations generally indicate that the sales price was a land sale and a house was subsequently built on the lot. To screen out these, observations were eliminated if the year of sale is earlier than the year built. If the year of sale is equal to the year built, then the 1991 assessed value is compared to the sale price inflated at a rate of 5 percent per year for each year that the sale pre-dates 1991. If the assessed value is greater than or equal to the sales price, then the observation is eliminated.

After these screens were applied, the remaining data in each county were used to calculate the mean and standard deviation of the price per square foot for each year. One final screen was then applied to eliminate outliers--prices that are unreasonably high or low and not representative of the distribution of prices in the county. The final screen eliminated all observations more than three standard deviations removed from the mean. The mean and standard deviation was then recalculated, resulting in a data series of the mean price change per year per county. This work was all completed in the statistical data base SAS.

Electric Utilities

7

Thomas W. Moore
Manager, Economic
Planning and Forecasting
and
William R. Ashburn
Administrator, Pricing
Tampa Electric Company
Tampa, Florida

There are fifty-eight electric utilities in the state of Florida, falling under the categories of: 1) investor-owned, 2) municipal and 3) rural electric co-operatives. Of this total, twenty-five generate electricity.

Despite the large total, a handful of utilities provides the bulk of electric power in the state. Specifically, Florida Power and Light, Florida Power, Tampa Electric, Jacksonville Electric Authority and Gulf Power account for 84 percent of Florida's electrical sales. With the exception of Jacksonville Electric Authority, all are investor-owned utilities.

The Florida Public Service Commission (FPSC) is responsible for regulating the rates of the investor-owned electric utilities in the retail sector. This encompasses the price of electricity charged to households and businesses that the utility serves directly. In addition, the commission also makes rules controlling utility operations, including the certification of all new power plants in the state. The FPSC consists of five members appointed by the governor from a list of nominees selected by the Public Service Commission Nominating Council. These appointments then are confirmed by the Florida Senate.

In the wholesale market, which represents the sale of electricity between utilities, the Federal Energy Regulatory Commission (FERC) is responsible for regulating the rates of the state's investor-owned

Table 1. Fuel Type of Electricity Generation in Florida
(percent)

Fuel Type	1980	1993
Fuel Oil	46.2	30.0
Coal	20.6	40.8
Nuclear	17.5	17.0
Natural Gas	15.5	12.1
Hydro	0.2	0.1

Source: Florida Public Service Commission, *Statistics of the Florida Electric Utility Industry*, various years.

electric utilities. For the municipal utilities, the retail rate levels and the wholesale rates are regulated locally either through the city council or a separately constituted municipal board or authority. Finally, rates charged by rural electric cooperatives, which are joint ventures of the users, are set through an overseeing board that is normally subject to a vote of the members.

The state has more than 38,000 MW of generating capacity. About 41 percent of the total electricity produced in Florida during 1993 was generated using coal while 30 percent was provided by oil. Of the remainder, nuclear power supplied 17 percent and gas represented 12 percent. This marked a dramatic change from 1980 (Table 1), when Florida was heavily dependent on oil as a production fuel. The reduced dependence on oil-fired generation is the result of federal and state emphasis on conservation of this resource.

Looking ahead, the percentage of oil-fired generation in Florida should remain on a downward course during the coming years. While coal will continue to increase its share, natural gas will be the primary replacement for oil as utilities are planning to build gas-fired facilities over the next decade because of their environmental advantages and low capital costs.

Florida's pattern of electricity consumption reflects the service-based nature of its economy. In 1993, 82 percent of the state's electricity was used by the residential and commercial sectors. Industrial activity, on the other hand, consumed only 14 percent. This is considerably different from the rest of the country, where residential/commercial usage makes up only 62 percent of the total while the manufacturing sector represents a 34 percent share.

Electricity Trends in Florida

Almost everyone is familiar with Florida's dramatic economic growth. Since 1980, population additions have exceeded four million as Florida has climbed from seventh to fourth place in the state rankings. Employment gains also have been impressive, as two million new jobs have been created, producing a tripling in state income and a solid increase in the individual family's standard of living.

Economic expansion has been the driving force behind the state's 54 percent increase in electricity sales during the past decade, which represents a 4.4 percent average annual growth rate. The sharp rise in residential and commercial construction, resulting from household and employment growth, has been the largest single factor influencing the increasing demand for electricity. However, gains in family income during this period have also impacted sales by spurring increased appliance purchases.

Another element affecting electrical consumption has been the stability in utility bills. Over the past ten years the price of electricity in Florida has risen at a modest annual rate of 0.3 percent. This is due to the relative calm in world oil markets plus a reduction in new power plant construction resulting from conservation efforts. When compared to the increased costs of other products, the "real" or inflation-adjusted cost of electricity has actually declined by nearly 30 percent over this period. This reduction in the relative price of electric power has provided a considerable boost to customer usage.

The fastest-growing component of electricity sales over the past decade has been the commercial sector, which includes firms involved in service-related activities. Between 1984 and 1993, this group's consumption has advanced at a 5.2 percent annual rate. This trend, however, is not unexpected given recent economic patterns. More specifically, the majority of new jobs generated both at the state and national level have come from the service sector, reflecting the basic change in our economy from manufacturing to nonmanufacturing.

The second-fastest-growing class has been residential sales, which have increased at a 4.9 percent annual pace. About two-thirds of the consumption increases in this area have resulted from the state's rapid population growth over this period while the other third has been due to the advance in income and the decline in the "real" price of electricity.

Finally, industrial electricity sales have experienced only limited growth in the past decade, increasing at only a little over 1 percent per year. As previously noted, this modest advance can be explained partially by the economy's shift away from manufacturing. Moreover, the majority of growth occurring in the manufacturing sector is in "lighter," less energy-intensive processes.

Another development that has limited industrial electricity usage has been the move toward nonutility generation or cogeneration. In the industrial sector, this primarily involves the production of electricity using waste heat from the manufacturing process. This waste heat or steam had, in the past, been removed through a venting device such as a smokestack. The Public Utilities Regulatory Policies Act of 1978 (PURPA), however, provided certain regulatory and financial incentives to industrial customers. This legislation, along with improved technology, has made it cost-effective for some companies to use their residual steam to power turbines, producing electricity for their needs. This has reduced manufacturers' demand for power from electric utilities and dampened industrial electricity sales.

Slowing the Need for New Power Plants

Additional power plants have been required to accommodate the state's growing electrical needs. Between 1980 and 1993, Florida has added around 9,600 MW of new generation, which represents a 2.3 percent average annual increase in capacity.

This, however, is a considerable deceleration from the rapid growth in capacity that occurred during the 1970s. Specifically, the state's generating capacity more than doubled from 13,500 MW in 1970 to 28,500 MW in 1980 for a 7.8 percent average annual rate of growth. This development, along with the expectation of continued expansion, concerned both the Florida Legislature and the FPSC as the state entered the 1980s. Added to this was the state's heavy reliance on oil and the uncertainty in those markets resulting from the OPEC oil embargo.

These considerations led to the passage in 1980 of the Florida Energy Efficiency Conservation Act (FEECA). The primary purpose of this legislation was to reduce both the state's dependence on oil and the need for expensive new power plants.

To realize these objectives, the FPSC adopted goals for electric utilities between 1980 and 1989 limiting both energy sales and peak demand growth. This prompted utilities to develop comprehensive conservation programs aimed at minimizing electricity needs related to the state's future growth. These programs encompassed the two general categories of conservation and load management.

Conservation programs are designed to reduce both energy consumption and the state's peak demand for electricity. These programs provide consumers with information and/or incentives to install more energy-efficient appliances or to weatherize their homes.

Load management involves controlling appliances to reduce winter and summer peak electrical requirements. This consists of allowing the utility to install control devices on heating and cooling appliances as well as water heaters and pool pumps that turn off power to the appliances in order to smooth out peak usage periods.

The programs have produced dramatic results. Since 1981, conservation and load management have saved nearly 1,800 GWH of energy sales. The impact on the state's peak demand has been even more dramatic as it has been reduced by 2,200 MW or 23 percent of the state's load growth during this period. When industrial cogeneration is considered, these reductions are even greater. As a result of these actions, annual power plant additions (which include purchases from outside the state) between 1980 and 1994 have been only a third of the pace of construction in the 1970s.

Table 2 highlights the conservation impact. Between 1970 and 1980, electricity sales and power plant additions grew at a pace well above that of both population and employment. Since that time, however, these relationships have changed considerably with the ratios between generating capacity and the economic measures declining significantly.

Table 2. Conservation Impact

	1970-1980	1980-1993
Average Annual Growth Rate		
Population	3.7	2.6
Employment	5.2	3.5
Electricity Sales	6.1	4.0
Generating Capacity	7.8	*2.3
Ratios**		
Electricity Sales/Population	1.6	1.5
Electricity Sales/Employment	1.2	1.1
Generating Capacity/Population	2.1	0.9
Generating Capacity/Employment	1.5	0.7

*Includes purchases from outside the state.

**The ratios are a way of comparing growth rates. The 1.6 electricity sales/ population ratio for 1970-1980 is calculated by dividing sales growth of 6.1 percent by population growth of 3.7 percent.

In 1994, the FPSC set new conservation goals for the larger utilities that are based on individual program savings rather than the more general peak-demand and energy-sales objectives of the 1980s. These program-related targets will be set specifically for each utility over the coming year and will serve the industry during the next decade.

Florida's Electricity Growth in the Coming Decade

For the 1994-2003 period, utilities are projecting Florida electricity sales to increase at a 2.5 percent annual rate (Table 3), which represents some moderation from the 4.4 percent pace of the past decade. There are several factors behind this slower expected pace.

First, it is anticipated that national economic growth will be more subdued after the rapid advances of the 1980s that were fueled by dramatic tax cuts and an escalation in government spending. This deceleration in national growth will serve to moderate state employ-

Table 3. Florida Electrical Sales Growth
(average annual percent change)

	1984-1993	Forecast 1994-2003
Residential	4.9	2.5
Commercial	5.2	2.8
Industrial	1.3	1.9
Other	4.7	2.0
Total	4.4	2.5

Source: Florida Electric Power Coordinating Group, *Forecast Document--* FPSC Docket No. 890004-EU.

ment additions in the next decade, which will also ease population inflows.

Also important is that a major contributor to Florida population growth in the 1980s was the Baby Boom generation, the large group of people born between 1946 and 1964. During the 1980s, this group was in the highly mobile 20-40-year age category. This group is now older and less inclined to move around. Moreover, the size of the group replacing them is smaller. These patterns of migration are extremely important since 85 percent of Florida's population growth over the past twenty years has occurred from people moving into the state.

Despite the expected moderation in Florida's electricity growth, it is important to note that the 2.5 percent forecast for the state still represents a healthy rate of increase and is above the projected national pace. Looking at individual categories, some of the trends of the past are expected to continue over the next decade. For example, commercial energy sales should remain the major area of growth, followed by residential consumption.

While the industrial sector's expansion is still expected to lag behind that of the other categories, the forecast of 1.9 percent growth per year is above the rate experienced in the 1984-to-1993 period. This stems from the fact that much of the downsizing of heavy manufacturing, which partially offset the light industrial gains in the 1980s, is now over. Thus, the expansion of high-tech industrial activity anticipated in the coming years will not be curtailed by declines in the energy-intensive sector.

Also responsible for the faster industrial growth are cogeneration additions, which are projected to moderate in the manufacturing sector during 1994-2003. This is because many of the largest industrial companies already have shifted to this source of power.

The state's expanding demand for electricity in the 1994-2003 period requires a coordinated plan to accommodate this growth. As in the 1980s, the industry intends to utilize a combination of conservation, additional utility plants and nonutility generation to meet these requirements.

Both conservation and load management will continue to play an important role in limiting the need for future plant additions. Between 1994 and 2003, reductions in the state's peak demand from these programs will more than double from 2,200 MW to 4,870 MW. These savings are expected to represent 12 percent of the state's projected peak demand in 2003. Looked at another way, this projected future impact is equal to twelve 400-MW power plants.

The relative contributions from these two groups also will be changing over this period. Presently, 65 percent of total peak reductions are provided by load management programs but during the next ten years, new savings should be equally divided between conservation and load management. Thus, the conservation contribution to total savings will rise from its present level of 35 percent to 43 percent by 2003.

Even with these impressive reductions, however, Florida's peak demand needs will remain on an upward course. Therefore, the utilities plan to build 5,300 MW of additional generation as well as to continue purchasing electricity from outside the state over the next ten years. In addition, nonutility generation will also be rising. In fact, power from this source will expand by 1,470 MW between 1994 and 2003, representing 22 percent of the state's additional installed capacity over this period. In total, the planned capacity additions in the next ten years are less than in the past decade and substantially below the 15,000 MW constructed in the 1970s.

The challenge over the coming decade, therefore, is to develop an effective plan for meeting the strong electrical demand that will result from a growing state. From recent experience, a mix of conservation, nonutility generation and new utility facilities offers the best approach to meeting this objective.

A Look Ahead

Where PURPA provided incentives for industrial customers to serve themselves and also set up a guaranteed market for excess generation, the Energy Policy Act of 1992 (EPACT) has greatly modified the industry's legal structure by opening the door to greater wholesale competition and expanding the potential for future retail competition.

First, EPACT has created the concept of the Exempt Wholesale Generator (EWG). Whereas the cogenerator must provide both electric and thermal energy to qualify for the benefits of PURPA, under EPACT any entity can now own a generator as an EWG and provide wholesale power without its operations being regulated as an electric utility. Second, EPACT has given FERC the authority to order utilities to grant EWGs and other utilities access to their transmission network under appropriate pricing, including transmission system expansion if required.

These two changes were intended by Congress to foster a more competitive wholesale market for power generation with the expectation that competition will result in lower prices, thus improving the ability of the United States to compete in the increasingly competitive global economy. In part in reaction to these regulatory developments, a competitive market has begun to develop in Florida for the long-term supply of wholesale power.

EPACT specifically denied FERC the authority to order access to retail markets, yet the same motivations behind the opening up of the wholesale market to competition have stimulated groups to demand retail access and competition as well. Those demands are being heard in some state jurisdictions but there are legal and jurisdictional issues still to be worked out before retail electric competition can begin, including in Florida. This trend, however, is expected to increase in activity through the end of the decade and Florida will likely be affected.

One of the key issues in this deregulation trend, and in both whole-sale and retail competition, is that of wheeling and access to the trans-mission/distribution systems of the utilities. Wheeling describes a service provided by the utility where it receives delivery of power owned by another party at one point on its grid and delivers it for a price to another point on its grid. Wheeling has in the past been a voluntary act on the part of the utilities, and granting the authority to FERC to order a utility to provide this service was part of EPACT. How this service is priced, what additional services are offered to make the wheeling transaction acceptable from a reliability and con-trol perspective, what terms and conditions are placed on such trans-actions, and how comparable all the above will be to the way the transmitting utility serves its own power sales over its network are all important issues that are currently being litigated. This will bear on the speed and eventual ability of competitors to access and com-pete for wholesale and retail power sales.

Structural changes to the utility industry are also possible as com-petitive pressure is applied. One such change is called unbundling. This would entail disintegrating the current vertically integrated struc-ture of most large power companies into separate generation (i.e., power plants), transmission (i.e., high voltage power lines that are networked together and tie the power plants to distant load centers) and distribution (i.e., lower voltage lines that unidirectionally dis-tribute the power to the ultimate users) entities. Under this structure, generation would be essentially deregulated, transmission would be regulated by FERC and distribution would be regulated by the FPSC. This trend, and its impacts, is currently under discussion nationally and in Florida within the industry.

Natural Resources and the Environment

8

J. Walter Milon
Professor of Natural Resource
and Environmental Economics
Food and Resource
Economics Department
University of Florida
Gainesville, Florida

Everyone recognizes the importance of Florida's clean air and water, beaches and wildlife to the state's economy and the quality of life for residents and visitors. Despite the obvious importance, there is no simple way to measure the economic significance of these natural resources and the environment because there is no comprehensive data-gathering system and many services provided by the environment are not priced through everyday markets.

Indirect measures of economic significance such as expenditures for air- and water-quality protection and habitat preservation show that these governmental activities play an integral role in the state economy. Also, renewable resources such as fisheries are an important part of total economic activity. Available data indicate that, for some resources, the ecosystems are generally "healthy" or at a stage where careful management can prevent significant deterioration. But in many cases, there is considerable uncertainty about the direction of these systems.

Over the past few decades, Florida has made a substantial investment in environmental and natural resource protection and long-term preservation. But, the finite nature of these resources coupled with an ever-growing state population creates the need for innovative approaches to environmental and resource management to assure the sustainability of Florida's natural assets for future generations.

Environmental Quality Protection

The task of protecting the environment and managing the state's natural resources is the responsibility of the Florida Department of Environmental Protection (DEP). This "super agency" was created in 1993 from the Departments of Natural Resources and Environmental Regulation, two agencies that had been created in a 1975 reorganization. The DEP's responsibilities include, among others, regulation of air, water, toxic and noise pollution; maintaining and monitoring public drinking water standards; management of state-owned lands, parks and marine resources; land acquisition; management of solid and hazardous waste disposal; and oversight of the state's five water management control districts. This agency also coordinates the administration of federal environmental laws such as the Clean Water and Clean Air acts. The structure of the DEP reflects a need for "ecosystem management" that integrates decisionmaking for environmental protection on a broad scale so that the cumulative effects of decisions are recognized.

State expenditures for environmental protection in the past three years have been about $1.5 billion or about $115 per resident. Environmental protection expenditures have averaged about 3.5 to 4.0 percent of total state expenditures over the past five years (SAFE report 1994). These expenditures do not account for federal environmental program expenses in Florida or the expenses incurred by private businesses and government agencies to comply with environmental protection regulations.

Expenditures for environmental protection, however, provide little indication of the effectiveness of laws and regulations to protect the environment. Unfortunately, despite nearly two and one-half decades of federally coordinated environmental regulations, there still remains much uncertainty about the status of Florida's environment. A recent assessment of trends for the DEP (SAFE report 1994) indicated that the number of rivers, lakes and estuaries showing water quality improvements greatly exceeded those showing declines during the period 1984-1993. However, the change in water quality in the vast majority of these water bodies was unknown. Similar uncertainty characterizes groundwater quality. Although the Water Quality Assurance Act of 1986 established a groundwater quality-monitoring network, few trends are clearly identifiable from the monitoring data accumulated to date. Sampling results for 1989 to 1992 showed that water in nearly 17 percent of the test wells contained chemical concentrations that exceed established levels of concern but samples of water supplied by public drinking water systems (drawn mostly from groundwater) showed very few violations of maximum contaminant levels. Thus, while the average Floridian enjoys good-quality drinking water, the presence of chemicals in well test results suggests a need for concern about future groundwater quality.

Air quality is another important component of Florida's environment. In general, air quality in Florida has been, and continues to be, good due to natural prevailing winds and the relatively small industrial sector of the economy. Although total levels of carbon monoxide, nitrogen dioxide, sulfur dioxide and particulate matter have increased over the past decade due primarily to increased electric power generation and motor vehicle traffic, the number of reported violations of national and state emissions standards is very low. These indicators, however, do not capture aesthetic effects of degraded air quality such as reduced visibility and odor that occur in some areas. Moreover, long-term effects of air pollution from both within and outside of Florida may pose a more serious problem due to ecosystem effects of acid rain, nitrogen and mercury deposition, and sea-level rise from global warming.

Water Supply Management

Florida receives, on average, 50 to 55 inches of rainfall each year, one of the highest amounts in the U.S. The variability of this rainfall from year to year and from region to region can be quite large, ranging from more than 80 inches to less than 25 inches. To promote proper utilization of surface and groundwater supplies and to manage the flow of surface waters, the Florida Water Resources Act of 1972 created five water management district agencies whose governing boundaries are defined by regional hydrologic and demographic characteristics. Since 1972 these agencies have developed into powerful economic entities and their governing boards (with members appointed by the governor) influence all aspects of freshwater use in the state. Table 1 shows the 1994-95 budgets for each water management district to manage water supply and quality, ensure flood protection and maintain water-dependent natural systems. Given the diverse hydrologic and ecological characteristics of each region, the priorities and activities vary considerably from district to district.

The South Florida Water Management District, which includes the populous lower east coast and encompasses the Kissimmee River/ Lake Okeechobee/Everglades/Florida Bay drainage basin, is the largest of the districts and has more than 1,600 staff positions. By contrast, the Suwannee River District in north Florida is the smallest in area and population served and has a budget of $17.5 million with about 70 staff. Expenditures by all the districts amount to $597.4 million, or nearly 40 percent of the expenditures by the Department of Environmental Protection for all environmental protection programs in Florida.

Each district has the power to levy ad valorem taxes to support its activities, but the millage rates and share of total revenues supplied by ad valorem taxes vary by district and by the funding provided by the Legislature for special projects and priorities. Table 1 shows that the Northwest District has the lowest millage rate at 0.05 mills per $1,000 of taxable value while the Suwannee and St. Johns districts have the highest millage rates at 0.491 and 0.482, respectively. Payments for household or industrial water consumption or sewage discharges accrue to the local government entity or private company supplying the service, not the water management district.

Despite the relatively large amount of rainfall in Florida, withdrawals from freshwater supplies have increased dramatically. Between 1950 and 1990, average daily withdrawals increased from 2,926 million gallons per day (MGD) to 7,532 MGD, with about 62 percent of the 1990 total from groundwater. This increase reflects growth of the state's population and tourism, agriculture and industry. Figure 1 shows the changing pattern of use during this period. In

Table 1. Water Management District Budgets and
Millage Rates for 1994-95 by Region

	Budget (in millions of dollars)	Millage Rate (in mills per $1,000)
South Florida	290.30	0.248
Southeast Florida	140.40	0.422
St. John's River	115.10	0.482
Northwest	34.10	0.050
Suwannee River	17.50	0.491
Total	597.40	

Source: Florida Department of Environmental Protection, Office of Inspector General, *Expenditures and Revenues for the Fiscal Year Ended September 30, 1994 of the Water Management Districts.*

1950, withdrawal for thermoelectric power generation was the dominant use with agriculture and commercial-industrial users accounting for roughly equal shares of the total. By 1990, thermoelectric freshwater withdrawals decreased significantly while agricultural and public water-supply withdrawals increased by 915 and 1,033 percent, respectively. Agriculture and public water suppliers who serve residential and commercial users are now the dominant freshwater users. Although freshwater withdrawals by thermoelectric users have decreased, total water use by this group has actually increased due to withdrawals from saline surface water supplies.

Increased withdrawals from groundwater supplies and the construction of canals to facilitate access to coastal waters has caused saltwater intrusion into Florida's freshwater aquifers. As a result, reverse osmosis treatment plants to convert these saline waters to potable water are becoming more common, especially in coastal areas of the state. The majority of these plants are located in the Southwest Florida Water Management District on the southwest coast, south of Sarasota. Total water production from reverse osmosis plants in 1990-91 was about 52 MGD, or less than 3 percent of the total water withdrawals by public water suppliers.

University of Florida   *Bureau of Economic and Business Research*

Figure 1. Percentage Distribution of Freshwater Withdrawals by User Group 1950 and 1960

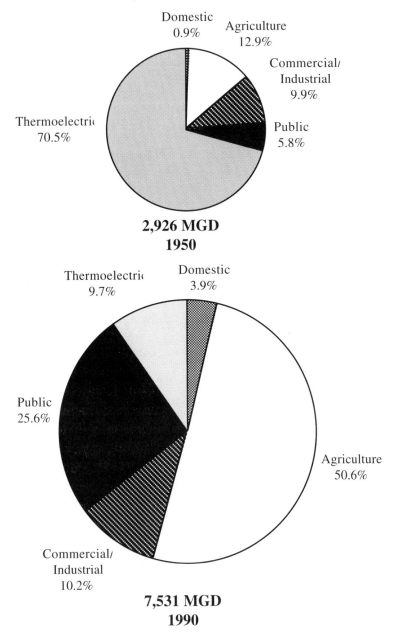

Source: U.S. Geological Survey, Water Resources Division, *Water Withdrawals, Use, and Trends in Florida.*

Several of the water management districts have recently under-taken major initiatives to promote sustainable use of surface and groundwater supplies. For example, the Southwest Florida Water Management District has adopted regulations for portions of the district to prevent future increases in permitted withdrawals from the Floridan aquifer (the deepest layer of groundwater in the region) and to encourage water-use efficiency through economic incentives. These regulations are intended to prevent economic damages caused by further deterioration of groundwater quality due to saltwater intrusion and the lowering of inland lake levels.

In addition, the South Florida Water Management District is co-ordinating a major restudy and redesign of the Central and South Florida Project (first authorized by the U.S. Congress in 1948) oper-ated by the U.S. Army Corps of Engineers to manage the flow of surface water from Lake Okeechobee and the Everglades to coastal areas. This effort is intended to restore more natural surface-water flows in the interest of environmental quality, water supply and other purposes. Also, the Everglades Forever Act of 1994 passed by the Florida Legislature provides funds to acquire and restore wetland areas and creates a trust fund from a special tax on agricultural pro-ducers in the Everglades Agricultural Area to be used for improving the quality of surface-water flows into Everglades National Park. Governor Lawton Chiles has also appointed the Commission for a Sustainable South Florida to recommend strategies for ensuring the long-term compatibility of the south Florida economy and ecosys-tem. The combined efforts of local, state and federal agencies in this south Florida effort may make this one of the largest environmental restoration projects ever attempted. Initial cost estimates for rede-signing surface-water control structures and land acquistion amount to as much as $2 billion but the full costs and benefits of these resto-ration efforts have not been estimated.

Fisheries and Wildlife

Florida's estuaries and offshore waters support one of the largest commercial and recreational marine fishing industries in the U.S. These fisheries are managed, in state waters, through the Florida

Marine Fisheries Commission and, in federal waters, by the South Atlantic and Gulf of Mexico Fishery Management Councils. Most of the state's fisheries are regulated to maintain the long-term biological productivity of the stocks. Commercial landings in 1994 were valued at more than $206.9 million in dockside value (prices paid to the fishing vessel). These landings were composed of $76.8 million in finfish (grouper, mullet, snapper, etc.), $74.3 million in invertebrates (clams, crabs, lobster, etc.) and $55.8 million in shrimp (Florida Department of Environmental Protection 1995). The total weight of landings was more than 162.4 million pounds in 1994. Landings have varied between 158 and 200 million pounds since 1986 with no clear trend for any of the three major product groups. There are more than 11,500 commercial vessels with more than 20,000 fishermen working in Florida waters. Seafood processing and wholesaling is also important, with more than 500 businesses and 5,000 employees. These businesses produce seafood products valued at more than $500 million, which is the highest of any state in the southeastern U.S. (U.S. Department of Commerce 1994).

The seafood industry will be impacted in future years by a constitutional ban on near-shore commercial net fishing that was approved by voter referenda in 1994. Harvesters and processors of mullet, pompano, spanish mackerel and other finfish will feel the greatest economic impact from the ban that took effect in 1995.

Recreational fishing is also an important economic activity although there are no reliable estimates of total recreational landings in Florida. More than 2.3 million residents participated in marine fishing in 1991-92, accounting for more than 20 million fishing trips. Estimated trip expenditures amounted to more than $1.3 billion and total investment in fishing-related equipment (rods and reels, boats, etc.) amounted to more than $29.3 billion (Milon and Thunberg 1993). In addition, more than 2.9 million visitors participated in marine fishing in Florida, generating more than $1.3 billion in fishing-related expenditures (Bell 1993). Recreational fishing license sales have averaged about 1.0 million per year since 1990-91 (the first year a saltwater license was required), resulting in revenues of more than $11.1 million for marine fishery programs. Freshwater fishing in Florida is also important, with more than 1.3 million resident and visitor anglers who engaged in more than 15 million days of freshwater fishing (U.S. Department of the Interior 1993). During the past three years, an average of 650,000 freshwater fishing licenses was sold, producing average revenues per year of more than $10 million.

Florida's environment sustains animals and birds that are the recreational focus of a large number of hunters and wildlife observers. In 1991, more than 253,000 residents and visitors hunted in Florida and the majority of the 4.5 million trips targeted game animals such as deer, turkey and rabbits. Resident hunters spent more than $323 million for trips and equipment (U.S. Department of the Interior 1993). Over the past three years, the Florida Game and Fresh Water Fish Commission sold an average of 134,000 hunting licenses that yielded an average of $1.8 million per year. The expenditures by hunters, however, are relatively small compared to the $1.2 billion spent by more than 3.8 million residents and visitors who participated in nonconsumptive wildlife observation. These activities focused on birds, reptiles and marine mammals such as alligators, manatees and sea turtles.

While fisheries and wildlife-associated recreation represent a significant contribution to Florida's economy, the habitat to sustain fish and wildlife populations has decreased dramatically over the past several decades. It is estimated that forest acreage in Florida decreased 38 percent between 1936 and 1987 and the loss of native forests to planted, monoculture tree farms has been even greater (SAFE 1994). In addition, wetlands acreage decreased by 28 percent during this period but the loss of wetlands habitat has been much greater around large estuaries such as Biscayne Bay and Tampa Bay. Regulations enacted in the past two decades have sharply reduced the conversion of wetlands to other uses, although runoff from developed areas continues to be a major problem for water quality in many bays and estuaries.

Land Acquisition

Regulations on water use and quality along with other restrictions on land use may not be sufficient to maintain natural ecosystem functions and the flora and fauna that are part of that ecosystem. In light of intense land development pressure throughout Florida, since 1963 the state has initiated new land purchasing programs to meet specific environmental management objectives. These programs, along with the year of authorization, are as follows:

Land Acquisition Trust Fund (1963)
Land Conservation Act (1972)
Conservation and Recreation Lands Act (1979)
Save Our Coast/Save Our Rivers (1981)
Preservation 2000 Act (1990)

These conservation programs resulted in the purchase of nearly two million acres of land. Combined with the 3.9 million acres held by the federal government in national forests and parks, more than 15 percent of the total land area in Florida is managed for environmental purposes. The bulk of acquisitions in the past two decades has been through state funds.

Since 1974, the state spent more than $1 billion to acquire environmental lands (Florida Department of Environmental Protection, Division of State Lands 1994). While a large share of these funds was spent in south Florida counties such as Collier, Dade and Monroe, purchases have been made in forty-six of Florida's sixty-seven counties. The largest area purchased was a 134,822-acre, $40 million addition to the Big Cypress National Preserve in Collier County. The most expensive purchase was a $66 million, 2,981-acre area in North Key Largo. Purchases in prime areas for development can be very expensive. For example, a 56.27-acre tract in Brevard County intended to protect sea turtle nesting areas as part of the Archie Carr National Wildlife Refuge cost $151,242 per acre.

In addition to state-funded acquisitions, several counties (currently sixteen) have initiated environmental land acquisition programs. Most of these programs have been approved through voter referenda, indicating the strong popular appeal of environmental protection programs in Florida. More than $615 million has been provided from these programs, with the largest programs in Hillsborough and Palm Beach counties ($100 million each) and Dade County ($90 million).

The Preservation 2000 Act proposed to raise over $3 billion for land acquisition over a ten-year period and the Legislature has approved $1.2 billion in bonds during the first four years. Even with this significant commitment, the Nature Conservancy estimates that more than $5 billion in land acquisitions could be made to protect Florida's environmentally valuable land. Regardless of the actual level of expenditures, it seems most likely that Florida citizens will continue to support local and state efforts to preserve important segments of the state's diverse ecosystems.

A Look Ahead

Based on current trends, expected growth of Florida's resident and visitor populations will continue to rank Florida as one of the most rapidly growing states in the U.S. Within the next twenty-five years, the resident population could increase from the current level of about 14 million to between 17 and 23 million. Extrapolating these trends to the year 2050 (when most of today's high school students will be starting their retirement), Florida's resident population could be as large as 43 million people. Given that Florida is already highly urbanized in many areas with an average statewide population density of more than 250 people per square mile, it is not difficult to anticipate that population growth will put an increasing burden on the natural resource and environmental assets that make Florida an attractive place to live and visit. While environmental protection has had, and continues to have, strong public support, other consequences of growth such as crime control, education and community development will provide strong competition for public funding. This competition will become more pronounced as a new constitutional amendment (passed by voter referenda in 1994) limits the growth of state spending.

The challenge for the future will be to develop laws and incentive systems that promote population and economic growth while maintaining environmental quality. Actions such as the Southwest Florida Water Management District's regulations to prevent future increases in freshwater withdrawals from the Floridan aquifer are a precursor of the type of rules that will be needed to maintain the integrity of these natural systems. These constraints will impose some economic costs but properly designed incentive systems can help to minimize the costs of compliance while attaining the benefits of resource protection. For example, the federal Clean Air Act of 1990 created an emissions permit trading program to allow electric utilities that emit sulfur dioxide to choose the most cost-effective control strategy rather than having to use prescribed control equipment. The utilities gain from lower costs to comply with air quality regulations and the public gains as total sulfur dioxide emissions are reduced by 10 million tons from 1980 levels and a permanent cap of 8.9 million tons per year applies after the year 2000. Variations on the permit trading concept could be developed in Florida for water allocation (e.g., Saarinen and Lynne 1993) and fisheries management (Milon et al. 1992).

A similar need for innovation may be necessary in land acquisition. The state's commitment to habitat preservation has been significant but funding may not keep pace with rising land costs and economic incentives for land development. As an alternative to direct state acquisition, it may be appropriate to consider more extensive private-public partnerships through nongovernmental organizations such as The Nature Conservancy and the Trust for Public Land. These groups can purchase whole parcels or specific easements and manage land for habitat preservation. For example, the Walt Disney Co. has purchased a large tract in central Florida to create the Disney Wilderness Preserve as mitigation for wetlands developed in another area. The entire preserve will be donated to the Nature Conservancy for long-term management. Other types of property-right transfers such as conservation easements or purchases of development rights may provide a less expensive alternative to protect Florida's environmental resources.

Finally, one immutable consequence of population growth is the need for additional waste handling and processing capacity. Although the Florida Legislature in 1988 established specific waste reduction and recycling objectives, there has been a steady increase in the amount of municipal solid waste generated. Here again, incentives to recycle and use alternative waste disposal methods may help to alleviate a growing problem. As in other areas, new ways of looking at old problems may help to maintain the natural resources and environment that are such an important part of the quality of life in Florida.

References

Bell, F.W. 1993. *Current and Projected Tourist Demand for Saltwater Recreational Fisheries in Florida*. Florida Sea Grant College Program Report No. 111, Gainesville.

Florida Department of Environmental Protection. 1994. *Strategic Assessment of Florida's Environment: SAFE*. Report prepared by the Florida Center for Public Management, Florida State University, Tallahassee.

_____, 1995. "Marine Fisheries Information System: 1994 Annual Landings Summary." St. Petersburg: Florida Marine Research Institute.

_____, Division of State Lands. 1994. *Conservation and Recreation Lands Annual Report*, 1994. Tallahassee.

Milon, J.W., K. Wellman and J. Gauvin. 1992. *Consideration of the Potential Use of Individual Transferable Quotas in the South Atlantic Mackerel Fishery*. Report to the National Marine Fisheries Service, National Oceanic and Atmospheric Administration, for the National ITQ Study. Washington, D.C.

Milon, J.W., and E.M. Thunberg. 1993. *A Regional Analysis of Current and Future Florida Resident Participation in Marine Recreational Fishing*. Florida Sea Grant College Program Report No. 112. Gainesville.

Saarinen, P.P., and G.D. Lynne. 1993. "Getting the Most Valuable Water Supply Pie: Economic Efficiency in Florida's Reasonable-Beneficial Use Standard." *Journal of Land Use and Environmental Law* 8(2), pp. 491-520.

U.S. Department of Commerce, National Marine Fisheries Service. 1994. *Fisheries of the United States, 1993*. Current Fishery Statistics No. 9300. Silver Spring, Maryland.

U.S. Department of the Interior, Fish and Wildlife Service. 1993. *1991 National Survey of Fishing, Hunting, and Wildlife-Associated Recreation.* Washington, D.C.: U.S. Government Printing Office.

Banking and Finance

9

Mark J. Flannery
Eminent Scholar
and
Joel F. Houston
Associate Professor
Department of Finance,
Insurance and Real Estate
University of Florida
Gainesville, Florida

The U.S. financial services industry has experienced a massive set of shocks and changes over the past decade.

1) The dramatic collapse of the savings and loan industry has eliminated nearly a thousand competitors from the financial marketplace.

2) Banking firms have been provided the opportunity to combine across state lines in a manner that was virtually unthinkable at the start of the 1980s.

3) Nonbanking firms such as mutual funds, retail and commercial finance companies have steadily encroached upon traditional banking market areas, reducing the banks' share of overall financial assets in the U.S. (Boyd and Gertler 1994, Kaufman and Mote 1994).

4) Securities markets have also replaced banking firms as suppliers of credit to the nonfinancial sectors, particularly in the areas of mortgage-backed securities, auto loans and credit card receivables.

These and other major factors have affected the profitability, size and number of banking firms operating throughout the U.S.

A variety of institutions operate in the financial services industry. Examples include commercial banks, savings institutions, credit unions, investment companies, mortgage bankers and brokers, secu-

The authors thank Richard Hume for his careful work in collecting most of the statistics reported here.

rity dealers, insurance companies and real estate corporations. Commercial banks offer the broadest array of financial services, including deposits and loans for corporations, small businesses and individuals. Because businesses require credit to operate effectively, a state's banking industry plays a vital role in its economic development, most importantly in the area of new and smaller businesses.

One set of financial service firms is distinguished by their legal power to take deposits as a source of funds. These so-called "depository intermediaries" include banks, thrift institutions (savings and loan associations and mutual savings banks) and credit unions. Deposits include both checking and savings accounts, each of which are held by individuals as well as corporations. Deposit accounts constitute an important investment vehicle for many individuals, as well as the most common means of payment. In addition, thrift institutions were created to promote housing finance, and therefore generally invest a large percentage of their assets in home mortgages. Thrift institutions are also separately regulated from commercial banks. Credit unions are cooperative organizations whose members ("customers") generally share a common bond such as working for the same firm, belonging to the same union or living in the same area. Credit unions are funded by their members' savings deposits and use the proceeds to provide consumer credit to other members.

Distinctions among the various types of financial institutions have blurred over the past decade, largely due to the gradual elimination of regulations that had restricted the activities of commercial banks. For example, many commercial banks now offer mutual funds, discount brokerage and insurance services--all of which were generally prohibited in the past. In recent years, the strict separation of commercial and investment banking, which was required by the Glass-Steagall Act (passed at the depth of the Great Depression), has been relaxed via Federal Reserve Board rulings. Recent proposals from the White House and the congressional banking committees raise the prospect that the Glass-Steagall Act may be repealed completely in the near future, opening the way for commercial bankers to help local firms sell securities directly to the public. At the same time, other financial institutions have begun to offer services very similar to those offered by commercial banks: thrift institutions and credit unions

Table 1. Employment in the Financial Services Industry in Florida 1985-1992

Year	Number of Employees in Finance, Insurance and Real Estate	Percentage of State Nonfarm Employment
1985	315,403	6.96
1986	332,106	7.00
1987	361,066	7.21
1988	365,336	6.98
1989	377,886	7.00
1990	383,505	7.07
1991	382,345	7.15
1992	375,196	6.90

Source: U.S. Department of Commerce, *County Business Patterns Florida* (various years).

now routinely offer transaction (checking-like) accounts, while money market mutual funds compete aggressively for individuals' savings business.

While the Florida banking industry has remained profitable over the past decade, its form has changed dramatically in response to the factors influencing financial services firms nationwide. The state's financial services industry will continue to evolve in response to changing regulations, technology and consumer preferences. Consequently, financial firms' strategic planners should find the next several years to be as interesting and exciting as the past ten.

The Changing Composition of the Financial Services Industry in Florida

Since 1985, Florida's financial services firms have employed about 7 percent of all nonfarm workers in the state (see Table 1). In 1992, just over 375,000 people were employed in the financial services industry in Florida, nearly 75,000 of these by commercial banks. While financial services, and the banking industry in particular, con-

Figure 1. - Employment in the Financial Services Industry
(Total employed in 1992: 375,196)

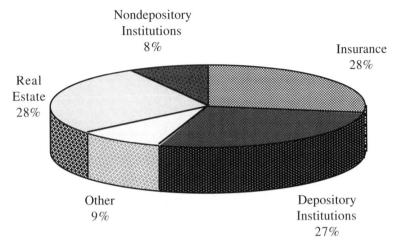

tinue to employ a significant number of Floridians, the number of workers employed by Florida financial institutions peaked in 1990 and has declined slightly since then.

Figure 1 shows the breakdown in employment among the various types of financial services firms for 1992. (This overall mix of employment has remained fairly constant since at least 1988). Depository institutions, insurance companies and agents, and real estate corporations each employ roughly 28 percent of the overall financial services industry. The remaining portion consists of nondepository institutions (which include security brokers and dealers, finance companies, and mortgage brokers and bankers), and "other" institutions (which include investment companies, holding offices, trusts, real estate investment trusts, and patent owners and lessors).

The Decline of the Thrift Industry

During the late 1980s, many thrift institutions failed nationwide in what is frequently referred to as the "S&L Crisis."[1] In Florida, the number of operating thrifts fell from 144 in 1985 to 89 in 1993. When

---

[1]See White (1991) for a good description of the factors causing the S&L crisis and the impact the crisis had on the U.S. financial system.

Figure 2. Total Assets - Florida Depository Institutions 1985-1993

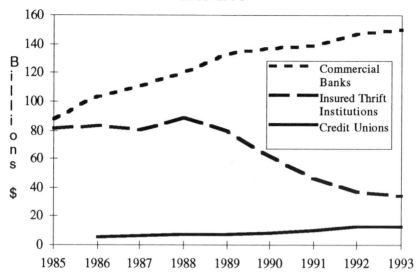

Sources: For Banks: FDIC *Historical Statistics on Banking*;
              For Thrifts: FDIC *Statistics on Banking* and Federal Home
                  Loan Bank of Atlanta;
              For Credit Unions: National Credit Union Administration
                  year-end statistics.

a thrift institution failed, another financial institution--usually a commercial bank--frequently took over its operations. Thus, the financial services industry did not so much shrink as change its form away from thrift institutions and toward commercial banks.

Figure 2 plots the total assets held by the various types of depository institutions in Florida, annually since 1985. The sharp decline in thrift assets after 1988 was accompanied by an offsetting rise in bank assets. Summarizing the implications of Figure 2: commercial banking assets have increased slightly, assets held by insured thrift institutions have declined sharply and credit unions have experienced strong growth, while still representing a relatively small part of the overall industry.

A similar impression emerges from the employment data. While depository institutions have provided about 28 percent of the financial sector's jobs in recent years, there have been significant changes in employment patterns among the different types of depository in-

Figure 3a. Employment Among Depository Institutions 1988
(Total employed in 1988: 103,060)

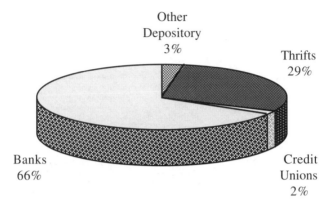

Figure 3b. Employment Among Depository Institutions 1992
(Total employment in 1992: 103,717)

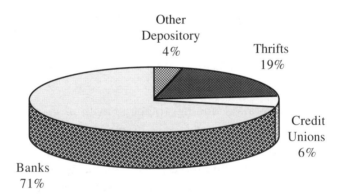

stitutions. Figures 3a and 3b break down employment among depository institutions for both 1988 and 1992. Commercial banks
represent the largest component of depository institutions, employing more than 70 percent of all depository institutions workers in
1992. Two trends are worth noting here. First, employment by thrift
institutions has declined from 29.4 percent of all depository institution workers to less than 19 percent, mirroring the reduction in thrifts'
total assets. Second, credit union employment, while still relatively
small, more than tripled. These competitors have been quietly expanding at the expense of other types of depository institutions.

Table 2. Commercial Bank Profitability

Year	ROA Florida Banks	ROA Southeast Banks	ROE Florida Banks	ROE Southeast Banks	LLE Florida Banks	LLE Southeast Banks
1985	0.86	0.91	13.68	13.09	0.66	0.75
1986	0.87	0.82	14.21	11.87	0.68	0.86
1987	0.75	0.78	12.06	11.18	0.77	0.80
1988	0.78	0.82	12.21	11.65	0.59	0.64
1989	0.61	0.68	9.53	9.50	0.78	0.79
1990	0.28	0.52	4.16	7.14	1.22	1.06
1991	0.48	0.66	7.12	8.96	1.03	0.90
1992	0.86	1.05	12.12	13.72	0.59	0.59
1993	1.15	1.26	15.41	15.56	0.36	0.32

ROA = return on assets (net income divided by year-end total assets).
ROE = return on equity (net income divided by year-end book value of equity).
LLE = loan loss expense as a percentage of all interest-earning assets.
Sources: Federal Reserve Bank of Atlanta *Economic Review*, various issues, and FDIC *Historical Statistics on Banking*.

The Recent Profitability of Commercial Banks

In years past, commercial banking was considered a stable industry, which manifested consistent and reliable profitability. Over the past fifteen years, however, increased competition, greater volatility in financial markets and deregulation have created an environment in which the profitability of commercial banks is no longer assured.

Table 2 demonstrates how the profitability of Florida banks has compared to that of all southeastern banks in recent years. Two measures of profitability are reported—return on assets (ROA) and return on stockholder's equity (ROE). Prior to 1988, all southeastern banks exhibited comfortable, relatively stable profitability.[2] Among southeastern banks, Florida banks realized slightly lower-than-average ROAs throughout the period shown. Before 1990, the Florida

----

[2]Frame and Holder (1994) provide a good explanation of how bank profitability numbers are computed.

Table 3. The Number of Bank Failures in the U.S. and Florida 1985-1993

Year	U.S. Failures	Percentage of all U.S Banks	Florida Failures	Percentage of all Florida Banks
1985	120	0.83	2	0.47
1986	138	0.97	3	0.72
1987	184	1.34	3	0.73
1988	200	1.52	3	0.72
1989	206	1.62	5	1.16
1990	168	1.36	7	1.62
1991	124	1.04	10	2.38
1992	120	1.05	2	0.49
1993	42	0.38	0	0.00

Source: FDIC *Statistics on Banking*, 1993, Table RC-8 and FDIC *Statistics on Banking*, 1990, Table RC-10.

banks' greater leverage provided them a higher ROE but this advantage was not sufficient to offset the relatively low Florida ROAs since that time.

Beginning in 1989, Florida banks' performance deteriorated, both absolutely and relative to that of other southeastern banks. The primary cause of this decline was a deterioration in banks' credit quality, particularly loans secured by commercial real estate. Banks typically operate with fairly narrow profit margins and can therefore incur great losses when a large number of loans go uncollected. One measure of credit quality, loan loss expense as a percentage of interest-earning assets (LLE), is presented in the last two columns of Table 2. Throughout the Southeast, credit quality deteriorated in the late 1980s and continued to worsen through the 1990-91 recession. As the real economy recovered both in Florida and nationwide, the southeastern banks' credit quality improved dramatically. Bank profitability numbers clearly reflect the effect of the reduced loan-loss expenses.

The interest-rate environment has also contributed to the recent rebound in bank profitability. In the early 1990s, many banks were well-positioned to profit from the sharp decline in interest rates that

Table 4. Top 10 Florida Bank Holding Companies
as of March 1994

Institution	Total Assets ($ billions)	1993 Net Income ($ millions)	1993 Return on Assets (ROA) (percent)	1993 Return on Equity (ROE) (percent)
1. **Barnett Banks - Jacksonville**	38.1	421	1.10	15.54
2. First Union Corp. of Florida - Jacksonville	27.4	416	1.59	19.58
3. Nationsbank of Florida - Tampa	22.3	151	0.71	13.30
4. SunBanks Inc. - Orlando	20.3	250	1.27	15.84
5. Amsouth Bank of Florida - Tampa	2.6	19	1.12	13.97
6. Southtrust of Florida Inc. - Jacksonville	2.4	16	0.90	11.09
7. Northern Trust Bank of Florida - Miami	1.3	29	2.39	30.12
8. **Republic Banking Corp. of Florida - Miami**	1.1	12	0.96	12.06
9. **Capital Bancorp - Miami**	1.1	12	1.02	14.71
10. **Ocean Bankshares Inc. - Miami**	1.0	11	1.26	19.10

Note: Florida-owned in bold.

Source: Koenig 1994, p. 31.

accompanied the recession. The record level of bank profits experienced nationwide during 1993 was importantly related to the fact that banks dropped their deposit rates much more quickly than loan rates as market yields (e.g., on government bonds) fell. Despite the fact that market rates reversed themselves in 1994, bank profitability remained fairly robust on account of continuing strong real economic performance.

A similar impression of the impact of real economic activity on bank soundness emerges from inspection of bank failure rates in Table 3. In the years leading up to 1991, bank failures were more common than at any time since the Great Depression. Particularly noteworthy for Florida was the fall of Southeast Banking Corporation, which was the state's second-largest bank when it failed in 1991. As the economy recovered from recession, however, the number of bank failures fell off quite sharply in 1992 and 1993. Not only has the Florida banking system been doing well in general but the state's

Table 5. Number of Banks and Banking Offices
in the State of Florida 1985-1993

Year	Number of Banks	Number of Banking Offices	Average Offices per Bank	Average Asset Size ($ million)
1985	422	2,453	5.81	208.5
1986	418	2,665	6.38	246.9
1987	410	2,818	6.87	270.7
1988	417	2,935	7.04	288.5
1989	430	3,125	7.27	309.5
1990	432	3,183	7.37	317.6
1991	421	3,244	7.71	329.9
1992	407	3,087	7.58	362.4
1993	375	3,025	8.07	400.5

Source: FDIC *Historical Statistics on Banking* (for number of banks), Freer 1994 (for number of banking offices).

largest banks have posted good profits and maintained strong equity capital positions over this time period.

Recent data for the ten largest Florida banks are reported in Table 4. These large firms are important because they hold a very large share of all banking assets in the state. The ten holding companies shown in Table 4 comprise only 2.7 percent of all Florida banks, yet they hold 78 percent of Florida banking assets. (The largest four banks alone account for roughly two-thirds of the state's banking assets.) Moreover, in many local markets these firms' branches have an important effect on loan and deposit rates. Table 4 clearly indicates that, almost without exception, these firms are highly profitable and well-capitalized.

To summarize, the health of the banking industry in Florida has improved in recent years, largely due to a favorable economy and interest-rate environment. While the industry appears to be fundamentally sound, increased competition assures that banks will have to compete more aggressively in the years ahead just to retain the same level of profitability. Moreover, deregulation and macroeconomic uncertainties mean that large fluctuations in year-to-year profitability appear to be here to stay.

Table 6. Assets of Commercial Banks in the United States and Florida 1985-1993

Year	Assets Held by Banks in Florida ($ billions)	Assets Held by Banks in the U.S. ($ billions)	Percentage of Banking Assets Held by Florida Banks	Percentage of U.S. Population in the State of Florida
1985	88.0	2,731	3.20	4.77
1986	103.2	2,941	3.50	4.86
1987	111.0	3,000	3.70	4.95
1988	120.3	3,131	3.80	5.03
1989	133.1	3,300	4.00	5.12
1990	137.2	3,389	4.00	5.19
1991	138.9	3,431	4.00	5.26
1992	147.5	3,506	4.20	5.29
1993	150.2	3,613	4.20	5.30

Sources: Freer 1994 (for assets held by banks in Florida), FDIC *Reports of Income and Condition* (for assets held by banks in the U.S.) and *Statistical Abstract of the United States 1994* (for population figures).

The Changing Face of Florida Banking

Table 5 shows that 375 banking institutions were operating slightly more than 3,000 branch offices at the end of 1993. The number of banks has declined steadily over the past decade, reflecting both the addition of new firms and the departure (through failure or, more commonly, merger) of old ones. Since 1985, 104 new banks and trust companies (de novo institutions) were opened in the state, while 35 institutions failed. The net 11.1 percent decline in the number of banks operating in Florida results from the large number of banks that were acquired by other institutions. Table 5 further indicates that the average Florida bank became larger: the average number of offices per bank has risen from slightly less than six in 1985 to just over eight in 1993, while the average bank's asset size rose 92 percent (from $208.5 million in 1985 to $400.5 million in 1993).

Table 6 compares recent Florida history to the nationwide banking experience. While the U.S. banking system's assets rose 32.2 percent between 1985 and 1993, the increase in Florida banks' assets was nearly

71 percent. As a result, Florida banks' share of U.S. banking assets rose over this period (from 3.20 percent to 4.20 percent). The last column in Table 6 indicates, however, that about a third of this increased asset share is due to the increase in Florida's share of the total U.S. population. That leaves a majority of Florida's asset share growth due to competitive gains by the state's banks. Another sense in which Florida banks have differed from the nationwide trend is in their declining numbers: Florida's 11.1 percent decline in operating banks is less than half of the decline nationwide, where the number of banks fell by nearly 24 percent (from 14,404 in 1985 to 10,957 in 1993).

Banking in Florida has undergone a number of changes over the past decade. One of the most dramatic has been the influx of out-of-state institutions. As was shown in Table 4, six of the state's seven largest banks are affiliated with or owned by an out-of-state holding company. By contrast, in 1982 Florida had no large banks controlled from out of state (see Table 7). Of the state's ten largest banks in 1982, only Barnett Banks remains controlled within the state of Florida. (Barnett itself has been the subject of occasional, intense takeover rumors in recent years (Koenig 1994).) This rapid consolidation can be attributed primarily to economic forces that encourage banks to merge and changing laws that have made it easier for banks to merge. Consolidation can raise bank profitability by reducing operating costs, because mergers can enable them to realize economies of scale by closing overlapping offices, integrating computer systems, pooling advertising and marketing expenditures and cutting back the number of employees.

Prior to 1985, with a few exceptions based on legal loopholes, out-of-state banks were unable to enter Florida. In 1985, the Florida Legislature agreed to allow regional interstate banking--banks in the Southeast were allowed to acquire Florida banks as long as Florida banks were allowed to enter the acquiring bank's home state. In the years that followed, institutions such as NCNB (currently Nationsbank), First Union, Trust Company of Georgia and Citizens and Southern (since acquired by Nationsbank) made significant inroads into the Florida market.

This trend toward out-of-state ownership has raised the concern that the acquiring banks have entered Florida for the purpose of using

Table 7. The Ten Largest Florida Bank Holding Companies as of December 1982 and their Current Status

Bank Holding Company	Total Deposits as of 12/31/82 ($ billions)	Current Status
1. Barnett Banks, Inc., Jacksonville	5.8	independent
2. Southeast Banking Corp. Miami	5.2	seized by regulators/ assets acquired by First Union in 1991
3. SunBanks of Florida, Inc., Orlando	4.1	merged with Trust Co. in 1985
4. Florida National Banks, Inc. Jacksonville	2.9	acquired by First Union in 1989
5. Flagship Banks Inc. Miami	2.7	acquired by SunBanks in 1984
6. First Florida Banks of Fla. Inc. Tampa	2.0	acquired by Barnett Banks in 1986
7. Atlantic Bancorp Jacksonville	2.0	acquired by First Union in 1985
8. Ellis Banking Corp. Bradenton	1.3	acquired by NCNB (Nationsbank) in 1985
9. Southwest Florida Banks Inc. Ft. Myers	1.3	acquired by Landmark Banking Corporation in 1984
10. Landmark Banking Corp., Ft. Lauderdale	1.2	acquired by C&S Corp., Ga. in 1985

Source: Freer (1994), p. 16.

the state's rich deposit base to fund loans elsewhere. This argument would suggest that while regional integration has probably worked to increase the rate of return earned by depositors, some individuals and small businesses may now find it harder to obtain credit. However, it must be recognized that *de facto* regional integration existed long before interstate banking. Banks operating in Florida could always choose to participate in loans outside the state and to make other investments such as Treasury securities, mortgage securities and municipal bonds--all of which could (indirectly) provide credit to residents of other states. Even more directly, Florida banks could lend money (via the interbank "federal funds" market) to distant banks that need extra funds to satisfy their customers' loan demands.

Furthermore, any bank's interest in maximizing its return to share-holders leads it to make profitable loans wherever they may be lo-cated. To the extent that Florida businesses continue to generate profitable investment opportunities for themselves, any bank should be eager to advance credit for such projects. For example, David Humphrey, a professor at Florida State University, has observed that a tremendous amount of capital entered the state to rebuild south Florida following Hurricane Andrew (Koenig 1994).

Nor have these large regional juggernauts proven to be the in-domitable competitive forces that many feared. In particular, and to the surprise of some analysts, the development of interstate banking has not led to a collapse in community banks, which are most likely to concentrate their lending within the state. Community banks, which are locally owned and managed, continue to thrive by providing ser-vices to local customers that larger institutions are less able or will-ing to provide. A recent survey, reported in the *American Banker,* suggests that Florida community banks expected a 16 percent in-crease in their loan portfolios during 1994--compared to only 4 per-cent for larger banks in the state (Atkinson 1994).

Despite these narrowly economic reasons for out-of-state banks to seek profitable loan business through their Florida networks, Arnold Heggestad, a finance professor at the University of Florida, fears that acquisitions by out-of-state banks may reduce the contributions that banks make to their local communities (Koenig 1994). While the Florida subsidiary of an out-of-state holding company is likely to sup-port activities in Florida, he argues, they may do so less intensively than they would if the holding company were incorporated in the state.

Changing Technology and the Financial Services Industry

Along with the thrift industry's decline and the banking industry's consolidation, another major trend over the last decade has been the

Table 8. Transaction at the HONOR Network
Automated Teller Machines (ATM) and
Point-of-Sale Terminals (POS)
1985-1993

	ATM			POS		
Year	Terminals	Transactions	Trans- actions per Terminal	Terminals	Transactions	Trans- actions per Terminal
1985	2,145	22,194,518	10,347	1,403	790,761	564
1986	2,328	28,082,664	12,063	1,476	1,193,218	808
1987	2,660	34,621,785	13,016	2,511	1,358,626	541
1988	2,891	41,672,547	14,415	2,981	2,342,250	786
1989	3,253	50,615,761	15,560	3,043	4,016,424	1,320
1990	3,228	54,703,591	16,947	3,276	5,746,965	1,754
1991	8,040	137,890,420	17,151	6,221	9,166,761	1,474
1992	8,769	155,086,038	17,686	8,172	13,000,378	1,591
1993	9,164	181,324,676	19,787	14,485	19,196,424	1,325

Note: The large jump in terminals and transactions between 1990 and 1991 reflects the merger of the HONOR system with the AVAIL network in Georgia and with the RELAY network operating in North Carolina, South Carolina, Virginia and Maryland.

Source: Freer 1994, p. 51.

increased use of technology to deliver banking services. In 1985, there were 2,560 Floridians for every office of a depository intermediary. By 1993, this number had risen to 3,262 (Freer 1994). Despite this (relative) decline in the number of banking offices, however, the rise of Automatic Teller Machines (ATMs) and Point of Sale (POS) terminals has dramatically increased the availability of banking services to most consumers.

Prior to the spread of ATMs and POS terminals, consumers could conduct their banking business only at a branch office during normal working hours. Now consumers may use banking services several times a week without ever entering a bank. Many workers have their paychecks deposited directly into their bank accounts and have arranged for banks automatically to pay their mortgages, insurance premiums, utility bills, etc. Depositors may withdraw cash from an ATM outside a restaurant late in the evening, use a POS terminal to pay for groceries and pay bills through their home computer. Table 8 demonstrates the phenomenal growth of the HONOR network of electronic banking terminals over the past decade. Not only have the number of ATM and POS terminals risen very sharply over the period but the increased number of transactions per terminal clearly indicates the public's willingness to conduct routine banking business using the new technology for delivering banking services.

A Look Ahead

The financial services industry remains a large and important component of the Florida economy. Over the last several years the industry has undergone a number of changes. Most significant among these changes are the decline in the thrift industry, the increased use of technology and the consolidation of the banking industry arising largely from acquisitions by out-of-state institutions. Moreover, an increasing number of consumers obtain financial services from institutions other than banks and thrifts.

Many of these trends are likely to continue in the years ahead. Further advances in technology, and a changing population which grows increasingly comfortable with the use of computers, suggest that the nature of banking services will continue to evolve. Recent legislation allows for a limited type of nationwide banking and it seems increasingly likely that federal legislation will soon make full interstate branching a reality. Accordingly, the past decade's trend toward consolidating financial firms should continue. Other federal legislation has recently been proposed that would permit banks to combine with securities firms, insurance companies and even with industrial firms. This regulatory reform would hasten the tendency of financial institutions to offer an increasingly similar set of products. In short, it appears that financial institutions in the years ahead will operate in a more competitive, less regulated environment. This environment will provide numerous challenges as well as opportunities.

References

Atkinson, B. 1994. "Beaming Florida Bankers Report A Lending Boom." *American Banker* (September 7).

Boyd, J. H., and M. Gertler. 1994. "The Role of Large Banks in the Recent U.S. Banking Crisis." *Quarterly Review* 18 (Winter), pp. 2-21. Federal Reserve Bank of Minneapolis.

Frame, W. S., and C. L. Holder. 1994. "Commercial Bank Profits in 1993." *Economic Review* (July/August), pp. 22-39. Federal Reserve Bank of Atlanta.

Freer, J. 1994. *A Decade of Distinction: Florida Banking 1983-1993.* Encino, California: Jostens Publishing Group, Inc.

Kaufman, G. G., and L. R. Mote. 1994. "Is Banking a Declining Industry? A Historical Perspective." *Economic Perspectives* (May/June), pp. 2-21. Federal Reserve Bank of Chicago.

Koenig, J. 1994. "And Then There Was One." *Florida Trend* (October), pp. 22-32.

White, L. 1991. *The S&L Debacle - Public Policy Lessons for Bank and Thrift Regulation.* Oxford University Press.

Telecommunications Industries

10

Sanford V. Berg
Executive Director
Public Utility Research Center
Professor of Economics
University of Florida
Gainesville, Florida

Every citizen is affected by state policies toward telecommunications. Historically, the telephone industry was viewed as a natural monopoly. Local service, long distance, inside wiring and even telephone equipment in businesses and residences were provided by a single company for much of the nation. Florida had a number of companies providing local service but these firms did not compete with one another. The Florida Public Service Commission (FPSC) ensured that local prices remained low and that returns to suppliers were not excessive. In recent decades, the Florida Office of Public Counsel represented residential customers at FPSC rate hearings, providing additional pressure to hold down prices. However, the advent of the Computer/Information Age and the AT&T divestiture are changing the ways telecommunications costs are recovered from local and long distance customers. The Federal Communications Commission has overseen the introduction of competition into the interstate long distance market as well as the vertical disintegration of the industry. These developments have altered the services available

This chapter draws upon a "White Paper on Telecommunications Legislation: Approaches to Resolving Telecommunications Issues in Florida" prepared by the author. The views expressed here do not necessarily represent those of organizations sponsoring the Public Utility Research Center or the Telecommunications Industries Analysis Project.

and the number of alternative suppliers in many telecommunications markets.

The regulatory system in Florida changed in 1978, when the FPSC went from a three-member elective commission to a five-member appointive one. Under the new law, the governor appoints commissioners from nominees selected by the FPSC Nominating Council, who are then confirmed by the state senate. Perhaps the governor and the Legislature viewed the expansion of the commission as a way of incorporating a more diverse set of backgrounds into the regulatory process. By the mid-1990s, the commission included an African-American and a Hispanic-American—with three of the five being women. It is also argued that the appointive process enables the assembly of a greater pool of expertise than might arise under an elective system. Recent commissioners serving four-year terms have had backgrounds in accounting, economics, energy, engineering, finance, law and public affairs.

In the past, rate hearings served as the primary mechanism for obtaining information about actual and projected costs and revenues. Local telephone companies, intervenors and staff presented testimony on allowed rates of return on investment, prices for different services and different customers, cost containment and other aspects of the business. Lest one see regulation as only being a battle over pricing and identifying which customer groups should pay which categories of costs, many other issues arise, including modernization of facilities, disaster recovery, quality of service and new incentive mechanisms for regulated firms. Today, technical workshops and generic hearings are often used to address the complicated issues facing regulators.

As of December 1993, the FPSC regulated or provided oversight for 13 local exchange telephone companies, 281 long distance interexchange telephone companies, 776 competitive pay telephone service providers, 50 shared tenant service (STS) providers and 14 alternative access vendors (AAVs). The latter two groups illustrate the impact of new technologies on the industry. AAVs provide networks that allow businesses and other users (including government) to connect with long distance interexchange carriers for access to a wide variety of services, including voice grade private lines, digital data, video and other services requiring high bandwidth capacity. These

Table 1. Sizes of Florida's Local Exchanges, September 1993
($000s)

	Gross Plant in Service	Operating Revenues
ALLTEL	147,714	45,699
Centel	514,149	181,952
GTE	3,497,654	1,084,027
Southern Bell	9,319,695	3,166,576
United	2,207,580	709,190
Other LECs	157,363	55,218
TOTAL	15,844,155	5,242,662

bypass the local exchange. Similarly, STS firms supply common switching or billing arrangements to commercial tenants in a single building--again substituting for local exchange company services.

Based on an FPSC annual report, the sizes of Florida's local exchange companies (as of September 1993) are significant, as shown in Table 1. Thus, about $16 billion of investment in local exchange facilities serves Floridians. Additional investments in facilities have been made by long distance carriers and recent entrants into the industry. Furthermore, cellular, cable, satellite and other firms are beginning to enter market niches.

Over the last thirty years the industry has undergone a dramatic reconfiguration, with regulatory and technological changes transforming it. First, equipment became competitive (in the 1960s) as computers and silicon chips opened up new possibilities for customers. In the 1970s, the entry of MCI and others into long distance and changes in Federal Communications Commission regulation turned interstate long distance into a more competitive market. The 1982 court decision led to full divestiture of AT&T--with the regional operating companies remaining under the regulatory jurisdiction of state commissions. However, the pace of innovation has meant that state regulators, including the Florida PSC, have had to develop new ways to promote efficiency and fairness in telephony.

In particular, the "universal service" objective may have to be achieved via new funding mechanisms. Rate averaging and payments to local carriers by long distance (interexchange carriers) have enabled Floridians to have some of the lowest basic residential telephone rates in the Southeast. However, both of these funding sources are being eroded by competitive pressures. Thus, rate averaging has led to "postage-stamp" pricing, keeping prices down in low-density rural areas with high cost of service. However, emerging competition in the urban (especially, business) markets places downward pressure on urban rates--encouraging rate de-averaging and relatively higher rural prices.

The monthly $10 to $12 basic residential telephone rates characterizing much of Florida are low relative to other parts of the Southeast: Atlanta, Ga. ($15.90), Birmingham, Ala. ($20.10) and Columbia, S.C. ($16.90). None of these rates includes taxes or the $3.50 federal subscriber line charge (for long distance access) but they indicate the bargain Florida citizens currently receive. Toll rates within Florida have also fallen. For example for a three-minute daytime call spanning 100 miles, AT&T's rates have dropped from $1.25 in 1984 to $0.71 in May 1994. Given general inflation, the real reduction in price is even greater. Entry and new technologies have tended to lower prices but further entry into the local market will add pressure to raise rural rates.

Thus, Florida regulations are in a transitional phase. The Legislature has considered major telecommunications bills in recent years, even as our national Congress considers how cable television, fiber optics, satellite, cellular and other systems will fit into the emerging national information infrastructure. Regulators want customers who will be early users of more exotic systems to foot the bill for them (rather than having subscribers in general subsidize early users). Yet regulators also want to encourage the development and introduction of new services that can make Floridians more productive and meet the needs of our citizens. As the world goes digital, the possibilities for network interconnection and competition raise numerous public policy issues.

New strategic alliances among firms illustrate how suppliers are trying to discover the best ways to meet customer needs. Recent developments include a GTE announcement that it planned to provide cable television service in St. Petersburg. BellSouth has a venture with Disney to provide cable television services. Teleport and other providers of fiber optic networks are constructing rings through the business districts of major Florida cities. These competitive access providers enable heavy users of long distance service to avoid the local exchange.

Note that increased competition is not an unambiguous benefit to customers. For example, quality of service is being monitored from the standpoint of final customers and features of each system, since interconnecting networks are only as good as their weakest link. Similarly, operator service providers assist the hotel and pay telephone industries, raising questions regarding final customer access to preferred long distance companies. Competition has brought with it some customer confusion. "Slamming"--the unauthorized switching of a customer to another long distance carrier--has been another activity that the FPSC has attacked via tougher enforcement actions.

The most important issue for Florida to consider is the process whereby competition is introduced into telecommunications markets. We know that local telephony, long distance, information services, television and mobile services will be organized very differently in the future due to technological innovations and changes in public policy. The precise steps whereby incumbent firms in one industry become entrants into another will be determined by laws drawn up and passed by the Legislature and by rules established by the Florida Public Service Commission. The rules will depend on the priorities set in state law.

The problem facing Florida can be defined as follows: *How can policymakers ensure that the benefits of competition flow to those who successfully commercialize new services and to consumers who desire those services?* We want innovative suppliers to benefit because they will then have an incentive to continue to take the risks associated with telecommunications investments. We want consumers to benefit because that is the purpose of market systems--getting the right mix of goods and services to consumers at the lowest possible prices using the most efficient production techniques. An associated problem facing Florida is the following: *How can the introduction of greater competition in telecommunications markets be accomplished without jeopardizing universal service?*

Status quo regulation would impose huge costs on the state economy in terms of lost opportunities. On the other hand, "flash"

total deregulation of all telecommunications markets is neither politically feasible nor economically desirable. Some consumers would
face residual market power for a period of time--and the existence of
bottleneck facilities would require some oversight from regulators
regarding terms and conditions of access during the transitional
period ahead.

Most observers would agree on four general points:

(1) Competition is increasing in telecommunications markets due to technological change and new regulatory initiatives.

(2) This development is likely to be beneficial to many
consumer groups, but not all.

(3) It will not be easy to regulate portions of the marketplace so that least-cost suppliers emerge during this transitional period.

(4) Finally, because segments of the industry are likely
to have market power in the near future, some regulatory
constraints will be needed (a) to protect those customers with
no competitive alternatives and (b) to ensure that entrants have
equal, nondiscriminatory access to remaining bottleneck
facilities.

Consider each point in turn. With regard to the first point, it
should not be necessary to go through the entire litany of technological developments that are transforming telecommunications. The
convergence of the communications and computer industries via digi-
talization, the expansion of spectrum-using technologies (cellular,
personal communications systems, satellite) and developments in fiber optics (and associated electronics) represent only a few of the
production alternatives promising new services and lower costs in
the future. Beyond technology, the FCC and state regulatory commissions are providing greater flexibility to incumbents and are allowing new entry into various telecommunications markets.

The second point, that many customer groups are likely to benefit from such developments, has substantial empirical support. Historically, cost-of-service regulation could ensure that neither monopoly profits nor the savings associated with new technologies were
captured by suppliers of telephony. Local rates were held down (to

promote universal service) and long distance rates declined (though more slowly than costs were falling). However, innovations disrupted traditional industry structures even as costs fell. The AT&T divestiture and entry in markets that had once been regulated signaled the beginning of a new era for consumers. Competition is recognized as a powerful factor pushing some prices down, forcing formerly subsidized prices up and encouraging innovation.

The fundamental tension between regulation and competition, the third point noted above, is widely recognized. Reliance on the competitive marketplace to set prices and determine new service introductions is inconsistent with having an agency set prices for an incumbent. Continued command and control regulation creates opportunities for corporate gaming of the political system. When government intervention, rather than actual performance in the marketplace, determines which firms are winners and which are losers, corporate executives have an incentive to devote resources to lawyers and consultants rather than to scientists and engineers. Similarly, when regulators have substantial discretion (without clearly defined objectives articulated in the law), cohesive customer and supplier groups are encouraged to plead for special treatment. The hearing room rather than the industrial laboratory becomes the focus of attention. This tendency is most unfortunate (though nearly irresistible--since such stakeholders have political power). Elected officials will be tempted to continue to micromanage the industry.

The fourth point identifies the key issue facing legislators and regulators today--how to ensure that the benefits of competition flow to those who successfully commercialize new services and to consumers who desire those services. If government has a broad mandate to "regulate in the public interest," then the regulatory process becomes a relentless source of controversy. The term "public interest" is vague, leaving the prioritization of worthy economic and social objectives up to the chaotic political process. "Politics as usual" drives the evolution of the industry--at least until the configuration of firms (and artificial partitioning of markets) is so inefficient that stakeholders re-open the process. Thus, we find ourselves with a unique opportunity to structure the rules of the game to increase reliance on basic market forces--recognizing that competition can also

be chaotic and unpredictable. Depending on the market (local telephony, information services, inter-LATA toll or cable television), a
firm can find itself as an incumbent in one, entrant in another and
potential supplier in a third! Each stakeholder would like to protect
its established position while gaining access to new markets. The
positions are not necessarily inconsistent, since these participants
perceive "special circumstances" in each firm's core market.

The complexity of the sub-issues is illustrated by the three broad
categories: legal/regulatory, technical and universal service. The
first involves current barriers to competition, appropriate roles for
regulators during transitional regulation and interconnection. All three
topics are contentious. For example, the appropriate level of unbundling and the pricing of network elements will affect the revenues of
incumbents and costs of entrants. Too high a price will unduly dampen
competition, too low a price will confer unjustified savings onto entrants in the local exchange market. Establishing prices that are efficient, fair and nondiscriminatory will be a challenge. In addition,
compensation for access to networks also raises important issues regarding value-based versus cost-based pricing.

The technical issues are probably less important politically but
their resolution will not be simple. This group includes
telecommunications infrastructure development, open network
architecture, resale and mechanisms for sharing technologies.
Network interoperability and number portability raised the most
serious issues.

The third set of issues revolves around the potential impacts on
universal service of competitive entry in the local exchange. Linked
to this issue is the appropriate definition of basic service, the current
level of subsidies (or contributions) from other services, possible
future mechanisms for keeping local calling rates low and costs (or
benefits) of carrier-of-last-resort obligations. Again, these issues must
be addressed if we are to ensure that the benefits of competition are
to be partly captured by consumers.

Note that continuation of traditional regulation is not the only
option involving continued oversight activities by the FPSC. There
are a number of models being adopted in other states that are worthy
of investigation: price caps, sharing rules, infrastructure moderniza-

tion plans—each with (or without) increased reliance on competition. It may not be reasonable to "leap" to full competition. The chasm could be too wide. On the other hand, a series of half-built, disconnected bridges would waste resources. Until the probable consequences of each policy option are understood, it is likely that dramatic regulatory changes will be avoided.

In telecommunications markets, voice, data, information and video seem to be converging. Technological change is bringing telecommunications markets together. The delivery technologies are diverse: traditional wireline via twisted copper pair, coaxial cable, fiber optics and new uses of the radio spectrum (especially Personal Communications Systems). The formats can be analog or digital. No single firm is likely to be the least-cost supplier for all these services, using all these technologies, in all possible formats. The fundamental issues facing the national and state regulators revolve around the transition from what were once viewed as natural monopolies to clusters of interconnected delivery systems that are becoming competitive with one another. The transition is clearly affected by where the burden of proof is placed when considering policy initiatives.

The irony is that the transition to greater competition involves new types of regulation rather than less regulation during the evolution to new industry structures. Numerous contentious issues have been identified: universal service, network interoperability, service quality, number portability, supplier-of-last-resort obligations, the appropriate extent of unbundling and the efficient pricing of network components. The politics of regulation are such that regulators dare not withdraw from the field before they are confident that politically powerful consumer groups are, indeed, protected from the exercise of residual market power. Similarly, to the extent that policymakers can operate as honest brokers in the development of complex contracts in vertical markets, they may be able to make the transition to competitive markets less disruptive. However, involvement in these negotiations (or dictating new supply arrangements) requires different types of regulation than in the past. To some extent, hearing rooms will continue to serve as the arbiters of outcomes--limiting the role of the marketplace in rewarding good performance.

A Look Ahead

While regulatory micromanagement of this rapidly changing sector is inappropriate, Florida regulators cannot avoid taking on two tasks: (1) serving as umpires who ensure that the game of competition is played according to well-defined rules and (2) protecting those customers who continue to face residual market power. Completing these tasks will require great discipline on the part of legislators and regulators. It will require substantial analysis and the beginning of an educational process informing stakeholders (large and small) of the rationale behind the new initiatives. In addition, the approach requires all suppliers to exercise self-restraint—trying negotiation and economic compromise rather than seeking political victory in the hearing room. The "league office" (the Legislature) can ease the burden on "umpires" (regulators) by clearly articulating the desired objectives and establishing a mechanism for maintaining universal service. The impacts of transitional regulation can then be evaluated and policies recalibrated. Well-crafted legislation today means that less bickering is likely to arise in the future.

In June 1995, a new Telecommunications Bill (CS/SB 1554) took effect--setting Florida's local telecommunications industry onto a path toward competition. Facilities-based competition was authorized and the local monopolies were eliminated. Price (rather than cost-based) regulation was established as the transitional mechanism for protecting consumers who might face few alternatives. The price caps for local service will be in effect for three to five years, depending on the current local exchange carrier. Resolution of many issues was left to future policymakers. Such issues include universal service obligations and access by competitors without extensive wire networks.

Although this brief overview provides only a partial catalogue of the types of issues addressed by Florida regulators and legislators, it illustrates the scope of the problems and the techniques being used to resolve conflicts. The promotion of competition has raised numerous concerns, including potential cross-subsidization, predatory pricing and determining when a market is effectively competitive. Despite these issues, the convergence of computer and communications technologies promises to open up new possibilities for Florida citizens.

Florida's Transportation Funding Shortfall

11

Gary L. Brosch
Center for Urban
Transportation Research
University of South Florida
Tampa, Florida

"A substantial part of [Florida's] roads are now obsolete, as they fail to provide reasonable standards of convenience and safety. Congestion in many cities has reached the saturation point, and automobile travel therein is now slower than the horse and buggy was in 1900." -- 1954 Florida legislative report as quoted in "Roadblock," *Florida Trend*, March 1995, p. 58.

"There can be little question that Florida is seriously underinvesting in the transportation infrastructure." -- Gary Brosch, *The Economy of Florida*, 1990.

Since 1990, much has changed at both the state and national levels concerning transportation policy and funding. Yet, the fundamental conclusion remains the same--as a state and a nation we are still seriously underinvesting in transportation infrastructure.

State Transportation Policy Initiative

In 1992, the Florida Legislature and the Governor's Office asked the Center for Urban Transportation Research (CUTR) at the University of South Florida to undertake a multiyear comprehensive study of Florida's transportation system. The purpose of the study

Table 1. State Transportation Committees

State Transportation Policy Initiative
Steering Committee

Chester "Ed" Colby, *Metro-Dade Transit Agency*
Donald Crane, Jr., *Floridians for Better Transportation*
The Honorable Mario Diaz-Balart, *Florida State Senate*
The Honorable James Hargrett, Jr., *Florida State Senate*
Wallace Hawkes III, *Greiner, Inc.*
The Honorable Ed Healy, *Florida House of Representatives*
Arthur Kennedy, *Florida Transportation Commission*
David Kerr, *Florida Transportation Commission*
Michael G. Kovac, *Interim Provost, University of South Florida*
The Honorable Vernon Peeples, *Florida House of Representatives*
Linda Loomis Shelley, *Secretary, Florida Department of Community Affairs*
Ben Watts, *Secretary, Florida Department of Transportation*
Virginia Bass Wetherell, *Florida Department of Environmental Protection*
Jack Wilson, *The Wilson Company*

State Transportation Policy Initiative
Technical Advisory Committee

Jane Mathis, *Florida Transportation Commission*
John Johnston, *Florida House of Representatives, Committee on Transportation*
Dorothy Johnson, *Florida State Senate, Transportation Committee*
Robert P. Romig, *Florida Department of Transportation*
Richard McElveen, *Florida Department of Environmental Protection*
John Outland, *Florida Department of Environmental Protection*
Patricia S. McKay, *1000 Friends of Florida*
Ben Starrett, *Florida Department of Community Affairs*
Charles Pattison, *Florida Department of Community Affairs*
Wes Watson, *Florida Transit Association*
Lucie Ayer, *Hillsborough County Planning Commission*

was to examine a wide variety of transportation policy and planning issues under the direction of a broad-based Steering Committee and a Technical Advisory Group (see Table 1).

Nine major reports have been issued, with four more completed by July 1995 (see Table 2). Although the transportation, land use

Table 2. State Transportation Policy
Initiative Reports

Statewide Transportation Needs and Funding Study—Summarizes the methodology and results of a forecasting model used to define and evaluate Florida's transportation needs in relation to four alternative scenarios. The study addresses roads and bridges, transit, paratransit, rail, airports and seaports. Needs are evaluated against Florida's current and potential capacity to raise revenue for transportation improvements under these various scenarios.

Transportation and Growth Management: A Planning and Policy Agenda— Addresses methodologies for determining future land use needs, transportation planning and modeling, coordinating land use and transportation, and intergovernmental coordination.

Impact of Community Design on Transportation—Contains eighteen case studies of development types, evaluated in relation to their context, dimension, function, form and development process, with emphasis on interaction of each development type with its surroundings.

Transportation, Land Use, and Sustainability—Reviews the concept of sustainability as it relates to community design and transportation, evaluates community development types and presents guidelines for achieving more sustainable development patterns.

Moving People in Florida: Transit, TDM, and Congestion—Reviews a range of transportation alternatives that relieve traffic congestion by moving more people in fewer vehicles, including various forms of public transportation and transportation demand management (TDM) strategies that reduce single-occupant vehicle travel.

Transportation Planning for State Purposes—Surveys state transportation planning in a sample of eleven other states across the country to examine the approach used by other states in making transportation decisions and what lessons this offers for Florida for its statewide transportation planning program.

Trends and Forecasts of Florida's Transportation Needs—Describes trends in transportation in Florida over the past twenty years using a model of motor fuel usage and vehicle miles driven, resulting in forecasts of motor fuel demand and vehicle miles driven to the year 2010 and potential impacts on revenues in the State Transportation Trust Fund.

The Role of Level of Service Standards on Florida's Growth Management Goals—Reviews level of service (LOS) standards and measures developed in response to Florida's concurrency mandate, including a detailed summary of innovative approaches to measuring LOS in five local governments in Florida.

A Review of Mobile Source Air Quality Practices in Florida—Describes the air quality analysis practices for mobile sources and transportation planning in Florida and evaluates the status of current practice, concluding with recommendations for strengthening the effectiveness of air quality practices in the state.   Continued . . .

Table 2. State Transportation Policy
Initiative Reports (continued)

Transportation Costs of Urban Sprawl: A Review of the Literature—Reviews findings and theoretical underpinnings of the various studies conducted between 1965 and 1990 on the costs of urban sprawl.

Analysis of the Statewide Future Land Use Map—Evaluates the implications of a statewide future land use map compiled using the adopted future land use maps of Florida's 452 local governments.

A New Strategic Urban Transportation Planning Process—Explores the limitations of the transitional long-range transportation planning process and strategies to manage uncertainty in planning public systems, concluding with practices that can make transportation planning more strategic, dynamic and flexible in responding to future uncertainties.

Planning, Zoning, and the Consistency Doctrine: The Florida Experience—Addresses technical considerations and political and legal issues that affect the relationship between comprehensive plans and land development regulations, concluding with guidelines from the literature, practice and case law to promote greater consistency between plans and development regulations.

---

and growth management reports contain significant recommendations for improvement, this paper focuses only on the forecasts of transportation needs and revenues.

Defining Needs

Developing a consensus on the definition of transportation "needs" remains an elusive goal. Environmentalists, truckers, neighborhoods, commuters, shippers, employers and manufacturers all have different perspectives on transportation needs. Many papers (including mine in 1990) and books have been written that verify the complexity of defining "needs" for transportation systems.

STPI Needs Approach

The State Transportation Policy Initiative (STPI) project has taken a direct, pragmatic approach to defining transportation needs in hopes of developing credible needs forecasts that can be accepted by professionals and understood by the public at large.

First, it was decided to provide separate forecasts for each of the major components of the transportation system, including:

- highways and bridges
- new fixed guideway
- airports
- transit
- paratransit
- rail
- seaports

Second, each element was examined under three basic scenarios:

Maintain Funding (Scenario 1)—assumed no change in existing revenue sources or tax and fee rates.

Maintain Conditions (Scenarios 2 & 3)—assumed completion of improvements needed to maintain current physical condition and levels of service. The third scenario assumed the same improvements as the second but added a policy limit on the maximum number of lanes for various roadway classifications. This limit is based on the Florida Department of Transportation's maximum lane policy for Interstate highways and proposed lane standards for other state highways. The third scenario further assumed that corresponding reductions in roadway expenditures would be transferred to transit and rail, increasing the emphasis on those modes.

Improve Conditions (Scenario 4)—assumed that all current deficiencies in physical condition and levels of service would be corrected over the twenty-year planning period. This scenario does not include the maximum lane policy but does assume a substantial increase in the emphasis on transit and rail modes.

A Few Assumptions

Providing estimates of transportation needs for the next twenty years involves a complex mixture of mathematical models, financial forecasts and engineering standards, as well as a number of exogenous assumptions. These assumptions can have a significant impact on final results. This study has attempted to use reasonable, widely accepted assumptions. When faced with a choice, researchers chose assumptions that would tend to <u>underestimate</u> the cost of transportation needs. The primary assumptions are listed below.

- Road/bridge needs included product, product support, operations and maintenance, and administration needs.
- The Highway Performance Monitoring System (HPMS) analytical process was used for the calculation of needs on interstates, arterials and collectors.
- Florida Department of Transportation (FDOT) design standards and construction costs were used.
- FDOT's long-term construction cost forecast was used and varied from an annual low of 0.3 percent to a high of 3.7 percent over the next twenty-year period.
- Right-of-way cost was assumed to inflate at a rate of 5 percent per year.
- Federal revenues for roads and bridges were forecast to increase 1 percent per year for the next twenty years.
- State revenues for roads and bridges were forecast to increase 4 percent per year for the next twenty years.
- Local revenue sources were assumed to grow at a rate of 3.1 percent per year.
- All sources of revenue will continue at current tax and fee rates; all growth in revenue is caused by growth in the tax base, or through indexation (where applicable).
- Transit needs included both operating and capital needs.
- Transit system revenue will continue to supply the same percentage of total funding that it did in 1992.
- The supply of transit service will grow at 1.7 percent annually in the maintain-conditions scenario.
- Transit's mode split will increase by 100 percent by 1997 in the improve-conditions scenario. This would move the overall mode share for transit back to its 1970 level of 2 percent of all trips.
- Tri-County Commuter Rail Authority (Tri-Rail) needs included both operating and capital needs.
- Airport needs included only capital needs.
- Seaport needs include only the state's portion of needs.
- Seaport needs assumed a need equal to the proposed state

spending of $25 million per year plus FDOT central office spending for administration and planning.

The Results

The analysis yields results that should not be surprising, given similar results in other studies. Current funding for transportation simply does not come near keeping up with growth in demand for transportation services nor are enough funds available to maintain the existing system.

Without an infusion of new revenue, congestion will become significantly worse in the next twenty years on virtually all roadways, in both urban and rural areas (see Figure 1). For example, the percentage of traffic that is congested on rural interstates will become five times worse, increasing from about 7 percent to about 35 percent. Similarly, congestion on urban arterials will become about five times worse and congestion on urban interstates will increase from 44 percent to 75 percent.

Similarly, the physical condition of pavements such as potholes and ruts will worsen significantly, with most areas experiencing a doubling of the percentage of pavement in poor condition (see Figure 2).

The estimated funding shortfall to maintain the current condition of our transportation system for the next twenty years is $26.7 billion ($16.2 billion state/$10.5 billion local) (see Table 3). This level of additional funding would allow the system to keep up with growth in population and demand for transportation services and keep the system in its current condition. It would not provide sufficient funding for any improvements to the system beyond what is necessary to keep it from becoming worse.

In order actually to improve our transportation system, reduce congestion and improve mass transit, it is estimated that $58 billion ($34 billion state/$24 billion local) more than current funding would be required. This level of funding would provide for such improvements as reducing congestion to levels approved in local comprehensive plans and a doubling of mass transit usage.

There are, of course, a number of potential revenue sources to meet these shortfalls. These include the obvious gas tax as well as

Figure 1. Peak-Hour Congestion Given Current Funding
(percentage of peak-hour travel in congested condition)

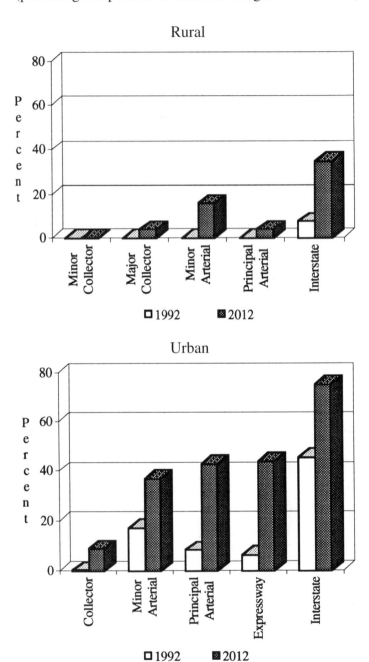

Rural

Urban

Figure 2. Pavement Condition Given Current Funding
(percentage of pavement in poor condition*)

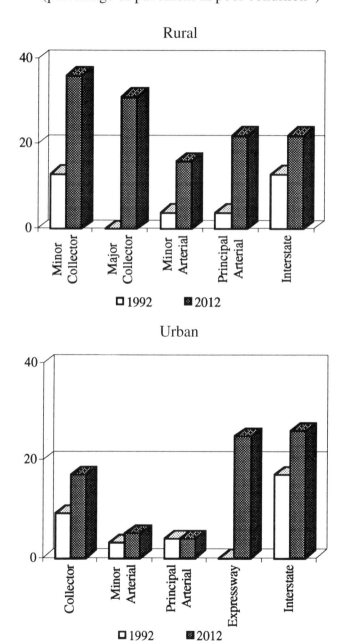

Rural

Urban

☐ 1992   ■ 2012

*Based on highway industry standards.

Table 3. Twenty-Year Revenue Needs and
Shortfalls, All Modes
(billions of 1992 dollars)

	Needs Scenarios		
Needs	Maintain Funding	Maintain Conditions*	Improve Conditions
Roads and Bridges	68.8	83.3	109.6
Transit, Paratransit and Rail	12.9	27.4	34.9
Seaports and Airports (State Share)	2.0	2.9	2.9
Total Needs	83.8	113.6	147.4
Available Revenue	83.8	86.9	89.3
State Shortfall	0.0	16.3	33.5
Local Shortfall	0.0	10.5	24.6
Total Shortfall	0.0	26.7	58.1

*With maximum lane policy.

infrastructure sales tax, port and airport fees, tag fees, rental car surcharges and increased use of toll facilities.

One method of translating billions of dollars into terms easily understood by the public is to express the shortfalls in terms of new taxes. Table 4 is not a recommended funding strategy but is merely an illustration of the possibilities. This table assumes most transportation revenue sources are increased proportionally to cover the shortfalls.

For example, in order to raise the additional $26.7 billion necessary to maintain conditions, the state gas tax would have to increase 5.7 cents per gallon, the local gas tax would have to increase an average of 3.8 cents per gallon and other local sources would have to increase an average of 39 percent. If the entire burden were to fall on the gas tax, the increases would be 9.2 cents state and 5.1 to 6.2 cents local for this scenario.

A Look Ahead

In conclusion, the CUTR State Transportation Policy Initiative demonstrates conclusively that in order to sustain Florida's quality

Table 4. Increases in Taxes and Fees Required
to Make Up Twenty-Year State
and Local Shortfalls

Tax or Fee	1994 Typical Charge	Increase Needed for Each Scenario		
		Maintain Funding	Maintain Conditons*	Improve Conditions
State Shortfalls				
Motor Fuels Taxes				
(per gallon)	12.6¢	0	5.7¢	11.9¢
Aviation Fuel Tax				
(per gallon)	6.9¢	0	3.8¢	3.8¢
Motor Vehicle				
License Fee	$35.10	0	$15.87	$33.28
Initial Registration Fee	$100.00	0	$45.21	$94.82
Rental Car Surcharge				
(per day)	$2.00	0	$0.90	$1.90
Incremental Title Fee	$24.00	0	$10.85	$22.76
Local Shortfalls				
Motor Fuels Taxes				
(per gallon)	10¢	0	3.9¢**	8.1¢**
Other Local Sources	Variable	0	39%**	81%**

*With maximum lane policy.
**This statewide average will vary among counties.

of life and economic productivity, we must address the needs of our transportation system. The economic cost of <u>not</u> making transportation improvements is staggering. It is estimated the public would save $47 billion if we invest the $26.7 billion necessary to maintain conditions and save $95 billion if we invest the $58 billion needed to improve conditions. These savings do not include the tremendous negative impact a worsening transportation system will have on tourism, manufacturing and other businesses.

Changes must be made in how we plan, design and implement transportation improvements. Although this chapter focuses primarily on the needs and funding study, many of the thirteen STPI reports provide research, conclusions and recommendations on ways to improve the coordination of transportation and growth management, urban design and state planning. Doing it "better" is important but, alone, will be insufficient to address our transportation challenges. Similarly, simply throwing more money at the problem without addressing policy, planning, land use and coordination issues would be imprudent. We must do <u>more</u> and do it better.

Military Bases and Defense Manufacturing

12

David G. Lenze
Associate in Research
Bureau of Economic
and Business Research
University of Florida
Gainesville, Florida

The end of the Cold War brings with it a major reduction in U.S. military spending and a geographic redistribution of the remaining military-industrial complex. This period of declining defense spending completes the third defense cycle since the end of World War II.

Like business cycles, defense cycles are periods of growing real defense spending followed by a period of declining spending. In this chapter the period of expanding defense spending will be called the rearmament phase of the defense cycle and the period of declining defense spending, the disarmament phase.

The economic repercussions of disarmament deserve serious attention. Among other things:

- Abrupt defense cutbacks after the Korean War are widely believed to have caused a national recession in 1953-54, while the current disarmament is believed to have impeded the recovery from the 1990-91 recession.

- Even when disarmament proceeded at a slower pace to avert a national recession (as after Vietnam and in the current disarmament), some have claimed that regional recessions developed in places like California and New England because of the extremely high regional concentration of defense spending there.

- Disarmament alters migration patterns to reflect the new geographic distribution of job opportunities in expanding civilian industries and losses in contracting defense-oriented industries.

■ Disarmament also causes obsolescence of capital stock (both physical and human) because much of the highly specialized plant and equipment as well as engineering and marketing skills of defense manufacturers are not easily transferable to civilian uses. The situation is similar with military bases and armed forces personnel.

This chapter describes the current phase of defense cutbacks (both what has occurred already and what is yet to come) and the implications for Florida, by putting it into historical and regional perspective. From a regional perspective, defense expenditure for the construction, operation and maintenance of miltary bases and the expenditure for research, development, testing and production of military goods are most important. As will become clear, the two types of expenditure differ substantially in their impacts on regional economies.

This chapter first briefly describes the actual and planned cutbacks 1987-1998 at the national level and then puts them in historical perspective by comparing them to cutbacks after the Korean and Vietnam wars. Next, it presents a detailed picture of the military industrial complex in Florida in 1987, the peak of the current defense cycle, followed by a discussion of the implications of the planned base realignments and cutbacks in Florida.

Disarmament 1987-1998, National Overview

National defense purchases of goods and services peaked in 1987 at $292 billion.[1] DRI/McGraw Hill forecasts the amount will fall to $197 billion by 1998, a $95 billion or 33 percent decline (Probyn 1994).

Defense purchases of durable goods will bear a disproportionate amount of the decline, falling at least 38 percent while employee compensation will decline only 23 percent. Declines in armed forces personnel will vary by branch, with the Air Force declining the most

---

[1]Unless otherwise stated all money values are expressed in constant 1987 dollars.

Figure 1. National Defense
Purchases of Goods and Services
(annual change, billions of 1987 dollars)

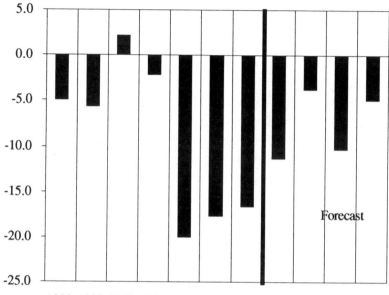

Sources: U.S. Department of Commerce 1992, Probyn 1994 and calculations by the author.

(37 percent) and the Marine Corps the least (13 percent) (U.S. Department of Defense 1988b, 1995).

About one-third of the decline has already occurred (see Figure 1). Total defense spending in 1994 is down $66 billion from the 1987 peak, compensation down $17.6 billion and other purchases down $48.2 billion. Civilian employment is down 20 percent and active duty employment is down 26 percent.

Defense cutbacks are not new. From 1953 (the peak year of Korean War spending) to 1965, defense spending declined 28 percent, while from 1968 (the peak year of Vietnam War spending) to 1976 it declined 38 percent. The $82.4 billion post-Korean War decline was 4.9 percent of 1953 GDP while the $108.2 billion post-Vietnam War decline was 3.9 percent of 1968 GDP. The current $95 billion post-Cold War decline is 2.1 percent of 1987 GDP. These cutbacks compare with GDP growth rates of 3.2 percent in 1953-1965, 2.4

percent in 1968-1976 and an expected 2.4 percent in 1987-1998. In both prior cutbacks, compensation was reduced by a smaller percentage than other goods and services.

It should also be noted that though the Korean War cutbacks were spread over twelve years, 81 percent of them were accomplished in just two years. Similarly the bulk of the cutbacks after the Vietnam War (90 percent) was spread over five years though the complete decline took eight years. The current cutbacks will be spread over eleven years, with 80 percent concentrated in five (nonconsecutive) years.

Disarmaments and recessions seem to go together. The association is more than just coincidence, although the duration of previous disarmaments ensured that they would overlap at least one or two recessions. The rapidity of the Korean War disarmament probably caused the 1953-54 business recession (Bolton 1966, p. 30). Though not a primary causative factor, the disarmament after the peak of the Vietnam War probably aggravated the 1969-70 recession. Similarly, the current round of defense cutbacks probably contributed to the unusually slow recovery from the 1990-91 recession (U.S. Congress 1992, Chapter 6).

When the current cutbacks are completed, defense spending as a share of GDP will be the lowest in the post-World War II era; however, the level of spending in 1998 will nevertheless be high. It will be higher than the $179.9 billion spent in 1976 (during the "detente" thaw in the Cold War) and the $80.7 billion spent in 1947.

The Military-Industrial Complex in Florida: 1987

Military Bases. In 1987, at the peak of the current defense cycle, Florida had nineteen major military installations (Table 1). The Navy maintained a naval station at Mayport plus five naval air stations elsewhere in the state, while the Air Force maintained five airbases (plus Hurlburt Field). In addition, the Navy had three training centers plus four other support facilities. The Army had no major installation in Florida. Except for NAS Key West, these installations were all located in Metropolitan Statistical Areas.

Although Orlando and Ft. Walton Beach each had about the same number of active-duty military--14,800 (Table 2)--Orlando's huge

Table 1. Major Military Installations in Florida 1987

Installation	Location
Navy	
NS Mayport	Jacksonville MSA
NAS Cecil Field	Jacksonville MSA
NAS Jacksonville	Jacksonville MSA
NAS Key West	Monroe County
NAS Whiting Field	Pensacola MSA
NAS Pensacola	Pensacola MSA
Naval Training Center	Orlando MSA
Naval Tech Training Center, Corry Station	Pensacola MSA
Naval Education and Training Center	Pensacola MSA
Naval Aviation Depot	Jacksonville MSA
Naval Aviation Depot	Pensacola MSA
Naval Coastal Systems Center	Panama City MSA
Naval OLF Saufley	Pensacola MSA
Air Force	
Eglin AFB	Ft. Walton Beach MSA
Homestead AFB	Miami MSA
MacDill AFB	Tampa MSA
Patrick AFB	Melbourne MSA
Tyndall AFB	Panama City MSA
Hurlburt Field	Ft. Walton Beach MSA

Note: NAS = Naval Air Staton, NS = Naval Station, AFB = Air Force Base.
Source: Based on information in U.S. Department of Defense 1991.

population meant that the military was far less important to its economy. The armed forces made up only about 1.4 percent of Orlando's resident population, a bit more if military dependents were counted. In Ft. Walton Beach they accounted for 11 percent of the population. Clearly, it is the metropolitan area most dependent on the military. It is also interesting to note that although Tampa and Miami have major military installations, active-duty personnel made up a smaller share of the resident population (0.3 percent) than they did statewide (0.6 percent). Florida had about 5.5 percent of the nation's domestically based military personnel, slightly more than its share of population (4.9 percent).

Table 2 also presents the distribution of civilian defense employees within Florida. These data underestimate the civilian presence of the

Table 2. Resident Population, Active-Duty and Civilian
Military Employees by Area 1987

| Area | Population | Active-Duty Personnel | | Civilian Military Employees | |
		Number	Percent of Population	Number	Percent of Population
Metropolitan Areas					
Daytona Beach	354,869	0	0.0	0	0.0
Ft. Lauderdale	1,178,730	21	**	82	**
Ft. Myers	295,080	0	0.0	0	0.0
Ft. Pierce	218,868	0	0.0	0	0.0
Ft. Walton Beach	134,057	14,752	11.0	4,724	3.5
Gainesville	173,776	128	0.1	13	**
Jacksonville	864,193	12,319	1.4	8,750	1.0
Lakeland	380,203	0	0.0	0	0.0
Melbourne	360,510	3,845	1.1	1,640	0.5
Miami	1,835,520	5,360	0.3	1,247	0.1
Naples	127,170	0	0.0	0	0.0
Ocala	173,831	0	0.0	0	0.0
Orlando	1,084,600	14,800	1.4	2,853	0.3
Panama City	125,093	4,435	3.5	2,420	1.9
Pensacola	329,461	11,278	3.4	8,498	2.6
Punta Gorda	92,999	0	0.0	0	0.0
Sarasota	453,958	0	0.0	0	0.0
Tallahassee	214,321	169	0.1	38	**
Tampa	1,958,530	6,431	0.3	1,230	0.1
West Palm Beach	793,893	19	**	213	**
Other Areas					
Monroe County	73,638	1,795	2.4	675	0.9
Florida	12,000,200	75,713	0.6	33,344	0.3
United States	243,080,000	*1,377,431	0.6	*979,328	0.4

*Excluding those stationed overseas.
**Less than 0.05 percent.
Sources: Active-duty and civilian data from U.S. Department of Defense 1988a; population (except U.S.) from West, Lenze and Tracy 1995; U.S. population from CITIBASE; calculations by the author.

military because they do not include all employment in ancillary activities such as base exchanges. It is important to note that the civilian military jobs typically pay wages higher than the average prevailing in other local industries.

University of Florida   *Bureau of Economic and Business Research*

Table 3. Military Earnings as a Percent of Total Earnings and Total Personal Income 1987
(millions of current dollars)

Area	Military Earnings	Total Earnings	Total Personal Income	Millitary Earnings as Percent of	
				Total Earnings	Total Personal Income
Metropolitan Statistical Areas					
Ft. Walton Beach	322	1,325	1,838	24.3	17.5
Jacksonville	759	10,097	12,987	7.5	5.8
Melbourne	101	3,697	5,501	2.7	1.8
Miami	173	21,951	28,040	0.8	0.6
Orlando	303	12,621	16,452	2.4	1.8
Panama City	106	1,072	1,518	9.9	7.0
Pensacola	338	2,962	4,197	11.4	8.1
Tampa	209	18,501	29,948	1.1	0.7
Other Areas					
Monroe County	67	688	1,236	9.7	5.4
Florida	2,496	119,684	189,558	2.1	1.3
United States	42,094	2,768,360	3,789,392	1.5	1.1

Source: U.S. Department of Commerce 1994 and calculations by the author.

Table 3 displays military earnings as a percentage of total earnings and as a percentage of personal income for the nine areas with major military bases. Although active duty personnel accounted for only 11 percent of Ft. Walton Beach's population, they generated about 25 percent of earnings. In all the metro areas with major military installations, the military's economic importance (share of earnings) is greater than its demographic importance (share of population). This suggests a three-tiered ranking of MSAs: those in which the military is very important, generating at least 7.5 percent of earnings (Ft. Walton Beach, Jacksonville, Panama City and Pensacola); those where it is somewhat important (Melbourne, Miami, Orlando and Tampa), generating between 0.8 and 2.7 percent of earnings; and those where it is negligible, generating less than 0.5 percent. All told, the military paid about $2.5 billion as earnings in 1987.

Table 4. Government Retirement Benefits: Military and Other as a Percent of Total Income 1987
(millions of current dollars)

| | | As a Percent of Income | |
Area	Military Retirement Transfers	Military Retirement Transfers	Other Retirement Transfers
Metropolitan Statistical Areas			
Daytona Beach	56.6	1.1	12.6
Ft. Lauderdale	52.4	0.2	8.1
Ft. Myers	38.7	0.8	11.3
Ft. Pierce	22.8	0.6	10.0
Ft. Walton Beach	130.6	7.1	6.9
Gainesville	18.5	0.8	6.2
Jacksonville	200.6	1.5	6.5
Lakeland	36.9	0.7	9.7
Melbourne	155.1	2.8	9.0
Miami	72.4	0.3	5.7
Naples	14.3	0.5	7.4
Orlando	244.8	1.5	7.0
Ocala	21.3	1.0	13.0
Panama City	58.7	3.9	8.2
Pensacola	152.3	3.6	8.4
Punta Gorda	22.6	1.6	15.7
Sarasota	61.2	0.7	11.4
Tallahassee	24.2	0.9	5.8
Tampa	313.7	1.0	10.3
West Palm Beach	51.2	0.3	7.5
Other Areas			
Monroe County	15.1	1.2	5.9
Florida	1,876.8	1.0	8.5
United States	18,398.0	0.5	7.2

Source: U.S. Department of Commerce 1994 and calculations by the author.

Table 4 presents military retirement pay as a percentage of total personal income by MSA. For Ft. Walton Beach, Panama City, Pensacola and Melbourne, military retirement pay ranges from 2.8

to 7.1 percent of total personal income, the highest shares in the state. In fact, Ft. Walton has the highest share in the nation, except for a rural county in Nevada. (By comparison, for the state as a whole military retirement pay is only 1.0 percent of total personal income and for the U.S. as a whole it is only 0.5 percent). In Ft. Walton, military retirement pay is larger than retirement pay from all other sources including Social Security. The common factor in the four MSAs is the presence of a military base with a commissary and base exchange.

It is important to point out that the MSAs with relatively high concentrations of military retirees are not the same as the MSAs with relatively high concentrations of other retirees. Among MSAs, Punta Gorda, Ocala, Daytona Beach, Sarasota and Ft. Myers have the highest percentages of total personal income from nonmilitary government retirement programs.

Defense contracts. The state's major defense contractors are listed in Table 5. The table lists all Florida firms receiving a prime contract from the Department of Defense of $50 million (current dollars) or more in fiscal years 1985-87. The table also lists the location (MSA) of the contracting firm. (Multiple contracts received by the same firm or by divisions of the firm were not aggregated).

Prime contracts cover everything from construction to base supplies and from research and development to production of air-craft engines. Contracts by MSA are tabulated in Table 6. Orlando received the largest amount by far ($1.7 billion), followed by West Palm Beach ($1.1 billion). Melbourne and Tampa each received more than $500 million.

Table 6 also presents the value of contracts per resident. This helps to indicate the relative importance of prime contracts in some of the smaller MSAs. For instance, although Ft. Walton Beach received only $204 million of contracts (seventh in the state), on a per capita basis its $1,523 ranks third. Panama City, Daytona Beach, Jacksonville and Pensacola all rank higher than Tampa on a per capita basis.

It should be noted that neither Daytona Beach nor West Palm Beach has military bases; the contracting in those metro areas is pri-marily for research and development, services and supplies.

Table 5. Select Recipients of Defense Prime Contracts
Fiscal Years 1985-87

Company	Location (MSA)
Brunswick	Daytona Beach
General Electric	Daytona Beach
Sparton	Daytona Beach
Jacksonville Shipyards	Jacksonville
Grumman	Melbourne
Harris	Melbourne
McDonnell Douglas	Melbourne
Pan Am World Services	Melbourne
Southern Air Transport	Miami
Martin Marietta	Orlando
MDTT	Orlando
E Systems	Tampa
Honeywell	Tampa
Reflectone	Tampa
Sperry	Tampa
United Technologies	West Palm Beach

Source: Based on information in U.S. Department of Defense 1986 and other editions.

A Look Ahead

Progress on the current disarmament has reached an advanced stage; much has already been completed and plans for the remaining cutbacks are under review. The base closure and realignment recommendations released by the Secretary of Defense in March 1995 are the fourth and final phase of a process begun in 1988 and repeated in 1991 and 1993.

Accurate and complete regional data are not available for 1993 and 1994 so a precise statement of how Florida fared cannot yet be made. The data which are available, however, suggest that Florida

Table 6. Total and Per Capita Defense Prime Contracts,
Average of Calendar Years 1985-87
(constant 1987 dollars)

Area	Total (millions of dollars)	Per Capita (dollars per person)
Metropolitan Statistical Areas		
Daytona Beach	243	684
Ft. Lauderdale	114	97
Ft. Myers	3	9
Ft. Pierce	29	134
Ft. Walton Beach	204	1,523
Gainesville	15	85
Jacksonville	283	327
Lakeland	19	50
Melbourne	692	1,920
Miami	153	83
Naples	16	123
Ocala	12	71
Orlando	1,748	1,612
Panama City	93	740
Pensacola	104	314
Punta Gorda	5	57
Sarasota	45	100
Tallahassee	11	52
Tampa	591	302
West Palm Beach	1,095	1,380
Other Areas		
Monroe County	30	404
Florida	5,582	465
United States	135,619	558

Note: Deflated by the implicit price deflator for national defense purchases (excluding compensation).

Sources: Contract data from U.S. Department of Commerce 1986 and later editions; price deflator based on data in U.S. Department of Commerce 1992 as updated in the *Survey of Current Business*; population data from West, Lenze and Tracy 1995; and computations by the author.

University of Florida   *Bureau of Economic and Business Research*

Table 7. Projected Change in Active-Duty and
Civilian Defense Jobs 1987-2000

Area	Active Duty	Civilian
Metropolitan Statistical Areas		
Ft. Walton Beach	3,010	299
Jacksonville	-3,900	1,149
Melbourne	305	156
Miami	-5,360	-1,065
Orlando	-14,800	-2,853
Panama City	1,581	680
Pensacola	5,228	-3,151
Tampa	-1,059	634
Other Areas		
Monroe County	-20	-5
Florida*	-16,359	-4,213
United States	-729,000	-384,000

*Including changes in areas not listed in table.

Sources: Based in part on data in U.S. Department of Defense 1995 and earlier editions.

has fared better than other states. By 1992 only 9,600 active-duty and 2,400 civilian positions had been lost.

Ultimately, the Department of Defense will probably reduce its presence in Florida by 19 percent (16,000 military and 4,000 civilians). This is much less than the 34 percent cutback occurring nationally. Major reductions will occur at Homestead AFB, MacDill AFB, Naval Air Station Cecil Field, Naval Aviation Depot Pensacola, Naval Hospital Orlando and Naval Training Center Orlando. Major gains will occur at Naval Air Station Pensacola, Naval Aviation Depot Jacksonville and Naval Station Mayport.

The net effect of the gains and losses is summarized in Table 7. Ft. Walton Beach, Melbourne, Panama City and Pensacola MSAs will gain active duty personnel while Jacksonville, Miami, Orlando and Tampa MSAs will lose. Ft. Walton Beach, Jacksonville, Melbourne, Panama City and Tampa MSAs will gain civilian personnel, while Miami, Orlando and Pensacola MSAs will lose.

Orlando's losses are the greatest among MSAs: almost 15,000 active-duty personnel and 3,000 civilians. Although Jacksonville will see a net decline in total defense personnel (military plus civilian), it will nevertheless have the greatest number of personnel (about 43,500) of all MSAs in the year 2000.

After the proposed cutbacks take effect, the military will no longer have a major presence in the Orlando and Miami MSAs; the bulk of the remaining jobs will be part-time reserve and guard positions. It is fairly certain that these MSAs will lose their attractiveness to military retirees. The loss is perhaps less important for Miami; its retiree population had been declining for many years prior to the announcement of the closure of Homestead AFB.

Not surprisingly, the cutbacks in the armed forces have increased military retirement nationwide. The pool of retirees nationwide was growing at a 1.1 percent annual rate (about 15,000 persons per year) in 1987. By 1992 it was growing at a 2.1 percent rate. Florida's growth rate has not increased so much but that is partly because these retirees tend to be relatively young with many years of potential labor force participation ahead of them.

In contrast to the centralized planning behind the geographic distribution of cutbacks in military and civilian defense personnel, the geographic distribution of cutbacks in defense contracting will be accomplished through the decentralized decisions of thousands of independent firms. There is therefore less certainty about their ultimate magnitude. However, it does seem reasonable to expect Florida to continue to expand its share of national contracts (Lenze 1995).

The experience in Florida so far (through calendar year 1992) is quite varied regionally (Table 8). Contracting peaked as early as 1982 in West Palm Beach and 1983 in Daytona Beach but not until 1985 for the nation and 1986 for Florida. Surprisingly, contracting was still rising in 1992 in the Melbourne and Miami MSAs.

From their 1986 peak, Florida's prime contracts had fallen 25.5 percent by 1989. Since then, contracting has actually increased 12 percent. Contracting also troughed in 1989 in Daytona Beach, Panama City and West Palm Beach. In Ft. Walton Beach, Jacksonville,

Table 8. Size and Timing of the Current Disarmament
Real Prime Contracts by MSA and County
(calendar-year data)

Area	Percent Change	Peak-Trough
Metropolitan Statistical Areas		
Daytona Beach	-61.4	1983-89
Ft. Walton Beach	-22.3	1991-92
Jacksonville	-27.6	1987-92
Melbourne	*	*
Miami	*	*
Orlando	-54.2	1987-92
Panama City	-39.6	1986-89
Pensacola	-9.7	1991-92
Tampa	-23.8	1990-92
West Palm Beach	-59.3	1982-89
Other Areas		
Monroe County	-44.8	1986-89
Florida	-25.5	1986-89
United States	-27.4	1985-92

*Peak not reached yet.

Note: Deflated by the implicit price deflator for national defense purchases (excluding compensation).

Sources: Contract data from various editions of U.S. Department of Commerce (1986) and U.S. Department of Defense (1986); price deflator based on data in U.S. Department of Commerce (1992) as updated in the *Survey of Current Business*; calculations by the author.

Orlando, Pensacola and Tampa, contracting set new lows for the current defense cycle in 1992.

Cutbacks in defense contracting will have the most noticeable impact on manufacturing jobs (Henry and Oliver 1987, p. 8). Table 9 presents the current forecast of manufacturing employment for the regions of the state with relatively large amounts of military prime contracts. It incorporates not only the defense cutbacks but also the effects of compensating growth and trends in other factors affecting manufacturing. (Other important determinants of manufacturing

Table 9. Manufacturing Employment in 1987 and
Projected 2000 by MSA and County

Area	1987	2000	Percent Change
Metropolitan Statistical Areas			
Daytona Beach	13,003	11,248	-13.5
Ft. Walton Beach	5,200	3,629	-30.2
Jacksonville	38,167	34,128	-10.6
Melbourne	28,150	26,984	-4.1
Miami	94,017	74,033	-21.3
Orlando	59,830	50,149	-16.2
Panama City	3,400	2,876	-15.4
Pensacola	11,450	11,006	-3.9
Tampa	92,783	89,466	-3.6
West Palm Beach	35,725	31,203	-12.7
Other Areas			
Monroe County	596	532	-10.7
Florida	530,967	485,622	-8.5
United States	18,999,000	18,227,000	-4.1

Source: West, Lenze and Tracy 1995; unpublished data from the U.S. Bureau of Labor Statistics; and calculations by the author.

employment include productivity growth, population change and housing starts.)

Ft. Walton Beach is the hardest hit percentagewise (30.2 percent decline). Miami declines 21.3 percent, Orlando 16.2 percent and Panama City 15.4 percent. Statewide about 45,000 manufacturing jobs (8.5 percent) are lost between 1987 and 2000.

As in previous disarmaments, the effect of defense cutbacks on aggregate regional economic indicators has been relatively mild in Florida. The recovery from the 1990-91 recession was probably slowed by the cutbacks but no MSA appears to have suffered population loss (aside from those who left Dade County after Hurricane Andrew). Only in the recessionary year 1991 were other sources of growth insufficient to keep the number of nonfarm jobs increasing in the MSAs identified as being relatively dependent on defense.

If history is any guide, at some point the U.S. will probably embark on another cycle of military buildup and disarmament. As international relations continue to evolve in the post-Cold War world, additional geographic reallocations of defense resources may also become desirable. In the past, economic impact studies of new bases and defense contracts have focused solely on the building and operation of the base or contractor's facility, disregarding its eventual abandonment. It should be clear from this paper that assuming an infinite lifetime for military spending in a particular geographic locale is untenable.

References

Bolton, Roger E. 1966. "Defense spending: Burden or prop?" in Roger E. Bolton, ed., *Defense and disarmament: The economics of transition*, pp. 1-53. Englewood Cliffs, New Jersey: Prentice-Hall.

CITIBASE: Citibank economic database, machine-readable magnetic data file 1946-present. New York: Citibank, N.A.

Henry, David K., and Richard P. Oliver. 1987. "The defense buildup, 1977-85: effects on production and employment." *Monthly Labor Review* (August), pp. 3-11.

Lenze, David G. 1995. "Military contract expenditures rose in Florida 1989-93." *Economic Leaflets* Vol. 54 No. 3. Gainesville: University of Florida, Bureau of Economic and Business Research.

Probyn, Christopher. 1994. "The long-term outlook." *Review of the U.S. Economy* (November), pp. 26-45. Lexington, Massachusetts: DRI/McGraw-Hill.

U.S. Congress, Office of Technology Assessment. 1992. *After the Cold War: Living with lower defense spending.* Washington, D.C.: U.S. Government Printing Office.

U.S. Department of Commerce, Economics and Statistics Administration, Bureau of the Census. 1986. *Consolidated Federal Funds Report, Volume 1: County Areas.* Washington, D.C.: U.S. Government Printing Office.

_____ Economics and Statistics Administration, Bureau of Economic Analysis. 1992. *National Income and Product Accounts of the United States, Volume 2, 1959-88.* Washington, D.C.: U.S. Government Printing Office.

_____ Economics and Statistics Administration, Bureau of Economic Analysis, Regional Economic Measurement Division. 1994. *Regional Economic Information System.* (CD ROM)

U.S. Department of Defense. 1986. *Prime Contracts by State, City, Contractor.*

_____ Washington Headquarters Services, Directorate for Information, Operations, and Reports. 1988a. *Distribution of Personnel by State and by Selected Locations, September 30, 1987.*

_____ 1988b. *Selected Manpower Statistics, Fiscal Year 1987.*

_____ 1991. *Worldwide List of Military Installations (Major, Minor & Support).*

_____ 1995. *Base Closure and Realignment Report.*

West, Carol T., David G. Lenze and Tony L. Tracy. 1995. *The Florida Long-Term Economic Forecast, Volume 1: State and Metropolitan Statistical Areas.* Gainesville: University of Florida, Bureau of Economic and Business Research.

The Health Industry

13

Gary M. Fournier
Professor of Economics
Florida State University
and
Ellen F. R. Fournier
Legislative Analyst
Florida Senate
Tallahassee, Florida

Health care expenditures in the United States have been rising rapidly and now account for about 14 percent of Gross Domestic Product (GDP). In Florida, about 13 percent of Gross State Product is spent on health care, compared to 8.9 percent in 1980. While Florida is the fourth-largest state, it ranks nineteenth among states in personal health care costs per capita, reflecting both lower average costs of services and lower levels of health care consumption by Floridians.

Supply-Side Developments

The health care industry is made up of diverse enterprises including hospitals, both acute care and long term; private-practice physicians; various medical treatment and health care facilities; home health care services; pharmacists and other health care specialists. The industry has undergone significant changes in recent years in response to the introduction of new technologies, changes in Florida's demographics and attempts by health service payers to control costs. Several new types of health care institutions have flourished, including Health Maintenance Organizations (HMOs) and Preferred Provider Organizations (PPOs). Hospitals and physicians have been

forced to adapt to constraints placed on their behavior by governments and insurance companies. This section surveys some important developments in the supply of health care in Florida.

Hospitals. Relative to other states, the ownership of Florida's
hospitals and institutions is more highly represented by for-profits.
About 35 percent of the acute-care beds in the state are in investor-
owned hospitals, compared to 10.8 percent nationally (Florida Hospital Association 1993).[1] Hospitals have been adjusting to new circumstances in recent years. The occupancy rate in the state has been
declining for some years; after reaching a high of 74 percent in 1982
it stood at 53 percent in 1993. Beginning with the implementation of
a prospective payment system for inpatient services under Medicare
in 1983, pressure from federal and state regulators and insurance
companies to achieve cost controls on health care has tended to exacerbate the problem of low occupancy by encouraging hospitals and
physicians to reduce hospital admissions and inpatient lengths of stay.
Moreover, it is well-known that the prospective payment system fos-
ters the substitution of outpatient services. Despite these pressures
and the financial difficulties of rural hospitals, hospital closures were
not a significant problem in the last five years.

Two trends in Florida's hospital industry should be pointed out.
First, the expansion of multihospital systems, both geographically
and across lines of business, raises interesting questions about future
consolidations in the industry. Second, the extension of specialized
medical treatment and health service facilities into activities that were
formerly the domain of community hospitals continues to shape the
way health care services are delivered.

Multihospital Systems. Two companies exemplify the changing
marketplace for health care today: Humana Inc. and Columbia/HCA
Healthcare Corporation. Until March 1993, Humana Inc. owned the
second-largest multihospital system in Florida, including seventeen
hospitals with 3,914 licensed beds throughout the state. Its managed-
care operations included about 1.7 million members nationwide.
Constrained in their ability to attract managed-care patients and their
physicians, while at the same time having financial interests in hos-

---

[1]Cowart and Serow (Table 11.1, p. 194) find this is true not only for hospitals
but also for nursing homes, home health agencies and hospices.

pitals, the management of Humana left the acute-care hospital market. As a result of its nationwide reorganization, Humana no longer owns hospitals and concentrates exclusively on its managed-care services. Those services include HMOs and PPOs, with memberships totaling about 1.6 million in 1994.

Following the acquisition of Humana's former hospital group by Columbia Healthcare, and the merger of Columbia with HCA, the largest consolidation in the industry's history was completed in the spring of 1995 with Columbia/HCA's acquisition of Healthtrust, Inc. Columbia/HCA now operates 320 hospitals and, following its acquisition of Medical Care America (MCA), 125 outpatient centers in thirty-six states and Europe. Some restructuring of its hospitals has occurred in Florida. For example, Victoria Hospital was consolidated into Cedars Medical Center in Miami. Subsequently, Cedars Medical Center was consolidated and now provides laboratory services for other hospitals in the area. These moves are expected to yield benefits from the renegotiation of supply contracts as a group, information sharing, integration and coordination of information systems, as well as cost savings in obtaining financial capital. In addition, by achieving a more complete geographic coverage of the state, the firm hopes to become more attractive to managed-care companies. The company has also entered into joint-venture agreements with large nonprofit hospitals in Jacksonville and Orlando.

A trend being aggressively pursued by Columbia/HCA is the development of comprehensive integrated health care delivery networks in key localities. In the Orlando area the company owns three hospitals and operates a joint venture with Winter Park Memorial, as well as numerous ambulatory surgery centers, psychiatric and home health service operations. This co-ownership of facilities in the local market reduces the duplication of services and technology and makes it easier for the various units to share information and other services.

Proliferation of Special-Service Facilities. The Florida health industry is being transformed by supply-side developments that include a proliferation of new service-delivery enterprises that were largely unknown fifteen years ago. Table 1 charts some examples of these institutions. Small-scale treatment facilities are cost-effective for many

Table 1. Growth in Selected Treatment and Health Service Facilities in Florida 1987 and 1992-93

	1987	1992-93	Percent Change
Adult Congregate-Living Facilities	1,362	1,666	22
Number of Beds	52,059	60,338	16
Ambulatory Surgical Centers	42	146	248
Birthing Centers	22	22	0
Clinical Laboratories	823	856	4
Dialysis (ESRD) Centers	95	164	73
Home Health Agencies (Certified and Not Certified)	457	1,316	188
Hospices	30	37	23
Nursing Homes	481	603	25
Number of Beds	55,388	69,439	25

Source: *Florida Health Care Atlas*, various years.

health services and their popularity with patients and payers provide growth potential for the next several years.

Managed Care. "Managed care" describes various arrangements for providing health care that attempt to control costs by managing the utilization of services. Two types of arrangements are HMOs and PPOs. These are risk-pooling enterprises that act as intermediaries between consumers, employers and health care providers, and both have enjoyed significant growth in recent years in Florida and nationally.

HMOs offer a stated range of health services at a predetermined price to persons enrolled in the plan. HMO members have access to all services included as part of their contract with limited out-of-pocket expenses for copayments and drugs. Members must use physicians and other service providers who are affiliated with the HMO and all referrals are authorized through their primary-care physicians.

Table 2. Growth of Health Maintenance Organizations
(total enrollment)

Year	Florida	U.S.
1985	519,873	21,051,657
1986	768,571	25,777,130
1987	1,010,605	29,286,020
1988	1,144,776	31,940,494
1989	1,232,065	33,092,954
1990	1,319,655	34,071,646
1991	1,547,139	35,051,645
1992	1,661,215	36,149,313
1994	*2,400,000	

*Estimate.

Source: Florida Hospital Association 1993, from Interstudy, Inc., data.

HMOs combine the financing and administration of health care plans with cost-control features achieved by direct provision of primary-care facilities and by contracting with selected providers.

In 1994, over 16 percent of Florida's population belonged to an HMO according to the Florida Department of Insurance. The thirty-four organizations had a membership of almost 2.2 million. Table 2 shows HMO enrollment for Florida and the U.S. since 1983. Currently, enrollments are growing at an annual rate of about 20 percent. News reports this year have called attention to the high profitability of HMOs.

HMOs have become a source of health care for Medicaid and Medicare recipients. In 1995, fifteen commercial HMOs and ten exclusively Medicaid HMOs had 433,173 Medicaid recipient members. The Florida Agency for Health Care Administration also reports that HMOs enrolled 203,415 Medicare recipients in the state.

HMOs are paid a fixed amount per enrollee per month regardless of the services used, plus small copayments for certain services. Profitability hinges on their success in limiting the use of services by enrollees while meeting their contractual requirement to provide a high quality of health care. HMOs have been promoted as a way to lower the cost of health care because of this incentive system. In general, research supports this concept and shows that HMOs can reduce costs by 10 to 40 percent compared to fee-for-service indemnity plans.[2] These cost savings appear to be the result of lower rates of hospitalization.

PPOs are contractual arrangements under which a group of health care providers agrees to deliver care on a fee-for-service basis to a defined group of patients at an agreed-upon schedule of charges. PPOs are similar to traditional health insurance plans in that the cost of covered services is paid by the plan after the services have been provided. They differ, however, in two ways: the insurer negotiates payment rates with providers *ex ante*, and providers are subject to strong controls over the use of services. On this last point, the few studies that have been done suggest that PPOs have not been entirely successful in containing costs.[3]

A PPO encourages its members to choose physicians and other service providers from a "preferred" list by setting reduced copayments or deductibles. Plan members may consult with physicians who are not on the list but must pay more in copayments or deductibles.

PPOs were established in the 1980s and have grown rapidly. They are attractive to health care consumers who want more freedom to choose doctors than an HMO will typically allow. PPOs are not licensed or regulated by the state and have no reporting requirements. Consequently, accurate data on enrollments and the growth of these organizations are not readily available. According to one source.[4] however, there were seventy-eight PPOs in Florida in 1994 and PPO enrollment in 1993 was estimated to be 3,039,137.

Workforce Developments. In the 1980s, health planners voiced concerns about the adequacy of health care practitioners in Florida and it has been perceived by some that shortages of certain occupations, especially nurses, are a serious perennial problem. While temporary shortages have been observed in some years, these fears have proven to be largely unfounded, as the supply of health care special-

---

[2]For example, Freeborn and Pope provide a comprehensive survey of the available research on HMOs.

[3]For example, Freeborn and Pope.

[4]American Managed Care and Review Association.

Table 3. Employment Growth in Selected Health
Occupations in Florida 1987-1993
(active, licensed practitioners)

	1987	1993	Percent Change
Medical Doctors	18,213	28,539	56.7
Osteopathic Physicians	1,180	1,962	66.27
Chiropractic Physicians	2,403	3,002	24.93
Podiatric Physicians	635	886	39.53
Physician's Assistants	505	1,146	126.93
Registered Nurses	85,784	119,982	39.87
LPNs	33,349	42,906	28.66
Dentists	6,193	7,558	22.04
Dental Hygienists	4,276	5,791	35.43
Emergency Medical Technicians	12,196	18,501	51.7
Paramedics	4,679	7,799	66.68
Occupational Therapists	3,406	2,797	-17.88
Physical Therapists	1,265	6,609	422.45
Respiratory Therapists	2,371	1,187	-49.94
Pharmacists	10,770	8,306	-22.88
Radiologic Technicians	11,487	15,136	31.77
Psychologists	1,470	2,248	52.93
Optometrists	1,153	1,396	21.08

Source: *Florida Health Care Atlas*, compiled from the Florida Department of Professional Regulation.

ists is responsive. Table 3 shows the number of active practitioners for the years 1987 and 1993. Scholars researching the nature of the nursing shortage have discovered that institutions can usually cure the problem with appropriate adjustments in wages and other benefits (Cowart and Serow, Chapter 11). Table 4 shows the estimated average wages for three consecutive periods for Florida health workers in selected occupations that are adequately represented in the Census Bureau's *Current Population Survey*. Real wages have not risen to a great extent over these years but in certain categories there is some improvement, especially where alleged shortages have been reported in the early period--for registered nurses and licensed practical nurses.

Table 4. Average Weekly Earnings and Hourly Wages
for Selected Health Occupations
(in real 1994 dollars)

Occupation*	1986 - 1988		1989 - 1991		1992 - 1994	
	Earnings†	Wage††	Earnings	Wage	Earnings	Wage
EXECUTIVE ADMINISTRATIVE						
AND MANAGERIAL	738	16.90	709	16.10	707	15.90
Managers, Medicine and Health	708	15.98	735	16.96	673	15.44
PROFESSIONAL SPECIALTY						
OCCUPATIONS	691	16.98	665	16.39	673	16.83
Registered Nurses	609	16.09	659	17.55	659	17.49
Pharmacists	821	20.56	879	22.26	973	23.72
Dietitians	446	11.88	527	12.48	455	11.76
Respiratory Therapists	625	14.61	711	16.48	506	12.77
Physical Therapists	646	15.76	460	13.37	759	20.46
TECHNICIANS AND RELATED						
SUPPORT OCCUPATIONS	542	13.88	547	13.8	532	13.45
Clinical Laboratory Technologists						
and Technicians	504	12.92	502	12.92	535	13.43
Dental Hygienists	526	15.88	504	15.83	505	17.39
Radiologic Technicians	449	12.16	512	12.33	521	13.31
Licensed Practical Nurses	390	10.27	420	11.03	470	12.66
Health Technologists and Technicians,						
not elsewhere classified	388	11.19	417	10.69	424	10.25
SERVICE, EXCEPT PRIVATE						
HOUSEHOLD, AND PROTECTIVE	248	7.05	256	7.23	249	7.23
Dental Assistants	264	7.95	340	9.32	311	9.17
Health Aides, except Nursing	279	7.55	292	8.01	277	7.31
Nursing Aides, Orderlies and Attendants	270	7.28	316	8.36	271	8.06

*Categories shown in all-capital letters measure, for comparison purposes, earnings and wages in similar occupation categories throughout Florida industries.

†Estimated average weekly earnings.

††Estimated average hourly wage.

Source: Hirsch and Macpherson 1995, computations from the Census Bureau's *Current Population Survey.*

Demand for Health Care

The demand for health care is overwhelmingly influenced by third-party payment arrangements, where private or government insurance plans pay for the services being consumed. Inherent in the

Table 5. Growth in Health Care Expenditures
(billions of dollars)

	1980	1991	Percent Change
Total Expenditures, Florida	8.6	32.5	278
Expenditures Per Capita, Florida	962.0	2,427.0	152
Percent of Gross State Product	8.9	13.0	
Expenditures Per Capita, United States	1,087.0	2,896.0	166

Source: *Florida Health Care Atlas 1993*, Florida Agency for Health Care Administration.

shifting of costs to third parties is the tendency of consumers and their physicians to choose excessive levels of health care, a problem known as "moral hazard," because they do not shoulder the full burden of the costs. Among the most important issues facing Florida and the rest of the nation regarding the demand for health care are the large number of people lacking health insurance and the rising cost of Medicaid and Medicare. Florida, which ranks highest among states in numbers of elderly in the population, is obviously affected by these programs. For example, some hospitals get more than 50 percent of their revenues from Medicare, and nursing home care is the second largest component of Medicaid spending in the state. This section looks at several of these issues.

Health Care Costs and Health Insurance. Since 1980, the cost of health care services has grown twice as fast as the general price level.[5] The growth of health care expenditures has been much reported in the media. Table 5 gives a thumbnail sketch.

The cost of health insurance has risen even faster than the medical Consumer Price Index. For example, state employees' health in-

---

[5]As measured by the medical Consumer Price Index, costs grew by 118 percent from 1980 to 1990 while the general Consumer Price Index grew only 59 percent during this period.

Table 6. Insurance Coverage of Workers in Florida

Firm Size (number of employees)	Percent Not Offering Health Insurance
1 - 4	66.4
5 - 9	41.0
10 - 24	30.1
25 - 50	15.8
Over 50	6.5
All Firms	45.1

Source: Florida Agency for Health Care Administration 1993, from a study by RAND Corporation.

surance premiums for family coverage were $840 per year in 1980 and $3,212 per year in 1990, an increase of 282 percent. Because of its cost, many Florida employers do not offer health insurance to their employees and many others offer insurance only for employees, not their families. This practice has contributed to a burgeoning population of uninsured Floridians, persons who do not qualify for Medicaid or Medicare but cannot afford commercial insurance. The average premium for conventional employer-sponsored health insurance is almost $5,000 per year for family coverage, and individual policies are even costlier.

Two-and-a-half million Floridians were uninsured in 1994 and 75 percent of them are employed or dependents of employed persons. Uninsurance is most prevalent among males, people with incomes below $25,000 and those aged 18-39. In 1993, 45.1 percent of all businesses in Florida did not offer health insurance. These firms employ 16 percent of the workforce. Table 6 shows that small businesses are least likely to offer insurance. Uninsured persons with serious health problems often are treated in hospital emergency rooms, which by law may not turn them away. If they are unable to pay their bill, the cost of their treatment is shifted to other patients and their insurance carriers, driving up the cost of health insurance further.

Medicaid. Medicaid is a federal program that pays for health care services for certain defined categories of persons. Federal money accounts for about 55 percent of the funding; the rest is from state

Table 7. Growth in the Medicaid Program in Florida
1986-87 through 1995-96

	1986-87	1995-96	Percent Growth
Total Expenditures ($ millions)	1,212.4	6,932.9	472
Caseload	547,432	1,612,294	195
1986-87 Base Caseload	547,432	1,238,691	126
Percent of Population Eligible	4.6	11.3	145
Average Cost Per Case (dollars)	2,215.0	3,853.0	94

Source: Calculated by the authors from Florida Social Services Estimating Conference data.

sources. Eligible groups include families and children, and the aged, blind or permanently disabled. Within these groups there are several categories of eligibility for Medicaid, based on household income and asset level. Thousands of persons who would qualify on the basis of income or assets, however, are not eligible because they are not members of the two eligible groups.

Medicaid was created thirty-two years ago. It remained relatively small until the 1980s, when it began to show significant growth due to rising service costs, increasing categories of eligibility and large increases in the eligible population. As indicated in Table 7, Florida Medicaid spending grew an average of slightly over 20 percent a year over the whole period. This growth rate has slowed since 1994.

Medicaid benefits are directed by the program's eligibility requirements primarily toward the young and old. It provides health insurance for one in every four Florida children and pays for 43 of every 100 live births. Pregnant women and children have been targeted by expansion of Medicaid benefits, increasing the income cutoff for eligibility. Elderly people receive benefits from both Medicare and Medicaid but only Medicaid pays for long-term nursing home care, which is the second-largest single component of Medicaid spending in the state.

Because the federal government requires state matching funds for Medicaid, states have some discretion about the services for which they will pay. Coverage of certain services and categories of people is mandated for participation in the program, but states may provide more than this mandated level and receive matching funds. Florida has chosen to provide little beyond the mandatory coverage and ranks forty-third in spending per Medicaid recipient. If the Medicaid program is converted to a fixed-growth block grant, Florida will be doubly penalized because it receives a low level of federal dollars per case and because its eligible population is growing far faster than the eligible population nationwide.

Florida has begun to move to managed care for Medicaid recipients through the MediPass program and prepaid health plans, including HMOs. Payments to prepaid health plans for Medicaid recipients grew from $106.2 million in 1990-91 to $875.6 million in 1995-96 (estimated). The AHCA has been directed by the Legislature to work toward requiring all Medicaid recipients to be covered by a managed-care program, either a prepaid health plan or MediPass.

In the MediPass program, each Medicaid recipient is assigned a primary-care physician who serves as a case manager, providing primary care and making referrals for other care. Recipients may not consult other doctors without going through their primary physician, who receives a monthly payment for case management in addition to reimbursement for medical services.

Policy Developments

This section will explore more details about key policy developments. First, we want to look at the antitrust (competitive) effects of multihospital-system mergers and joint ventures in the context of recent changes like Columbia/HCA and the FTC Guidelines. Then we will discuss the statutory reforms affecting Florida's health care system.

The Role of Competition and Antitrust. Competition among health care providers is viewed to some degree ambiguously because of the industry's unique institutional context and the complex nature of interaction among decisionmakers.[6] Nevertheless, it is widely accepted that competition can be helpful in improving efficiency in health care provision, as well as price and quality conditions for con-

---

[6]The economics literature lacks a full consensus on the nature of competition among hospitals and other health services facilities, e.g., Dranove and White.

sumers and insurers. The merger trend underway in the past few years suggests that companies perceive enormous private benefits from diverse forms of consolidation and integration. Recently, the federal enforcement agencies issued detailed guidelines concerning health care mergers.[7] These guidelines act to signal the business community about the circumstances that might trigger an antitrust investigation or injunction. In substance, these guidelines embody an important evolution in antitrust law, suggesting that the federal authorities are more cognizant of the benefits of integration than ever before. At the same time, the complex types of business arrangements that are unique to this industry require special attention to prevent the abuses associated with market power.[8]

The approach known as "managed competition" introduces limited government intervention to promote and protect access to health care through the establishment of purchasing alliances of employers. In Florida, the model being adopted involves voluntary participation of employers around the state. The countervailing power of the health alliances in bargaining for services is intended to generate better terms for consumers in local communities. The negotiations between purchasing alliances can aid in reducing costs and designing health plan features that are more responsive to the preferences of participants, as well as facilitate in the dissemination of information needed for making sound decisions about health care.

Health Care Reform. Congress in 1993 debated, but rejected, an attempt at dramatic reforms for health care proposed by the Clinton administration. While such moves are likely to be held in abeyance for some years, there are substantial developments at the federal level

---

[7]These guidelines were issued jointly by the U.S. Department of Justice and the Federal Trade Commission--"Statement of Enforcement Policy and Analytical Principles Relating to Health Care and Antitrust," September 27, 1994.

[8]A related development in the industry is the growth of joint ventures between physicians and health care facilities. In the last few years, physicians have been much more strictly regulated than previously to prevent abuses. Provisions of Section 1877 of the Social Security Act were amended by the "Stark Bill" to restrict the scope of physician self-referrals. Also, the Medicare and Medicaid Patient and Program Protection Act of 1987 regulates certain business practices, as does the Antifraud Amendments under Section 1128B(b) of the Social Security Act. These developments are discussed in Grosfield 1995.

that will affect the health care sector of Florida's economy. Federal proposals to limit the growth of spending for the Medicare or Medicaid programs would have a significant impact on participants, as well as on health provider companies that rely upon Medicare and Medicaid beneficiaries.

State programs and policies that deal with health care issues have been dominated by the rapidly rising cost of and demand for health care services. As noted above, Medicaid spending grew faster than any other major category of state spending in the past five years, becoming the single largest component of the state budget. The large number of working people without health insurance prompted health care reforms, which were enacted to improve access to health insurance for small businesses.

Agency for Health Care Administration. In 1992, the Legislature created the Agency for Health Care Administration (AHCA), combining the functions of the Health Care Cost Containment Board and the certificate of need and health facilities regulation functions of the Department of Health and Rehabilitative Services (HRS). The Division of Medical Quality Assurance and its health-related boards were later transferred to the agency July 1, 1994. Supervision of Medicaid and state employees' health insurance was transferred to the agency July 1, 1993.

The AHCA was created to reduce fragmentation in the administration of Florida's health care system and to improve the coordination of health care policy development and regulation. Several health-related entities and functions were brought together to initiate health care reforms intended to improve the distribution of health care in Florida, making it available to more people and controlling costs.

Insurance Reforms. The Health Care and Insurance Reform Act of 1993 (HCIRA) implements changes that would bring about these ends by addressing a wide range of health-related issues. Its most important feature is the establishment of managed competition in the market for small-group health insurance. Covering each of the eleven HRS districts in the state, the act creates eleven "community health purchasing alliances" (CHPAs) to assist small employers in obtaining health insurance. CHPAs are nonprofit, private corporations that serve as intermediaries to facilitate the provision of affordable health insurance plans. Newly formed CHPAs pool together groups of purchasers, such as small businesses, to obtain better rates from health care providers. The AHCA certifies and supervises these alliances and collects data about them. HCIRA also makes changes in health insurance regulations, the Medicaid reimbursement system, rural health policies and the development and use of practice parameters.

It was recognized when this legislation was being drafted that managed competition would have little effect unless certain practices in the insurance industry were changed. In 1991 and 1992 various insurance reforms had been enacted and the 1993 legislation carries these further. It requires insurers and HMOs that issue policies to small employers to offer all plans, not just the "basic" and "standard" plans, on a "guarantee issue" basis. Insurers must apply a modified community rating standard to the policies, based on age, gender, family composition, tobacco usage and location; rates may not be based on health status or claims experience. Finally, the definition of "small employer" is increased from 3-24 eligible employees to 1-50 eligible employees.

Medicaid reforms included in the 1993 act raise the copayment for hospital outpatient and physician services from $1 to $2 per visit, with exceptions for children, pregnant women and institutionalized persons. The AHCA is directed to adopt a new fee schedule for physician services, shifting emphasis toward primary care and away from specialities. MediPass, Medicaid's case management program, is now expanded to include all districts in the state.

Rural Health Initiatives in the 1993 act provides incentives for health care professionals to serve in rural areas and establishes the Rural Health Network Program to promote coordinated delivery of health care services in these areas. It also provides financial assistance for rural hospitals that care for large numbers of Medicaid and indigent patients.

The 1993 act creates two programs to provide low-cost insurance for Floridians with incomes below 250 percent of the poverty level. First, MedAccess is a state health insurance program for persons whose incomes are less than 250 percent of the poverty level and who have not had health insurance for at least one year. Premiums are paid by insured individuals or their employers; there are no state or federal subsidies. Health care providers are compensated at Medicaid reimbursement rates and benefits are limited, emphasizing primary care and prevention. Second, the act directs the agency to seek federal authorization to establish a Medicaid "buy-in" program for low-income persons. This program would tie Medicaid eligibility solely to income instead of providing benefits to specific categories of persons.[9]

Health Care Cost Containment Policies. Some policy changes attempt to improve the cost controls on hospitals and other health care providers.[10] Tort reforms aimed at malpractice litigation are another way policies have addressed the inflation in health care costs. In the mid-1980s, there was a substantial increase in the number and size of malpractice claims, leading to a rapid escalation in insurance premiums and the threat of exit by insurance carriers in selected specialties and areas. In many states, a popular approach to cost containment in malpractice is the use of physician practice parameters. This approach sets guidelines for physicians so that in the event a malpractice claim is filed, clearer standards exist in adjudication and physicians may have an affirmative defense.

In the Health Care Reform Act of 1992, the Legislature approved the development of practice parameters by AHCA in conjunction with professional medical organizations. A demonstration project was authorized to examine the effect of practice parameters on the cost of medical care and professional liability insurance. The 1993 act goes beyond this stage by requiring practice parameters to focus on cost effectiveness as well as the quality of medical care. It directs acute-care hospitals to provide patient outcomes data to AHCA, which will provide a data base for evaluating practice parameters.

---

[9]Neither MedAccess nor the Medicaid buy-in program has been implemented. Federal authorization for the buy-in has been approved but the Legislature has not passed laws needed to implement these health care reforms, despite repeated calls from the governor to do so, including a special legislative session in 1994.

[10]Florida law incorporates "rate regulation," to the extent that a hospital may increase its gross and net revenues per admission by no more than 2 percent plus an adjustment for increases in costs of its purchased goods and services.

A Look Ahead

Further amendments to this string of reforms may well be adopted in the coming years. It remains to be seen whether the newly reorganized AHCA will have any substantive benefits in terms of regulatory effectiveness or simply become yet another cosmetic attempt at "reinventing government." In addition, the insurance reforms to expand access to health care are welcome but are not likely to have a substantial impact. Even if every small business could purchase health insurance at rates comparable to large purchasers like the State of Florida, many would still be unable to meet the expense. As a workforce issue in small enterprises, to the extent they succeed, these reforms will improve working conditions in the state and contribute favorably to the business climate.

Florida's health care industry has shown itself to be very responsive to changes in the market conditions, producing new forms of health care organizations and delivery systems. Severe problems remain, however, in the distribution of health care services, with a significant portion of the population lacking access to timely, adequate service. If proposed changes in federal funding are implemented, Florida will face a growing population of underserved children, working aged and elderly persons.

References

Cowart, Marie E., and William J. Serow. 1992. *Nurses in the Workplace*. Newbury Park, California: Sage Publications.

Dranove, Dave, and William D. White. 1994. "Recent Theory and Evidence on Competition in Hospital Markets." *Journal of Economics and Management Strategy* 3:1 (Spring), pp. 169-209.

Florida Agency for Health Care Administration. 1987-93. *Florida Health Care Atlas*. Tallahassee: State Center for Health Statistics, AHCA.

_____. 1993. *The Florida Health Security Plan*. Tallahassee: AHCA.

Florida Hospital Association. 1993. *Environmental Assessment and Hospital Fact Book 1993*.

Freeborn, Donald K., and Clyde R. Pope. 1994. *Promise and Performance in Managed Care.* Baltimore: Johns Hopkins University Press.

Grosfield, Alice G., ed. 1995. *Health Law Handbook: 1995 Edition.* New York: Clark, Boardman and Callaghan.

Hirsch, Barry T., and David A. Macpherson. 1995. *Union Membership and Earnings Data Book 1994.* Washington, D.C.: Bureau of National Affairs, Inc.

Tourism 14

David R. Williams
President, Florida
Economics Consulting
Group, Inc.
Miami, Florida

Tourism is a major contributor to Florida's economy, with approximately forty million domestic and international tourists visiting the state in 1994 (see Table 1). These visitors spend money, create jobs in industries that serve them and pay state taxes while vacationing here. Since 1980 the total number of tourists visiting Florida has doubled from twenty million to forty million. Tourism accounts for one in eight nonagricultural jobs in Florida (see Table 5).

Factors in the Importance of Florida as a Tourist State

Florida is such a popular vacation state because of its climate, geographical location and natural resources. Its warm temperate climate is an obvious attraction, together with approximately 8,000 miles of shoreline, second only to Alaska. Activities related to the beach and water are virtually innumerable and the state also has numerous state parks for tourists to enjoy. The state has capitalized on its natural resources that attract visitors to also become the premier state in offering attractions and theme parks. Florida is also the

The author would like to thank H. Frank Williams of the Division of Economic and Demographic Research, Florida Legislature, for his invaluable assistance and also the staff of the Florida Department of Commerce, in particular Chip Coggins, for their research help in writing this chapter.

Table 1. Domestic and International Tourist
Visitors to Florida 1980-2000
(in millions)

Year	Total	Air Visitors	Auto Visitors
1980	20.0	9.3	10.7
1981	21.2	10.4	10.8
1982	23.0	11.1	11.9
1983	23.6	10.3	13.3
1984	27.3	12.7	14.6
1985	28.9	13.1	15.8
1986	31.8	14.8	17.0
1987	34.2	16.6	17.6
1988	37.1	18.1	19.0
1989	38.8	17.4	21.4
1990	41.0	20.7	20.3
1991	39.6	19.2	20.4
1992	40.5	19.4	21.1
1993	41.0	19.7	21.3
1994	39.9	21.4	18.5
1995 (projected)	41.9	22.7	19.2
2000 (projected)	48.6	26.3	22.3

Sources: Office of Tourism Research, Bureau of Economic Analysis, Florida Department of Commerce and Florida Economics Consulting Group, Inc.

Number One destination for college students for the annual "Spring Break," with Daytona Beach overtaking Ft. Lauderdale in recent years as the place to be.

Relatively recently there has also been a movement to turn Florida into a major movie-making state. The Disney/MGM Studio tour opened in Orlando on May 1, 1988, and the Universal Studios tour in 1990. The list of television shows and movies that have been shot on location in Florida ranges from the popular children's TV show Nickelodeon based in Orlando to the blockbuster movie "True Lies" shot on location in Miami and the Florida Keys. Disney's continuous stream of new attractions will lead to even more tourism growth in the Orlando area, helping maintain its position as the Number One vacation spot in the world.

The plethora of major worldwide events such as the Summit of Americas, World Cup of soccer, Super Bowl and Olympic games qualifying events all help attract additional visitors each year. Also, the cruise industry in Florida has grown by leaps and bounds, with approximately seven million passengers served annually. Over five million of these cruise passengers come through the Port of Miami and Port Everglades annually. Disney is planning a $24 million cruise facility at Port Canaveral to open in 1998 for exclusive use by Disney cruise ships.

Characteristics of Tourists Visiting Florida

Air Visitors. Nearly 40 percent of the domestic air visitors to Florida come from five states, led by New York with 14 percent, or three million air tourists annually. The other four top origin states, in order, for air tourists are New Jersey, Illinois, California and Pennsylvania, according to data from the Florida Department of Commerce annual exit survey of visitors.

The top three destinations of air visitors surveyed, in order, are Dade County, the Orlando area and Broward County. Their primary purpose for visiting was a vacation (35 percent), with business (30 percent) and visiting friends/relatives (29 percent) their second and third purpose, respectively. Nearly a quarter of the survey respondents indicated they visited Walt Disney resorts and attractions, followed by Universal Studios (11 percent) and then state parks/preserves (6 percent).

The estimated expenditure per party per day was $98.27 with an average number of nights stayed of 8.5. Very encouraging responses were that 93.6 percent were repeat visitors while 97.9 percent indicated that they will return to Florida in the future. In 1994 just over 6.5 million air visitors flew to Florida through Orlando airport, while 5.4 million air visitors came through Miami airport and 2.9 million through Tampa airport.

Auto Visitors. The top origin state for auto visitors in 1994 was neighboring Georgia with 15.8 percent, or 2.9 million, of the total auto visitors. Rounding out the top five origin states, in order, for auto tourists were Ohio, Tennessee, North Carolina and New York.

The top three destinations of auto visitors surveyed, in order, were the Orlando area, Bay County (Panhandle beaches) and Volusia County (Daytona Beach and Spring Break). Over half indicated that their primary purpose for visiting was a vacation, with visiting friends/relatives (35 percent) and business (10 percent) their second and third main purpose, respectively. A quarter of the survey respondents indicated they visited Walt Disney resorts and attractions, followed by visiting Universal Studios (12 percent) and then Sea World (8 percent).

The estimated expenditure per party per day was $50.22 with an average number of nights stayed of 16.9. Similar to air visitors, 93.9 percent of auto tourists were repeat visitors while 96.1 percent indicated that they will return to Florida in the future.

As one of the main purposes for both auto and air tourists visiting Florida is to see friends and/or relatives, this augurs well for the future of the number of tourists to Florida as the state is forecast to experience considerable population growth through the turn of the century and beyond, though at a slower pace than before. Florida is scheduled to become the third-most populous state in the nation, after California and Texas, early in the next century. However, these visitors tend to spend less on lodging and food as they take advantage of the facilities and hospitality of their family and friends.

Areas Visited by Tourists. Perhaps somewhat surprisingly to some people, the southeast region (including Broward, Dade, Monroe and Palm Beach counties) continues to outdraw the Orlando area in terms of tourists. In 1994, 13.3 million tourists visited southeast Florida compared to 9.9 million visiting the Orlando area. The Orlando area was down over 800,000 tourists in 1994 compared to 1993.

Tourism Lodging and Restaurants in Florida

Table 2 shows changes in the number of lodging accommodations and rooms (all sizes) and the number of restaurants and seating capacity in 1975, 1985 and 1995. The number of hotels and motels has actually decreased since 1975 but the number of rooms has increased--a clear movement toward bigger hotel and motel facilities. Anyone who has traveled to Miami Beach would notice that the number of rental condominiums has increased substantially over the past

Table 2. Lodging Accommodations (all sizes) and Restaurants in Florida 1975, 1985 and 1995

	1975	1985	1995
Hotels	990	781	783
Rooms	87,565	96,015	132,884
Motels	5,321	4,379	3,929
Rooms	180,286	196,399	204,224
Rental Condos	294	1,924	6,535
Units	7,731	29,366	62,180
Restaurants	21,506	28,901	34,796
Seating	1,281,441	1,794,733	2,875,352

Source: Master File Statistics, Division of Hotels and Restaurants, Florida Department of Business Regulation.

three decades. There have been numerous conversions of hotels to long-term leases, i.e., to rental condominiums, especially along the coastal areas.

International Tourism in Florida

Florida was the Number One destination for international tourists to the United States in 1994 with 3,952,941 foreign visitors from overseas; California is a distant second at 2,829,379. This is based on first-address data from the Immigration and Naturalization Service's I-94 forms (which excludes Canada and Mexico) and is more detailed than other survey methods.

Florida attracts one of every five international visitors to the United States, with these over four million travelers (including Mexico) spending over $9 billion annually. Not surprisingly, about half of the tourists to the U.S. from Central and South America and from the Caribbean visit Florida due to the state's proximity and close cultural and ethnic ties with these regions. A third of the British tourists to the United States choose Florida for their holidays, probably because of the extreme change in climate. Table 3 shows tourist totals to Florida from selected countries in 1983 and 1992-1994, plus the percentage of all U.S. foreign tourists visiting Florida in 1994.

Table 3. International Tourists (excluding Canada): Florida as Intended First Address in the U.S.

	1983	1992	1993	1994	Percent*
Total Overseas					
Visitors	1,685,950	4,299,584	4,619,256	4,189,459	20.1
Europe	479,743	2,215,422	2,231,128	1,849,321	22.4
France	27,981	106,725	110,314	104,903	12.2
Germany	82,781	453,559	455,046	312,667	18.3
United					
Kingdom	221,817	1,071,401	1,127,739	954,998	32.7
South America	519,759	964,510	1,124,277	1,135,849	53.0
Brazil	91,052	254,890	294,791	334,793	50.6
Columbia	160,937	108,347	127,329	129,427	56.7
Venezuela	132,585	208,477	268,992	262,997	62.0
Central America	160,968	205,607	245,328	230,640	44.2
Other Countries					
Japan	4,372	104,537	112,695	107,169	2.6
Caribbean	383,587	473,882	536,177	477,800	47.4
Mexico	89,503	232,052	230,408	236,518	14.3

*1994 as a percent of all U.S. international visitors.

Source: U.S. Travel and Tourism Administration, *Summary and Analysis of International Travel to the United States* (various issues).

In addition to these international tourists, 1.9 million Canadians visited Florida in 1994. Canadians spent $1.7 billion in Florida last year and stayed an average of 22.3 nights, significantly higher than the average air or auto visitor. Nearly two-thirds of the Canadians visited from the province of Ontario while a quarter came from the province of Quebec.

The fall in the dollar's value against most major currencies has helped make Florida a relatively inexpensive spot for international tourists. The dollar's fall also makes foreign travel for Americans a relatively more expensive proposition. Thus, Americans are more likely to take a vacation stateside, where Florida is a prime destination.

University of Florida   *Bureau of Economic and Business Research*

Table 4. Tourist/Recreation Taxable Sales
Categories 1984 and 1994
($ millions)

Kind		Taxable Sales	
Code	Description	1984	1994
8	Restaurants and Lunchrooms	6,464.3	13,351.3
9	Taverns and Nightclubs	1,643.3	1,760.5
16	Jewelry, Leather and Sporting Goods	1,026.2	2,234.4
39	Hotels, Apartments and Rooming Houses	869.5	6,599.5
43	Cigar Stands and Tobacco Shops	19.5	29.0
52	Photographers and Photo Supplies	479.0	832.7
55	Gift Card and Novelty Shops	795.9	1,623.6
56	Newsstands	42.0	56.7
59	Admissions	1,013.1	3,396.6
60	Holiday Season Vendors	2.8	7.0
61	Rental of Tangible Property	1,129.9	2,824.6
83	Parking Lots, Boat Docking and Storage	163.5	270.8
85	Hotels and Transient Rentals	2,460.2	712.3
	Total	16,109.2	33,698.9

Source: Florida Department of Revenue.

Tourists and Taxes

Tourists have a significant impact on tax collections of the state. The tourism/recreation taxable sales category represents the portion of total taxable sales most influenced by tourists. However, it does combine visitor and resident sales. Therefore, the sales tax paid by a Florida resident buying an admission to the EPCOT Center is included under this definition. Table 4 highlights the individual categories of tourism/recreation taxable sales in calendar years 1984 and 1994.

Not surprisingly, tourist expenditures on food and lodging, kind codes 8, 39 and 85, make up over 60 percent of this category. In fiscal year 1994-95 the tourism and recreation category accounts for $2.1 billion or 19.7 percent of total sales tax collections of $10.5 billion. Tourists do spend a lot in the other five categories of sales tax, although less than on food and lodging.

Table 5. Tourist-Related Employment in Florida
1974, 1984 and 1994

	1974	1984	1994
Eating and Drinking Establishments	145,433	295,358	414,891
Hotels and Lodging	72,075	104,267	137,408
Amusement Services	40,283	72,092	117,717
Air Transportation	33,175	43,200	49,242
Total Tourist-Related	290,966	514,917	719,258
Total Nonagricultural Employment	2,863,820	4,205,130	5,796,560
Tourist-Related as a Percent of Nonagricultural Employment	10.2	12.2	12.4

Source: Bureau of Labor Market Information, Current Employment Statistics Program, Florida Department of Labor and Employment Security.

Estimated percentages of selected state taxes directly paid by tourists are as follows: sales 15 percent, fuel 14 percent, beer 19 percent, cigarettes 10 percent, alcohol 30 percent and pari-mutuel betting 22.5 percent. There are also a number of other state taxes, such as documentary stamp and intangible taxes, of which tourists pay an undetermined percentage. Tourists also pay tolls on state highways and a whole range of other user fees, such as park and campground admissions. In many counties they also pay a "bed" tax, otherwise known as the tourist development tax. In fiscal year 1994-95 it is estimated that out-of-state tourists will contribute approximately $3.5 billion, or 9 percent, of the total state budget of close to $40 billion.

Tourism and Job Growth

Table 5 details job growth in four of the primary tourist employment categories in the state for each decade between 1974 and 1994. These categories by no means include all Florida workers in tourist-related jobs; however, they are a strong indicator of the direct impact of tourism on employment trends in the state.

As the table shows, the share of tourist-related jobs in total nonagricultural employment has risen gradually from 10.2 percent

Table 6. State Tourism Promotion Expenditures
in the U.S. 1991-92 and 1994-95
($ millions)

State	1991-92	Rank	1994-95	Rank
Hawaii	23.0	2	33.9	1
Illinois	25.3	1	30.5	2
Texas	16.2	3	20.8	3
New York	—	—	15.4	4
Florida	**13.1**	**5**	**15.1**	**5**
Massachusetts	9.2	10	14.0	6
Louisiana	13.5	4	13.4	7
Pennsylvania	12.2	6	12.6	8

Source: U.S. Travel Data Center.

in 1974 to 12.4 percent in 1994. This trend should continue, and by the turn of the century over 13 percent of total nonfarm employment in Florida will be in these tourist-related categories. In other words, one in eight nonfarm jobs in Florida is tourist related. The continued expansion of the Disney empire in the Orlando area is a major reason for this continued growth in the tourist-related employment share.

Tourism and Advertising

Florida is not only a major player as a tourist destination in the U.S., but also in the world. There is a risk that other countries and states in the U.S. will capture some of Florida's large share of tourists if advertising in the state falls flat or is reduced. One current example is Myrtle Beach, South Carolina's aggressive courting of Canadian tourists away from Florida.

As Table 6 shows, whereas the State of Florida has increased tourism advertising and promotion by only a modest 15 percent to $15.1 million between fiscal years 1992 and 1995, other states--notably Massachusetts (52 percent) and Hawaii (47 percent)--have increased their tourism budgets significantly more. The competition for tourists is fierce and Florida cannot afford to rest on its laurels and let other states chip away at its market share. Although data on advertising budgets of the private sector are not available, they greatly exceed what the state spends. In fact, the state's own spending is merely a drop in the bucket when compared to the advertising of, say, Disney. Advertising by the state obviously helps the private-sector attractions, and vice versa.

Is the only modest increase in Florida's tourism advertising relative to spending by its major competitors a problem? Should Florida's local and state governments advertise more? Before tackling these questions, it is helpful to discuss why any tax money at all should go to boosting tourism, instead of leaving it to the private sector entirely.

One reason for the government to become involved is that when a resort or theme park draws tourists, it benefits dozens of other businesses. A hotel that hosts a convention fills restaurants for blocks around. A theme park fills neighboring campgrounds. When the managers of the hotel or theme park budget funds for advertising, they will not weigh the added profits for the restaurants and campgrounds; and the restaurants and campgrounds are unlikely to advertise out of state. They gain from being free riders on the hotel and theme park.

Because of the incentive to free riding, advertising by the private sector may fall short of what it should be when the higher revenues of all businesses--theaters, stores, resorts, taxis--that gain from tourists are added together. Consequently there may be good reason for the state and local governments to step in.

But this argument could go in the other direction. With their dollars, tourists bring congestion and pollution. They swarm the beaches, crowd the roads and deplete the water. Perhaps the state should even urge people to stay away, warning would-be visitors of the dangers of sharks and sunburns, in order to preserve Florida's beauty for those lucky enough to live here. At least residents need to ask whether encouraging more tourism is good.

From the perspective of governmental taxing and spending, the state probably wins by having more tourists. With minor exceptions, tourists as a group pay the same taxes as residents, such as sales and gasoline taxes. While most of them pay no local property taxes directly, they do raise the values of hotels, restaurants and malls, thus enhancing the base for the property tax and boosting revenues. Moreover, in 1990 they are spending at a daily rate that ranks them with high-income residents, who contribute more than average to taxes.

This is offset by what tourists add to nearly all forms of governmental spending, from roads to police. There is one major difference between tourists and most citizens in this regard, however: tourists require little or no service from education, which accounts for about a quarter of state and local spending in Florida. In this way residents gain from having more tourists, who pay almost all the same taxes but place no extra burden on this major component of public spending.

This seeming net gain from taxes on visitors makes a strong case for a larger state and local role in encouraging tourism but it does not settle the issue, especially if the congestion and pollution tourists cause more than offset the net gain in revenue. The question of more advertising should be weighed against the damage tourists do. Unfortunately, this can only be guessed, since there are no data to provide an answer.

Perhaps what irritates people most frequently is road congestion, and while tourists add to the revenues from the gasoline tax, clearly they add to the congestion. But how much? Travel during off-peak hours seldom slows other drivers, and tourists are less likely than residents to swell rush-hour traffic for the simple reason that they do not come to Florida to work. Tourists may, however, be more likely to use the roads during the winter, when they are already crowded by seasonal residents, but this effect may be small. Florida now has two tourist seasons. Though one covers November through March and makes the winter crowding worse, the other is in July and August when the snowbirds are gone. The winter tourists, moreover, usually arrive by air and use the roads less.

It is human nature to deplore the stress others cause more than to praise the vitality they bring. The tourists who crowd the roads also enable residents to enjoy a wider variety of restaurants and amusements. The per capita availability of amusement and recreation services in Florida exceeds the national average by approximately 75 percent, giving residents more options for entertainment than they

Table 7. Florida Tourist Breakdown 1993 and 1994
(in millions)

	1993	1994	Percent Change
Total Visitors	41.0	39.9	-2.8
International (Excluding Canada)	4.6	4.2	-9.3
Canada	2.3	1.9	-17.4
Domestic	34.1	33.8	-0.9

Source: U.S. Travel and Tourism Administration, *Summary and Analysis of International Travel to the United States*; Statistics Canada, *Canadian Residents Visiting Florida*; Bureau of Economic Analysis, Florida Department of Commerce.

would otherwise have. If diversity is the spice of life, residents owe a lot to tourists. On balance, it appears that spending more on advertising to bring more tourists to Florida would be wise.

Tourism and Crime

The shock waves caused by the high number of vicious crimes against mainly international visitors to Florida in 1993 sullied the state's reputation and caused in effect a recession in state tourism in 1994. As Tables 3 and 7 show, the biggest negative impact was felt among certain segments of international visitors. About 390,000 fewer Canadian, 173,000 fewer British and 142,000 fewer German tourists visited Florida in 1994 compared to 1993, mainly as a direct result of all the worldwide negative publicity surrounding crime in the state in 1993. Perhaps somewhat surprisingly, given the deluge of bad press Florida received in the U.S. as well, the number of domestic visitors from other U.S. states was down only minimally in 1993 compared to 1994. This is significant because domestic visitors make up about 85 percent of the state's tourists, while Canadian and other international visitors make up the remaining 15 percent of our visitor base.

South American tourism to Florida was actually up in 1994 over 1993, which speaks volumes for the much higher crime rate there compared to Florida, particularly in Brazil and Colombia. A report by the Latin American Economic System found that Latin America has become the world's most murderous continent. It is therefore not surprising that people from Latin America have not been put off from visiting Florida because of crime here.

The reaction in Florida by the authorities and tourism industry was quite swift with changes in car rental license plate markings, 24-hour patrols at rest areas, better road sign directions, beefed-up police presence at airports and attractions and more information centers to greet visiting tourists. A degree of paranoia entered into the proceedings with some car rental companies offering rental cars equipped with radar and sporting bulletproof glass to already fearful visitors.

The peak of bad publicity has subsided due to the above efforts, but the visions of international tourists as the deadly victims of carjackings and the like has not been totally forgotten around the world. It has probably permanently changed some people's perceptions and future travel plans related to Florida.

However, the current outlook is brightening with respect to international visitor arrivals to Florida with a strong rebound forecast in 1995 over 1994, barring a repeat of high-profile deadly crime stories broadcast around the world.

A Look Ahead

The outlook for tourism in Florida through the year 2000 and beyond is generally excellent, although there are always potential dark clouds on the horizon which could alter expected outcomes. The projections in Table 1 show that by the turn of the century close to fifty million domestic and international visitors will come to Florida. In fact, data for the first quarter of 1995 indicated that Florida tourism is up about 7.5 percent over the same time period of 1994. This translates into about forty-two million tourists to visit Florida in 1995, a new record and a strong rebound over a disastrous 1994.

The reasons for the increase are many. Clearly, the state's climate and natural resources will still be in place over the course of the next ten years. Additionally, Florida has the benefit of history as a tourist state which other states, apart from California, do not have. Florida's infrastructure of attractions is already in place, with many more new projects in the pipeline, giving it a tremendous advantage over other states. Disney is planning a fourth major theme park in the Orlando area, at an estimated cost of $800 million, scheduled to open in 1998.

On the downside, any national economic slowdown would depress tourism in Florida. Recessions have a stagnating effect on consumer expenditures on non-necessity items such as vacations, which tend to get postponed until personal finances and confidence are restored. Looking back at Table 1, the number of tourists to the state fell in 1980 and 1991 because of recessions and accompanying high energy costs.

However, the outlook for gasoline prices through the turn of the century is excellent, with only moderate growth expected. Low energy prices imply that the costs of driving or flying to Florida can be kept at reasonable levels. Also, with more than twenty-six million air tourists expected to visit the state by the year 2000, the competition among air carriers should continue to be intense, resulting in relatively low fares.

The prognosis for international tourism is also favorable; in fact the growth rate in international tourist arrivals is expected to exceed that of domestic arrivals. The dollar is forecast to remain weak relative to most major currencies for the foreseeable future. As the Latin American economies are projected to go through a recovery phase, there should be steady growth in tourists to Florida from this volatile region too.

As the population of Florida continues to increase, so too does the number of friends and relatives that tourists can visit in the state. By the turn of the century, the state's population is projected to reach about sixteen million, an increase of two million from the fourteen million residents today.

Another important factor is that Florida no longer promotes itself as purely a beach state. The state's tourism industry has diversified over the last twenty years along with Florida's total economy, promoting convention and cruise business along with the attractions, parks, campgrounds, festivals, museums and other traditional lures.

This diversification should help maintain the state's position as a major domestic and international visitor destination well into the next century. However, the growing number of other states and destinations aggressively marketing themselves will mean that Florida's tourism industry (public and private) will not be able to relax and must continue to be on the cutting edge in terms of innovative marketing and new attractions; otherwise market share will be eroded.

References

Canadian Residents Visiting Florida in 1994. Statistics Canada.

Espino, M. 1986. "The Impact of Tourist Exports on Florida's Economy." Unpublished Ph.D. dissertation. Tallahassee: Florida State University.

Florida Visitor Study (various years). Tallahassee: Florida Department of Commerce, Bureau of Economic Analysis, Office of Tourism Research.

Redman, Milton B. 1979. "The Proportion of State Taxes Paid by Tourists." *Financing Florida State Government.* Tallahassee: Florida State University.

Trager, Kenneth. 1990. *The Impact of Fiscal Year 1988-89 Out-of-State Tourism on the Florida Economy.* Tallahassee: The Florida Legislature, Division of Economic and Demographic Research.

Trager, Kenneth, and H. Frank Williams. 1992. *Who Pays Florida's Sales Tax? An Empirical Examination of Florida's Sales Tax.* Tallahassee: The Florida Legislature, Division of Economic and Demographic Research.

Trager, Kenneth, William Bales and Michael Clark. 1986. *Florida's Population Influx : A Methodology to Capture Tourism Monthly for each of Florida's 67 Counties with Applications for the Law Enforcement Community.* Tallahassee: Florida Statistical Analysis Center.

Mining Activity

15

Thomas W. Moore
Manager, Economic
Planning and Forecasting
Tampa Electric Company
Tampa, Florida

Florida's mining industry employs about 6,600 people (Table 1). Although this represents only a small portion (0.1 percent) of the state's total number of jobs, these companies provide products and support services that are critical to many sectors of the economy. In addition, processing and shipping these minerals creates further employment opportunities.

About 35 percent of this sector's employment is involved in the mining and quarrying of limestone, dolomite, sand and gravel. These materials are used primarily to build roads and manufacture cement. In addition, oil and gas extraction accounts for another 8 percent of employment. The largest single area of mining, however, is phosphate, which accounts for almost 45 percent of total employment. Because of its predominance, the remainder of this chapter is devoted to discussing the phosphate industry.

The Phosphate Industry

Phosphate mining is one of the oldest industries in Florida, as deposits were first discovered in the 1880s. About 90 percent of the rock mined is used in the production of agricultural fertilizers, which are sold both in domestic and foreign markets. Most of the remaining application of phosphate is for livestock feed supplements.

Table 1. 1993 Florida Mining Employment

Metal Mining (est.)	175
Coal and Lignite Mining (est.)	10
Oil and Gas Extraction	434
Mining and Quarrying of Nonmetallic	
Metals, Except Fuels	5,947
Stone, Sand and Gravel (est.)	2,401
Chemical and Fertilizer	2,893
Other Nonmetallic Minerals, Except Fuels	363
Clay, Ceramic and Refractory Minerals	243
Nonmetallic Minerals (Except Fuels)	
Services (est.)	47
Total	6,566

Source: Based on information from State of Florida Department of Labor and Employment Security.

Within the phosphate industry Florida is a dominant player, as it supplies over 70 percent of the rock mined in the United States. Florida also plays an important role in the world market, providing more than one-fifth of the world's phosphate production (Figure 1). Other major producers include China and Morocco as well as the countries formerly in the U.S.S.R. Total U.S. production combined with that of these other countries represents over 70 percent of the world's phosphate output.

There are two regions of phosphate mining in Florida. One is in the northern part of the state along the Suwannee River in Hamilton County. The bulk of industry activity, however, is in the "Bone Valley" of west central Florida, a ten-million-year-old deposit of phosphate ore and prehistoric animal bones. This is where the majority of phosphate mining occurs, not only in Florida but also in the U.S. Production takes place in the five-county area of Hardee, Manatee, Pasco, Hillsborough and Polk--with the primary activity in the latter two counties.

The phosphate process can be divided into two major phases. The first involves mining of raw phosphate, which includes cleaning and separating out impurities. The second step involves processing

Figure 1. World Phosphate Rock Production 1994

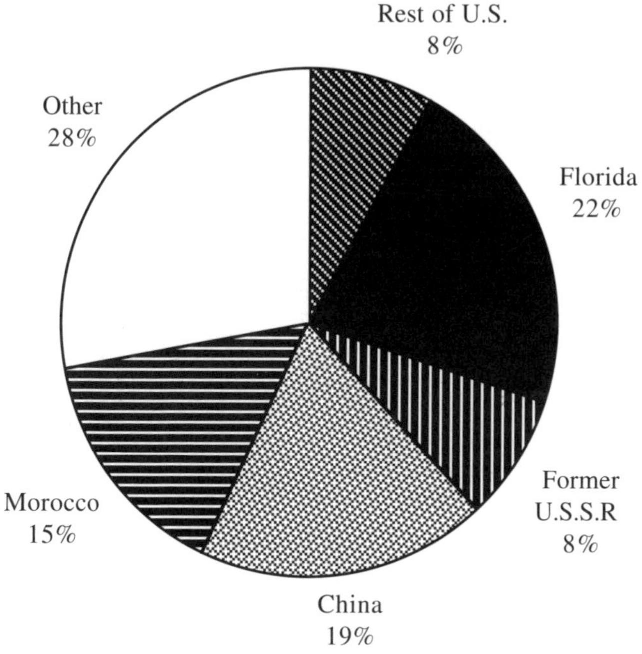

Source: Bureau of Mines.

phosphate to make it suitable for commercial applications. The most widely used fertilizer derived from the raw phosphate is diammonium phosphate, better known in the industry as DAP.

In 1994, the phosphate industry employed roughly 7,900 workers with around 40 percent involved in mining and 60 percent in processing. The majority of these employees are located in Polk County.

Since phosphate products are used all over the world, most of west central Florida's production finds its way through the Port of Tampa. In 1993, more than 25 million tons of phosphate were shipped through this facility. This represented 55 percent of the port's tonnage and has helped make Tampa the seventh-busiest terminal in the United States.

Economic Cycles

Florida's phosphate industry is extremely sensitive to the business cycle. Since 1980, there have been three major cycles that

Table 2. Florida Phosphate Mining

Year	Millions of Tons	Change in Tons	Percent Change
1980	43.0	—	—
1981	42.8	-0.2	-0.5
1982	30.2	-12.6	-29.4
1983	33.4	3.2	10.6
1984	37.9	4.5	13.5
1985	39.0	1.1	2.9
1986	29.7	-9.3	-23.8
1987	30.0	0.3	1.0
1988	34.6	4.6	15.3
1989	38.2	3.6	10.4
1990	35.4	-2.8	-7.3
1991	36.2	0.8	2.2
1992	36.2	0.0	0.0
1993	25.2	-11.0	-30.4
1994	29.0	3.8	15.1

Source: Florida Phosphate Council.

have caused dramatic change in the industry's dynamics and structure.

Each of the three phosphate recessions that occurred during these cycles has been influenced by different factors. The first downturn, from mid-1981 through 1982, resulted primarily from the impact of a serious national recession on the agricultural sector as falling crop prices combined with escalating operating costs (increasing interest rates and gasoline prices) to squeeze the farmer's profit margins. This led to a sharp reduction in the use of phosphate fertilizer.

Also impacting the industry at this time was the rising value of the U.S. dollar against foreign currencies, which increased the cost of American goods to overseas buyers and, thereby, reduced foreign demand for U.S. phosphate products. With both domestic and foreign demand weakened, Florida's phosphate production fell nearly 30 percent in 1982 (Table 2).

The second phosphate recession began in mid-1985 after the dollar reached its highest level of the 1980s relative to foreign currencies.

Figure 2. Phosphate Inventory
(millions of metric tons)

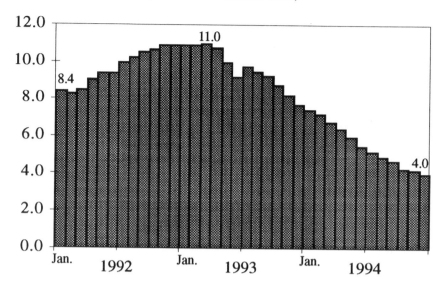

The strong dollar so dramatically raised U.S. phosphate prices in international markets that foreign demand fell sharply. At the same time, falling agricultural crop prices at home hampered domestic fertilizer sales. The combined effect of these two factors resulted in phosphate production dropping 24 percent in 1986 to under 30 million tons.

After the 1985-86 recession, the phosphate industry began a period of gradual improvement in which both domestic and international demand expanded. By 1992, Florida mining activity had climbed back to around 36 million tons.

The first signs of the third cycle surfaced during the end of 1992 when international markets began to soften. This weakening was related to political considerations as three of the largest purchasers of fertilizer--China, India and Russia--attempted to decentralize their procedures for purchasing phosphate. The result was disastrous as phosphate demand in the three countries plummeted. The falloff in foreign consumption soon affected producer inventories, which in Florida jumped from around 9 million tons in mid-1992 to 11 million tons by the spring of 1993 (Figure 2).

The deteriorating situation was even more apparent in the industry's inventory-to-sales ratio. The Florida companies presently

Figure 3. Phosphate Inventory/Sales Ratio
(millions)

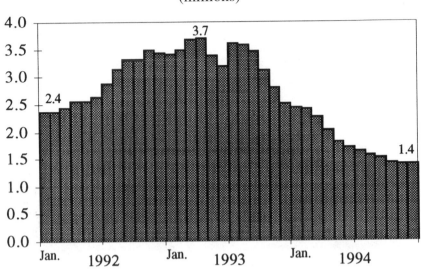

attempt to keep 1.5 to 2.0 months of sales in stock in order to respond quickly to any acceleration in product demand. The falloff in phosphate sales and the resulting increase in inventories, however, combined to push the ratio to 3.7 during the spring of 1993, twice the industry target (Figure 3). With sales slumping and inventories bloated, phosphate companies began to reduce production substantially to get their stocks back in line.

To accomplish this task, companies cut phosphate production well below the level being demanded so that inflated inventories could be absorbed. By the end of 1993, phosphate stocks had returned to a more manageable level and the inventory-to-sales ratio was down to 2.5. At the same time that production and inventories were being adjusted, demand began to improve. Although demand from the former Soviet states remained sluggish, China and India returned to the market in the second half of 1993 and picked up their pace of purchases. Still, the phosphate recession dramatically impacted Florida's 1993 production as output fell to 25 million tons, the lowest level that the industry had experienced since the mid 1960s.

International markets, however, continued to gather forward momentum in 1994. In addition, domestic phosphate sales also strengthened. The reasons behind the improvement in U.S. demand go back to the summer of 1993, when midwestern floods reduced grain yields. This pushed up corn, wheat and other farm commodity prices since the reduced harvest sapped industry inventories. At the same time, farm income was bolstered by government insurance payments to the flood-ravaged regions. With farm income stabilized and crop prices up, farmers sharply increased their 1994 plantings, which boosted domestic fertilizer sales.

With demand accelerating in both the domestic and foreign markets, phosphate activity recorded a solid advance in 1994. The industry met the increase in fertilizer sales by expanding production and further reducing inventories. In fact, stocks declined to an extremely lean 4 million tons by the end of 1994, a 64 percent plunge from the 11 million peak in early 1993. As further evidence of the industry's trim position, the inventory-to-sales ratio was at an alltime low of 1.4 in December 1994.

Given this dramatic correction in industry stocks, it appears that no further inventory reductions are needed at this time. Therefore, 1995 should show another sturdy improvement in the phosphate sector as companies escalate production to meet expanded demand.

Changing Industry Patterns

The volatility that has occurred in the phosphate sector during the past fifteen years has produced numerous changes in the way firms do business. All the adjustments that companies have initiated have had the objective of lowering costs.

One adjustment has been in the workforce, which has declined by nearly half since 1980 (Table 3). While much of the decrease is due to lower production levels, there has also been a trend toward a more capital-intensive process. This can be seen by the fact that the number of tons mined per employee has risen 25 percent from 2,945 to 3,671 between 1980 and 1994.

Phosphate companies have also become extremely cost-sensitive. One major step the industry is taking to control expenses is the move toward self-generation of companies' electricity needs. During the past ten years, nearly every major phosphate plant in Florida

Table 3. Florida Phosphate Employment
and Productivity 1980-1994

Year	Employees (thousands)	Percent Change	Tons Mined Per Employee
1980	14.6	—	2,945
1981	14.0	-9.3	3,057
1982	12.7	-9.4	2,378
1983	11.5	-9.4	2,904
1984	12.5	8.7	3,032
1985	11.7	-6.4	3,333
1986	9.8	-16.2	3,031
1987	9.4	-4.1	3,191
1988	9.8	4.3	3,531
1989	9.8	0.0	3,898
1990	9.9	1.0	3,576
1991	9.8	-1.0	3,694
1992	9.0	-8.2	4,022
1993	7.8	-13.3	3,231
1994	7.9	1.3	3,671

Source: Florida Phosphate Council.

has installed its own electrical generating system driven by the waste heat from its facilities.

Another cost-control measure companies are employing is monitoring inventories more closely. In the early 1980s, the industry attempted to maintain phosphate stocks at three to four months of sales. This ratio has since been cut in half to one and one-half to two months of sales.

Finally, the phosphate industry has experienced consolidation as the weaker companies have been forced to downsize, merge or face dissolution. Since the mid-1980s, the number of phosphate companies in Florida has declined by nearly half from fifteen to the present number of eight.

Some major consolidations have occurred since the 1993 downturn. In the beginning of that year, Cargill Fertilizer Inc. bought Seminole Fertilizer while IMC absorbed Conserv. In addition, Consolidated Minerals Inc. was purchased by a Japanese investor and the name was changed to Coronet Industries.

The most highly publicized merger, however, took place when IMC and Agrico, the two largest companies in the industry, joined forces in the middle of 1993. This resulted in a new IMC-Agrico group that presently controls more than half of the market. During the next several years the shakeout is expected to continue, with more firms likely to be absorbed.

International Situation

Foreign agricultural markets are an extremely important source of revenue to the U.S. phosphate industry. About half of the phosphate mined in the U.S. finds its way overseas. Some is shipped in its raw rock form, with South Korea and Western Europe being the largest buyers. The majority of phosphate exports, however, are sold as processed fertilizer. Major foreign customers of DAP, the most common fertilizer, include China, India and Pakistan. In addition, sales to Western Europe are also considerable.

An aggressive expansion by foreign producers has eroded the U.S. phosphate producers' market share in the European and Asian markets. Specifically, Morocco, Jordan and Togo have accelerated mining production. This foreign expansion has reduced the U.S. share of world reserves to 25 percent from the 33 percent level of several years ago.

In addition to expanding their mining capacity, many countries are also building their own processing plants. Fertilizers and Chemicals, a subsidiary of Israel Chemicals Ltd., has recently formed a joint venture with Turkey's Trans Turk to build a liquid fertilizer plant in southern Turkey. At the same time, plants are also being constructed in Jordan, Pakistan and China.

The increased foreign supply of phosphate has put downward pressure on prices, requiring U.S. producers to trim back costs. In fact, the present price of rock in world markets is below the level of the early 1980s. And with further expansions likely, these markets should become even more competitive.

A Look Ahead

From the recent experience, U.S. phosphate producers can expect continued volatility driven by fluctuations in crop prices, the value of the dollar and the political landscape. These patterns will likely move the industry to greater cost efficiency, consolidation and even tighter inventory control in the coming years.

Looking beyond these cycles, however, world phosphate demand is expected to grow at an average annual rate of 1.5 percent to 2.0 percent over the next twenty years. Given Florida's deposits, many of the reserves presently being used will be mined out over this period. Therefore, mining operations will be moving south from Hillsborough and Polk counties into Manatee, De Soto and Hardee counties.

In fact, this migration is already occurring. Many companies have been purchasing land south of existing mines in preparation for the move. In addition, Estech and Mobil have closed depleted mines in Polk County during the past few years. Anticipating the closing of their Haynesworth, Phosphoria and Kingsford mines during the coming years, IMC-Agrico has been relocating draglines out of Polk County to new reserves in Hardee County.

The phosphate in these new fields is generally of lower quality and less concentrated than deposits now being worked, resulting in higher production costs. This has led to differences of opinion as to whether Florida will be able to supply the growing world demand in the coming years.

Certain experts believe that the higher mining costs of these new locations will prevent their development given the present low price of phosphate. These individuals expect Florida's phosphate production to slide sharply over the next twenty years. A more optimistic viewpoint, however, anticipates technological breakthroughs that will allow the recovery of these reserves at a cost that is competitive in world markets. This second group predicts a greater level of mining activity.

There are also environmental considerations to address as the industry moves toward the next century. The United States has the toughest reclamation laws of any phosphate-producing country. Both companies and governmental authorities will be challenged to balance the needs of industry with the environment.

The importance of the phosphate industry, however, is beyond debate as it provides an essential input to the agricultural sector. With the need for American agriculture to remain viable, the U.S. phosphate industry must also be maintained.

International Trade and Investment

16

Thomas M. Fullerton, Jr.
Senior Economist
Bureau of Economic
and Business Research
University of Florida
Gainesville, Florida

Many changes have occurred in international trade practices and volumes since the publication of the 1990 edition of *The Economy of Florida*. The most interesting involve trade agreements, both regional and global. Florida trade flows have also been impacted by international economic performance, with the latter responding to cyclical as well as structural factors. As pointed out by Ramsey (1990), the world economy is present in nearly every aspect of the average Floridian's daily existence, from the food we consume to the clothes we wear, to the cars we drive, to the jobs many of us hold. Recognition of the benefits provided by trade and international investment is sometimes absent but the overall economic welfare of the state is undeniably enhanced by their presence.

International trade brings two major gains. First, trade simply provides goods and services to consumers at lower prices. This may occur due to lower production costs abroad or it may result from increased competition. For example, home electronics and automobile prices are lower in the United States due to imports from Europe and Japan, generating significant consumer savings on these types of purchases. Second, trade helps create and is driven by new goods, information and technology flows. The latter ultimately result in additional welfare enhancements plus higher real growth rates.[1] A

[1]For a brief, nontechnical summary, readers are referred to a magazine article published in the July 16, 1994, issue of *The Economist*.

well-known modern example is provided by computer chip technology in the 1980s. Each successive chip generation helped increase computer speed and capacity, as well as lower machine prices. These eventually led to productivity improvements in other segments of the economy.

To identify some of these factors, this chapter surveys recent trends in international trade, tracing business patterns, local and international, which have affected export flows or benefited from them. It also summarizes some of the highlights associated with trade agreements signed by Florida's principal trading partners, most of which are in Latin America. Given the looming importance of Cuba, prospects for change spurred by international diplomacy are briefly considered. Recent developments in state trade flows and direct foreign investment are also reviewed using data compiled by the Florida Department of Commerce.

Realignment in the Global Marketplace

Few policy issues have generated controversy and headlines in recent years such as those associated with international trade agreements. The most highly publicized trade treaty went into effect on January 1, 1994, and is called the North American Free Trade Agreement, or NAFTA. Other agreements important to Florida include the Uruguay Round of the General Agreement on Tariffs and Trade (GATT) of 1994, the new Andean Pact of the late 1980s, the Southern Cone trade treaty (MERCOSUR) of the early 1990s and the recently renegotiated Central American common market treaty (CACM).

NAFTA is an extension of an earlier trade treaty negotiated between Canada and the United States by the Mulroney and Reagan administrations. The previous agreement, which went into effect in the late 1980s, now includes Mexico. Going well beyond merchandise trade to cover areas such as services, copyrights and foreign investment, NAFTA represents a huge turnabout in international relations between the United States and Mexico. During most of its 75-year post-revolution history, Mexican foreign policy was dominated by efforts to minimize trade and investment flows with the United States. Signaling a reversal of this stance, NAFTA is also the

Table 1. Major Florida Export Markets

Country	1993 Value ($ billions)	1994 Value ($ billions)
World Total	18.204	20.514
Canada	1.618	1.569
Brazil	0.843	1.412
Colombia	1.086	1.260
Argentina	0.933	1.058
Dominican Republic	0.815	0.997
Venezuela	1.225	0.882
Mexico	0.755	0.844
Japan	0.570	0.748
China	0.244	0.694
Paraguay	0.347	0.594

Source: Florida Department of Commerce.

first trade agreement of this magnitude to link industrialized economies like the U.S. and Canada directly with a developing economy such as Mexico. As such, NAFTA represents a watershed event in global politics and diplomacy.

Adoption of market-oriented economic measures in Eastern Europe spurred the 180-degree change in Mexican policy goals, first by the Salinas administration and later by the Zedillo government. While most of the increased trade to and from Mexico will flow through California and Texas, history and geography also bring Florida into the NAFTA ballgame. As shown in Table 1, Mexico is the seventh-largest export market for goods produced in the Sunshine State and sold abroad. Greater volumes of Florida merchandise were shipped to Mexico in 1993 and 1994 than to larger trading partners such as Japan or traditional trading partners such as Costa Rica or Honduras.

When negotiations for NAFTA intensified, one of the more interesting responses was Banco Nacional de Mexico's (Banamex) application to open a representative office in Miami. One of Mexico's largest banking groups, its goal is to service growing trade not only between Mexico and Florida but also between Mexico and the rest of Latin America. Banamex selected Miami due to its status as a major transportation and communications hub for the entire region from the Petén jungles in Guatemala to the windswept hills of Patagonia in Argentina. This was not just a symbolic act on the part of Banamex. Mexico has also negotiated lower trade barriers with its "Group of Three" trading partners, Colombia and Venezuela.

Other interesting aspects of the Florida-Mexico trade nexus include centuries-old shipping routes from Pensacola and Tampa to Veracruz. Merida, the capital of what is sometimes referred to as "the independent and autonomous state of Yucatan," is closer to Miami than to Mexico City. In fact, one Tampa bakery ships its finest products daily to premier Mexican hotels and resorts on the Caribbean. Florida export sectors expected to benefit from expanding sales on the western perimeter of the Gulf of Mexico include processed foods, transportation equipment, electronic machines and parts, telecommunications equipment, clothing apparel and medical equipment (Hufbauer and Schott 1992).

Despite existing and potentially profitable new business linkages between Florida and Mexico, residents on this side of the Gulf are somewhat ambivalent with respect to the new treaty. At the height of the NAFTA debate in Congress, the Bureau of Economic and Business Research at the University of Florida conducted a survey on popular attitudes toward the proposed treaty. Most survey respondents expressed indifference toward the treaty or did not know whether they favored it. Because this complex piece of legislation, negotiated on a "fast-track" basis off and on over the course of two presidential administrations, dealt with an arcane subject, it is perhaps not surprising that fully 30 percent of the survey respondents had not even heard of NAFTA (Denslow, Fullerton and McCarty 1993).

Responses among those who did express an opinion regarding NAFTA were fairly evenly divided, with 49 percent in favor of the agreement and 51 percent opposed. Econometric analysis of the survey results indicated that education, perceptions regarding future financial prospects and familiarity with foreign affairs are among the factors influencing opinions regarding NAFTA (Denslow and Fullerton 1995). For example, the most significant factor behind opposition to the treaty was uncertainty with respect to U.S. economic performance. Support for NAFTA was bolstered by consumer confidence, educational attainment and experience. Ethnicity also played a role, with Hispanic respondents more likely to support NAFTA, perhaps reflecting familiarity with Latin America in general.

One source of the divided public opinion over NAFTA in Florida is concern regarding import competition from Mexico, especially in agriculture. Speculation exists that Mexico may soon challenge Florida citrus producers for dominance in the domestic juice market and supersede Florida farmers in winter markets for fresh vegetables. Both scenarios are implausible. Historically, segments of the state's vast agricultural sector that come under competitive pressure respond by increasing productivity (Cook et al. 1991). If this continues to be the case, NAFTA may prove beneficial for the entire state economy, even Florida agriculture.

Fears regarding farm import competition from Mexico may be overstated for other reasons. Given the size of Mexico's domestic food markets, as incomes there rise it is not clear that production will always outstrip consumption. It is possible that Mexico could eventually become an importer of fruits and vegetables as incomes and diets improve (Cook et al. 1991, Barkema and Drabenstott 1994). Mexican production also faces potential hydrologic constraints that could hinder export capacity in the long run.

Of course, during periods when U.S. fall, winter or spring harvests are unexpectedly below normal, Mexican imports help moderate the resulting price increases faced by consumers throughout the nation. Examples of such occurrences include the weather-related supply disruptions in Florida in 1993 and California in 1995. Ultimately, it is not clear that Florida fresh vegetables will ever face one-to-one overlapping harvests with Mexican output. If that eventuality arises, however, it is likely that the Mississippi River valley will still serve as the general line of demarcation for output from the two regions. Florida output would likely predominate along the eastern seaboard, while State of Sinaloa exports would reach markets west of the Rocky Mountains. This geographic market division is not new, dating back at least to the 1930s.

There are other reasons that NAFTA, despite the potential for increased competition in citrus crops and winter vegetables and fruits, may ultimately benefit Florida agriculture. In 1986, Mexico accounted for just over 4 percent of all U.S. agricultural exports. By 1992, its share of this important category of international sales had more than doubled to nearly 9 percent (Barkema and Drabenstott 1994). Although the volume of farm output sold to Mexico varies, consumers there represent a vast market for manufactured food items. Since 1986, consumer food items have been the largest segment of the world agricultural market. Florida is well-positioned to take advantage of growing demand for processed foods in Mexico and throughout the globe.

This is not to say that all farm and nonfarm producers will benefit from expanding trade with Mexico and the world. Increased competition can drive less efficient companies out of particular markets. When this occurs, workers lose their jobs and may find that their skills do not match new labor-market requirements. To mitigate these types of impacts, the U.S. Department of Labor created the NAFTA Transitional Adjustment Assistance Program. Designed to facilitate retraining efforts for workers displaced by Canadian and Mexican imports, it also provides extended unemployment benefits (Narisetti 1994). By late 1994, more than nine thousand participants were enrolled nationwide in this program's multiple training programs.

Trade negotiations have also occurred on a global scale in recent years. In a rare post-election lame duck session of Congress held in December 1994, the Clinton administration gained legislative approval for the Uruguay round of GATT. This round of negotiations was the most ambitious ever, extending GATT into previously untouched arenas such as agricultural products, services, trade and intellectual property protection via copyright and patent enforcement. The new global trade agreement also attempts to strengthen member participation and rules observance by creating a new governing body, the World Trade Organization (WTO).

Extending WTO coverage to include agriculture, services and copyrights helps Florida in two ways, directly and indirectly. Most important, all three areas play significant roles in the state economy and will enable the business community to obtain greater market shares abroad. Examples include orange juice and citrus sales in Western Europe and Japan, export/import trade financing provided to clients in developing countries and health services diagnostic software for usage with new medical practices.

Broader GATT/WTO coverage to farm output helps Florida indirectly, as well. First, this decision encouraged many of our most important trading partners to become signatories to the agreement since it affords some protection to the commodities they produce. In becoming parties to the agreement, these nations must liberalize their own import restrictions, thus benefiting Florida exporters. Second, external market disruptions caused by the Organization for Economic Cooperation and Development (OECD) government impediments to farm products should eventually be reduced. The latter should help our Southern Hemisphere trading partners improve their overall economic growth performances and lead to more stable conditions in these important target markets for Florida exports.

Latin American Realignments

The historical roots of the Andean Pact date back more than twenty-five years to the signing of the Agreement of Cartagena in 1969 under the auspices of the Lleras administration in Colombia. Reflective of the general mistrust of multinational business activity then prevailing in Latin America, the original agreement did virtually nothing to encourage international trade among its members. It did, however, actively discourage direct foreign investment. That practice, which would eventually hamstring member-country efforts to extricate themselves from the international debt crisis in the 1980s, caused Chile to withdraw from the group in the mid-1970s.

Venezuela and, more recently, Bolivia joined the remaining original members, Colombia, Ecuador and Perú, to give the pact its current line-up. Following the inward-looking development scheme period of the 1970s, the Andean Pact has haltingly come to embrace market-oriented trade and investment policies. Member nations have worked hard to lower import barriers and deregulate international trade among themselves. In fact, the Andean Pact was the first regional trading bloc in the world to open commercial air traffic to international competition on a wide-scale basis.

Of particular interest to Florida companies doing business in this region of Latin America are ongoing efforts to adopt a universal code of trade regulations governing imports from nonmember nations. Adoption of common import codes throughout the five-member trade area would greatly simplify the tasks faced by local businesses that export goods to more than one country in the pact. Further progress in this direction depends on the policy orientation of member governments. Venezuela, in particular, has wavered in recent years and has reversed previously implemented market-oriented trade and investment measures. Examples include strictly regulated retail merchandise, foreign currency and financial markets.

Other important regional trade associations in Latin America include MERCOSUR and CACM. MERCOSUR, an acronym that stands for "common market of the south," includes Argentina, Brazil, Paraguay and Uruguay, and has a combined regional income in excess of $400 billion. Negotiations are underway that may bring Chile into the agreement. Doing so would further reduce member-nation import barriers since Chile has freer trade than any other country in the region (Inter-American Development Bank 1991). Of course, the future of MERCOSUR will be influenced by business-cycle fluctuations and face ongoing risks associated with sometimes-volatile Latin American nationalism. The importance of MERCOSUR is underscored by the fact that prior to 1990, Brazil traded more with the Netherlands than with Argentina (Moffett 1994).

CACM stands for the Central American Common Market, an organization whose negotiations paralleled those for NAFTA. Ironically, business groups in Panamá voiced the same concerns as many in Florida and other parts of the United States with respect to cheap-labor availability resulting in unfair trade advantages and investment losses to other CACM member nations. Florida trade with this region has historically been high and was boosted by the Caribbean Basin Initiative. Similar to other regions of the hemisphere, however, Florida's marketing inroads there will be influenced more by structural adjustment policies and future economic performance than by trade agreements (for more on this topic see Williamson 1990).

Of course, no Latin American economy is more in need of market-oriented adjustments than the "centrally planned" recession-plagued island of Cuba. Although Cuban economic performance is hampered by the ongoing trade embargo imposed by the United States, the greatest source of stagnation arises out of self-inflicted policy errors. The risks implied by disastrous economic practices in Cuba became fairly obvious yet again in 1994 when approximately thirty-five thousand "balseros" left the island and roughly three thousand made landfall in Monroe County.

Adoption of market-oriented policies is the only long-term method for reducing pressures for widespread migration from the island. If Cuba ever enacts political and economic reforms, and rejoins the world economy, there will be opportunities for immense flows of trade and investment to and from Miami. The latter will probably trigger a similar trade boom throughout the rest of the Caribbean basin (for discussion, see Jenkins and Haines 1994).

Although the timing remains uncertain, negotiated diplomatic agreements between Washington and Havana may eventually lift the current economic embargo. If (or when) this occurs, huge quantities of Florida-produced goods and services will be in demand. Potential merchandise exports include computers and peripherals, telecommunications equipment, medical machinery, engineering and laboratory devices, automobile parts and fertilizers. The market for service exports to Cuba is also expected to be very large. Examples include accounting, advertising, banking, educational, health care, insurance, legal and franchising. Of course, some Florida businesses can expect Cuban competition in world export markets for items produced in both regions. Agricultural products such as sugar, cigars and tobacco, fresh fruits and vegetables are historical examples. In the service arena, winter tourism is probably the primary area of overlap, while in manufacturing, apparel output in Cuba is likely to increase.

Florida Trade Flows

Common methods for classifying regional trade flows include countries of origin, product destination and product categories. Analyzing Florida's export-import mix in this manner underscores the diversity

Table 2. Major Florida Exports

Category	1993 Value ($ billions)	1994 Value ($ billions)
Total	18.204	20.514
Industrial Machinery and Computers	3.460	4.013
Electrical and Electronic Equipment	2.592	3.173
Transportation Equipment	2.665	2.836
Chemical Products	2.020	2.601
Scientific Instruments	1.238	1.332
Apparel and Textile Products	0.874	1.023
Food and Kindred Products	0.936	1.006
Paper Products	0.630	0.668
Unprocessed Crops	0.515	0.544
Fabricated Metal Products	0.553	0.521

Source: Florida Department of Commerce.

of the state's international business sector. Although Florida is known throughout the world for its high-quality citrus output, food and kindred product exports ranked only sixth in total trade volume among state merchandise exports in 1993. Despite growing to more than $1 billion in 1994, this category's ranking fell one spot to seventh, overcome by surging international apparel sales (see Table 2). It comes as a surprise to most casual observers of the Sunshine State that the top export category is industrial machinery and computer equipment.

In fact, industrial machinery and computer equipment exports (Standard Industrial Classification, or SIC, 35) make up a larger proportion of Florida exports than they do of overall U.S. exports. Other top-five export categories include electronic equipment (SIC 36), transportation equipment (SIC 37), chemical products such as phosphatic fertilizers (SIC 28) and scientific instruments (SIC 38). For a region of the nation that is not located near major domestic markets for manufactured goods, international trade is one means by which Florida can compete in these high-value-added segments of the national industrial sector. More than half of all Florida-origin exports in 1993 and 1994 were high-tech manufactured products.

An interesting characteristic of U.S. trade not shown in Tables 1 or 2 is that Florida accounts for more than 15 percent of the nation's exports in both apparel and forestry products (Evans et al. 1995). Other items of note include the fact that seven of the state's top ten export markets (and ten of its top fourteen) are in Latin America. One of the most contentious aspects of the NAFTA treaty was that it dismantled trade barriers between industrial and developing economies, a step that had never been attempted by any previous agreement of this nature and was consequently viewed with suspicion. As seen in Table 1, this type of arrangement seems eminently logical from a Florida sales perspective.

As it is for the rest of the United States, Canada is the largest destination market for export goods made by Florida manufacturers and primary commodity producers. Ranking next in order of magnitude are Brazil, Colombia, Argentina, the Dominican Republic and Venezuela. Colombia and Argentina have removed many tariff and nontariff barriers to imported goods during the 1990s, directly benefiting many Florida companies. Venezuela and Brazil have more-checkered trade practices and growth patterns but still represent large markets. Cracking the top ten list for exports for the first time in 1994 was mainland China, a potentially huge market with nearly 1.1 billion consumers.

Size is not the only factor that determines which region becomes an important export market. For example, proximity is probably the principal reason that the relatively small island economy of the Dominican Republic is among Florida's top ten export markets. Mexico may eventually work its way up on future versions of this list as NAFTA and other trade efforts help strengthen economic links across both the Gulf of Mexico and the Rio Grande. The presence of Japan in Table 1 is not surprising since it represents an important target market for the entire country. Another small nation, Paraguay, was Florida's tenth-largest export destination in 1994. Other economies ranking among the top fifteen export markets but not appearing in Table 1 include Chile, Great Britain, Guatemala, Panamá and Ecuador.

International business is not without risks, especially when important overseas markets are subject to severe business-cycle volatility. For example, Florida merchandise exports fell by more than

$500 million in 1993. The decline was attributable to a number of different causes. Some of the principal complicating factors include an intense recession brought about by self-imposed congressional economic policy mistakes in Venezuela; output collapses in the agricultural sectors of Eastern Europe and mainland China leading to lower global demand for phosphatic fertilizers; and generally weak demands for imports in advanced markets such as the United Kingdom and Japan. Events such as those of 1993 underscore why Florida firms engaged in international marketing must be nimble.

From a strictly regional perspective, international trade contributes to the economic well-being of the state through demands for financial, port, warehouse, freight and distribution services. Demand for these nontradable services is associated with both exports and imports. This translates into business and job-opportunity benefits that go beyond the standard output and welfare improvements normally analyzed in theoretical studies. Florida firms are actively engaged in providing financing, insurance and freight services to support export and import flows to and from the United States. As shown in Tables 3 and 4, huge volumes of goods are involved and servicing them generates immense earnings.

Table 3 also illustrates an important point with respect to U.S. (and Florida) export volumes to Latin America and the Caribbean: economic performance matters more than negotiated trade agreements. Although Florida goods are marketed throughout the world, the principal destinations of merchandise that departs the nation via the Tampa and Miami customs districts are generally located in points south (Evans et al. 1995). Figure 1 shows the impact of the 1980s international debt crisis on U.S. trade, as real exports remained below their 1981 level for six consecutive years. Economic stagnation combined with debt-servicing difficulties to severely constrain the demand for imports throughout the region.

Income performance in Latin America finally stabilized as country after country began adopting structural reform measures in the late 1980s (Fullerton 1993). This trend accelerated following the introduction of the Brady Initiative for debt restructuring in 1989 and the emergence of market-oriented policy reforms in Eastern Europe in the early 1990s (Cline 1995). The upsurge in Florida exit

Table 3. Value of Florida-Exit Exports 1980-1994

Year	Nominal ($ billions)	Constant (1987 $ billions)
1980	10.012	11.495
1981	10.967	11.807
1982	9.868	10.366
1983	7.832	8.091
1984	8.987	9.087
1985	8.986	9.197
1986	9.319	9.617
1987	10.837	10.837
1988	13.552	12.870
1989	14.444	13.411
1990	15.518	14.224
1991	18.626	16.826
1992	21.276	19.202
1993	21.820	19.711
1994	25.074	20.723

Source: Florida Department of Commerce.

exports accompanied these developments even though they predated NAFTA and any future North-South trade agreements that will result from the 1995 Summit of the Americas held in Miami. While treaties of this nature will undoubtedly have important implications for business trends and practices, international sales volumes will continue to be determined primarily by economic performance patterns abroad. The change in the respective rankings in Table 1 for Brazil and Venezuela underscores this point.

One final note with respect to the importance of international exports for the economy of modern-day Florida warrants mention. Much of the state's rapid economic growth over the past fifty years has been related to defense spending, space exploration and retiree relocation. These sources of growth are expected to taper off and remain below their levels attained during the 1980s for the foreseeable future. In the year 2000, the depression-era birth dearth will effectively cap the pool of potential retirees nationwide. The latter is

Table 4. Value of Florida-Entry Imports 1980-1984

Year	Nominal ($ billions)	Constant (1987 $ billions)
1980	6.436	6.347
1981	7.427	7.107
1982	7.184	7.206
1983	7.950	8.290
1984	10.380	10.960
1985	11.244	12.236
1986	13.357	14.332
1987	13.283	13.283
1988	14.035	13.354
1989	13.814	12.815
1990	15.065	13.547
1991	15.065	13.646
1992	16.885	15.406
1993	18.057	16.813
1994	20.863	18.892

Source: Florida Department of Commerce.

expected to cause net migration to be approximately 25 percent below its level in 1987 (West, Lenze and Tracy 1994). Separately, lower defense spending is projected to contribute to an ongoing decline in durable manufacturing employment in Florida over the 1995-97 period, in addition to that caused by technological improvements (West and Fullerton 1994).

As a result, state industries must find new markets in which to compete if the local standard of living is to continue to rise. For high-tech manufacturing and service firms that formerly served the defense industry and aerospace activities associated with NASA, seeking new markets abroad in this era of global technological investment is a natural response to the changes occurring domestically. Given the international policy trends described above, the timing for this type of market diversification effort is probably the best that it will ever be. International trade is thus likely to remain one of the major engines of growth in the Florida economy for years to come.

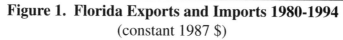

Figure 1. Florida Exports and Imports 1980-1994
(constant 1987 $)

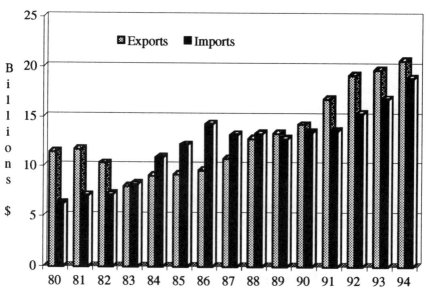

Import entry points also enjoy benefits associated with trade flows. These disembarkation areas include cities with seaports and airports, and occasionally cities with airports only. Anecdotal evidence regarding the advantages provided by international commerce was reported by the construction sector in Florida during the early 1990s. Excess capacity in the form of empty space combined with the 1990-91 recession to force statewide industrial construction to a virtual standstill. With the exception of Lakeland and Ocala, and to a lesser degree Daytona Beach, the only metropolitan economies in Florida to observe any serious volumes of industrial construction were those in which international trade was increasing (Moss and Kessel 1992). Types of industrial construction occurring included seaport and airport cargo units, warehouse sites and distribution facilities.

The import product mix entering the United States via Florida continues to diversify and expand. In 1993, Miami International Airport replaced JFK in New York as the nation's top international cargo airport (Stumpfl 1994). Chilean fresh fruit such as table grapes and apples traditionally has entered the country via the Philadelphia customs district. Winter produce from this South American country is now unloaded in Jacksonville too, for distribution among south-eastern U.S. retail points of sale. Miami and Port Everglades (Ft. Lauderdale) have been designated as coffee exchange ports, meaning that coffee can be imported and stored for later sale. More than simply importing merchandise already purchased by manufacturers, coffee trading centers serve as commodity exchange markets for brokerage deals. This type of activity goes well beyond serving as a transshipment facility and will foster new business opportunities in Broward and Dade counties.

Direct Foreign Investment in Florida

Trade in goods and services enhances consumer welfare by allowing these items to be acquired in excess of the levels at which they are produced within a given economy. Direct foreign investment (DFI) also improves social welfare in a given region by expanding the total volumes of goods and services produced there. When capital investment occurs, it raises the productive capacity of the area in which it takes place. The capacity expansion is realized irrespective of where the funding for the investment originates. In that sense, DFI is doubly beneficial because it makes available financial resources in excess of the savings pool already present in a regional economy. As output rises subsequent to the new investment, employment and incomes increase in a parallel fashion.

Table 5 lists the primary sources of DFI in Florida. Not surprisingly, nearly all of the capital inflows to Florida come from industrialized regions of the world such as Western Europe, Japan, Australia and Canada. That is because DFI occurs when excess savings in one country are invested in another. In order to invest abroad, surplus capital resources must be available. This is obviously not the case in capital-starved regions of the world where industrial development lags behind that of the OECD nations. It should be pointed out that prior to 1981, the United States was a net creditor to the global financial system. Due to ongoing federal budget deficits that increased enormously during the past fourteen years, this nation is now a net debtor similar to Florida's neighbors to the south.

Table 5. Direct Foreign Investment in Florida
($ billions)

Region	1988	1990	1992
Total	11.905	18.659	21.758
Europe	5.963	9.483	11.883
United Kingdom	1.853	3.517	4.396
France	0.547	1.185	1.930
Germany	0.729	1.203	1.508
Netherlands	0.986	0.897	1.035
Asia and the Pacific	0.739	3.240	3.997
Japan	0.335	1.685	2.553
Australia	0.200	0.852	0.659
Canada	3.021	3.599	2.788
Latin America	1.072	1.319	1.687
Middle East and Africa	1.109	1.019	1.202

Source: Florida Department of Commerce.

In 1992, Florida's most important source of foreign investment was the United Kingdom. In second place was Canada, closely followed by Japan. Similar to the country trade rankings in Table 1, the volumes of DFI arriving from source countries vary annually and can change the ordering from year to year. Within the state manufacturing sector, electrical and electronic equipment is the segment receiving the highest level of DFI (Ondrich and Wasylenko 1993). Nearly all DFI flows are predicated on the basis of business criteria. Factors influencing the choice of Florida as an investment location for international corporations include its domestic market size and the presence of other firms within given industries. Among the few fiscal-policy instruments that may significantly influence DFI decisions, expenditures on higher education are perhaps the most effective.

As shown in Table 5, not all of Florida's DFI comes from industrialized trading partners. In fact, there are many instances in which some of the most important services produced in the state economy result from Latin American DFI. One well-known example is the large volume of trade financing provided by the "Brickell Avenue" international banks in Miami (Ramsey 1990). Less well-known is that the Chilean telecommunications company Americatel is the first foreign-held long-distance company to open its headquarters in a North American city (Stumpfl 1994). Latin American subsidiaries from a variety of industries are being set up in cities around the state, although mostly in Dade and Broward counties.

A Look Ahead

As opposed to the old saying in real estate, international trade is governed by more than just location, location, location. In the case of Florida, however, geographic proximity has provided important comparative advantages to the state's international business sector. A large percentage of all U.S. exports to, and imports from, Latin America and the Caribbean are shipped via Florida ports situated throughout the state. These factors will resurface as never before if (or when) political barriers to trade with Cuba are removed. Once that occurs, more than thirty years of pent-up demand for Florida goods and services will be unleashed.

In addition to the commercial opportunities awaiting Florida businesses in Cuba, trade between the two nations makes sense from another regional perspective. Intensely substandard economic performance is destroying the collective standard of living on the island. Undeniably, the bulk of the negative income growth results from poorly designed policies. According to recent refugee accounts, the downward economic spiral is making residents want to leave. Nearly all the potential migrants want to reach the United States, especially Dade County. If a mass wave of new refugees left the island, it would probably generate significant financial, economic and social responsibilities for the state.

Poor economic performance is forcing the Cuban government to grudgingly allow markets to emerge along with a new business sector. As seen in Eastern Europe, the transition from a centrally planned economy to one where resource allocation is determined by market interactions can be fraught with uncertainty. In the case of Cuba, if transition dislocations are severe, the pressures to migrate will intensify. One way of reducing migration pressures would be to make the transition from central planning be less disruptive by lifting the trade embargo. If economic conditions in Cuba continue to deteriorate, Florida can expect to receive further outpourings of unemployed Cubans.

Nongeographic factors will also influence future trends in Florida international commerce. One deals with mainland China, another economy making the transition from central planning to market-oriented resource allocation. As shown in Table 1, Florida-origin exports to China surged in 1994, causing it to become one of our top ten markets abroad. Widely projected to become the world's largest economy by the year 2010, it is fairly certain that the Chinese economy looms large in Florida's economic future. Because other Asian economies have also adopted growth-oriented approaches to economic policymaking, the region as a whole will probably figure prominently as a trade partner for the state. The upward trend in Asian direct foreign investment in Table 5 is likely to persist, also.

Unfortunately for the state economy, governments in Florida's most important Latin American trading partners generally take longer to enact many structural adjustment measures now spreading across Asia. Significant roadblocks to privatization and other helpful reform measures still exist throughout Central and South America (McCoy 1993). Cyclical markets for many of their major primary commodity exports such as coffee and petroleum are also likely to affect current account balances and demands for imports from Florida and elsewhere. Consequently, while Latin America is expected to remain a hugely important factor in the state's economic future, sales volumes to the region will probably oscillate. At least over the short run, Florida enterprises conducting business in Latin America should prepare to operate in as flexible a manner as possible in order to respond to potentially rapid shifts in regional market conditions.

References

Barkema, Alan, and Mark Drabenstott. 1994. "A New Agricultural Policy for a New World Market." *Economic Review* 79 (Second Quarter). Federal Reserve Bank of Kansas City.

Cline, William. 1995. *International Debt Re-examined.* Washington, D.C.: Institute for International Economics.

Cook, Roberta, C. Benito, J. Matson, D. Runsten, K. Schwedel, T. Taylor, T. Spreen, R. Muraro and G. Fairchild. 1991. "Fruit and Vegetable Issues." *NAFTA Volume 4.* Park Ridge, Illinois: American Farm Bureau Research Foundation.

Business Focus. 1994. "The Tyranny of Triangles." *The Economist* (July 16).

Denslow, David, and Thomas M. Fullerton, Jr. 1995. "Consumer Attitudes toward Trade Liberalization." *Applied Economics Letters* (forthcoming).

Denslow, David, Thomas M. Fullerton, Jr., and Christopher McCarty. 1993. "What NAFTA Means to Florida." *Economic Leaflets* 52 (November). Gainesville: University of Florida, Bureau of Economic and Business Research.

Evans, Patricia, A. Gay, K. Reeves and R. Ribeiro. 1995. *The Impact of Foreign Trade on Florida's Economy.* Seventh Annual Report. Tallahassee: Division of Economic Development, Florida Department of Commerce.

Fullerton, Thomas M. Jr. 1993. "Development Trends in Latin American Economies" in Soo-Keun Kim, Chul-Hwan Kim and Yoosik Gong, eds. *Comparison of Development Experiences: Latin America and Korea.* Seoul, Korea: Ajou University Press.

Hufbauer, Gary C., and Jeffrey J. Schott. 1992. *North American Free Trade: Issues and Recommendations.* Washington, D.C.: Institute for International Economics.

Inter-American Development Bank. 1991. *Economic and Social Progress in Latin America.* Washington, D.C.: Johns Hopkins University Press.

Jenkins, Gareth, and Lila Haines. 1994. *Cuba: Prospects for Reform, Trade, and Investment.* New York: The Economist Intelligence Unit.

McCoy, Terry L. 1993. "Democratic Transition and Economic Reform in Latin America" in Soo-Keun Kim, Chul-Hwan Kim and Yoosik Gong, eds. *Comparison of Development Experiences: Latin America and Korea.* Seoul, Korea: Ajou University Press.

Moffett, Matt. 1994. "Spreading the Gospel." *The Wall Street Journal* (October 28).

Moss, William, and Gregory W. Kessel. 1992. "Florida Commercial Real Estate Markets." Paper presented at the University of Florida-Goodkin Research Florida Economic Development Outlook Conference.

Narisetti, Raju. 1994. "Not Everybody Wins." *The Wall Street Journal* (October 28).

Ondrich, Jan, and Michael Wasylenko. 1993. *Foreign Direct Investment in the United States.* Kalamazoo, Michigan: W.E. Upjohn Institute.

Ramsey, Sally. 1990. "International Trade and Investment" in David Denslow, Ann Pierce and Anne Shermyen, eds. *The Economy of Florida: 1990 Edition.* Gainesville: University of Florida, Bureau of Economic and Business Research.

Stumpfl, Amy. 1994. "Florida, A New Beginning." *Plant Sites & Parks* 21 (November/December).

West, Carol, and Thomas M. Fullerton, Jr. 1994. "Forecast Summary: Florida Economy." *The Florida Outlook* 18 (Third Quarter). Gainesville: University of Florida, Bureau of Economic and Business Research.

West, Carol, David Lenze and Tony Tracy. 1994. "Volume 1: Metropolitan Statistical Areas." *The Florida Long-Term Economic Forecast.* Gainesville: University of Florida, Bureau of Economic and Business Research.

Williamson, John. 1990. *Latin American Adjustment: How Much has Happened?* Washington, D.C.: Institute for International Economics.

State and Local Government Finance

17

J. F. (Dick) Scoggins
Associate Director
Bureau of Economic
and Business Research
University of Florida
Gainesville, Florida

State and local governments comprise a large sector of the economy of Florida. As Figure 1 indicates, the number of people employed by the state and local governments as a percentage of all employed Floridians has remained over 10 percent since 1969 and is about four times the percentage of civilians employed by the federal government.

As Florida's population and economy grow the state and local governments' respective revenue streams are not keeping pace (see

Figure 1. Federal and State and Local Civilian Government Employment as a Percentage of Total Employment 1969-1993

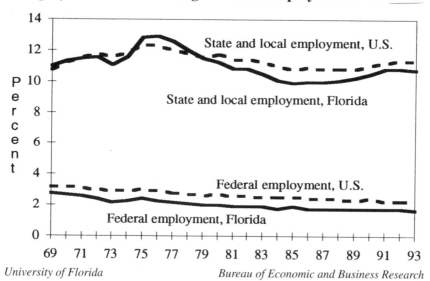

Robertson 1995). As will be shown below, government revenues in Florida are partially linked to tourism. Over the past decade the number of tourists that visit the state each year has been stagnant, while the number of permanent residents has grown. Today there are three tourists for every resident. Ten years ago this ratio was nearly four to one. This has made it increasingly difficult for governments to provide services at previous levels. There are no easy answers to this problem, but a careful analysis of how these governments finance their expenditures might provide an insight into the most likely solutions.

Why Have State and Local Governments?

Perhaps the best way to start this analysis is to describe the reasons why a government sector is a necessary component of a well-functioning state economy. Basically, there are only two rationales for state and local government revenue collections and expenditures, which will be referred to respectively as efficiency and equity.

Efficiency for Expenditures. All resources are scarce and no goods or services are ever truly free. But the production and distribution method that minimizes the costs to the producers and maximizes the benefits to the consumers is by definition efficient. For most goods and services efficient production can be achieved only by the private (nongovernment) sector. The interplay of supply and demand generates a market price that provides an adequate incentive for suppliers to produce and sell the good or service. The market price also conveys to the consumer the cost of producing a certain good relative to an alternative good and allows for the least costly way of satisfying the consumer's preferences.

However, under certain conditions, the efficiency of the private market breaks down. When this happens it is known as "market failure." The causes of market failure are few and very specific. One of them is the "free-rider" problem. Once a good with this kind of problem is produced, its consumption or enjoyment cannot be denied to any specific group of individuals. Hence failure to pay for the good will not prevent an individual from benefiting from its production. And consequently the supplier cannot recoup production costs.

Police protection is a prime example of the free-rider problem. Almost everyone benefits when a habitual criminal is put behind bars. But excluding this benefit from individuals who refuse to pay for it is impossible. Without the economic incentive of revenue from free riders, there will be no private suppliers of police protection, even though the benefits of such protection greatly outweigh the costs.

A related cause of market failure is known as the "spillover" problem. This happens when either the cost or the benefit of a good affects someone other than the supplier or the consumer of the good. For most goods and services there are no spillovers. All the costs of production are incurred by the producers and all the benefits of consumption are enjoyed by the consumers. But for some goods, this is not the case. Primary education, for example, has many positive spillovers. Literate people are less likely to commit crimes against others. They are also able to make more informed decisions with regard to political candidates. They better understand how contagious diseases are spread and are better able to prevent that from happening. If the quantity and quality of primary education were determined solely by the private market, fewer resources would be devoted to that sector than would be economically efficient.

Many spillovers are negative. Wildlife habitat degradation is an example. Land development often destroys forests and wetlands. Declining populations of animals, such as the Florida cougar, are a cost borne by society, not just by the commercial land developers. Since most of this cost is not incurred by the suppliers, it need not be recouped in order to make the enterprise feasible. If left strictly to market forces, more land would be developed and more wildlife habitat degradation would occur than would be economically efficient.

Efficiency for Revenues. In order for a government to spend money it must have revenues. Other things the same, the efficient revenue system inflicts the smallest cost to the economy for each dollar collected. This may seem paradoxical since the cost of giving away a dollar is a dollar. However when a dollar is taken away involuntarily, such as by taxation, the economic cost is greater than one dollar.

The extra cost occurs because of the disincentives that arise with all taxes. For example a sales tax either lowers the revenue the producer receives or raises the price the consumer pays or both. Either way the information conveyed in the market price is distorted and the incentive to produce and consume the good is diminished. Thus the producers and consumers not only lose the money they pay in taxes; they also suffer because of the change in their selling and buying decisions caused by the change in the price of the taxed good relative to the prices of the other goods.

There are various strategies to implementing an efficient tax system. One is to impose as broad-based a tax system as possible. Theoretically, if all goods were taxed in the same proportion then their prices would rise proportionately and their relative prices would not change at all. This would minimize the extra cost of the tax.

Another strategy is to tax only the sale of those goods and services produced in markets in which the supply and demand do not react much to a price change. For example, if the supply of labor were little affected by a change in the wage rate, then a tax on the sale of labor would have little cost to the laborer other than the income given to the government.

Still another strategy is to "export" the tax by taxing out-of-state residents. For example, when a tourist from New York buys gasoline in Florida, the tax she pays provides revenue that could be used to supply education or to maintain roads in Florida. This practice is not necessarily efficient from a national perspective but it is efficient from a state and local perspective.

Yet another strategy is to charge directly for the use of government goods and services that have no free-rider problems. These include medical care at publicly owned hospitals and instruction at institutions of higher learning. Given that taxes always entail a total cost which exceeds their revenues, charges are always preferable on efficiency grounds.

Equity for Expenditures. The other rationale for government expenditures is equity or wealth redistribution. Many people see our unevenly distributed wealth as a major source of our social problems. Consequently, taking from the rich and giving to the poor is seen by these people as a constructive government function. Without arguing the pros and cons of the best way to approach the poverty problem, let it suffice to say that the existence of poverty in

Florida is undeniable. According to the most recent census, over 12 percent of Floridians live below the official poverty level. Death rates, crime rates and illiteracy rates are much higher for this group than for the general population.

There are two basic ways of redistributing wealth. One is by transfer payments. These payments are simply government revenues given to individuals. An example of a transfer-payment program at the state government level would be Aid to Families with Dependent Children (AFDC). This is a program in conjunction with the national government by which the state government gives monthly payments to low-income families with children.

The other way of redistributing wealth is by subsidizing the production of goods and services consumed by low-income groups. Primary education is an example. By providing primary education free to all income groups, people from low-income groups, who could not otherwise afford to pay for education and who pay little taxes, are made wealthier through increased lifetime income. People from high-income groups pay more in taxes than they would have to pay for a private education of equal value. Thus public support for primary education is justified on both efficiency and equity grounds.

Equity for Revenues. Wealth redistribution can also be facilitated through progressive taxation, which extracts a smaller percentage of a poor person's income than a rich person's income. Regressive taxes are counterproductive in terms of equity since they extract a greater percentage from low-income groups.

An example of progressive taxation is the property tax. Since most low-income people do not own real estate, they pay no property taxes, at least not directly. Hence their property tax bill as a percentage of their income is zero. This is not so for people with high incomes, who own most of the real estate property. Conversely, sales taxes are typically regressive, because a sales tax is levied only on consumption expenditures and not investment expenditures. Poor households spend a much greater percentage of their incomes on consumption goods than do rich households.

Equity vs. Efficiency. A source of many a political argument is the confounding dilemma between equity and efficiency. It seems that any program or practice that promotes the one, detracts from the other. For example, the most efficient tax in theory is the "head" tax. Under this tax each individual would pay the same fixed quantity of money to the government, regardless of income. No relative prices are distorted and so there is no extra cost of the tax beyond the transfer of funds to the government. Unfortunately, such a tax would be extremely regressive and is therefore undesirable on equity grounds.

Another example is the corporate income tax. This tax is thought by many to be a good vehicle for wealth redistribution because the corporate stockholders bear most of the burden of this tax and they are relatively wealthy. However, a corporate income tax is tantamount to a tax on capital investment, the supply of which is very sensitive to changes in price. Financial capital can easily be transported across state lines or even internationally to areas with less capital-investment taxation. Therefore this seemingly equitable tax is also very inefficient.

This dilemma has given rise to the search for the holy grail of government finance, a revenue and expenditure system that promotes both equity and efficiency. Although a worthwhile objective, such a system, called "first best" by economists, may not be possible. Any system that tends to neglect one goal or the other will not long meet with political success. Government policymakers should keep this in mind.

Revenues and Expenses

In 1992 Florida's state and local governments' combined budgets were in excess of $47 billion.[1] Tables 1 and 2 present the specific items of revenue and expenditure in per capita terms for Florida and the rest of the nation. As one can see, the combined per capita revenues and expenditures of state and local governments in Florida are smaller than that for the rest of the nation. This gives credence to the notion that Florida is a fiscally conservative state with a relatively small government sector.

Florida's allocation of revenues and expenditures between the state and local governments is also atypical. Nearly half of all rev-

---

[1]This figure excludes employee trust funds and publicly owned utilities and nets out the expenditures of the Florida lottery.

Table 1. Revenues for State and Local Governments Fiscal Year 1992

Sources	Florida							All Other States and D.C.						
	State and Local		State		Local			State and Local		State		Local		
	Per Capita	% of Total	Per Capita	% of Total	Per Capita	% of Total	% of State & Local	Per Capita	% of Total	Per Capita	% of Total	Per Capita	% of Total	% of State & Local
Taxes (Total)	1,922	56.4	1,075	61.9	846	50.7	44.0	2,192	57.2	1,299	54.9	893	60.8	40.7
Sales	965	28.3	844	48.6	121	7.2	12.5	758	19.8	626	26.5	132	9.0	17.4
Property	738	21.7	36	2.1	702	42.0	95.0	697	18.2	26	1.1	671	45.7	96.3
Individual Income	0	0.0	0	0.0	0	0.0	—	477	12.4	433	18.3	44	3.0	9.2
Other Taxes	219	6.4	195	11.2	23	1.4	10.5	260	6.8	214	9.0	46	3.1	17.7
Federal Grants	471	13.8	401	23.1	70	4.2	14.9	715	18.6	636	26.9	79	5.4	11.0
Charges (Total)	567	16.6	95	5.5	472	28.2	83.2	535	14.0	214	9.0	321	21.9	60.0
Transportation	81	2.4	21	1.2	60	3.6	74.1	50	1.3	16	0.7	34	2.3	68.0
Hospital	168	4.9	7	0.4	161	9.6	95.8	147	3.8	52	2.2	95	6.5	64.6
Higher Education	63	1.8	42	2.4	21	1.3	33.3	129	3.4	116	4.9	13	0.9	10.1
Environ. & Housing	145	4.3	4	0.3	141	8.4	97.2	117	3.0	11	0.5	106	7.2	90.1
Other Charges	110	3.2	21	1.2	89	5.3	80.9	92	2.4	19	0.8	73	5.0	79.3
Interest Earnings	247	7.2	65	3.7	182	10.9	73.7	215	5.6	106	4.5	109	7.4	50.7
Other	202	5.9	102	5.9	100	6.0	49.5	178	4.6	111	4.7	67	4.6	37.6
Total	3,409	100.0	1,738	100.0	1,671	100.0	49.0	3,835	100.0	2,366	100.0	1,469	100.0	38.3

Source: Government Finances: 91-92 (Preliminary Report), U.S. Department of Commerce.

Table 2. Expenditures for State and Local Governments Fiscal Year 1992

| Function | Florida | | | | | | | All Other States and D.C. | | | | | | |
| | State and Local | | State | | Local | | | State and Local | | State | | Local | | |
	Per Capita	% of Total	Per Capita	% of Total	Per Capita	% of Total	% of State & Local	Per Capita	% of Total	Per Capita	% of Total	Per Capita	% of Total	% of State & Local
Education (Total)	1,090	31.2	195	16.0	895	39.4	82.1	1,292	33.7	348	21.4	944	42.9	73.1
Primary & Secondary	819	23.4	0	0.0	819	36.0	100.0	902	23.6	9	0.6	893	40.5	99.0
Higher	228	6.5	152	12.5	76	3.3	33.3	336	8.8	276	17.5	51	2.3	15.2
Other	43	1.2	43	3.5	0	0.0	0.0	54	1.4	54	3.3	0	0.0	0.0
Public Safety	405	11.6	109	8.9	296	13.0	73.1	324	8.5	107	6.6	217	9.9	67.0
Public Welfare	399	11.4	382	31.3	17	0.7	4.3	616	16.1	477	29.3	139	6.3	22.6
Environ. & Housing	351	10.0	71	5.8	280	12.3	79.8	304	7.9	64	3.9	240	10.9	78.9
Transportation	323	9.2	149	12.2	174	7.7	53.9	305	8.0	166	10.2	139	6.3	45.6
Interest on Debt	230	6.6	55	4.5	175	7.7	76.1	216	5.6	99	6.1	117	5.3	54.2
Hospital	223	6.4	38	3.1	185	8.1	83.0	231	6.0	106	6.5	125	5.7	54.1
Government Adm.	201	6.0	79	6.5	122	5.4	60.7	197	5.1	78	4.8	119	5.4	60.4
Other	271	7.8	141	11.5	130	5.7	48.0	344	9.0	181	11.1	163	7.4	47.4
Total	3,493	100.0	1,219	100.0	2,274	100.0	65.1	3,829	100.0	1,626	100.0	2,203	100.0	57.5

Source: Government Finances: 91-92 (Preliminary Report), U.S. Department of Commerce.

enues are collected by the local governments in Florida. For the rest of the nation, this figure is less than 40 percent. The local governments in Florida account for over 65 percent of all expenditures whereas for the rest of the nation this figure is less than 58 percent. Therefore, in Florida the local governments control a larger share of revenues and expenditures than in the other states. In fact the per capita *levels* of revenues and expenditures of local governments in Florida are greater than those for the rest of the nation on average. This partially offsets the comparatively small role of the Florida state government.

The above-mentioned figures indicate that the local governments in Florida, like those for the rest of the nation, account for a greater percentage of expenditures than they do revenues. This occurs because the state governments transfer funds to the local governments. However, the local governments in Florida, which receive $630 per capita on average, depend on this form of revenue less than local governments in other states, which receive $772 per capita.

For discussion purposes, we will analyze individual revenue and expenditure programs by grouping them into three categories: pure revenue, pure expenditure and combined revenue-expenditure.

Pure Revenue. Pure revenue consists of revenue sources that are not associated with nor create a specific expenditure other than incidental collection costs. These would include all taxes and federal government grants. In Florida pure revenues account for 70.2 percent of total revenues, whereas in the rest of the nation they account for 75.8 percent. This difference is due almost entirely to Florida's relatively low share of federal government grants. In 1992 Florida's $471 per capita share ranked it last among all the states in federal government grants per capita. The average for the rest of the country was $715. Florida's last-place allocation that year was typical since it had held that position since at least 1983.

The reasons why Florida receives so little federal grant money were detailed in Scoggins (1995). The major reason is that the Florida governments spend much less per capita on welfare programs than the other states' governments do on average ($399 vs. $616 in 1992), even though per capita income in Florida is very close to that for the rest of the nation ($19,664 vs. $20,137 in 1992). The allocation formulas for over half of all federal grant funds give more to states that spend more on welfare programs and also to states with well-below-average income. Florida misses out on both scores.

Although Florida's governments receive in taxes the same percentage of total revenues as the rest of the nation, the mixture of the types of taxes is quite different. Most significantly Florida has no revenues from individual income taxes. Such taxes account for over 12 percent of the revenues for the other states. This difference is made up by Florida's relatively high sales and property taxes.

The individual income tax is thought by many economists to be a relatively efficient tax. Recall that the less sensitive to a price change the demand or supply is for a good that is taxed, the less distorted are the choices to buy and sell goods and thus the more efficient is the tax. Since an individual income tax is largely a tax on the sale of labor, the sensitivity of the supply of labor is a major determining factor of the efficiency of the income tax. Hansson and Stuart (1985) cite numerous studies that find the sensitivity of labor supply to a wage change to be very small. The implication is that the income tax is an efficient tax.

However a tax is more efficient, at least from the point of view of state residents, the more the tax burden is borne by tourists. The fact that an income tax is levied only on state residents diminishes its efficiency. An income tax is also harder to enforce and it places a larger tax-preparation burden on the taxpayer than do sales and property taxes. Thus it is unknown what net effect the absence of an individual income tax has on the efficiency of Florida's tax system.

The individual income tax is also thought by many economists to be a relatively equitable tax because its tax rate can be adjusted upward with an individual's income, thus making it progressive. However, since property taxes are considered progressive while sales taxes are considered regressive, it is unknown whether Florida's tax system is relatively equitable or not compared to those of other states.

During the previous two recessions in 1991 and 1982, the state government saw sales tax revenue fall dramatically while demands for state assistance grew. These fiscal crises were blamed by many on the procyclical nature of sales tax revenues and led to calls for a broadening of the tax base by implementing an individual income tax. Although there is ample evidence that sales tax revenues are greatly affected by the business cycle, the relevant point is the degree of the procyclicality of sales tax revenues *relative to income tax revenues* (see Fox and Campbell 1984). In two separate studies, White (1983) and Holcombe and Sobel (1994) find income tax revenues to be more procyclical than sales tax revenues. If these findings are correct, then implementation of an income tax would exacerbate the state's fiscal crises during recessions rather than alleviate them.

Pure Expenditure. Areas of pure expenditure include primary and secondary education, public safety, public welfare and government administration. Like tax revenues as a percentage of total revenues, Florida's pure expenditures as a percent of total expenditures are quite similar to those of the rest of the country. In Florida pure expenditures total $1,867 per capita or 53.4 percent of total expenditures. For the rest of the nation, pure expenditures total $2,093 per capita or 54.7 percent of total expenditures.

The differences lie in the relative allocations among areas. As a percentage of total expenditures, Florida spends much more on public safety and a little more on government administration than the rest of the nation on average. Much less is spent on public welfare in Florida, while primary and secondary education expenditures are the same.

The emphasis on public safety is not surprising, given that Florida's location makes it a prime entry point for drug trafficking and illegal immigration. It is perhaps somewhat surprising to find that in spite of Florida's low cost of living and fiscal conservatism, the per capita cost of administering the state government is higher in both relative and absolute terms than it is for the rest of the nation.

As has already been noted, Florida's low expenditures on public welfare have had a sizable downward effect on federal grant revenues. For the rest of the nation over a fifth of all public welfare expenditures are made by local governments. In Florida less than 5 percent come from local governments. The fact that Florida's municipal governments are much less powerful than the county governments might explain this divergence.

Outside of Florida, a large city's population will typically have a high percentage of individuals from low-income households. Most of the wealth consists of corporate office and production facilities. Taxing the corporations, usually in the form of high property taxes, is a politically viable means of financing public welfare expenditures.

In Florida, county governments are more powerful and control a larger percentage of resources than do municipal governments. Furthermore, Florida has few counties (sixty-seven) relative to its population (14,000,000). These large counties encompass both urban and suburban areas, making large public welfare expenditures less politically viable.

Combined Revenue-Expenditure. Recall that one of the major justifications of government taxation is that the free-rider problem makes it impossible to charge for the use of certain goods. Many publicly provided goods do not have a free-rider problem, however, and users can be required to pay a price. Publicly provided goods for which significant amounts of revenues are raised through charges include higher education, environment and housing, transportation and hospitalization.[2] Florida relies more on charges than the rest of the nation on average, since it receives $567 per capita or 16.6 percent of its total revenues from charges versus $535 per capita or 14 percent for the rest of the nation. Florida spends $1,125 per capita or 32.2 percent of its total expenditures on these publicly provided goods, so their production is highly subsidized. The rest of the nation spends $1,266 per capita or 33.1 percent of total expenditures on these same goods.

Although Florida spends the same percentage of total expenditures on primary and secondary education as the rest of the nation, the same is not true for higher education. Florida spends only $228 per capita or 6.5 percent of total expenditures on higher education. The rest of the nation spends $336 per capita or 8.8 percent of total expenditures on higher education. The reason for this sizable difference lies chiefly in how these expenditures are financed. Florida finances only 27.6 percent of its higher education expenditures through charges, which are mostly tuition. The rest is financed

---

[2]Theoretically, primary and secondary education students could be charged for admission. However, no government in Florida or any other state has chosen this means of financing.

through tax revenues. The rest of the nation finances 38.4 percent of its higher education expenditures through charges.

This greater reliance on lagging tax revenues during a time of a burgeoning student-age population has created a difficult financial situation for Florida's institutions of higher learning. An obvious solution would be to raise tuition levels to more accurately reflect the costs of providing higher education. The increased tuition revenues could be used to bring per capita expenditures closer to that of the rest of the nation (a means of improving quality) and also to reduce the excess demand. To see how far below the rest of the nation are Florida's tuition levels for its colleges and universities, it should be noted that it would take a 63 percent increase to bring the percent of higher education expenditures financed through charges up to that for the rest of the nation.[3] Unfortunately, tuition levels are legally restricted to rise no faster than tax revenue expenditures on higher education. Until this price ceiling is relaxed, Florida's institutions of higher learning will have difficulty succeeding in a competitive national environment.

Other than in the area of higher education, Florida finances a relatively high percentage of its combined revenue-expenditure programs through direct charges. Florida finances 25.1 percent of transportation expenditures by charges versus 16.4 percent for the rest of the nation. The net result is that even though Florida spends a relatively large amount on transportation (i.e., road construction, etc.), $323 per capita versus $305 per capita for all the other states, it spends a relatively small amount from pure revenues, $242 per capita versus $255 per capita for the rest of the nation. In the area of environment and housing, Florida finances 41.3 percent of expenditures through charges versus 38.5 percent for the rest of the nation. In the area of hospitalization the respective figures are 75.3 percent and 63.6 percent. In both areas Florida spends a greater percent of its expenditures than the other states on average.

---

[3]If the increased tuition revenues were spent only on colleges and universities, a $40 per capita increase in charges (63 percent of $63 per capita) would increase per capita charges to $103 and per capita expenditures to $268. The ratio of these two figures is 38.4 percent, the same as the percent financed through charges for the rest of the nation.

University of Florida   *Bureau of Economic and Business Research*

Financial Assets and Liabilities

As in other enterprises, the flow of revenues and expenditures of state and local governments varies over time. This creates a need to borrow funds and hold financial assets. At the end of fiscal year 1992, the state and local governments in Florida held $4.8 billion worth of financial assets and almost that amount of debt. The state government alone held $1.3 billion in financial assets and $1.2 billion of debt. These facts may seem surprising for a state government that is supposedly constitutionally banned from deficit financing. In reality the so-called "deficit financing ban" is just a set of conditions under which the state government must operate when borrowing money. These conditions generally determine the type of debt instruments allowed and the purposes for which the funds can be used. Since funds are fungible and there is broad discretion in the allocation of services and responsibilities between state and local governments, the net effect of the ban on the state in general is negligible.

As Table 3 reveals, the asset and debt portfolios of the state and local governments in Florida are quite large relative to the population of the state compared to those for the rest of the nation. At the end of fiscal year 1992, Florida governments held $3,427 per capita in financial assets compared to $3,031 per capita for the rest of the nation. Likewise, the debt of Florida's governments was $3,384 per capita compared to $3,115 per capita for the rest of the nation. Florida is a rapidly growing state and its greater use of financing is to be expected.

Even though the total asset and debt amounts for all governments combined in Florida are relatively large, the state government's share is relatively small. Whereas the state governments' share of assets and debt in the other states is a little less than 50 percent, in Florida that figure is less than 30 percent. The constitutional limitations faced by the state government have merely shifted some services and responsibilities onto Florida's local governments.

Although Florida's debt and asset portfolios are relatively large, the more relevant statistic is the debt portfolio compared to assets. Table 4 reveals that Florida's debt to cash and securities ratio is only 98.7 percent compared to 102.8 percent for the rest of the nation.

Table 3. Cash and Securities, Debt and Capital Outlay of State and Local Governments Fiscal Year 1992*

Item	Florida							All Other States and D.C.						
	State and Local		State		Local			State and Local		State		Local		
	Per Capita	% of Total	Per Capita	% of Total	Per Capita	% of Total & Local	% of State	Per Capita	% of Total	Per Capita	% of Total	Per Capita	% of Total	% of State & Local
Cash & Securities (Total)	3,427	100.0	980	100.0	2,447	100.0	71.4	3,031	100.0	1,471	100.0	1,560	100.0	51.5
Beginning Balance	3,310		901		2,409		72.8	2,890		1,380		1,510		52.2
Change in Balance**	117	3.5	79	8.8	38	1.6	32.5	141	4.9	91	6.6	50	3.3	35.5
Ending Balance														
Offsets to Debt	1,685	49.2	418	42.7	1,267	51.8	75.2	1,508	49.8	873	59.3	635	40.7	42.1
Bond Funds	370	10.8	74	7.5	296	12.1	80.0	313	10.3	82	5.5	231	14.8	73.8
Other	1,372	40.0	487	49.8	885	36.2	64.5	1,210	39.9	517	35.1	693	44.4	57.3
Long-term Debt (Total)	3,384	100.0	912	100.0	2,472	100.0	73.0	3,115	100.0	1,420	100.0	1,695	100.0	54.4
Beginning Balance	3,219		822		2,397		74.5	2,935		1,319		1,616		55.1
Change in Balance**	165	5.1	90	10.9	75	3.1	45.5	180	6.1	101	7.7	79	4.9	43.9
Ending Balance														
Private Purposes	1,287	38.0	219	24.0	1,068	43.2	83.0	1,209	38.8	704	49.6	505	29.8	41.8
Education	652	19.3	378	41.4	274	11.1	42.0	447	14.3	161	11.3	286	16.9	64.0
Other	1,445	42.7	315	34.5	1,130	45.7	78.2	1,459	46.8	554	39.1	905	53.4	62.0
Capital Outlay	520		168		352		67.8	455		189		266		58.5

*Excludes Insurance Trust Funds and Utilities.
**For the Change in Balance row the Percent of Total column is percentage of Beginning Balance.
Source: Government Finances: 91-92 (Preliminary Report), U.S. Department of Commerce.

Table 4. State and Local Government Fund Ratios and Interest Rates
(percent)

Item	Florida			All Other States and D.C.		
	State & Local	State	Local	State & Local	State	Local
Ratio of Debt to Cash and Securities	98.7	93.1	101.0	102.8	96.5	108.7
Ratio of Change in Debt to Capital Outlay	31.7	53.6	21.3	39.6	53.4	29.7
Interest Rate on Debt	7.0	6.3	7.2	7.1	7.2	7.1
Interest Revenue Rate	7.3	6.9	7.5	7.3	7.4	7.0

Not only is the ratio small relative to that of other states, it is less than 100 percent. Theoretically these financial assets are primarily held as security for the holders of the state and local government debt instruments. A ratio of more than 100 percent or even close to 100 percent would appear overly cautious.

In a private corporation this excessive caution would be very expensive because the interest rate paid to borrow funds is greater than the interest rate earned on financial assets. However, such is not the case for state and local governments. The average interest rate earned was 7.3 percent in 1992 and the average interest rate paid was 7.1 percent. This occurs because interest income earned by investors in state and local bonds is not subject to the federal income tax, causing the cost of borrowing to be very low for these governments. The competitive advantage this tax loophole provides to the state and local governments acts as an incentive to both borrow and save. Table 5 indicates that state and local governments externally finance (through debt) a much greater percentage of the sources of their funds than do private corporations that do not enjoy this loophole. For Florida governments this figure is 35.9 percent versus 21.0 percent for private corporations in the U.S.

Notice in Tables 1 and 2 that in 1992, the governments of Florida earned more in interest revenue, $247 per capita, than they paid in interest expense, $230 per capita. While this practice of generating net revenues by circulating funds through the governments' portfolios makes sense from a local perspective, it is clearly bad economic policy

Table 5. Sources and Uses of Funds for State and Local
Governments and Private Corporations 1992
(percentage)

Item	Florida			All Other States and D.C.			Private Corp.
	State & Local	State	Local	State & Local	State	Local	
Uses of Funds							
Capital Expenditures	81.6	68.3	90.1	76.2	70.8	90.2	70.1
Increase in Financial							
Assets	18.4	31.7	9.9	23.8	29.2	9.8	29.9
Sources of Funds							
Internally Financed	64.1	75.9	56.6	63.7	64.7	62.9	79.0
Externally Financed*	35.9	24.1	43.4	36.3	35.3	37.1	21.0

*Financed by debt.

Source: Government Finances: 91-92 (Preliminary Report), U.S. Department of Commerce and *Statistical Abstract of the United States, 1993.*

from a national perspective. The resources used to channel and manage these funds are largely wasted and could be put to better use.

A Look Ahead

In 1994 Floridians passed an amendment to the state constitution severely limiting increases in revenues from tax hikes. There is a clear and strong preference for no further increases in tax rates in the state of Florida. The 104th U.S. Congress has shown a strong bent for cutting federal grant dollars shared with the states. The forecast is for no increases in pure revenue sources. Yet the projected growth of the state of Florida would indicate an increasing need for government services.

The most likely outcome is one of more active participation by local governments and an increased reliance on privatization and direct charges for services. In a survey conducted by the Bureau of Economic and Business Research at the University of Florida, a majority of households preferred an increase in local expenditures on crime prevention and education even if it required an increase in local tax rates (see Scoggins and Horn 1994). There are numerous restrictions on local tax rates and education expenditures, but as political pressures mount and state government dollars dwindle, these restrictions can be rescinded.

Direct charges for services will likely rise, especially for higher education. Privatization of many services, such as prison management and waste collection, have been implemented in other states with promising results. This greater reliance on direct charges for services and competitive processes, such as public school vouchers, has two benefits. One is that the increased flow of revenues will help local governments meet the demands of a growing population. The other is that increased competition will force public institutions to operate more efficiently.

The process will not be rapid or painless. The state and local governments will grapple with increasingly tight budgets for years to come. It is hoped the political process will have reached some kind of solution before the next economic recession. Otherwise a fiscal crisis that dwarfs the previous two could result.

References

Fox, William F., and Charles Campbell. 1984. "Stability of the State Sales Tax Income Elasticity." *National Tax Journal* 37 No. 2 (June), pp. 201-212.

Hansson, Ingemar, and Charles Stuart. "Tax Revenue and the Marginal Cost of Public Funds in Sweden." *Journal of Public Economics* 27 No. 3, pp. 331-54.

Holcombe, Randall G., and Russell S. Sobel. 1995. "The Relative Variability of State Income and Sales Taxes over the Revenue Cycle." *Atlantic Economic Journal* 23 No. 2 (June), pp. 97-112.

Robertson, Glenn W. 1995. "Storm Warnings." *Florida Trend* Vol. 37 No. 10.

Scoggins, John F. (Dick). 1995. "Florida lags in federal revenue." *Economic Leaflets* Vol. 54 No. 1. Gainesville: University of Florida, Bureau of Economic and Business Research.

Scoggins, John F. (Dick), and Randolph Horn. 1994. "Popular attitudes change toward local public finance in Florida." *Economic Leaflets* Vol. 53 No. 10. Gainesville: University of Florida, Bureau of Economic and Business Research.

White, Fred C.   1983.   "Trade-Off in Growth and Stability in State Taxes." *National Tax Journal* 36 No. 1 (March), pp. 103-114.

Changing Urban Form: Lessons for Florida

18

William O'Dell
Research Associate
and
Marc Smith
Associate Director
Shimberg Center for
Affordable Housing
College of Architecture
and
Larry Winner
Lecturer
Department of Statistics
University of Florida
Gainesville, Florida

The standard monocentric model (see Alonso 1964, Mills 1967, Muth 1969), a staple of urban economics for at least twenty-five years, has a fundamental assumption that all employment is located in the central business district (CBD). This assumption is increasingly violated as transportation, telecommunication and other advances have reduced the importance of traditional centralizing influences. Today, by several measures, suburbia has more economic activity than downtown (Schwartz 1993; also see Muller 1981 and Erickson 1983).

A number of factors influence the location decisions of firms. Mieszkowski and Mills (1993) explore two explanations for suburbanization: a natural evolution theory that decentralization has been driven largely by transportation advances as embodied in the polycentric model of urban spatial structure, and a theory emphasizing the role of social and fiscal problems of central cities and a "flight from blight" (see, for example, Bradford and Kelejian 1973). Sasaki (1990) suggests that firms may move to the suburbs instead of concentrating in the CBD to attain cost savings in land, labor and transportation; if those costs dominate then a multiple-centered city will result. Similarly, Gordon and Moore (1989) argue that CBDs cease to grow when agglomeration benefits fail to dominate congestion costs and greater advantage can be obtained in other centers.

The extent of suburban development in a metropolitan area is therefore dependent on tradeoffs among commuting costs, congestion, benefits of agglomeration and labor costs (Ladd and Wheaton 1991), with these tradeoffs benefiting outlying areas at present. Danielson and Wolpert (1992) state that siting preferences in current markets are targeted to relatively undeveloped or well-off fringe communities with good highway access and sites suitable for campus environments, not toward poorer inner city communities. Those trends will continue as a result of clustering of activities and favorable property tax and public service balances. Thrall et al. (1995) suggest that the sequence of urban development begins with increased access through investment in transportation infrastructure, followed by demographic change and the movement of employers and then retailers to where employees want to live.

Cities that have had much of their growth in recent years are the most likely to display growth that varies from the monocentric pattern. Florida fits this profile of a recent growth area. Florida's rapid population growth, particularly in coastal areas in the southern and central portions of the state, has taken the low-density form of urbanization that characterizes development throughout the country.

But what are the characteristics of that pattern? The larger question may be whether there is a pattern at all or simply a scattering of development across the landscape. Finally, can we understand the forces that underlie the nature of development so as to be able to intervene to achieve a desired outcome?

To address these questions, this chapter uses a case study of Orlando and Orange County. The study examines the development of the county over time and space, allowing a different perspective from that of an analysis at one point in time.

Background on the Orlando Region

Orlando is of interest because it has experienced the rapid growth that typifies other areas of Florida and because it is relatively unconstrained in its growth compared to other areas that are bounded by water. The region is also heavily impacted by tourism as are other areas of Florida, although the impact on Orlando may be larger and more recent due to the theme parks.

The Orlando region has grown from a population of about 700,000 in 1980 to over one million in 1990. This growth has continued past trends, as the population was 338,000 in 1960 and 453,000 in 1970. Prior to 1970, the region was anchored by orange-growing and distribution activities. The opening of what is now the Kennedy Space Center and the location of Martin Marietta and related firms also impacted the area during this period.

In the 1970s, tourism became a major factor in the growth of the region. The Magic Kingdom at Disney World was the primary impetus as it opened in 1971. Expansion of the airport and the opening of EPCOT Center in the early 1980s furthered the growth. Complementing these developments were other tourist attractions and associated growth in retail, services, hotels and related businesses. Most recently, the opening of the Disney MGM Studios and Universal Studios continued the growth in tourism.

During the 1980s, the region also diversified with growth in high technology, regional headquarters and manufacturing and distribution. Much of this activity is housed in office space that has developed both downtown and in suburban office clusters. For example, the American Automobile Association recently relocated its headquarters from Washington, D.C., to the Heathrow development in Seminole County.

Most of the road network in the region, and therefore the spatial structure, was developed by the 1960s. Florida's Turnpike was built through the area in 1957, I-4 in the 1961-65 period, and the Bee Line Expressway in 1966-68. The airport was able to expand after the Strategic Air Command left in 1975. The University of Central Florida also opened in the 1970s.

Orange County Data. The analysis that follows is derived from county property appraiser data for Orange County. The data were prepared for the analysis by ARMASI, Inc. They include entries for every parcel of property in the county for the roll year 1993, the most recent available at the time of this study. For each parcel, available data include the use of the parcel as classified according to a 100-

category land use code, size of the parcel, size of any building on the parcel, units, year the building was built, assessed value and land value. The data were aggregated to the section (one square mile) level to determine the square footage of certain land use categories in each section.

Three major land use types--residential, commercial and industrial--aggregated all land use in each category. There are also mappable data for significant land use types (or a combination of types such as retail) in each of the three aggregate categories: residential--single-family, condominiums and multifamily; commercial--generally all major commercial uses such as retail, office and entertainment; industrial--light and heavy manufacturing, warehouses and distribution terminals.

The amount of development that occurred during certain time periods was determined according to the unit's year built. Earlier development may be underestimated to the extent that such a method does not account for demolitions or conversions of units built in earlier time periods. It is assumed that such actions are trivial relative to the amount of development in the county. A second weakness of the approach is that only Orange County is used; growth in the region also includes Seminole and Osceola counties. However, the inclusion of those counties, particularly the development path in Seminole, should only further confirm the findings.

Orange County--A Descriptive Case Study
of Spatial Patterns

Orange County's explosive growth over the last three decades may be more extreme than that of other areas but yet is typical of the state. The county's growth is more atypical in at least two major respects. First, it is located in the center of the state away from the dominant spatial influence of the Atlantic or Gulf coasts. Second, a dominant aspect in the growth of Orange County has been the presence of Disney World. As a spatial phenomenon Disney World's influence over the development of the county's urban form, at least in the scale of its impact, is probably replicated nowhere else in the state. Disney was like a rock thrown into a pool of water. This

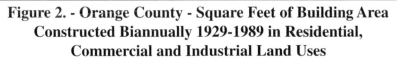

**Figure 2. - Orange County - Square Feet of Building Area
Constructed Biannually 1929-1989 in Residential,
Commercial and Industrial Land Uses**

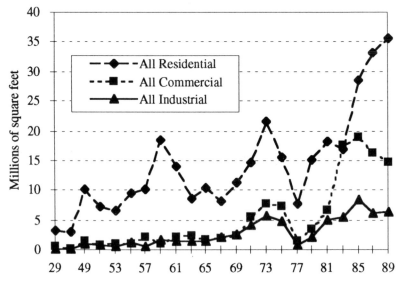

Source: Compiled from the 1993 roll year of Orange County Property Appraiser, ARMASI, Inc.

The following discussion takes four perspectives on analyzing growth in Orange County. First, total development in the county over time is examined to show the extent to which the county has grown in the past two decades and how its economy has diversified. Second, the location of growth across space in the county is explored to discover any locational patterns in the growth over time. The density attained by different sections in the county is reviewed to see if there appears to be a maximum density achieved before growth moves to other sections. Finally, the emergence of subcenters of activity is explored and placed in context with the literature on subcenters.

Extent of Development Over Time. It is not an exaggeration to say that Orange County's growth has been explosive over the past two decades (the Magic Kingdom opened in 1971). Figures 2-4 illustrate the growth of building area over the past seven decades. The decade of the 1980s was a period of particularly rapid expansion--over 40 percent of the county's cumulative industrial and resi-

Figure 3. - Orange County - Percent of Construction Activity (Square Footage) Biannually 1929-1989 in Residential, Commercial and Industrial Land Use

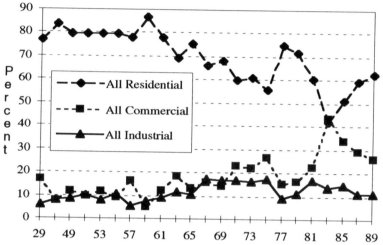

Source: Compiled from the 1993 roll year of Orange County Property Appraiser, ARMASI, Inc.

Figure 4. - Orange County - Percent of Construction Activity (Square Footage) Biannually 1929-1989 In Office, Retail and Tourist Land Uses

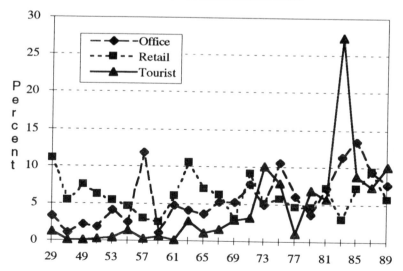

Source: Compiled from the 1993 roll year of Orange County Property Appraiser, ARMASI, Inc.

Figure 5. - Orange County Single-Family Residential Land Uses - Decade by Decade Growth in Square Feet of Building - Percent of Cumulative (Total as of 1989)

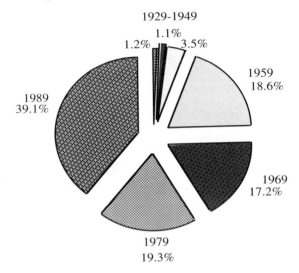

Source: Compiled from the 1993 roll year of Orange County Property Appraiser, ARMASI, Inc.

dential building area was constructed during the 1980s and over 60 percent of its cumulative commercial space (Figures 5-7).

The components of that construction activity show the mechanism by which that growth was fueled. In 1969 cumulative tourist-related building square footage was not quite 20 percent of retail space. By 1979 the gap had narrowed--the ratio of tourist-related to retail development was 61 percent and by 1989 cumulative tourist-related building area exceeded retail area by 17 percent. A similar phenomenon occured with office space. The ratio of cumulative office to retail space was 74 percent in 1969, 91 percent in 1979 and 120 percent by 1989. From the standpoint of building area, residential space is the dominant land use type. But residential building activity measured by the percent of square footage built by decade has declined relative to commercial and to a lesser extent industrial building activity over the last quarter century. A look within commercial building activity at its major components--retail, office and tourist--shows startling changes over time. The construction of retail square footage has

Figure 6. - Orange County Industrial Land Uses - Decade by Decade Growth in Square Feet of Building - Percentage of Cumulative (Total as of 1989)

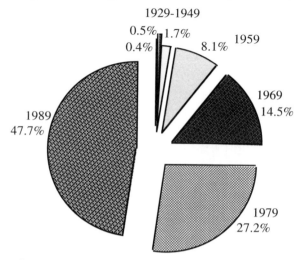

Source: Compiled from the 1993 roll year of Orange County Property Appraiser, ARMASI, Inc.

Figure 7. - Orange County Commercial Land Uses - Decade by Decade Growth in Square Feet of Building - Percentage of Cumulative (Total as of 1989)

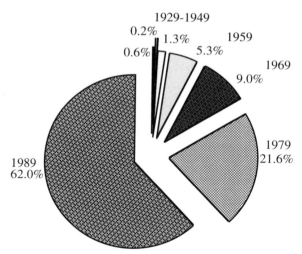

Source: Compiled from the 1993 roll year of Orange County Property Appraiser, ARMASI, Inc.

University of Florida   *Bureau of Economic and Business Research*

Figure 8. - Section at the Center of Gravity
of Residential Square Footage (Cumulative)

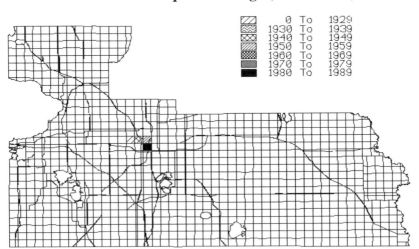

▨	0 To 1929
▧	1930 To 1939
▨	1940 To 1949
▨	1950 To 1959
▨	1960 To 1969
▨	1970 To 1979
■	1980 To 1989

remained surprisingly stable over the past forty years, generally accounting for between 5 and 7 percent of total building activity over each decade. Tourist-related land uses, however, have risen from approximately 2 percent of total building activity to over 10 percent in two decades, while office land uses have grown from approximately 5 percent of square footage built per decade to 10 percent. Both tourist and office uses passed retail in cumulative square footage in the early 1980s. These percentage changes do not show a decline in some land use categories but rather an increase overall in construction activity as the Orange County economy has grown and diversified.

Spatial Relationships Over Time. Despite or in some cases because of Disney, Orange County spatial patterns have remained surprisingly consistent over the seventy-plus years of land use evolution examined here. That consistency is most apparent when looking at the centers of gravity of various land uses over time. Centers of gravity are a geographical summation of activity rendered to a single point. In other words, a section is the center of gravity if it is the balance point for all the development of a particular type in the county. Growth may be moving outward but the center of gravity will remain the same if the growth is uniform away from the center.

Figure 9. - Section at the Center of Gravity
of Industrial Square Footage (Cumulative)

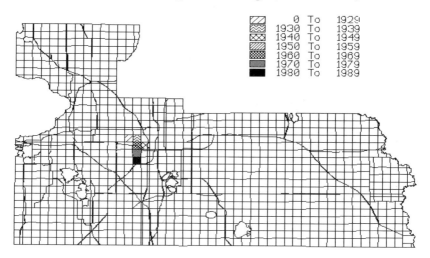

Figure 10. - Section at the Center of Gravity
of Commercial Square Footage (Cumulative)

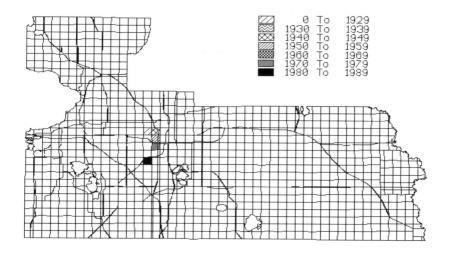

Figures 8-10 show the section at the center of gravity for commercial, industrial and residential land uses as measured by cumulative square footage through the end of each decade (centers of gravity by decade may lie atop each other). The center of gravity of residential land uses has remained tightly bound to the center of the city

Figure 11. - Orange County All Residential Land Use
(square feet building area developed 1970-79)

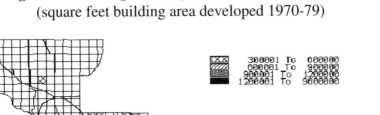

of Orlando, seeming to indicate that the downtown has remained the center from which commuting patterns evolve. Industrial uses have crept south, presumably influenced by Martin Marietta and associated facilities and the airport.

Commercial uses have crept south and east over the past seventy-plus years. Dissecting commercial use into component parts indicates the underlying causes of this movement and, not surprisingly, Disney World appears to have pulled commercial activity toward its location. The center of gravity of retail land uses has remained tightly wrapped around or in some cases coterminous with that of residential uses, and therefore near downtown. The office-use center of gravity has moved from west to east toward the central city of Orlando. The center of gravity of tourist-related activity has moved inexorably away from Orlando south and west toward Disney. The latter category has been the cause of the overall movement of commercial space.

Examining building activity section by section over time (in Figures 11-14), the county's spatial patterns take on more dimension but retain, interestingly, the same general formal characteristics. Residential land uses are fairly scattered prior to 1930, with some concentration near downtown. Through 1950, residential development fol-

Figure 12. - Orange County All Residential Land Uses
(square feet building area developed 1980-92)

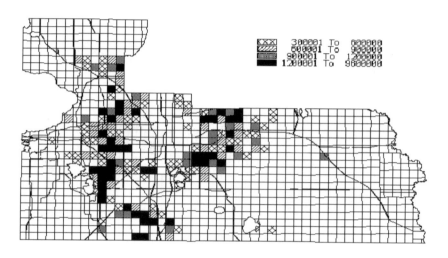

Figure 13. - Orange County All Commercial Land Uses
(square feet building area developed 1970-79)

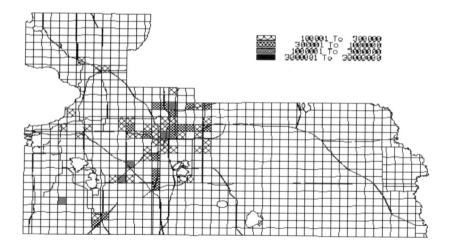

lows the past pattern but in the decade of the 1950s residential development began to spread in all directions from downtown. This pattern is arguably a series of concentric rings of activity with a focus on downtown Orlando--much as the center-of-gravity figure suggests.

Figure 14. - Orange County All Commercial Land Uses
(square feet building area developed 1980-92)

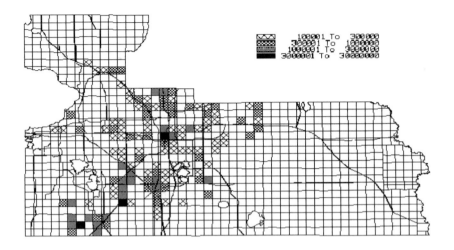

Commercial uses in Orange County prior to 1930 were concentrated near downtown and outlying towns. These uses remained largely near downtown, and fairly scattered, through 1970. In the 1970s, commercial uses began to spread through the southwestern portion of the county, the area in which Disney developed, and moved farther from the downtown node. Similar to the other land uses, the 1980s through 1993 saw commercial uses move away from downtown.

Suburban Subcenter Development in Orange County

While the discussion thus far has examined the spatial nature of development in Orange County, an additional issue is of interest. This is the character of subcenters or nodes of activity that locate in the suburbs.

As discussed earlier, urban form has evolved rapidly in the past two decades from the traditional pattern in which economic functions are found predominately in the central business district. While population has been suburbanizing for a longer period of time, businesses in the suburbs were generally household-serving retail and service establishments. Selection of suburban sites by industry, corporate headquarters and regional offices, and regional and national service firms is a more recent phenomenon.

These changes have meant that predicting the location of economic activity in the future will be more difficult. Modeling of urban growth has been evolving as urban economics and regional science move from the monocentric to the polycentric model of urban land use. Central to this model is the evolution of the city around multiple rather than single nodes of economic activity. The extent of polycentric development in an area is dependent on tradeoffs among the benefits of agglomeration, congestion and commuting costs (higher commuting costs encourage sprawl and decentralization), and labor costs (assumed to be lower in suburban areas) (Ladd and Wheaton 1991).

Identifying subcenters of economic activity is a difficult theoretical and empirical task, but the evolution of land use is even more complicated than that as some employers seem to be able to locate virtually anywhere and are less sensitive than in the past to the agglomeration economies inherent in central business areas. Thus there are scattered patterns of office parks and other commercial land uses. Compounding the analytical problem is the interrelationship of population and employment location.

Despite this scattering of employers, there do appear to be certain characteristics of locations that influence the locational choices of firms and the likelihood that certain locations will develop as subcenters of activity. Richardson (1988) suggests the development of a probabilistic model of the locational choice of new and expanding firms. The model would also determine subcenter location endogenously. Richardson notes that there is a degree of arbitrariness to subcenter location which is dependent on the role of the developer and the necessity for an anchor of critical mass to start the process, further justifying a probabilistic model. Richardson also notes that subcenters may specialize in particular activities such as an industrial park, a shopping mall, an office center or a university or hospital.

Defining Subcenters in Orange County. Several definitions have been offered in the literature for a subcenter. These definitions have been based on the amount of employment in an area compared to population or some other measure of the extent of commuting into

Figure 15. - Cumulative Square Feet of Building Area Developed Pre-1930 Through 1989 by Center - All Residential Land Uses

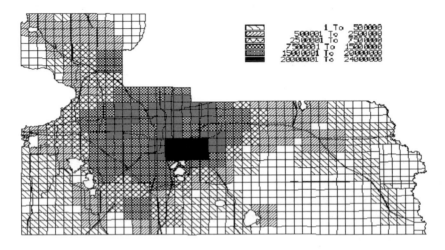

the area and intensity of nonresidential use. For this analysis, subcenters are defined for residential, commercial and industrial activity in a different fashion. A subcenter is defined as all adjacent sections within a 1.5-mile radius of a central section. The prototypical center thus contains nine contiguous sections forming a square three miles on a side. Because some centers occur at the edge of the county and because of some measurement error, centers can be composed of as few as four and as many as eleven sections. Centers may overlap each other at the edges up to one section deep. Figures 15-17 show spatial pattern by aggregations of sections defined as subcenters.

Residential location has developed in a dispersed, somewhat circular pattern radiating more or less out from Orlando, with the densest concentration of cumulative building activity developing south of the city center. Commercial and industrial uses have developed in a more linear fashion along transportation routes and at transportation nodes. Commercial activity by the end of the 1980s was concentrated on a northeast-southwest line running from Orlando to Disney World. The concentration of industrial activity had developed a linear north-south concentration orienting on Orlando and the concentration of activity west of the airport. By graphing the major centers by cumu-

Figure 16. - Cumulative Square Feet of Building Area Developed Pre-1930 Through 1989 by Center - All Commercial Land Uses

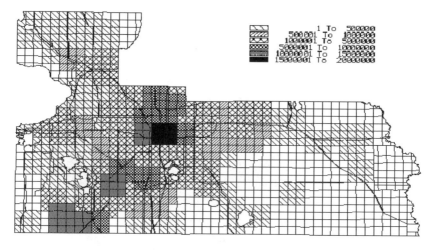

Figure 17. - Cumulative Square Feet of Building Area Developed Pre-1930 Through 1989 by Center - All Industrial Land Uses

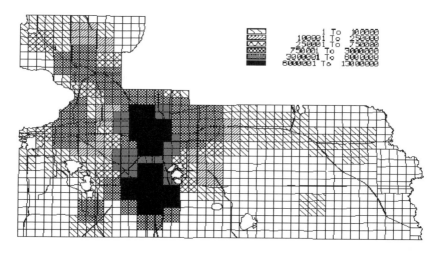

lative square footage and distance from the center of Orlando over time, a fourth picture emerges (Figures 18-20). Residential subcenters have developed over time at the periphery of development but by the end of the 1980s, with two exceptions, were of relatively equal size.

Figure 18. - Orange County Large Industrial
Centers - Cumulative Industrial Square Footage
Built to Distance from Orlando Central Business District

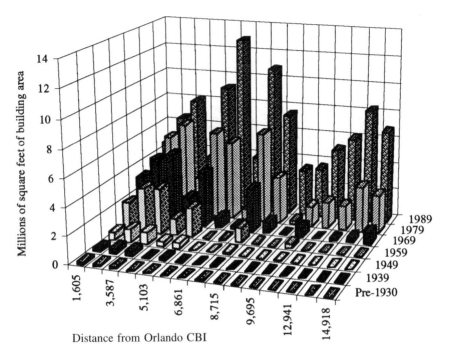

Note: Distance units are arbitrary; they denote relative distance.

Source: Compiled from the 1993 roll year of Orange County Property Appraiser, ARMASI, Inc.

Industrial and commercial uses, however, have developed clear nodes of concentration, subcenters, at various distances from the Orlando city center. This is even more pronounced when looking at activity decade by decade instead of cumulatively. In some cases the rise of large subcenters has occurred within one decade.

The location of subcenters appears to be consistent with factors that would be thought to influence their location. First, existing land use patterns are very important in creating inertia effects that lead to future development. There is a circular causality in residential and commercial development. Residential development may come first, creating market demand and a labor force. Commercial development follows that demand but in turn creates the need for more labor.

Figure 19. - Orange County Large Commercial
Centers - Cumulative Commercial Square Footage
Built to Distance from Orlando Central Business District

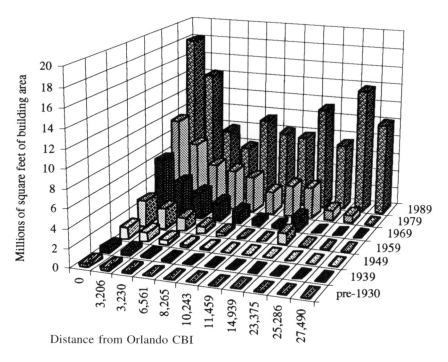

Note: Distance units are arbitrary, they denote relative distance.

Source: Compiled from the 1993 roll year of Orange County Property Appraiser, ARMASI, Inc.

The existing development pattern in an area is therefore a predictor of future development.

Wasylenko (1984) summarized six factors commonly hypothesized to affect business location choice. These factors are land rent or distance from the center of a city, proximity to interstate highways, agglomeration economies measured as proportion of firms in a metropolitan area located at a site, proximity to labor markets as measured by population density or number of employed residents within commuting distance of a site, fiscal variables and size of a local market for local-serving retail and office firms. While the role of all of these factors is not apparent from the maps, clearly interstate highways and agglomeration factors have been significant in Orange County's development.

Figure 20. - Orange County Large Residential Centers - Cumulative Residential Square Footage Built to Distance from Orlando Central Business District

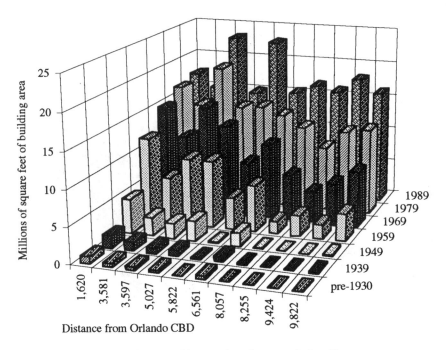

Note: Distance units are arbitrary, they denote relative distance.

Source: Compiled from the 1993 roll year of Orange County Property Appraiser, ARMASI, Inc.

The airport, University of Central Florida and of course Disney, Universal Studios, Sea World and other tourist developments have affected the location of nodes of activity. Finally, developers can play a major role by assembling land for a large-scale development, such as a Development of Regional Impact, that can affect the course of development by creating a certain environment.

Analyzing the level of development activity by section and center over time reveals another characteristic of development in the county. Other than the downtown sections, it appears that sections achieve a certain level of intensity of development consistent with the land use type that predominates in the section (residential, commercial, industrial), and development then moves to other sections for intense development activity. With most of the largest residential centers the pattern of development suggests a maximum level of intensity of use irrespective of distance from the Orlando CBD.

The data and maps provide an interesting overview of the spatial pattern of development in one Florida county. However, considerably more analysis is necessary to understand the forces that move growth in a particular direction, the location of concentrations or subcenters of activity and the evolution of those centers, and the causality between residential and nonresidential land uses (which comes first and drives the other, or is there mutual causality), among other research issues.

A Look Ahead

Florida cities have grown in a period in which polycentric urban form has been in ascendancy. The reasons for this form appear clear and relate to costs of business, access and urban problems. Relatively unexplained, however, are the reasons why nodes of activity emerge at one location and not others. For example, what are the roles of transportation access, developer decision-making, existing land uses and amenities in causing growth to occur at one location? A better understanding of forces leading to urban form would allow interventions, as through growth management, to work within those forces to achieve desired outcomes.

Among the policy questions that need to be addressed are the following: How can employment be attracted to the central city, and will certain types of regulatory initiatives drive employment growth out of a city or the state? Should efforts be made to locate housing closer to jobs? Continued technological development creates the potential to move beyond subcenters to general dispersion. Gordon and Richardson (1995), although discussing job, not residential centers, describe a phenomenon in Los Angeles which they contend is the evolution of city form beyond polycentricity to patterns of generalized dispersion. While social and other forces may ultimately preclude large-scale movement to general dispersion, there is evidence of it in residential development patterns. Perhaps the most important question is whether growth policies should even contend with economic forces and if they should, can they overcome the economic and technological forces that drive polycentric development?

References

Alonso, William. 1964. *Location and Land Use*. Cambridge: Harvard University Press.

Bradford, David, and Henry Kelejian. 1973. "An Economic Model of the Flight to the Suburbs." *Journal of Political Economy* 81:3 (May/ June), pp. 566-89.

Danielson, Michael N., and Julian Wolpert. 1992. "Rapid Metropolitan Growth and Community Disparities." *Growth and Change* 23 (4), pp. 494-515.

Erickson, Rodney A. 1983. "The Evolution of the Suburban Space Economy." *Urban Geography* 4 (2), pp. 95-121.

Gordon, Peter, and Harry W. Richardson. 1995. "The Myth of the Ideal Urban Form." Paper presented at conference on Growth Management, Development of Patterns and the Cost of Sprawl (June 22). Dania, Florida.

Ladd, Helen F., and William Wheaton. 1991. "Causes and Consequences of the Changing Urban Form." *Regional Science and Urban Economics* 21, pp. 157-162.

Mieszkowski, Peter, and Edwin S. Mills. 1993. "The Causes of Metropolitan Suburbanization." *Journal of Economic Perspectives* 7 (3), pp. 135-147.

Mills, Edwin S. 1967. "An Aggregative Model of Resource Allocation in a Metropolitan Area." *American Economic Review* 57 (May), pp. 197-210.

Muller, Peter O. 1981. *Contemporary Suburban America*. Englewood Cliffs, New Jersey: Prentice-Hall.

Muth, Richard F. 1969. *Cities and Housing*. Chicago: University of Chicago Press.

Richardson, Harry W. 1988. "Monocentric vs. Polycentric Models: The Future of Urban Economics in Regional Science." *Annals of Regional Science* 1-11.

Sasaki, K. 1990. "The Establishment of a Subcenter and Urban Spatial Structure." *Environment and Planning* A 22, pp. 369-383.

Schwartz, Alex. 1993. "Subservient Suburbia: The Reliance of Large Suburban Companies on Central City Firms for Financial and Professional Services." *Journal of the American Planning Association* 59 (3), pp. 288-305.

Thrall, Grant Ian, Mark McClanahan and Susan Elshaw-Thrall. 1995. "Ninety Years of Urban Growth as Described With GIS: A Historic Geography." *Geo Info Systems* (April), pp. 20-27.

Wasylenko, Michael J. 1984. "Disamenities, Local Taxation, and the Intrametropolitan Location of Households and Firms." *Research in Urban Economics* 4, pp. 97-116.

Data Appendix

Economic Profile
of the
State of Florida
1970 through 1994

(Data not available for all years in all categories)

University of Florida   *Bureau of Economic and Business Research*

Table 1. Florida Population and Bank Deposits 1970 to 1994 and Housing Starts 1976 to 1993

Year	Population Total (1,000)	Population 65 and Older (1,000)	Bank Deposits ($1,000,000)	Housing Starts Single-family	Housing Starts Multi-family
1970	6,791	986	13,938	-	-
1971	7,158	1,067	16,211	-	-
1972	7,511	1,137	19,714	-	-
1973	7,914	1,211	22,855	-	-
1974	8,299	1,289	24,094	-	-
1975	8,518	1,353	24,885	-	-
1976	8,667	1,415	26,764	58,989	35,897
1977	8,856	1,483	29,714	77,737	47,291
1978	9,102	1,567	32,194	90,422	60,519
1979	9,426	1,646	36,167	94,946	70,170
1980	9,746	1,688	40,537	87,219	75,464
1981	10,193	1,763	43,175	66,195	71,689
1982	10,471	1,824	49,623	56,579	43,698
1983	10,750	1,885	58,310	101,830	69,961
1984	11,040	1,949	65,847	100,746	88,502
1985	11,351	2,015	74,252	101,626	89,521
1986	11,668	2,084	87,187	107,238	79,991
1987	11,997	2,155	91,698	115,450	59,753
1988	12,306	2,223	100,306	112,725	56,374
1989	12,638	2,299	111,410	102,486	47,139
1990	12,938	2,356	116,977	86,042	44,098
1991	13,288	2,429	119,849	70,215	18,977
1992	13,510	2,473	124,406	83,359	17,562
1993	13,726	2,526	123,400	90,109	15,866
1994	13,953	2,571	135,300	-	-

Sources: Columns 1 and 2, U.S. Department of Commerce, Bureau of the Census, *Statistical Abstract of the United States, 1990* and previous editions for data prior to 1980. 1980 to present from U.S. Department of Commerce, Bureau of the Census (the Internet at http://www.census.gov); Column 3, Federal Deposit Insurance Corporation, *FDIC Historical Statistics on Banking, 1934-1992* and *FDIC Statistics on Banking, 1994* and previous edition; Columns 4 and 5, BEBR Database (calculated from housing-start ratios from Bureau of the Census).

Table 2. Florida Labor Force and Employment Status 1970 to 1994

Year	Labor Force (1,000)	Employ-ment (1,000)	Employment Status	
			Unemployment	
			Number (1,000)	Rate
1970	2,672	2,557	115	4.3
1971	2,792	2,655	136	4.9
1972	2,907	2,762	144	5.1
1973	3,169	3,033	136	4.3
1974	3,413	3,199	214	6.2
1975	3,554	3,175	378	10.7
1976	3,605	3,280	326	9.0
1977	3,717	3,411	305	8.2
1978	3,946	3,684	262	6.6
1979	4,132	3,884	248	6.0
1980	4,271	4,020	251	5.9
1981	4,519	4,211	308	6.8
1982	4,751	4,363	388	8.2
1983	4,936	4,512	424	8.6
1984	5,139	4,814	325	6.3
1985	5,343	5,023	320	6.0
1986	5,585	5,265	320	5.7
1987	5,868	5,556	312	5.3
1988	6,081	5,777	304	5.0
1989	6,193	5,845	348	5.6
1990*	6,440	6,057	383	5.9
1991	6,465	5,992	473	7.3
1992	6,541	6,006	535	8.2
1993	6,654	6,191	463	7.0
1994**	6,824	6,376	448	6.6

* Not strictly comparable with data for prior years due to revised population controls based on the 1990 Census.

** Not strictly comparable with data for prior years due to a major redesign of the Current Population Survey.

Source: U.S. Department of Labor, Bureau of Labor Statistics unpublished data, released February 3, 1995.

Table 3. Employment in Florida by Major Industrial Classification 1970-1994
(in thousands)

Year	Total	Nonagricultural Total	Mining	Con-struc-tion	Manufac-turing	Transporta-tion and Public Util-ities*	Whole-sale and Retail trade	Finance In-surance and Real Estate	Serv-ices	Govern-ment	Other**
1970	2,556.98	2,152.09	8.34	175.63	322.49	154.39	109.62	131.30	416.28	397.76	404.89
1971	2,654.88	2,276.26	8.86	186.83	322.71	161.67	121.70	143.66	449.86	419.14	378.62
1972	2,761.76	2,513.13	8.92	230.10	351.29	173.51	139.28	162.37	505.56	437.92	248.63
1973	3,032.68	2,778.57	9.25	290.18	380.55	186.73	151.76	182.61	556.17	469.91	254.11
1974	3,198.42	2,863.82	9.91	276.12	375.92	189.77	158.44	192.56	581.45	510.53	334.60
1975	3,173.30	2,746.35	9.34	182.46	339.39	182.91	152.03	188.35	584.27	546.05	426.95
1976	3,278.96	2,784.27	8.79	166.75	353.93	181.38	153.83	191.27	608.51	542.80	494.69
1977	3,409.99	2,933.41	9.14	179.03	380.88	185.07	160.91	202.51	639.99	565.73	476.58
1978	3,683.66	3,180.59	9.51	209.53	415.53	194.17	174.86	219.28	693.88	601.79	503.07
1979	3,883.37	3,381.22	10.16	241.37	443.62	208.48	190.30	235.06	752.58	600.49	502.15
1980	4,020.33	3,579.38	11.00	263.86	456.38	220.78	204.62	254.23	814.51	618.77	440.95
1981	4,210.62	3,735.95	11.25	283.08	472.15	229.76	215.00	274.35	860.96	620.15	474.67
1982	4,362.21	3,761.87	9.59	256.57	456.73	229.93	214.34	276.58	905.04	632.46	600.34
1983	4,512.19	3,905.41	9.58	268.79	464.23	231.40	218.18	283.23	974.39	639.33	606.78
1984	4,814.27	4,204.21	10.23	318.37	501.87	241.08	233.25	299.53	1,065.68	649.49	610.06
1985	5,023.41	4,410.01	10.15	334.24	514.43	242.99	245.63	319.19	1,129.81	674.39	613.40
1986	5,264.88	4,599.41	9.32	339.49	517.23	247.38	251.61	339.66	1,205.58	701.92	665.47
1987	5,555.70	4,848.10	8.72	341.54	530.97	254.78	266.33	359.27	1,304.35	731.83	707.60
1988	5,776.55	5,066.58	9.08	346.31	539.57	260.81	279.76	365.08	1,393.88	773.04	709.97
1989	5,844.65	5,260.86	9.20	340.23	537.88	266.35	290.28	370.26	1,504.32	800.08	583.79
1990	6,068.25	5,387.40	8.94	323.22	522.07	278.39	293.27	370.71	1,593.01	846.68	680.85
1991	6,000.68	5,294.29	8.18	276.89	492.79	274.88	288.07	358.21	1,621.48	859.31	706.39
1992	5,990.42	5,358.66	7.13	266.46	482.88	275.81	288.88	351.92	1,692.68	870.10	631.76
1993	6,166.35	5,571.43	6.33	285.34	485.18	287.14	293.93	360.33	1,809.23	881.63	594.92
1994	6,375.74	5,796.56	6.97	297.51	483.93	295.15	304.83	376.03	1,923.92	906.63	579.18

*Includes communications. **Includes agricultural and domestic workers.

Source: Florida Department of Labor and Employment Security, Bureau of Labor Market Information. Current Employment Statistics Program (790 data), in cooperation with U.S. Department of Labor, Bureau of Labor Statistics.

Table 4. Florida Gross State Product by Major Sector
1977 to 1992
(in millions of $1987)

| | | | | Private Industries | | | |
| | | | | | Mining | | |
Year	Total	Total	Agri-culture, For. and Fish.	Total	Oil and Gas	Non-metal Min-erals	Con-struc-tion
1977	115,092	97,288	2,701	956	379	558	7,001
1978	124,021	105,696	2,758	1,115	410	692	7,883
1979	130,787	112,278	2,795	1,114	386	717	8,794
1980	136,631	117,564	3,208	1,155	416	731	9,502
1981	142,070	122,494	3,128	1,039	379	649	9,973
1982	143,749	123,992	3,483	1,137	593	531	9,318
1983	155,859	135,162	4,197	1,154	541	594	9,601
1984	167,501	147,013	3,583	1,259	495	741	11,277
1985	176,468	155,259	4,278	1,075	427	622	12,336
1986	185,829	163,433	4,795	925	287	608	12,151
1987	197,096	173,864	5,201	740	169	546	12,156
1988	205,967	181,674	5,540	790	183	572	12,023
1989	213,343	187,545	5,190	756	103	616	11,888
1990	216,373	189,412	5,085	731	124	555	11,423
1991	217,501	189,895	5,861	735	131	552	10,096
1992	222,553	195,667	6,216	684	138	516	10,387

Continued . . .

Table 4. Florida Gross State Product by Major Sector
1977 to 1992 (continued)
(in millions of $1987)

		Private Industries (continued)				
		Manufacturing				
		Durable				
Year	Total	Total	Lumber and Wood Prod.	Fabri- cated Metal Prod.	Motor Vehicles and Trans- portation Equip.	NEC
1977	11,265	5,632	487	887	82	4,176
1978	12,313	6,251	484	948	89	4,728
1979	13,090	6,894	536	986	101	5,271
1980	13,638	7,431	567	1,057	92	5,715
1981	14,373	7,827	566	1,088	127	6,047
1982	15,063	8,274	589	972	146	6,568
1983	15,759	8,699	716	997	146	6,841
1984	17,813	10,247	864	1,200	154	8,032
1985	17,765	10,110	799	1,244	178	7,889
1986	18,380	10,521	771	1,262	182	8,307
1987	20,263	11,834	886	1,392	208	9,349
1988	20,980	12,243	838	1,336	241	9,829
1989	21,473	12,835	811	1,186	237	10,604
1990	21,324	12,586	737	1,094	236	10,520
1991	20,871	12,571	672	1,078	205	10,614
1992	20,893	12,610	626	1,060	259	10,665

Continued . . .

NEC - Not elsewhere classified.

Table 4. Florida Gross State Product by Major Sector
1977 to 1992 (continued)
(in millions of $1987)

		Private Industries (continued)					
		Manufacturing (continued)					
		Nondurable					
Year	Total	Food and Kind. Prod.	Text. and App. Prod.	Paper and Allied Prod.	Print. and Pub.	Chem- icals and Allied Prod.	NEC
1977	5,632	1,764	405	763	1,253	1,003	444
1978	6,063	1,973	500	743	1,367	982	499
1979	6,195	1,966	533	693	1,494	980	530
1980	6,207	2,101	500	615	1,534	915	543
1981	6,545	2,163	479	598	1,680	1,014	611
1982	6,790	2,484	436	569	1,725	1,021	553
1983	7,059	2,516	483	630	1,691	1,162	577
1984	7,566	2,469	503	734	2,021	1,220	620
1985	7,654	2,516	504	615	2,167	1,234	619
1986	7,859	2,536	543	699	2,154	1,333	593
1987	8,429	2,800	611	779	2,131	1,398	709
1988	8,738	2,829	664	949	2,167	1,382	745
1989	8,638	2,663	686	970	2,233	1,293	793
1990	8,738	2,805	721	937	2,178	1,294	803
1991	8,300	2,555	754	877	2,040	1,279	796
1992	8,282	2,452	781	943	1,967	1,301	838

Continued . . .

NEC - Not elsewhere classified.

Table 4. Florida Gross State Product by Major Sector
1977 to 1992 (continued)
(in millions of $1987)

		Private Industries (continued)			
		Transportation, Communications and Public Utilities			
		Transportation			
Year	Total	Total	Rail-road	Local and Interurban Passenger Transit	Trucking and Ware-housing
1977	11,544	3,845	318	280	1,343
1978	12,196	4,210	346	274	1,398
1979	12,890	4,461	356	279	1,370
1980	13,420	4,447	403	260	1,402
1981	13,630	4,418	425	234	1,338
1982	13,750	4,613	394	220	1,358
1983	15,162	5,211	501	219	1,602
1984	16,273	5,538	551	262	1,812
1985	16,532	5,597	517	268	1,898
1986	17,243	6,097	514	299	1,983
1987	18,973	6,656	558	324	2,069
1988	20,412	6,767	643	306	2,287
1989	20,642	6,835	721	349	2,487
1990	21,407	7,362	811	364	2,410
1991	22,535	7,443	772	384	2,537
1992	23,893	7,896	802	408	2,696

Continued . . .

Table 4. Florida Gross State Product by Major Sector
1977 to 1992 (continued)
(in millions of $1987)

	Private Industries (continued)				
	Transportation, Communications and Public Utilities (cont.				
	Transportation (continued)				Electric Gas and
Year	Water	Air	NEC	Communi- cations	Sanitary Services
1977	301	1,337	267	3,526	4,173
1978	356	1,530	307	3,962	4,023
1979	370	1,734	353	4,470	3,959
1980	409	1,597	377	5,007	3,967
1981	452	1,586	383	5,362	3,849
1982	449	1,786	407	5,482	3,655
1983	448	1,991	450	6,139	3,813
1984	476	1,952	485	6,699	4,037
1985	490	1,890	535	6,698	4,238
1986	493	2,219	589	6,860	4,286
1987	534	2,523	647	7,457	4,860
1988	577	2,248	708	7,888	5,757
1989	593	1,932	753	7,839	5,968
1990	669	2,370	737	8,096	5,949
1991	735	2,277	739	8,448	6,644
1992	716	2,484	790	9,063	6,934

Continued . . .

NEC - Not elsewhere classified.

Figure 1. - Broward County Residential Land Uses
(Square feet of building area developed 1970-79)

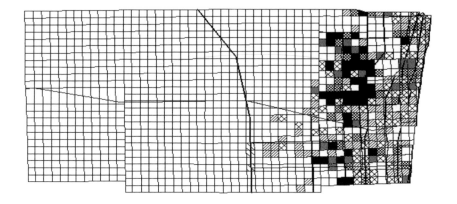

"complete vacation environment" was created in an area with an already established center and an evolved spatial pattern.

To explore the evolution of a specific urban form, this section describes the sequence of development in Orange County, summarizing this enormous building activity by mapping square footage of building area by land use and year built. These data were aggregated to trace the amount of building by section in ten-year (or sometimes biannual) increments for the last several decades. One limitation of this case study is the choice of a single county from a large and rapidly growing metropolitan area. A comprehensive look at spatial development over time should also include Seminole and Osceola counties.

Before proceeding to a description of Orange County's development it is helpful to contrast the evolution of its landlocked form with the development of a county whose urban form is shaped by a coastal amenity; the example is Broward. Figures 1 and 11 contrast the relatively linear north-south stratification of residential westward-moving development activity in Broward after 1950 with the dispersed, almost circular pattern of Orange County residential development activity radiating out in all directions from downtown Orlando after 1950.

Table 4. Florida Gross State Product by Major Sector
1977 to 1992 (continued)
(in millions of $1987)

			Private Industries (continued)			
	Whole-		Finance, Insurance and Real Estate			
	sale	Retail		Bank-	Insur-	Real
Year	Trade	Trade	Total	ing*	ance**	Estate
1977	5,961	12,959	22,215	4,693	2,705	14,816
1978	6,612	14,180	24,300	5,248	2,800	16,253
1979	7,174	14,579	26,142	5,490	2,876	17,776
1980	7,274	14,669	27,664	5,793	2,993	18,878
1981	8,062	15,715	28,357	5,674	2,936	19,748
1982	8,536	16,269	27,554	4,159	2,895	20,500
1983	9,082	18,078	31,432	6,857	2,988	21,588
1984	10,652	19,861	32,872	6,728	3,414	22,730
1985	11,710	21,498	34,929	7,779	3,564	23,586
1986	13,342	23,575	35,971	8,118	3,550	24,303
1987	13,802	24,020	38,050	8,695	3,553	25,802
1988	14,386	26,163	39,973	8,575	4,031	27,368
1989	15,011	27,029	41,622	8,876	4,104	28,642
1990	14,811	26,858	42,090	8,759	4,159	29,172
1991	15,025	26,208	42,348	8,612	4,426	29,310
1992	16,059	26,916	43,058	8,907	4,676	29,476

Continued. . .

*Includes depository and nondepository institutions and holding companies and investment services.

**Includes carriers, agents, brokers, and services.

Table 4. Florida Gross State Product by Major Sector
1977 to 1992 (continued)
(in millions of $1987)

Year	Total	Private Industries (continued)						
		Services						
		Hotels and Other Lodging Places	Auto- motive Repair and Garages	Amuse- ment and Recre- ation	Health	Legal	Educa- tional	NEC
1977	22,685	2,550	1,198	1,149	7,130	2,281	650	7,725
1978	24,339	2,690	1,361	1,241	7,395	2,443	675	8,536
1979	25,699	2,699	1,506	1,377	7,756	2,396	697	9,268
1980	27,034	2,450	1,563	1,501	8,381	2,370	762	10,006
1981	28,217	2,337	1,569	1,582	8,869	2,454	751	10,655
1982	28,881	2,421	1,531	1,737	9,385	2,502	750	10,555
1983	30,698	2,704	1,605	1,922	9,808	2,506	771	11,382
1984	33,422	2,864	1,759	1,974	10,334	2,672	799	13,021
1985	35,135	2,947	1,970	2,158	10,782	2,798	826	13,653
1986	37,051	3,160	2,003	2,288	11,070	3,004	830	14,697
1987	40,660	3,346	2,041	2,456	12,259	3,187	901	16,470
1988	41,406	3,476	2,123	2,498	12,420	3,273	977	16,641
1989	43,934	3,664	2,075	2,842	13,055	3,135	998	18,166
1990	45,684	3,615	2,112	3,037	13,746	3,174	993	19,008
1991	46,216	3,537	2,154	3,137	14,194	3,138	1,078	18,976
1992	47,561	3,612	2,103	3,417	14,394	3,240	1,075	19,720

Continued . . .

NEC - Not elsewhere classified.

Table 4. Florida Gross State Product by Major Sector
1977 to 1992 (continued)
(in millions of $1987)

Year	Total	Government Federal Civilian	Federal Military	State and Local
1977	17,804	3,055	3,150	11,599
1978	18,325	3,278	3,206	11,842
1979	18,509	3,201	3,060	12,248
1980	19,066	3,440	3,055	12,572
1981	19,576	3,306	3,204	13,067
1982	19,757	3,239	3,267	13,252
1983	20,697	3,784	3,285	13,627
1984	20,488	3,344	3,305	13,839
1985	21,209	3,419	3,392	14,398
1986	22,396	3,540	3,515	15,341
1987	23,233	3,666	3,552	16,015
1988	24,294	3,906	3,508	16,880
1989	25,798	4,204	3,608	17,986
1990	26,961	4,161	3,716	19,084
1991	27,606	4,416	3,721	19,468
1992	26,886	4,417	3,568	18,900

Source: U.S. Department of Commerce, Bureau of Economic Analysis, Regional Economic Information System, CD-ROM, May 1995.

Table 5. Florida Gross Sales by Major Sector 1980-1994 (in thousands of dollars)

Gross Sales by Major Sector

Year	Total	Food and Beverage	Apparel	General Merchan- dise	Auto- motive	Furniture and Appli- ances	Lumber Builders and Con- tractors	General Classi- fication
1980	136,318,331	18,456,101	2,110,880	11,784,919	23,595,731	5,510,566	9,824,127	65,036,010
1981	156,619,282	20,831,957	2,630,451	13,367,742	27,177,194	6,461,349	10,905,573	75,245,019
1982	161,796,459	22,480,948	2,616,237	13,520,199	27,797,852	6,980,449	10,080,111	78,320,666
1983	168,492,566	23,301,926	2,872,640	14,837,794	30,491,973	7,861,075	11,096,080	78,031,073
1984	195,758,800	24,806,296	2,846,886	16,664,867	35,884,011	8,880,835	12,963,684	93,712,223
1985	210,089,814	27,699,907	3,043,398	17,804,613	37,148,017	9,927,527	13,090,208	101,376,145
1986	223,601,586	29,176,725	3,597,500	19,355,072	38,880,206	10,933,708	13,414,839	108,243,535
1987	259,753,404	31,478,041	4,175,393	22,140,154	42,189,228	12,637,149	19,803,825	127,329,614
1988	277,485,535	32,840,089	4,542,280	23,488,414	45,418,184	13,223,744	18,432,504	139,540,485
1989	289,076,440	36,092,389	4,913,691	25,367,853	47,571,764	14,608,724	16,040,536	144,481,040
1990	303,465,606	38,539,862	5,296,288	27,475,135	48,149,872	15,107,911	14,744,603	154,151,207
1991	310,147,922	38,701,164	5,773,269	28,843,225	51,502,553	15,589,120	12,846,848	156,891,507
1992	330,770,070	40,699,905	6,095,056	31,619,440	56,424,660	16,519,929	13,234,310	166,176,769
1993*	360,267,714	42,644,792	6,436,195	35,031,212	59,268,411	18,933,339	15,127,409	182,826,356
1994*	385,110,860	43,657,229	6,556,484	37,866,542	64,504,180	20,876,602	16,038,165	195,611,656

*Audited data; not comparable to earlier years.
Source: Florida Department of Revenue unpublished data.

Table 6. Florida Personal Income: Derivation
by Place of Residence 1970-1993
(rounded to millions of dollars)

Year	Total Earnings by Place of Work*	Less Personal Contri- butions to Social Security	Plus Resi- dence Adjust- ment**	Plus Dividends Interest and Rent	Plus Transfer Payments	Personal Income by Place of Residence
1970	19,341	875	-19	5,385	3,168	27,000
1971	21,399	948	-13	6,020	3,794	30,251
1972	24,840	1,108	-11	6,632	4,470	34,823
1973	29,152	1,437	-10	7,748	5,402	40,855
1974	32,032	1,547	-2	8,971	6,522	45,976
1975	33,257	1,510	-11	9,554	8,397	49,688
1976	36,247	1,673	8	10,583	9,374	54,539
1977	40,507	1,891	19	12,079	10,393	61,107
1978	46,932	2,187	20	14,627	11,565	70,958
1979	53,525	2,612	15	17,865	13,346	82,140
1980	61,429	2,916	9	22,343	15,915	96,780
1981	68,508	3,478	34	27,951	18,552	111,566
1982	73,099	3,775	63	30,118	20,934	120,438
1983	81,338	4,229	91	32,950	22,759	132,908
1984	90,429	4,806	139	36,788	23,788	146,339
1985	99,267	5,557	180	41,102	25,991	160,983
1986	108,447	6,124	233	45,192	27,539	175,287
1987	119,684	6,529	291	46,805	29,306	189,558
1988	130,267	7,521	367	50,289	31,724	205,127
1989	139,640	8,255	450	60,909	35,280	228,024
1990	149,094	8,755	549	64,711	39,006	244,604
1991	154,628	9,078	602	65,261	43,616	255,029
1992	164,523	9,656	642	61,249	48,907	265,665
1993	174,652	10,364	664	66,266	52,220	283,437

*Consists of wage and salary disbursements, other labor income, and propri-etors income.

**An estimate of the net gain or loss to an area because of commuting from place of residence to place of work. Some persons earn income in the area in which they live, others earn income outside that area.

Source: U.S. Department of Commerce, Bureau of Economic Analysis, Re-gional Economic Information Service, CD-ROM, May 1995.

Table 7. Florida Personal Income: Earnings by Industry by Place of Work 1980-1993
(rounded to millions of dollars)

| Year | Total | Farm | Total Non-farm | Private Nonfarm | | | | Manufacturing | | | | | Finance, Insurance and Real Estate | Services | Nonfarm Govern-ment |
				Total	Agricul-tural Services*	Mining	Con-struction	Non-durable Goods	Durable Goods	Transpor-tation and Public Utilities	Whole-sale Trade	Retail Trade			
1980	61,429	1,766	59,664	49,803	594	638	5,138	3,114	4,763	5,073	4,102	7,970	4,586	13,825	9,860
1981	68,508	1,485	67,023	55,855	617	673	5,690	3,409	5,421	5,632	4,553	8,905	5,160	15,795	11,168
1982	73,099	1,941	71,158	58,840	645	575	5,503	3,526	5,773	6,085	4,752	9,340	5,026	17,616	12,317
1983	81,338	2,706	78,631	65,245	729	357	5,905	3,754	6,227	6,553	5,050	10,535	6,118	20,016	13,386
1984	90,429	1,984	88,444	74,012	829	461	7,313	4,136	7,130	6,965	5,666	11,759	6,533	23,219	14,432
1985	99,267	1,990	97,277	81,507	973	497	8,136	4,332	7,800	7,403	6,327	13,001	7,324	25,714	15,770
1986	108,447	2,140	106,307	89,208	1,054	265	9,082	4,542	8,256	7,784	6,741	14,224	8,693	28,566	17,099
1987	119,684	2,230	117,454	98,590	1,243	269	9,498	4,849	8,764	8,413	7,577	15,432	10,064	32,479	18,864
1988	130,267	2,751	127,515	106,926	1,308	302	10,083	5,279	9,390	8,701	8,433	16,632	10,715	36,084	20,589
1989	139,640	2,975	136,666	114,129	1,345	308	10,247	5,600	9,670	8,811	9,051	17,643	11,076	40,378	22,536
1990	149,094	2,424	146,670	121,610	1,554	301	10,191	5,824	9,803	9,611	9,572	18,422	11,533	44,798	25,060
1991	154,628	3,111	151,517	124,769	1,689	309	9,035	5,966	9,823	10,015	9,769	18,579	11,993	47,590	26,748
1992	164,523	2,736	161,787	134,006	1,766	316	9,038	6,288	10,241	10,698	10,584	19,676	13,312	52,086	27,781
1993	174,652	2,682	171,970	142,875	1,896	303	9,976	6,423	10,413	11,466	11,045	20,905	14,141	56,306	29,095

*Includes forestry, fisheries, and other. "Other" includes wages and salaries of U.S. residents employed by foreign embassies, consulates, and international organizations in the United States.

Source: U.S. Department of Commerce, Bureau of Economic Information Service, Regional Economic Information Service, CD-ROM, May 1995.

Table 8. Florida State Government Finances
1970-1992
(rounded to thousands of dollars)

		State Revenue by Major Source			
			General Revenue		
				Intergovernmental Revenue	
				From Federal Govern-ment	From Local Govern-ments
Year	Total Revenue	Total	Total		
1970	2,226,037	2,013,734	403,315	385,525	17,790
1971	2,548,063	2,308,731	508,295	493,137	15,158
1972	3,149,195	2,860,535	639,372	622,072	17,300
1973	3,882,857	3,534,005	762,920	742,754	20,166
1974	4,326,520	3,954,925	796,748	760,779	35,969
1975	4,666,797	4,253,460	1,023,773	991,221	32,552
1976	5,178,835	4,404,857	1,057,697	1,029,688	28,009
1977	5,707,077	4,851,120	1,153,534	1,126,802	26,732
1978	6,442,069	5,620,613	1,387,281	1,350,175	37,106
1979	7,286,206	6,298,323	1,450,111	1,413,924	36,187
1980	8,222,693	7,303,596	1,790,579	1,742,244	48,335
1981	9,028,662	8,063,292	1,971,345	1,916,484	54,861
1982	9,363,821	8,337,735	1,925,500	1,873,540	51,960
1983	10,569,129	9,056,548	1,963,069	1,884,745	78,324
1984	11,896,319	10,322,378	2,101,642	2,052,950	48,692
1985	13,798,172	11,882,029	2,408,396	2,361,618	46,778
1986	15,814,970	13,319,466	2,709,768	2,612,283	97,485
1987	17,394,294	14,435,691	2,902,105	2,799,133	102,972
1988	19,361,872	16,863,265	3,235,790	3,109,415	126,375
1989	22,159,704	19,288,967	3,626,033	3,546,388	79,645
1990	23,868,131	20,625,651	4,154,239	3,998,886	155,353
1991	25,754,050	22,079,594	4,826,682	4,581,729	244,953
1992	28,310,741	23,651,927	5,711,452	5,406,514	304,938

Continued . . .

Table 8. Florida State Government Finances
1970-1992 (continued)
(rounded to thousands of dollars)

State Revenue by Major Source (continued)

General Revenue (continued)

Taxes

| Year | Total | Sales and Gross Receipts | | | Corpo-ration Net Income | License | Other** |
		Total	General	Selec-tive*			
1970	1,421,109	1,148,775	658,197	490,578	-	176,524	95,810
1971	1,587,183	1,263,408	715,227	548,181	-	211,055	112,720
1972	1,989,970	1,515,643	875,775	639,868	27,874	245,092	201,361
1973	2,487,791	1,874,685	1,041,257	833,428	147,708	236,370	229,028
1974	2,786,602	2,085,893	1,196,571	889,322	188,778	262,545	249,386
1975	2,791,223	2,114,381	1,200,061	914,320	180,256	276,547	210,186
1976	2,935,507	2,218,934	1,254,086	964,848	180,740	291,704	244,129
1977	3,274,802	2,415,293	1,398,590	1,016,703	194,199	379,180	286,130
1978	3,764,283	2,807,830	1,644,747	1,163,083	256,189	328,910	371,354
1979	4,290,975	3,206,580	1,946,983	1,259,597	314,409	346,241	423,745
1980	4,804,298	3,544,031	2,252,113	1,291,918	371,405	379,845	509,017
1981	5,314,376	3,908,552	2,542,895	1,365,657	402,471	395,998	607,355
1982	5,555,936	4,189,571	2,783,889	1,405,682	383,827	399,933	582,605
1983	6,224,717	4,795,751	3,334,207	1,461,544	371,453	444,038	613,475
1984	7,329,368	5,731,434	3,980,949	1,750,485	365,446	453,504	778,984
1985	8,328,869	6,501,496	4,672,404	1,829,092	454,088	535,085	838,200
1986	9,120,166	7,062,173	5,027,376	2,034,797	486,925	620,928	950,140
1987	9,846,189	7,588,430	5,478,278	2,110,152	596,434	662,708	998,617
1988	11,460,299	9,122,497	6,862,627	2,259,870	624,032	685,279	1,028,491
1989	12,455,553	9,878,661	7,637,957	2,240,704	725,364	770,546	1,080,982
1990	13,289,492	10,577,503	8,191,414	2,386,089	698,825	840,499	1,172,665
1991	13,764,055	10,884,691	8,138,690	2,746,001	582,149	937,132	1,360,083
1992	14,411,775	11,284,828	8,325,978	2,958,850	695,114	997,465	1,434,368

Continued . .

*Sales and gross receipts taxes imposed on sales of particular commodities or services, apart from the application of general sales and gross receipts taxes. Includes taxes on tobacco products, alcoholic beverages, parimutuels and other businesses or services not enumerated.

**Includes severance, property, death and gift, and documentary taxes.

Table 8. Florida State Government Finances
1970-1992 (continued)
(rounded to thousands of dollars)

			State Revenue by Major Source (continued)				
			General Revenue (continued)				
		Charges and Miscellaneous General Revenue					Insur-ance Trust Revenue
			Miscellaneous General Revenue				
Year	Total	Current Charges	Total	Interest Earnings	Other*	Utility	
1970	189,310	132,486	56,824	41,506	15,318	-	212,303
1971	213,253	156,500	56,753	43,401	13,352	-	239,332
1972	231,193	173,520	57,673	38,849	18,824	-	288,660
1973	283,294	203,475	79,819	55,947	23,872	-	348,852
1974	371,575	232,419	139,156	111,896	27,260	-	371,595
1975	438,464	238,681	199,783	165,757	34,026	-	413,337
1976	411,653	272,252	139,401	106,064	33,337	-	773,978
1977	422,784	285,018	137,766	95,004	42,762	-	855,957
1978	469,049	300,625	168,424	114,236	54,188	4,085	817,371
1979	557,237	307,470	249,767	185,939	63,828	5,045	982,838
1980	708,719	343,642	365,077	298,276	66,801	5,515	913,582
1981	777,571	345,944	431,627	348,894	82,733	6,788	958,582
1982	856,299	361,844	494,455	392,662	101,793	6,635	1,019,451
1983	868,762	406,699	462,063	333,556	128,507	6,653	1,505,928
1984	891,368	421,442	469,926	342,735	127,191	6,915	1,567,026
1985	1,144,764	527,561	617,203	438,392	178,811	6,215	1,909,928
1986	1,489,532	692,795	796,737	440,416	356,321	5,662	2,489,842
1987	1,687,397	780,590	906,807	632,153	274,654	5,126	2,953,477
1988	2,167,176	840,152	1,327,024	708,955	618,069	5,155	2,493,452
1989	3,207,381	944,597	2,262,784	926,824	1,335,960	4,525	2,866,212
1990	3,181,920	990,186	2,191,734	985,090	1,206,644	4,513	3,237,967
1991	3,488,857	1,198,918	2,289,939	986,395	1,303,544	4,951	3,669,505
1992	3,528,700	1,281,046	2,247,654	882,050	1,365,604	4,834	4,653,980

Continued . . .

*Includes rents, donations, fines and forfeitures and other miscellaneous revenue.

University of Florida   *Bureau of Economic and Business Research*

Table 8. Florida State Government Finances
1970-1992 (continued)
(rounded to thousands of dollars)

			State Expenditure by Function			
				Insurance Trust		
				Un-employ-ment Compen-sation	Employee Retire-ment	Workers' Compen-sation
Year	Total	Utility	Total	sation	ment	sation
1970	2,116,316	-	86,674	26,133	59,557	984
1971	2,537,555	-	126,738	47,282	78,207	1,249
1972	2,862,509	-	137,491	45,651	90,111	1,729
1973	3,449,745	-	144,877	38,085	104,583	2,209
1974	4,084,511	-	180,187	55,409	121,578	3,200
1975	4,901,551	-	373,146	237,842	132,104	3,200
1976	5,157,603	-	672,791	527,365	140,264	5,162
1977	5,391,507	-	485,992	329,451	152,014	4,527
1978	5,712,824	10,134	364,430	185,614	168,902	9,914
1979	6,461,600	10,816	318,040	116,656	190,514	10,870
1980	7,386,754	*17,495	364,181	137,927	215,988	10,266
1981	8,273,745	*17,459	449,250	195,121	243,262	10,867
1982	9,322,355	*20,640	544,225	235,131	295,855	13,239
1983	9,873,718	*26,122	702,728	357,924	330,209	14,595
1984	10,320,305	16,756	622,812	233,730	374,487	14,595
1985	12,853,957	15,527	690,760	256,126	420,039	14,595
1986	13,739,762	17,738	754,669	280,705	473,964	NA
1987	15,426,277	22,910	833,093	279,434	532,209	21,450
1988	17,833,097	24,920	875,328	262,223	591,011	22,094
1989	19,977,374	32,963	1,003,609	304,299	656,925	42,385
1990	21,722,518	22,106	1,142,839	378,170	732,401	32,268
1991	25,167,779	24,241	1,515,101	646,881	813,145	55,075
1992	27,089,292	27,024	2,211,212	1,221,195	912,638	77,379

Continued . . .

NA - Not available.
*Expenditure for Jacksonville Transportation Authority.

University of Florida   *Bureau of Economic and Business Research*

Table 8. Florida State Government Finances
1970-1992 (continued)
(rounded to thousands of dollars)

| | | State Expenditure by Function (continued) | | | | |
| | | General | | | | |
Year	Total	Edu-cation	Public Welfare	Hos-pitals	Health	High-ways
1970	2,029,642	1,075,701	191,928	86,459	47,528	310,484
1971	2,410,817	1,185,232	263,509	97,233	58,257	449,219
1972	2,725,018	1,273,649	306,742	102,851	66,353	535,609
1973	3,304,868	1,412,135	382,057	141,517	75,700	586,833
1974	3,904,324	1,659,184	376,633	155,561	99,351	665,177
1975	4,528,405	1,942,131	422,829	171,463	156,668	725,917
1976	4,484,812	1,970,805	434,298	190,627	168,650	612,861
1977	4,905,515	2,205,579	442,093	223,368	198,476	584,523
1978	5,338,260	2,436,457	481,895	236,318	234,047	656,896
1979	6,132,744	2,785,354	621,022	270,130	276,175	773,854
1980	7,005,078	3,147,477	704,884	307,574	327,079	947,295
1981	7,807,036	3,601,647	891,430	310,128	381,122	891,428
1982	8,757,490	3,932,992	1,135,095	369,101	423,156	993,621
1983	9,144,868	4,076,586	1,141,738	401,134	493,771	956,301
1984	9,680,737	4,098,672	1,276,163	382,553	600,388	1,036,700
1985	12,147,670	4,976,742	1,546,774	255,672	694,783	1,209,796
1986	12,967,355	5,310,058	1,680,897	367,863	752,088	1,395,264
1987	14,570,274	5,744,313	1,905,156	392,391	981,880	1,466,365
1988	16,932,849	6,566,852	2,266,352	429,199	1,000,740	1,894,012
1989	18,940,802	11,958,189	2,772,531	465,360	1,190,144	1,969,871
1990	20,557,573	7,828,665	3,529,199	476,858	1,309,620	1,733,182
1991	23,628,437	9,096,937	4,556,120	491,279	1,457,379	1,778,850
1992	24,851,056	8,814,361	5,333,949	507,514	1,416,490	2,175,460

Continued . . .

Table 8. Florida State Government Finances
1970-1992 (continued)
(rounded to thousands of dollars)

| | | | State Expenditure by Function (Continued) | | | |
| | | | General (Continued) | | | |
Year	Police Protection	Cor- rections	Natural Resources	Govern- ment Adminis- tration	Interest on Debt	Other
1970	19,850	31,995	95,654	68,600	40,757	101,443
1971	29,011	36,057	105,216	78,790	39,479	108,293
1972	34,921	49,767	98,078	93,988	50,264	163,060
1973	40,338	75,404	115,645	119,711	63,587	355,528
1974	47,874	99,970	167,997	153,609	74,084	478,968
1975	53,966	140,165	222,305	179,439	77,244	513,522
1976	54,792	162,403	187,867	186,341	85,493	516,168
1977	65,294	174,275	269,247	206,864	99,500	535,796
1978	64,868	181,815	174,019	212,002	113,463	659,943
1979	76,848	194,048	183,256	216,764	141,025	735,293
1980	85,503	204,641	217,918	257,900	143,819	804,807
1981	97,488	224,485	232,318	283,264	150,622	893,726
1982	127,114	241,361	271,134	322,494	176,767	941,422
1983	116,188	293,032	337,574	356,526	210,936	972,018
1984	122,714	358,506	330,145	360,807	263,814	1,114,089
1985	151,094	411,997	420,325	401,526	273,957	2,078,961
1986	168,424	437,979	449,335	505,117	319,012	1,900,330
1987	206,985	508,194	516,356	576,527	568,347	2,272,107
1988	216,598	654,237	522,911	794,300	636,637	1,530,632
1989	207,337	758,719	548,079	952,784	668,057	1,644,317
1990	193,677	858,218	616,142	1,001,711	666,366	1,763,104
1991	251,709	924,210	690,528	1,021,173	694,414	1,988,645
1992	224,694	1,036,611	840,390	1,065,417	740,022	2,000,973

Continued . . .

Table 8. Florida State Government Finances
1970-1992 (continued)
(rounded to thousands of dollars)

| | | State Expenditure by Major Category | | | |
| | | | Direct | | |
Year	Inter-Govern-mental	Total*	Opera-tions	Capital Outlay	Assistance and Insurance Benefits
1970	846,892	1,269,424	719,769	296,412	212,486
1971	913,059	1,624,496	878,699	427,011	279,307
1972	1,024,986	1,837,523	992,859	484,847	309,553
1973	1,314,909	2,134,836	1,191,911	520,600	358,738
1974	1,560,305	2,524,206	1,492,698	592,749	364,675
1975	1,845,865	3,055,686	1,762,035	694,832	521,575
1976	1,834,215	3,323,388	1,838,699	579,882	819,314
1977	2,019,538	3,371,969	1,969,694	654,869	647,906
1978	2,235,987	3,476,837	2,166,369	654,785	542,220
1979	2,567,870	3,893,730	2,546,820	713,455	492,430
1980	2,925,889	4,460,865	2,837,944	898,467	580,635
1981	3,252,472	5,021,273	3,297,510	875,964	697,177
1982	3,512,218	5,810,137	3,811,328	965,228	856,814
1983	3,654,944	5,489,924	4,098,383	909,054	1,000,401
1984	3,561,701	6,758,604	4,400,984	1,100,981	992,825
1985	5,211,019	7,642,938	4,884,231	1,507,647	977,103
1986	5,198,824	8,540,938	5,782,411	1,249,341	1,190,174
1987	5,890,208	9,536,069	6,219,566	1,445,912	1,302,244
1988	6,500,752	11,332,345	7,469,221	1,823,380	1,403,107
1989	6,982,613	12,994,761	8,637,448	2,041,179	1,648,077
1990	7,204,813	14,517,705	10,034,565	1,890,512	1,926,262
1991	8,292,704	16,875,075	11,956,156	1,807,440	2,417,065
1992	8,405,800	18,683,492	12,404,979	2,266,801	3,271,690

Continued . . .

*Includes amounts not shown separately.

University of Florida   *Bureau of Economic and Business Research*

Table 8. Florida State Government Finances
1970-1992 (continued)
(rounded to thousands of dollars)

			State Indebtedness at End of Fiscal Year			
			Long-term			
				Net		
				Full Faith	Nonguar-	Short
Year	Total	Total	Total	and Credit	anteed	Term
1970	891,039	891,039	799,046	-	799,046	-
1971	1,021,038	1,021,038	924,311	-	924,311	-
1972	1,121,757	1,121,757	1,001,614	-	1,001,614	-
1973	1,260,271	1,259,320	1,090,233	-	1,090,233	951
1974	1,487,955	1,487,004	1,234,628	48,378	1,186,250	951
1975	1,597,560	1,579,860	1,306,979	76,374	1,230,605	17,700
1976	1,739,834	1,739,834	1,332,275	29,160	1,303,115	-
1977	2,003,353	2,003,353	1,500,605	167,252	1,333,353	-
1978	2,344,012	2,344,012	1,609,019	169,226	1,439,793	-
1979	2,670,982	2,670,982	1,868,041	168,941	1,699,100	-
1980	2,626,926	2,626,926	1,846,285	163,602	1,682,683	-
1981	2,815,714	2,815,714	1,940,870	552,149	1,388,721	-
1982	2,993,388	2,993,388	2,036,388	526,306	1,510,082	-
1983	3,566,782	3,566,782	2,167,977	502,454	1,665,523	-
1984	3,909,566	3,909,566	2,944,286	481,547	2,462,739	-
1985	5,014,494	5,014,414	2,734,690	785,165	1,834,240	80
1986	5,679,591	5,679,093	2,954,772	993,691	1,961,081	498
1987	7,805,781	7,805,781	3,282,199	1,069,434	2,212,765	-
1988	8,296,461	8,287,455	3,513,549	817,937	2,695,612	9,006
1989	8,967,093	8,961,136	4,162,888	883,103	3,279,785	5,957
1990	9,950,071	9,942,816	4,867,901	952,684	3,915,217	7,255
1991	11,083,642	11,074,300	5,923,221	574,866	5,348,355	9,342
1992	12,295,486	12,294,744	6,652,382	642,635	6,009,747	742

Continued . . .

Table 8. Florida State Government Finances
1970-1992 (continued)
(rounded to thousands of dollars)

| | Specified Per Capita State Revenue, Expenditure and Debt | | | |
| | Revenue | | | |
Year	Total	Inter-govern-mental	Taxes	Charges
1970	325.21	59.40	209.31	27.88
1971	361.89	72.19	225.42	30.29
1972	433.83	88.08	274.14	31.85
1973	505.78	99.38	324.06	36.90
1974	534.80	98.49	344.45	45.93
1975	558.43	122.51	334.00	52.47
1976	614.99	125.61	348.59	48.88
1977	675.23	136.48	387.46	50.02
1978	749.60	161.42	438.01	54.58
1979	822.37	163.67	484.31	62.89
1980	844.22	183.84	493.25	72.76
1981	926.36	202.27	545.27	79.78
1982	960.79	197.57	570.07	87.86
1983	989.62	183.81	582.84	81.34
1984	1,083.85	191.48	667.76	81.21
1985	1,213.99	211.90	732.79	100.72
1986	1,354.60	232.10	781.17	127.58
1987	1,446.75	241.37	818.95	140.35
1988	1,569.67	1,367.11	929.09	175.69
1989	1,748.85	1,522.29	983.00	253.13
1990	1,844.81	1,594.19	1,027.17	245.94
1991	1,939.75	1,663.00	1,036.68	262.77
1992	2,098.96	1,753.55	1,068.49	261.62

Continued . . .

Table 8. Florida State Government Finances
1970-1992 (continued)
(rounded to thousands of dollars)

| | | Specified Per Capita State Revenue, Expenditure and Debt (continued) | | | | |
| | | Expenditure | | | | |
Year	Total*	Educa-tion	Public Wel-fare	High-ways	Public Safety	Debt
1970	309.18	158.44	28.27	45.73	4.71	131.24
1971	360.40	168.33	37.42	63.80	5.12	145.01
1972	394.34	175.46	42.26	73.79	6.86	154.53
1973	449.36	183.94	49.77	76.44	9.82	164.16
1974	504.88	205.09	46.56	82.22	12.36	183.93
1975	586.52	232.40	50.60	86.86	16.77	191.16
1976	612.47	234.03	51.57	72.78	19.29	206.61
1977	637.90	260.95	52.31	69.16	20.62	237.03
1978	664.75	283.51	56.07	76.44	28.71	272.75
1979	729.30	314.37	70.09	87.34	30.57	301.47
1980	758.39	323.15	72.37	97.26	29.79	269.70
1981	848.91	369.54	91.46	91.46	33.03	288.90
1982	956.53	403.55	116.47	101.95	37.81	307.14
1983	924.51	381.70	106.90	89.54	38.32	333.97
1984	940.26	373.42	116.27	94.45	43.84	356.19
1985	1,130.91	437.86	136.09	106.44	49.54	441.18
1986	1,176.85	454.82	143.97	119.51	51.94	486.47
1987	1,283.06	477.78	158.46	121.96	59.49	649.24
1988	1,445.73	532.38	183.73	153.55	70.60	672.60
1989	1,576.62	578.20	218.81	155.46	76.24	707.69
1990	1,678.97	605.09	272.78	133.96	81.30	769.06
1991	1,895.59	685.17	343.16	133.98	88.57	834.80
1992	2,008.40	653.50	395.46	161.29	93.51	911.59

*Includes amounts not shown separately.

Source: U.S. Department of Commerce, Bureau of the Census, *State Government Finances in 1992* and previous editions.

Table 9. Florida Local Government Finances Fiscal Years Ending September 30, 1975, through 1992
(rounded to thousands of dollars)

Year	Total	Taxes	Licenses	Inter-Govern-mental	Charges	Fines and Forfeiture	Other
				Local Government Revenue by Major Source			
1975	4,008,585	1,033,218	50,884	769,035	599,572	62,431	1,493,445
1976	5,055,531	1,204,630	53,975	1,070,899	823,016	46,648	1,856,362
1977	5,543,218	1,311,354	65,165	1,152,336	889,613	50,988	2,073,762
1978	6,113,267	1,495,411	73,796	1,394,903	2,305,414	51,770	791,974
1979	7,760,911	1,586,643	94,396	1,389,176	2,405,182	55,627	2,229,883
1980	9,427,142	1,805,389	99,278	1,580,760	2,881,617	59,826	3,000,273
1981	11,486,356	2,155,637	120,698	1,700,316	3,289,173	69,668	4,150,864
1982	12,638,971	2,582,603	111,016	1,615,940	3,998,321	84,520	4,246,571
1983	17,794,683	2,647,020	137,319	2,045,956	4,904,746	92,425	7,967,216
1984	19,127,394	3,088,054	167,304	2,755,322	4,982,725	98,651	8,035,338
1985	22,634,850	3,484,640	180,569	2,022,891	5,372,566	110,930	11,463,252
1986	27,632,665	4,012,332	190,691	2,040,938	5,788,729	121,331	15,478,644
1987	22,613,385	4,527,470	203,623	2,180,931	6,309,487	148,032	9,243,843
1988	24,180,545	5,082,916	220,367	2,340,662	7,135,919	166,304	9,234,376
1989	27,421,411	5,599,515	253,951	2,600,026	8,072,561	181,400	10,713,957
1990	27,545,081	6,385,594	259,310	2,847,226	8,825,922	200,250	9,026,778
1991	29,675,330	6,962,304	243,780	2,773,084	8,847,610	214,159	10,634,391
1992	36,982,084	7,211,744	258,764	2,985,906	9,150,933	207,175	17,167,562

Continued . . . .

Table 9. Florida Local Government Finances Fiscal Years Ending September 30, 1975, through 1992 (continued) (rounded to thousands of dollars)

Year	Total	General Govern- ment	Public Safety	Physical Envir- onment	Transpor- tation	Economic Envir- onment	Human Services	Culture/ Recre- ation	Debt Service	Other
1975	3,873,736	647,940	609,649	101,646	508,027	258,039	482,461	223,127	-	1,042,847
1976	4,853,986	736,090	681,947	109,416	548,701	260,888	665,082	256,429	-	1,595,435
1977	5,231,032	814,845	759,105	86,711	614,113	303,687	681,768	278,894	-	1,691,910
1978	6,249,132	766,578	855,703	2,236,801	683,466	426,472	886,232	317,503	-	76,378
1979	7,749,238	672,071	976,818	1,560,835	712,792	382,620	843,050	352,480	391,112	1,857,460
1980	9,214,125	684,597	1,123,686	2,123,973	790,955	449,098	903,640	392,720	330,266	2,415,189
1981	11,451,236	932,030	1,303,171	2,644,933	942,593	400,563	1,031,770	451,590	610,327	3,134,258
1982	12,561,768	982,164	1,539,955	2,818,222	1,108,091	337,569	1,506,437	496,217	826,769	2,946,345
1983	16,657,605	1,307,157	1,747,651	3,198,838	1,150,689	371,131	1,987,994	568,062	1,447,771	4,878,311
1984	16,761,116	1,458,214	1,930,079	3,121,373	1,308,562	389,562	1,762,066	622,005	1,407,575	4,761,679
1985	22,493,647	1,654,674	2,186,736	3,384,238	1,507,376	438,268	1,841,510	665,190	2,297,947	8,517,709
1986	26,322,104	1,620,443	2,481,698	3,702,563	1,659,079	479,747	1,986,959	775,527	3,769,567	9,846,522
1987	22,596,090	1,805,305	2,819,369	4,084,372	1,870,147	533,548	2,063,780	875,166	1,763,824	6,780,579
1988	24,634,621	1,960,937	3,180,038	4,552,682	2,055,200	589,844	2,242,002	1,077,975	2,343,925	6,632,019
1989	27,000,124	2,218,633	3,601,094	5,177,234	2,375,645	648,352	2,528,608	1,100,018	2,441,682	6,908,859
1990	28,389,046	2,450,454	4,004,016	5,839,931	2,692,793	745,606	2,627,653	1,272,032	1,992,885	6,763,676
1991	29,867,838	2,548,170	4,387,149	5,655,283	2,933,771	785,510	3,070,427	1,241,093	2,627,974	6,618,460
1992	30,606,937	2,771,196	4,539,915	5,583,874	2,932,775	792,465	3,082,462	1,215,575	3,025,176	6,663,498

Source: Florida Department of Banking and Finance, *Local Government Financial Report, Fiscal Year 1991-92* and previous editions.

Table 10. Specified Per Capita State and Local Government Expenditure 1970-1992
(in dollars)

Year	Total Direct*	Educa- tion	Public Wel- fare	Health and Hospitals	High- ways	Police Pro- tection
1970	527.57	228.96	31.74	46.72	58.09	20.54
1971	613.34	251.87	42.58	54.49	76.87	25.17
1972	657.22	264.28	48.23	62.59	81.06	28.52
1973	689.31	248.81	54.00	66.33	81.05	32.64
1974	783.33	295.79	50.47	80.11	88.01	35.13
1975	943.55	365.59	55.25	94.44	98.81	43.05
1976	1,006.36	375.65	57.70	109.19	88.92	51.16
1977	1,098.85	406.79	57.77	121.40	85.89	56.50
1978	NA	NA	NA	NA	NA	NA
1979	1,291.34	449.38	76.41	148.69	110.85	68.74
1980	1,309.42	460.58	78.11	155.24	123.36	68.10
1981	1,468.70	527.41	98.60	169.35	126.07	75.65
1982	1,664.65	576.58	125.50	195.85	137.94	88.49
1983	1,644.65	564.86	116.52	207.48	128.91	91.63
1984	1,802.98	616.72	127.33	215.23	129.43	97.34
1985	1,955.63	669.29	147.27	213.72	147.92	102.43
1986	2,123.35	703.51	156.78	229.02	162.63	110.77
1987	2,351.37	751.35	171.23	242.15	174.98	123.59
1988	2,554.81	808.87	196.53	245.52	218.18	127.31
1989	2,832.59	911.14	232.43	271.42	221.86	135.28
1990	3,159.98	1,035.35	288.16	302.60	213.38	147.17
1991	3,412.17	1,113.97	358.38	235.44	225.90	162.81
1992	3,494.42	1,090.54	399.44	338.89	250.16	169.95

NA - Not available.

*All expenditure other than intergovernmental expenditure.

Source: U.S. Department of Commerce, Bureau of the Census, *Government Finances in 1991-92 Preliminary Report* and previous editions.

List of Authors

William R. Ashburn
Tampa Electric Company
PO Box 111
Tampa, FL 33601
813/228-4942

Bruce L. Benson
Department of Economics
Florida State University
Tallahassee, FL 32306-2045
904/644-7094

Sanford V. Berg
Public Utility Research Center
PO Box117142, University of Florida
Gainesville, FL 32611-7142
904/392-0132

Gary L. Brosch
Center for Urban Transportation Research
4202 E. Fowler Avenue, ENB 118
University of South Florida
Tampa, FL 33620-5350
813/974-3120

Mark Flannery
Department of Finance, Insurance and Real Estate
PO Box 117168, University of Florida
Gainesville, FL 32611-7168
904/392-3184

Ellen F.R. Fournier
The Florida Senate
Ways and Means Committee
Room 207, The Capitol
Tallahassee, FL 32399-1100
904/487-5140

Gary M. Fournier

Department of Economics
Bellamy 475
Florida State University
Tallahassee, FL 32306-2045
904/904/644-7080

Thomas M. Fullerton, Jr.

Bureau of Economic and Business Research
PO Box 117145, University of Florida
Gainesville, FL 32611-7145
904/392-0171

Carolyn Herrington

Learning Systems Institute
202 Dodd Hall, Florida State University
Tallahassee, FL 32306-4041
904/644-2573

Joel Houston

Department of Finance, Insurance and Real Estate
PO Box 117168, University of Florida
Gainesville, FL 32611-7168
904/392-7546

Lawrence W. Kenny

Department of Economics
PO Box 117140, University of Florida
Gainesville, FL 32611-7140
904/392-0151

David G. Lenze

Bureau of Economic and Business Research
PO Box 117145, University of Florida
Gainesville, FL 32611-7145
904/392-0171

J. Walter Milon

Department of Food and Resource Economics
Institute for Food and Agricultural Sciences
PO Box 110240, University of Florida
Gainesville, FL 32611-0240
904/392-1883

Thomas W. Moore

Tampa Electric Company
PO Box 111
Tampa, FL 33601
813/228-4111

Yasser A. Nakib

132 Willard Hall
Department of Education Development
University of Delaware
Newark, Delaware 19716-2915
302/831-4227

William O'Dell

Shimberg Center for Affordable Housing
College of Architecture
PO Box 115703, University of Florida
Gainesville, FL 32611-5703
904/392-5967

David W. Rasmussen

Policy Sciences Center
Florida State University
Tallahassee, FL 32306-2045
904/644-7649

J. F. (Dick) Scoggins

Bureau of Economic and Business Research
PO Box 117145, University of Florida
Gainesville, FL 32611-7145
904/392-0171

Marc Smith

Shimberg Center for Affordable Housing
College of Architecture
PO Box 115703, University of Florida
Gainesville, FL 32611-5703
904/392-9437

Stanley K. Smith

Bureau of Economic and Business Research
PO Box 117145, University of Florida
Gainesville, FL 32611-7145
904/392-0171

Carol Taylor West

Bureau of Economic and Business Research
PO Box 117145, University of Florida
Gainesville, FL 32611-7145
904/392-0171

David R. Williams

Florida Economics Consulting Group, Inc.
311 Ridgewood Road
Miami, FL 33133
305/669-8244

Larry Winner

Department of Statistics
PO Box 118545, University of Florida
Gainesville, FL 32611-8545
904/392-1941